ASP.NET Mobile Controls

Tutorial Guide

Adaptive Web Content For Mobile Devices With
The MMIT

Matt Butler
Matthew Gibbs
Costas Hadjisotiriou
Neil Raybould
Srinivasa Sivakumar

Wrox Press Ltd. ®

ASP.NET Mobile Controls
Tutorial Guide

Adaptive Web Content For Mobile Devices With The MMIT

© 2001 Wrox Press

Published by Wrox Press Ltd,
Arden House, 1102 Warwick Road, Acocks Green,
Birmingham, B27 6BH, UK
Printed in the United States
ISBN 1-861005-22-9

Trademark Acknowledgements

Credits

Authors
Matt Butler
Matthew Gibbs
Costas Hadjisotiriou
Neil Raybould
Srinivasa Sivakumar

Additional Material
Ewan Buckingham
Gerard Maguire

Technical Architect
Chris Goode

Lead Technical Editor
Ewan Buckingham

Technical Editor
Gerard Maguire

Index
Michael Brinkman
Andrew Criddle

Production Coordinator
Abbie Forletta
Tom Bartlett

Cover
Chris Morris

Author Agent
Avril Corbin

Project Administrator
Cathy Succamore

Technical Reviewers
Ken Avellino
Robert Bogue
Maxime Bombardier
Susan Connery
Chris Crane
Edgar D'Andrea
Robin Dewson
John Godfrey
Mark Harrison
Mark Horner
David Schultz
Keyur Shah
Kent Tegels
Sanjeev Yadav

Proof Reader
Keith Westmoreland

Category Manager
Steve Farncombe

Managing Editors
Viv Emery
Louay Fatoohi

About the Authors

Matt (.MAtt) Butler

Technology is an artistic subcategory, application architecture - its sculpture, the hum of servers - its music, and code is its poetry. Just as there are both 'artists' and 'entertainers' in the 'arts', so, too, with technology. .MAtt Butler is an artist, not an entertainer.

.MAtt went from a homeless, starving, jazz musician to a programmer holding numerous certifications, including MCSD (VB 6/SQL Server), a Sun Java Certified Programmer, BEA Certified Programmer (Java / Weblogic), and a few other miscellaneous certifications. He rode the wave of the .COM craze working on sizable profile-based search engines and transactional e-commerce applications using the Windows DNA architecture in return for 'stock options' and pizza.

.MAtt's interests include all things computer-oriented (especially .NET and security), math, science, physics, spoken word, composing and improvising introspective music.

<dedications>
To my parents (Kathy, Wayne, Deb, CR), Sisters (Brooke, Stacey), my daughter (Morgan), my soon-to-be wife (Daisey), the musicians that I have known (the Joe's (Y & C), Greg I., the John's (O & C), Ed R., Dennis B., Julie M., Tim S., Pete C., Ken N., Taylor E., Bill W., Ted R., Travis M., etc...). You have all inspired me to different levels throughout my existence.
</dedications>

Matthew Gibbs

Matt Gibbs is a software developer at Microsoft where he has been working on Internet technologies since 1997. He is currently working on the Mobile Internet Toolkit. Matt is looking forward to finishing his graduate studies in Computer Science at the University of Washington soon, so that he can spend more time with his wife, son, and daughter.

Constantinos Hadjisotiriou

After graduating from various engineering degrees, Constantinos Hadjisotiriou has switched to working with databases, websites, and gadgets. WAP applications are a big fascination, almost as much as PDA programming. He is now busy with porting a new image compression format to PocketPC, writing PL/SQL procedures, and taking on various web programming contracts. For the last 2 years he has been successfully working from home in Spain, and advises everyone to do the same. Contact is via radvig@yahoo.com.

Neil Raybould

Neil works as a web developer and technical writer for Crossoft Incorporated, located in Pittsburgh, Pennsylvania. He enjoys working with the .NET Framework and hopes to stay as close to the forefront as possible. His current technical interests include .NET mobile applications and Web Services, and he hopes to expand his writing beyond computing-related topics.

Neil is co-author of Beginning ASP.NET using C# and Beginning ASP.NET using VB.NET, both from Wrox Press. He currently holds an MBA from Duquesne University and a BS from Virginia Tech, as well as MCSD and MCDBA certifications.

To my Savior and God, Lord Jesus. You continue to give me FAR more than I deserve.

To my wife, Victoria. Your support means more to me than you'll ever know. I love you!

To my daughter, Abigail. We're so happy you're finally here.

To my parents, David and Virginia Raybould and Walter and Claire Stone. Your combined encouragement has been a tremendous blessing.

To Chris and Drew. Thanks for making work not feel so much like work..

Thanks also to Judy, Roger and Payton Neyman; Bret, Polly, Daniel, Brenon, Cara and Marissa Parry; Thomas, Alison, Michael and Thomas Stone Jr. for your support and prayers.

Srinivasa Sivakumar

Srinivasa Sivakumar is a software consultant, developer and writer. He specializes in Web and Mobile technologies using Microsoft solutions. He currently works in Chicago for TransTech, Inc. He also writes technical articles for ASPToday.com, CSharpToday.com, .NET Developer, and others. In his free time he likes to watch Tamil movies and listen to Tamil sound tracks (Especially one's sung by Mr. S.P Balasubramaniyam).

I'd like to thank the Wrox Team for giving me the chance to work on this book, especially to Laura, Chris and Ewan. Thanks Guys.

I'd like to dedicate my section of the book to my beloved mother Mrs. Rajam Sathyanarayanan. Mother, thanks a lot for everything that you've done for me and I've no way of paying back the wonderful things that you've given me.

And also I'd like to thank my wife Annapoorna, my daughters Sruthi and Anusri.

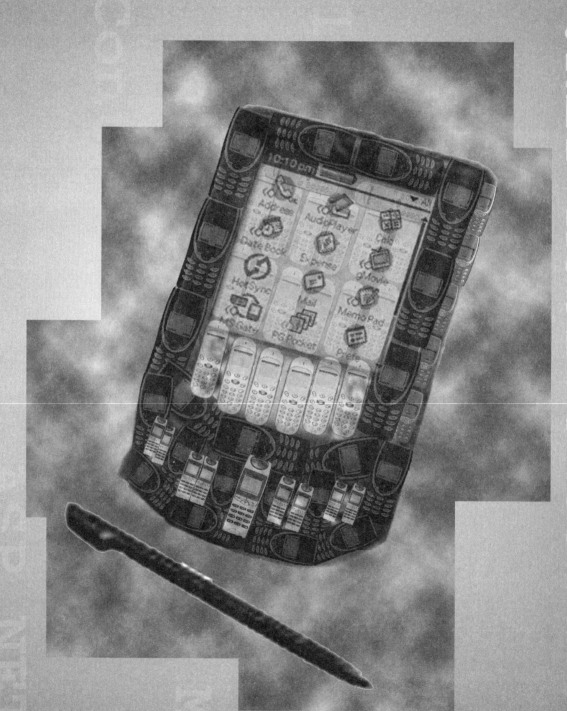

Table of Contents

Table of Contents

Table of Contents

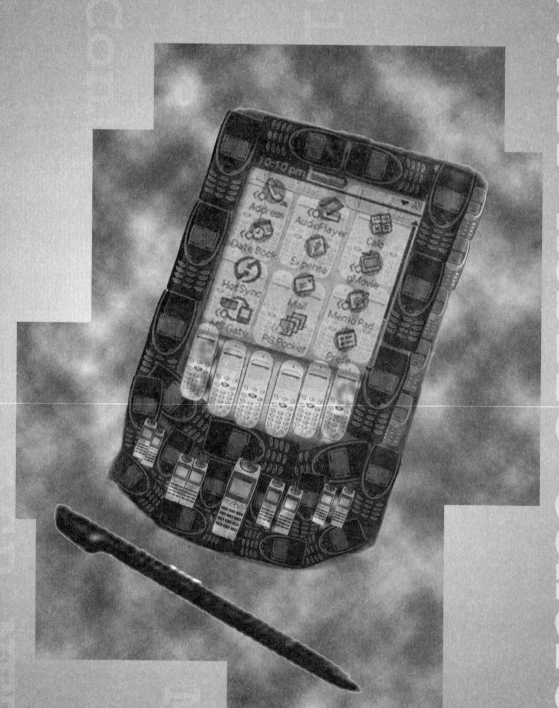

Introduction

ASP.NET Mobile Controls give developers the tools they need to create interactive web sites that are accessible from a wide range of mobile client devices. They are contained in an optional ASP.NET add-in, called the Microsoft Mobile Internet Toolkit, that comprises the controls themselves, together with additional functionality for integrating them into Visual Studio .NET.

This book is divided into three principal sections:

❑ An introduction to WAP, WML, and the conceptual ideas surrounding programming for clients with limited resources

❑ An explanation of how to use each of the ASP.NET Mobile Controls to produce targeted output tailored to each individual device that views your page

❑ A demonstration of how to utilize the controls in the Visual Studio .NET development environment, concluding with a complete case study mobile application

This book introduces the ASP.NET programmer to all the concepts and controls that they need to understand in order to create meaningful content for mobile client devices.

Who Is This Book For?

This book is aimed at anyone who is building, or planning to build, applications for mobile devices using the .NET Framework. Experience of ASP.NET is required, as is some exposure to C#. The reader of this book should feel comfortable about creating ASP.NET applications and not feel lost when viewing simple C# code.

A brief refresher of the basics of ASP.NET is included, but it may prove too advanced for the complete novice.

> **If you want more information about ASP.NET, to complement this book, you may find** *Beginning ASP.NET using C#* **useful (Wrox Press, ISBN: 1-861006-15-2).**

What Does This Book Cover?

This book is written against the Release Candidate of the Microsoft Mobile Internet Toolkit, running on the Release Candidate of the .NET Framework, and as such is designed to provide code that runs with the final release of .NET. The book covers the following topics:

An Introduction To The ASP.NET Mobile Controls

In Chapters 1 to 3, we'll talk about the principals of mobile communication, the strengths and weaknesses of mobile clients, and begin to discuss how developers need to think differently in order to maximize the potential of these devices. We'll go on to walk through the installation and setup procedures of the MMIT, and a selection of client browsers. We'll also recap the basics of how to serve your files using ASP.NET, and the mobile controls. We then move on to look at mobile communication in more detail, considering the communication technologies used, where those technologies have come from, and where they might be going in the future.

The ASP.NET Mobile Controls

In Chapters 4 to 9, we'll look in detail at the ASP.NET Mobile Controls. We'll begin by considering the lifecycle of an ASP.NET Mobile Web Form compared with its cousin, the traditional ASP.NET Web Form. Then we'll move on to consider the basic controls provided by the Microsoft Mobile Internet Toolkit and how they can be applied in a variety of ways to provide meaningful results. We'll demonstrate these ideas through the use of simple Try It Out examples, and present the output in a pair of different browsers so the differences in presentation between clients can clearly be seen.

Advanced Functionality And Optimization

In Chapters 10 to 16 we'll look at some of the more advanced ASP.NET Mobile Controls, such as those associated with validating user inputs, and dealing with rich outputs. We then move on to discuss how you can adjust the styling of the output your controls produce, and how to secure your mobile web applications against unauthorized access. We'll also consider how you can add support to the MMIT for new devices, and create your own mobile controls.

Visual Studio .NET Integration

The final chapters of the book will look at how to use Visual Studio .NET to create both standard, and mobile web applications. We'll walk you through the functionality provided by the IDE, and show how easily the MMIT is integrated into it. Finally, we'll conclude the book with a Case Study, created using the MMIT in Visual Studio .NET, bringing together all the concepts we've outlined in the book and using them to solve a real-world problem.

What Do I Need To Run ASP.NET?

In order to answer this, we need to consider the role that we'll be playing in this book – namely that of the web developer or webmaster. In this role, we'll be writing web pages, publishing them on a web server, and testing them to see what they look like and whether they work. This is just a list of items that you will need. Don't worry if you can't locate all the bits and pieces just yet, as we'll be looking at where to get them from in the opening chapter:

You'll need the following things to be able to use this book:

- ❑ The .NET Framework (this is available as a public download from Microsoft)

- ❑ An ASP.NET compliant web server (ASP.NET requires IIS 5.0 or later, which means you'll need to be running either Windows 2000 Professional or above, or Windows XP Professional)

- ❑ The Microsoft Mobile Internet Toolkit (this is also available as a free download from Microsoft. Details are given in Chapter 2)

- ❑ A selection of client device emulators for testing purposes (many are available as free downloads. Details are given in Chapter 2)

Optionally:

- ❑ Visual Studio .NET, for the integration chapters at the end of the book, and for the Case Study

> **The code in this book is designed to be run using the full release version of the .NET Framework, and as such it may not run correctly on pre-release versions.**

Conventions

We've used a number of different styles of text and layout in this book to help differentiate between the different kinds of information. Here are examples of the styles we used and an explanation of what they mean.

Code has several fonts. If it's a word that we're talking about in the text – for example, when discussing a For ... Next loop, it's in this font. If it's a block of code that can be typed as a program and run, then it's also in a gray box:

```
<%@ Page language="c#" runat="server" %>
```

Sometimes we'll see code in a mixture of styles, like this:

```
<%@ Page language="c#" runat="server" %>
<Invoice>
<script language="c#" runat="server">
  void Page_Load()
  {
      Response.Write("Welcome to ASP.NET Mobile Controls C#");
  }
</script>
```

When this happens, the code with a white background is code we are already familiar with; the line highlighted in gray is a new addition to the code since we last looked at it.

Advice, hints, and background information come in this type of font.

> **Important pieces of information come in boxes like this.**

Bullets appear indented, with each new bullet marked as follows:

- ❑ **Important Words** are in a bold type font.
- ❑ Words that appear on the screen, or in menus like File or Window, are in a similar font to the one you would see on a Windows desktop.
- ❑ Keys that you press on the keyboard, like *Ctrl* and *Enter*, are in italics.

Customer Support

We always value hearing from our readers, and we want to know what you think about this book: what you liked, what you didn't like, and what you think we can do better next time. You can send us your comments, either by returning the reply card in the back of the book, or by e-mail to feedback@wrox.com. Please be sure to mention the book title in your message.

How To Download The Sample Code For The Book

When you visit the Wrox site, http://www.wrox.com/, simply locate the title through our Search facility or by using one of the title lists. Click on Download in the Code column, or on Download Code on the book's detail page.

The files that are available for download from our site have been archived using WinZip. When you have saved the attachments to a folder on your hard-drive, you need to extract the files using a decompression program such as WinZip or PKUnzip. When you extract the files, the code is usually extracted into chapter folders. When you start the extraction process, ensure your software (WinZip, PKUnzip, and so on) is set to use folder names.

Errata

We've made every effort to make sure that there are no errors in the text or in the code. However, no one is perfect and mistakes do occur. If you find an error in one of our books, like a spelling mistake or a faulty piece of code, we would be very grateful for feedback. By sending in errata you may save another reader hours of frustration, and, of course, you will be helping us provide even higher quality information. Simply e-mail the information to support@wrox.com, where your information will be checked and, if correct, posted to the errata page for that title, or used in subsequent editions of the book.

To find errata on the web site, go to http://www.wrox.com/, and simply locate the title through our Advanced Search or title list. Click on the Book Errata link, which is below the cover graphic on the book's detail page.

e-mail Support

If you wish to directly query a problem in the book with an expert who knows the book in detail then e-mail support@wrox.com, with the title of the book and the last four numbers of the ISBN in the subject field of the e-mail. A typical e-mail should include the following things:

❑ The **title of the book, last four digits of the ISBN,** and **page number** of the problem in the Subject field.

❑ Your **name, contact information,** and the **problem** in the body of the message.

We **won't** send you junk mail. We need the details to save your time and ours. When you send an e-mail message, it will go through the following chain of support:

❑ Customer Support – Your message is delivered to our customer support staff, who are the first people to read it. They have files on most frequently asked questions and will answer anything general about the book or the web site immediately.

❑ Editorial – Deeper queries are forwarded to the technical editor responsible for that book. They have experience with the programming language or particular product, and are able to answer detailed technical questions on the subject.

❑ The Authors – Finally, in the unlikely event that the editor cannot answer your problem, he or she will forward the request to the author. We do try to protect the author from any distractions to their writing; however, we are quite happy to forward specific requests to them. All Wrox authors help with the support on their books. They will e-mail the customer and the editor with their response, and again all readers should benefit.

The Wrox Support process can only offer support to issues that are directly pertinent to the content of our published title. Support for questions that fall outside the scope of normal book support, is provided via the community lists of our http://p2p.wrox.com/ forum.

p2p.wrox.com

For author and peer discussion join the P2P mailing lists. Our unique system provides **programmer to programmer**™ contact on mailing lists, forums, and newsgroups, all in addition to our one-to-one e-mail support system. If you post a query to P2P, you can be confident that it is being examined by the many Wrox authors and other industry experts who are present on our mailing lists. At p2p.wrox.com you will find a number of different lists that will help you, not only while you read this book, but also as you develop your own applications. Particularly appropriate to this book are the **aspx** and **aspx_professional** lists in the .NET category of the web site.

To subscribe to a mailing list just follow these steps:

1. Go to http://p2p.wrox.com/

2. Choose the appropriate category from the left menu bar

3. Click on the mailing list you wish to join

4. Follow the instructions to subscribe and fill in your e-mail address and password

5. Reply to the confirmation e-mail you receive

6. Use the subscription manager to join more lists and set your e-mail preferences

Why This System Offers The Best Support

You can choose to join the mailing lists or you can receive them as a weekly digest. If you don't have the time, or facilities, to receive the mailing list, then you can search our online archives. Junk and spam mails are deleted, and your own e-mail address is protected by the unique Lyris system. Queries about joining or leaving lists, and any other general queries about lists, should be sent to `listsupport@p2p.wrox.com`.

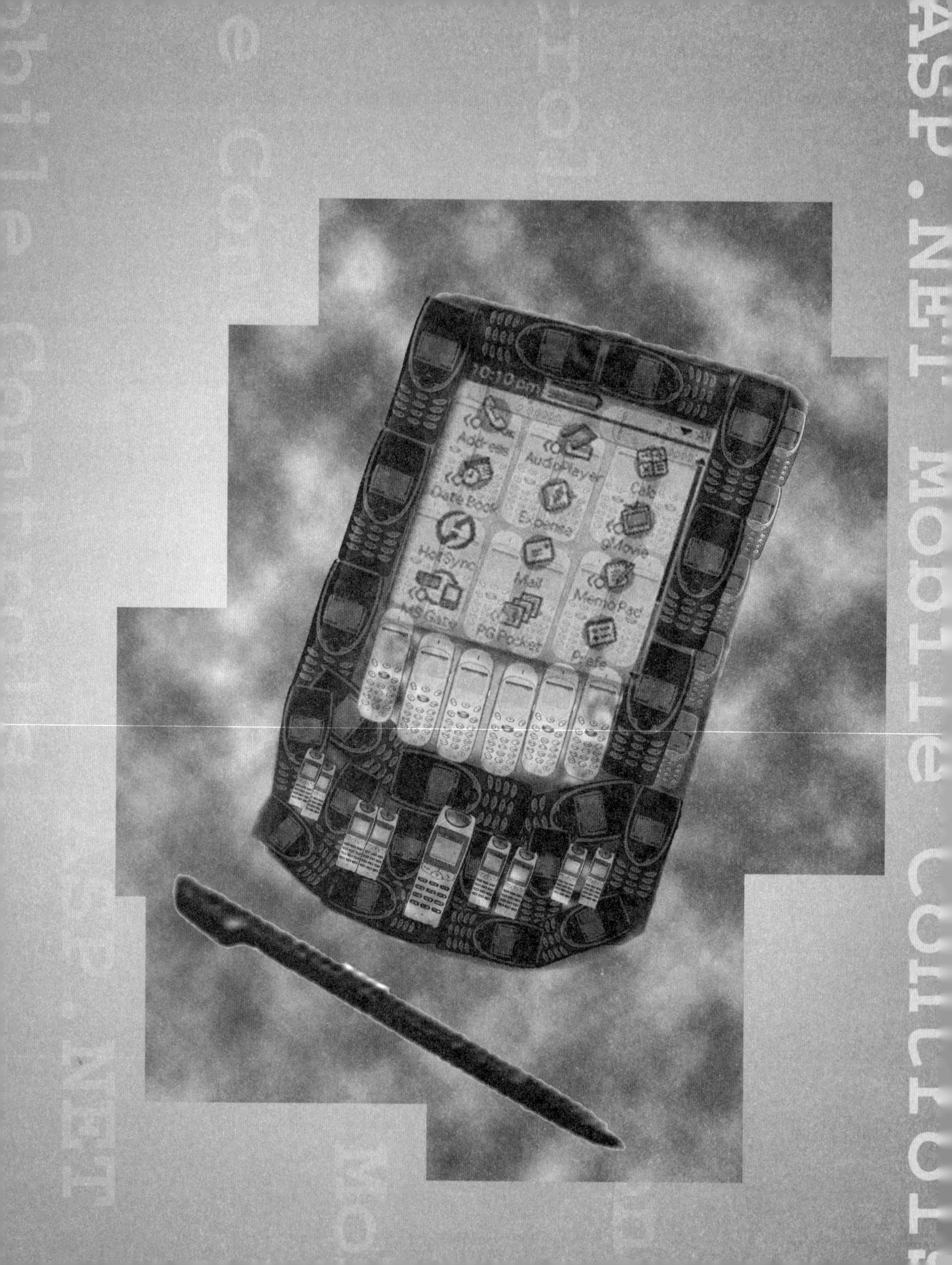
ASP.NET Mobile

Introducing The .NET Mobile World

The age of mobile development is upon us, but that doesn't mean that it has only just begun. Mobile application development has been around for quite a while; certainly long enough for developers to have a fairly big wish-list and 'diss-list'. Thankfully, some of those wishes may have come true with the rise of .NET, and perhaps we can scratch off a few lines of the 'diss-list', too. Microsoft has produced a tool far superior to its own previous offerings in the form of the **.NET Framework**. **ASP.NET** and the **Microsoft Mobile Internet Toolkit** are a very powerful set of tools that enable you to produce content accessible on any device.

The goal of this book is to get you comfortable with mobile development using ASP.NET and the Microsoft Mobile Internet Toolkit. By the end of this book, you should feel confident to take advantage of the many opportunities that .NET mobile content development creates.

In this chapter, we'll be looking at:

- ❑ Some of the challenges that traditional ASP programmers have had to face, and the ways that ASP.NET and the .NET Framework have resolved them

- ❑ An overview of the Microsoft Mobile Internet Toolkit, and show a very simple example page rendered in a mobile emulator

- ❑ And we'll talk a bit about some of the compatibility issues between ASP.NET applications and Mobile Web Controls

To put all these new technologies in context, cast your mind back to what it was like to program only a few years ago.

Business was dictating that we start moving away from the traditional Client-Server/Desktop application model and start thinking in terms of web services (ASP, JSP, and so on). At the time it could almost have been perceived as a regressive step: The way that applications resided on the Internet resembled old school mainframe architecture too closely for comfort – they were server-centric, with browsers in place of the original dumb terminals. To make matters worse, the new languages used to program web applications were wrought with imperfections when compared to trusty stalwarts like Visual Basic and Delphi. These problems threw up a number of challenges for developers to face, some of which are listed here:

- ❑ The early HTML controls used to develop User Interfaces (UI) were paper thin. The developer had to provide their own 'wiring' code to simulate events using Dynamic HTML (DHTML) or JavaScript (DHTML uses JavaScript to dynamically change an HTML element's properties, or react to events raised by them). In an attempt to ease this burden an event model was fitted onto a language originally intended for direct layout. To make matters worse, the output was rendered in a client that had originally been intended for delivering static pages, not for emulating desktop applications.

- ❑ State management was a big problem due to the stateless nature of the protocols that the Internet is comprised of. These protocols are connection-less which means that each time a user hits the server, it may as well be the first time as far as the server is concerned. Developers had to carry the user's state from page to page, using hidden variables or by packing it into a cookie. They then had to reconstruct the view state after each trip to the server. This meant lots of extra code had to be written where previously (under the Client-Server model) state was simply stored in memory on the user's box.

- ❑ Efficient, reliable debugging was impossible due to the distributed nature of web applications.

- ❑ A common ground for applications to share data between disparate systems was non-existent.

- ❑ Securing applications and data became a much bigger issue due to moving mission critical applications to the Internet. This just opened a major point of entry.

- ❑ Code reuse is limited due to the spaghetti-type relationship of the presentation code and business logic.

- ❑ Most often, developers were coding to unknown client capabilities (and even more so now) because of how quickly changes were being made to browser software and new additions being made to the client pool.

With this abbreviated list of obstacles it might invite the question "is it worth moving in this direction?" I believe so, but it is not the developer's job to pose that kind of question, rather it is our job to provide what the business world demands in software functionality. The pace that business moves now requires that workers in the field have ready access to inventory, scheduling, and a myriad of other enterprise-level data. Business demands mobility.

Developers came up with ever more creative ways of dealing with the obstacles of this new environment, while vendors feverishly developed tools and products to help compensate (read: placate) developers while they scrambled to figure out how to handle the sudden changes on the playing field.

.NET

The .NET Framework is Microsoft's move towards a toolset that is ready-made for the type of development challenges that the Internet does, and will, present. Within the brief overview of the framework that follows is **ASP.NET.** ASP.NET promises to completely change the world of web application development.

.NET isn't just a 'patch' for the problems we talked about, it is an entirely new platform that is designed to bridge the technical gap between traditional windows development and web application development, and at the same time, be extensible enough to handle the constant addition of new computing devices and their linguistic demands.

Some of what the .NET framework gives us is:

- The ability to easily build component-based applications.

- **XML Web Services** that let otherwise disparate systems share data. An XML Web Service can securely expose programmatic functionality over the Internet and allow the client application to treat it as though it were a local object or API. An example of a Web Service is Microsoft's Favorites Service that will allow any system that can make SOAP (Simple Object Access Protocol) calls over HTTP/S to implement functionality to allow users to store favorites on their site.

- **Common Language Runtime** (CLR):

    - A runtime environment that has enhanced security features, such as making sure that any code that runs is 'trusted'.

    - Memory management by way of a new Garbage Collection mechanism. One of the advantages to the new mechanism is that it solves the circular reference problems.

    - **Just In Time (JIT) compilation** to native code specific to the processor type on which the framework is running. This is a two-step compilation process that will allow easy porting between platforms. The compiler first compiles to MS Intermediate Language and then to the processor/operating system-specific machine code.

    - Support for multiple languages (**VB.NET, C#**, and **JScript.NET**, as standard).

- Language interoperability with CLR-compliant languages:

    - A common, binary type system that allows cross-language inheritance.

    - Exception handling across languages.

- Easier application deployment and maintenance:

    - **XCOPY** deployment for ASP.NET applications so there is no need for the application installation to make registry entries.

    - Easy code revision due to a system-level mechanism for handling versioning.

- Seamless interoperability with COM:

- **ASP.NET**, which includes:

    - **Web Forms Server Controls** – This is a set of controls that allows you to quickly develop event driven web applications. Using Visual Studio .NET makes programming Web Forms feel very much like programming a Visual Basic form.

    - **Web Services** allow access to the functionality of a server remotely.

    - Browser independent behavior and UI rendering.

    - Enriched support for state management.

    - **Code Behind** mechanism enables developers to separate HTML code from their program logic.

    - Because ASP.NET pages are compiled into native code by JIT compilers, this allows early binding in a strongly-typed programming environment.

Though .NET provides a wonderful new platform for developing web applications, don't be surprised or discouraged when associated new difficulties arise in spite of it all. This is the natural order of progress in the art or field. Over time developers explore new technology and push its limits, which is how each successive 'fixit' list is compiled for a platform or technology.

Now we've set the scene, we can start looking at the fun stuff! In the next section we'll review a few things you should know about ASP.NET, then we'll introduce the **Mobile Controls**.

Tone Your Web Application With ASP.NET

ASP.NET is what programming the Web **should** be like. Microsoft has successfully blurred the distinction between the Desktop and the Internet. They've taken the best parts of the Visual Basic programming paradigm and made them a part of the ASP.NET programming experience. Windows desktop programmers will now be able to leverage most of their existing skill-set to build web applications.

We're going to look in a little bit more detail now at the ASP.NET Server Controls, as they relate directly to the **Mobile Web Form Controls** that we'll be using in this book. The other controls are beyond our scope, but you can read about them in a couple of other books by Wrox – *Beginning ASP.NET with C#,* ISBN 1-861006-15-2, or *Professional ASP.NET,* ISBN 1-861004-88-5.

ASP.NET Server Controls

The ASP.NET server controls are new classes that provide functionality for everything from validating forms to enabling events to fire. A great many server controls are provided by ASP.NET out of the box, but it's pretty simple to create custom controls of our own that we can re-use in other ASP.NET applications. We're going to give a brief overview of the controls provided by ASP.NET, and then discuss what parallels are in the Microsoft Mobile Internet Toolkit (MMIT).

We will be considering the following groups of controls:

❑   **HTMLControls** and **WebControls**

❑   Server-side User controls

❑   Validation controls

HTMLControls And WebControls

The HTMLControls and WebControls will undoubtedly make our lives as developers much easier. They can automatically maintain their own state (using a feature called **postback,** which you will know from your study of ASP.NET), detect browser type and tailor the HTML that they send, and automatically reconstruct view state upon returning from a trip to the server. The days of having to write our own code to repopulate our controls are gone.

How Does This Work?

The HTML and web server controls exist as objects within the containing page and are consequently exposed programmatically to the server, on which they are processed (hence the name *server* controls). This allows client-side events to be detected in the form POST and handled just as they would be if they were raised in a Desktop application. So, from a control's instance, a developer has access to its properties and methods in the same way that they would with traditional Visual Basic form controls.

Here are a couple of factors that might help you choose whether to use HTML or web server controls:

❑ If you're working with legacy HTML code and need to add some additional functionality, then choosing HTML server controls will enable you to interact with your existing client-side code while taking advantage of an event-driven programming model. Bear in mind that you will not be able to take advantage of the typed object model if you do this, however, as all values are passed as strings.

❑ If your user interface design includes nested controls and you want a more granular style of event handling, then web server controls will suit you better than HTML server controls, since not only will you be able to catch events at the container level, but you will also have the added benefit of type safety.

❑ Both types of control will detect the client browser type and render the proper mark up language.

For reference, here is an example of the WebControls class:

```
<asp:Button runat="server" Text="Click" id="MyButton"></asp:Button>
```

and an example of the HTMLControls class:

```
<INPUT type=button value="Click" id="cmdMyButton" name="cmdMyButton"
runat="server">
```

User Controls

User Controls are useful ways of creating bundles of reusable logic that you can distribute much as you would an ActiveX control. The ease with which this can be done encourages much greater code reuse for web applications. Where previously, with Classic ASP, 'reuse' meant importing a Cascading Style Sheet or tweaking some JavaScript or VBScript to fit our page, now we can easily re-use code and also embed it into subsequent ASP.NET pages. To 'embed' these User Controls into a page we use the Register directive:

```
<%@ Register tagprefix="myTagPrefix" Tagname="myTagName"
Src="myUserControl.ascx"%>
```

and we then place the control where you need it in our page:

```
<myTagPrefix:myTagName runat="server"/>
```

> **A User Control must be embedded into an ASP.NET page – it cannot be called independently.**

Validation Controls

The validation controls that ship with .NET are intended to alleviate some of the burden of validating client input. These controls take the responsibility of client-side coding off the developer's shoulders. These controls break down into the following categories:

❑   `CompareValidator` – Compares a user's value against a constant value, or a property of another control.

❑   `CustomValidator` – Runs the validation against logic that the developer writes. This is useful if we need to check for values that are produced at run-time.

❑   `RangeValidator` – Checks to make sure that the value the user supplied is within certain boundaries. These boundaries can be a pair of numbers, dates, or alphabetic characters. Again, the ranges can be implemented as constants, or the properties of other controls.

❑   `RegularExpressionValidator` – Checks user input against a regular expression. This is useful in validating phone numbers, social security numbers, e-mail addresses, and so on.

Now that we've reviewed the Server Controls that ASP.NET uses as a base, we can go on to look at the wireless controls that build on top of that.

> We are only dealing with the Server Controls briefly in this book. For a more in-depth look at how they are developed please see either *Beginning ASP.NET* or *Professional ASP.NET*, both from Wrox Press.

The Mobile Thing

Just when developers thought limitations on the client-side couldn't become any more painful, someone figured out how to connect a cell phone to the Internet. That really put a dent in the paradigm! Suddenly there were many more potential client devices that were even more particular about what they would accept than the common web browser.

These new clients are arriving in the form of PDAs, cell phones, you name it; and someone is trying to connect these to the Internet (there's a guy I know who is working on a server that sits in his car and downloads and plays music using a wireless connection). These new clients further limit what developers can use to construct their user interfaces due to the reduced onboard memory and disparate markup languages the devices require. These subjects will be discussed in depth in Chapter 3.

Mobile computing will not *replace* the current state of web applications, rather it will be something that is a *part* of them in instances that require it. I can see those instances becoming quite frequent, though.

In order to keep pace with the constant addition of new computing devices, Microsoft developed an SDK for .NET called the **Microsoft Mobile Internet Toolkit (MMIT)**. The controls that ship with the MMIT, at first glance, look identical to ASP.NET's **Web Form** controls, but they are specifically geared for mobile devices, so there are some cool things going on behind the scenes to let them work with the different hardware.

The controls are designed to detect the client type and render the correct markup code. The idea behind the Mobile Controls is that you will be able to code once, and then run that code on many clients, the same way that you do with ASP.NET Web Form Controls.

It is also expansible. If John Doe writes a new browser for a mobile MP3 download gizmo that uses a homemade markup language that the MIT doesn't support, then he can write a **Device Adapter** (a Device Adapter is code written to implement support for a new device within MIT, discussed in Chapter 14), to get it to work with the MIT.

Let's look at a brief example of a Mobile Web Form in action.

> **If you don't already have the Mobile Internet Toolkit installed, this code will not work. We go through the installation process in Chapter 2. Don't worry for now about the specific details of what's going on, we'll be getting into that in later chapters, just look at this as a high level overview.**

Try It Out – Our First Mobile Control Example

This code is going to create a `Command` button on a Mobile Web Form. Like all the code in this book it can be downloaded from **www.wrox.com**.

As we are not writing an event handler for the button, nothing happens if we click it, other than posting the form back to the server.

1. Open your chosen text editor and enter the following code:

```
<%@ Page Inherits="System.Web.UI.MobileControls.MobilePage" Language="C#"%>
<%@Register TagPrefix="mobile" Namespace="System.Web.UI.MobileControls"
                               Assembly="System.Web.Mobile" %>

  <mobile:Form id="Form1" runat="server">
    <mobile:Command id="Command1" runat="server">It Worked!</mobile:Command>
  </mobile:Form>
```

2. Save the page as `WroxExample1.aspx` in your `/wwwroot` folder, or you can create a new virtual directory or this purpose as outlined in the next chapter.

3. Navigate your browser to http://localhost/WroxExample1.aspx and you will see one of the following (remember, if you have not installed the MMIT, this code will not work! See Chapter 2):

With the Microsoft Desk Pocket PC emulator, you'll see the following:

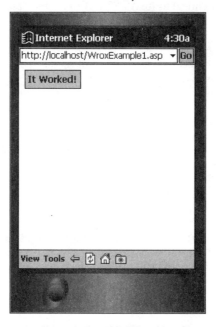

With the Nokia standard emulator, available as part of the Nokia Mobile Internet Toolkit:

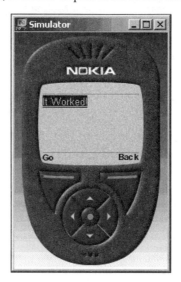

With the Openwave browser:

Image courtesy Openwave Systems Inc.

And lastly, with Microsoft Internet Explorer 6.0:

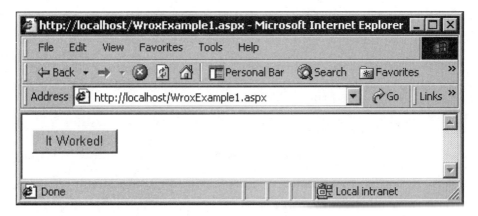

How It Works

Let's look at the code that spawned these views, piece by piece:

```
<%@ Page Inherits="System.Web.UI.MobileControls.MobilePage" Language="VB"%>
<%@Register TagPrefix="mobile" Namespace="System.Web.UI.MobileControls"
                                Assembly="System.Web.Mobile" %>
```

First come the **directives**. The Page directive tells the CLR that the page's instance is derived from the System.Web.UI.MobileControls.MobilePage base class (which is installed with the MMIT) using the Inherits attribute. The Language attribute is then used to inform the compiler that, in this case, it should use the C# compiler. Next, the Register directive sets aside the tag prefix that will be used to group and identify the Mobile Controls within the page that they are being implemented on. The Namespace attribute specifies where the button control resides and the Assembly attribute points to the assembly where the namespace resides.

```
<mobile:Form id="Form1" runat="server">
```

Next comes our mobile form. You will recognize that mobile is the tag prefix that we just set in the register directive. This statement declares the type of control that we are instantiating, in this case a Form, then the id attribute gives it a name to allow the server to access it as a container and use the controls within. Finally there is the runat="server" attribute that marks the control as a **server control**. We will look into the details of how this control renders the correct representation of a form on multiple clients in detail in Chapter 5.

```
<mobile:Command id="Command1" runat="server">
```

Residing within the Form control is the Command control. This is responsible for tailoring the output so it is rendered differently on each of the three clients that we used previously. Hopefully, you can now see how little code you need to write to render controls on different clients – just like with ASP.NET Server Controls the hard work of tailoring output to device is done for you.

A Few Compatibility Issues between ASP.NET and Mobile Controls

As closely related as ASP.NET and the Mobile Internet Toolkit are, there are still a few compatibility issues that we need to be aware of. We'll mention them briefly here, and then deal with them in depth in the chapters corresponding to them.

Error Handling and Reporting

When an ASP.NET application encounters an **unhandled error**, or any other type of error, it automatically generates an error page. These errors can include those that occur while compiling or running the page, or from bogus information in the Web.Config file. If your application is configured to generate default error pages, some mobile devices may encounter problems when trying to display the output. A good portion of mobile devices cannot handle the detailed contents of the returned error page. They will usually show a device-specific error, instead, telling you almost nothing about what is really going on to cause the error. To address this, you should always make a point of testing mobile forms on a common desktop browser to see if there are any initial compilation or configuration errors.

Tracing

ASP.NET provides a debugging feature called **Tracing**. This feature allows the developer to monitor the path of execution that a page request spawns. Tracing shows us a snapshot of what happened during the processing of the page.

This mechanism appends the trace results to the code sent to the client. As is the case for the above error-handling scenario, mobile clients may not have an easy time rendering the results. This limitation can be overcome by enabling tracing at the application level and viewing the results with a desktop browser.

Session State and Cookies

ASP.NET has some wonderful session management capabilities that are somewhat limited when working with Mobile Web Forms. In Chapter 16 we will discuss this in detail, for now, here is a brief overview:

❑ Some mobile devices and wireless gateways don't support cookies. In order for your application to support these situations you must configure your application to use **cookieless mode session management.**

❑ Some mobile devices incorrectly handle relative URLs after being redirected using the technique that cookieless session management uses. There is a workaround for this which is detailed in Chapter 16.

Summary

In this chapter we have talked about some of the problems that developers faced, and what the .NET framework, ASP.NET, and Server Controls have done to solve them. We also saw how the Mobile Web Form controls sit within this structure and the active part they are playing in helping developers deal with a rapidly expanding range of web clients.

We have looked at:

❑ Some of the obstacles that early last-generation web application developers had to deal with

❑ A brief overview of the .NET Framework and how it is a new platform that bridges the gap between traditional desktop development and web application development and solves many of the past problems

❑ A bullet-point overview of ASP.NET

❑ An introduction to the Microsoft Mobile Internet Toolkit (MMIT)

❑ A simple example using a mobile Web Form control

❑ We were alerted to the idea that there will be some compatibility issues to lookout for

Over the course of the book we will dig deeper into the MMIT, and specifically mobile Web Form controls, to get you up and running with your own mobile applications.

Chapter 3 will lay down some basics about mobile computing and what is involved for developers when working in those environments. But firstly, in the next chapter we'll get set up so that we're able to create and view the example code provided in this book.

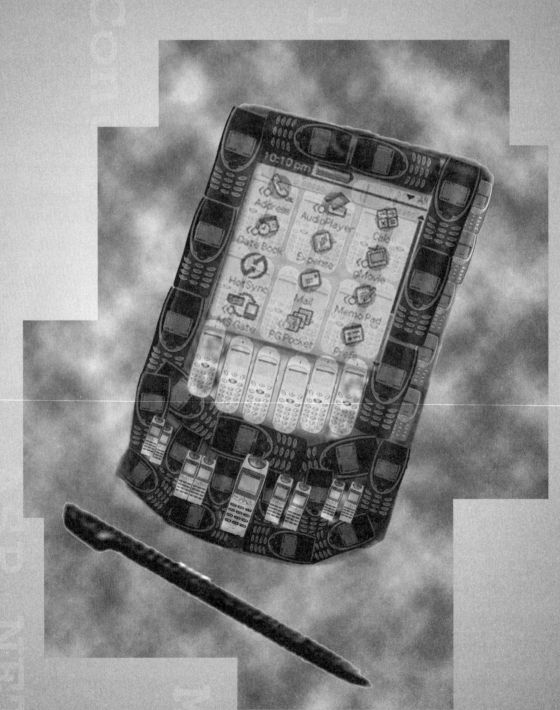

Prepare For Development!

In the previous chapter we saw a basic example of a Mobile application, and hopefully that will have whetted your appetite for more. This chapter will show you how to set up the various devices shown in Chapter 1 and, in no time at all, you will be pleased to see the words 'It Worked' on a multitude of different browsers! We will work through the setup and installation of some of the most popular browsers and highlight any possible problems with getting started.

In this chapter, we'll be looking at:

❑   Installing the Microsoft Mobile Internet Toolkit, which includes everything we need to use the mobile controls

❑   Installing simulators for mobile phones

❑   Installing simulators for handheld PDA devices, such as the MME and Pocket PC

❑   Setting up virtual directories and web applications using IIS

❑   Testing our installation.

Buckle up, settle down, and enjoy the ride – we're getting mobile!

Installation

We assume that you will have the Microsoft .NET framework, and possibly Visual Studio .NET installed on your PC before you start. Visual Studio .NET isn't a prerequisite for this book, but those of you who own a copy, or who have MSDN subscriptions, should have it installed before we go any further. Don't worry if you're just running the .NET Framework – the majority of this book is editor-neutral, so you won't be at a disadvantage. If you have not yet downloaded the Framework, you can find it on the MSDN web site (http://msdn.microsoft.com/).

Microsoft Mobile Internet Toolkit

Installing the Microsoft Mobile Internet Toolkit is a relatively painless process. Currently you can find the installer for the release candidate on the public downloads section of MSDN at the following URL:

http://msdn.microsoft.com/downloads/default.asp?url=/code/sample.asp?url=/MSDN-FILES/027/001/516/msdncompositedoc.xml&frame=true&hidetoc=true

> *The final release of the MMIT will probably be at a slightly different URL that is not known at the time of going to press, but you should be able to find it quite easily using MSDN's Search functionality.*
>
> *If you can't find it, stay tuned to http://www.wrox.com//, where you will be able to download the code samples for this book. In this download, we will be able to place up-to-date information, including the URL for the location of the latest MSDN download.*

Just point your browser at the appropriate URL, and the following page will appear:

Simply click on Download and away we go! You should then be invited to read, and accept, the terms of Microsoft's license agreement:

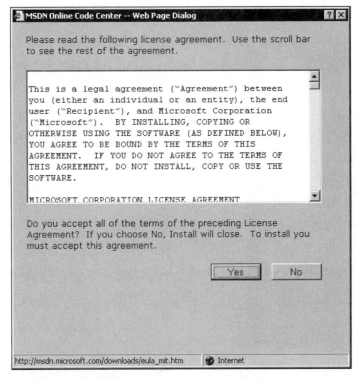

After accepting the terms of this agreement, save the program to disk, as shown in the screenshot below:

After clicking on the OK button, you're prompted to save the file to your local file system. Choose the appropriate download location and click Ok. Once the download is complete, double-click the downloaded file. You should see the following:

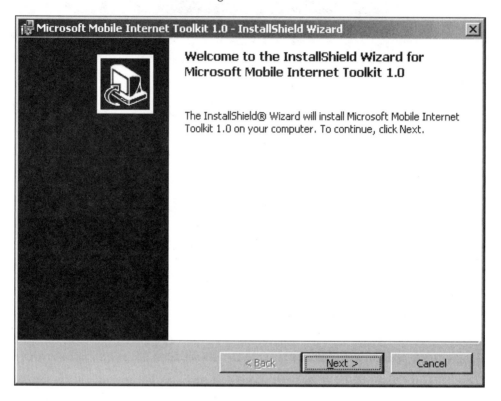

Simply click the Next button and you're presented with another license agreement. After reading through the legal information, and as long as you have no objections, click the radio button that says 'I accept the terms in the license agreement' and once again, click 'Next'.

We are now faced with a choice of the level of installation that we require, Complete, or Custom. We recommend that you select the Complete setup type which is the default setting, so all that is needed is to press Next again:

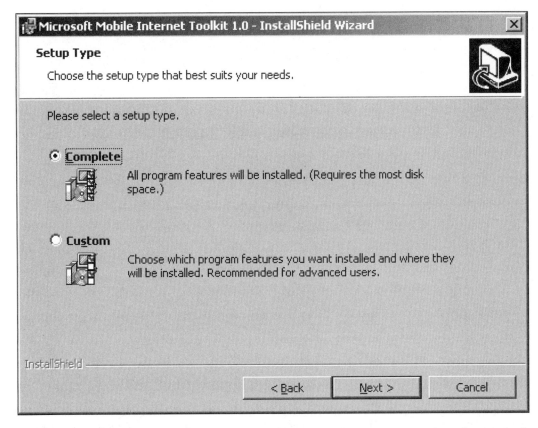

The Microsoft Mobile Internet Toolkit is now installed, and that's stage one complete! Our next task is to install some software clients to test our code on. We'll begin with the Nokia Mobile Internet Toolkit:

The Nokia Mobile Internet Toolkit

Downloading the Nokia MIT is really straightforward – it doesn't take very long, and there are no dead-ends to go down. The first stage is to visit the Nokia web site. This can be found by navigating to http://forum.nokia.com/ as shown here:

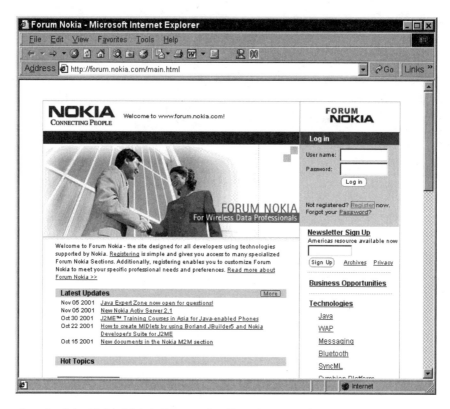

In order to download the Nokia Mobile Internet Toolkit 3.0, we need to register our details with Nokia. Simply click on the 'Register' button, as shown in the top right-hand corner of the screenshot above, and we will be transported to the registration page. We need to register our details with Nokia in order to gain access to their Mobile Internet Toolkit, so you'll need to fill in the various fields before we can proceed.

After registering your details, you can log in to the site in order to access the downloads that you're interested in. The screenshot below shows the link to the Nokia Mobile Internet Toolkit 3.0 download facility. This link can be found by scrolling down the http://forum.nokia.com/main page:

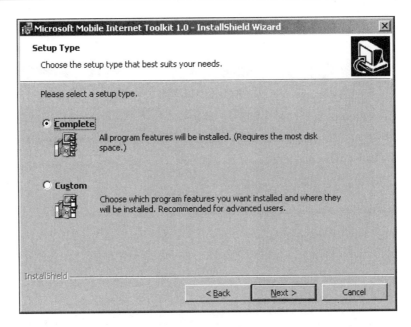

If we click on the hyperlink titled 'Nokia Mobile Internet Toolkit 3.0 Now Available' we are taken to the screen as shown below:

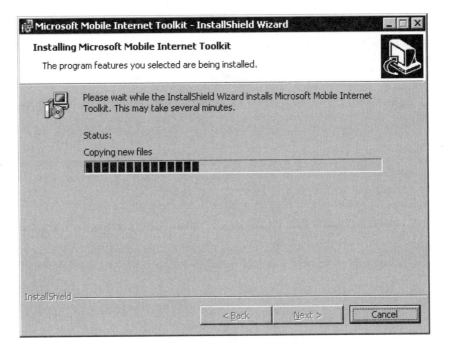

If we click on the Download link, as shown on the right of the previous screen, we are taken to the following page:

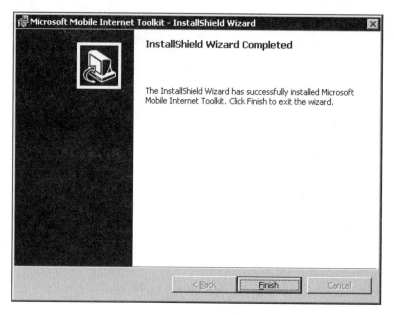

As you can see from the screenshot above, the Nokia Mobile Internet Toolkit 3.0 requires that we have the Java Runtime Environment 1.3.1 (or higher) installed. Don't worry if you haven't got it, as the download will try to find it on your system, and, if it's not there, will install it automatically. We'll discuss this again later in the chapter.

Simply click on the NokiaToolkit3_0.zip hyperlink, and you will be presented with a standard dialog box for saving the file to your local system or for opening it from its current location. Saving is usually the best option so that you can keep a copy of the toolkit download locally in case you need to reinstall it at any time. The toolkit is quite a large download, so it will take a while to complete.

After downloading the NokiaToolkit3_0.zip file, you will need to uncompress it using whichever tool you prefer. We can then read the license.txt file, the ReleaseNotes.txt file, or can simply set it up by running the setup.exe file. Once you start the setup process, you will need to read through and accept the Nokia license agreement in order to use the toolkit.

As we mentioned earlier, we need the JRE 1.3.1 installed on our machines before we can download the Nokia Toolkit. If JRE 1.3.1 isn't installed on your machine, then a message box similar to the one on the next page will appear. If we want to continue to download, then we have to click the Yes button.

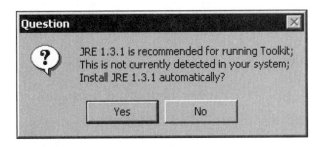

The Toolkit will then install the Java Runtime Environment, taking you through yet another set of installation screens. As before, you'll need to accept the license agreement, accept the default installation path, and then watch some exciting progress bars (the modern-day equivalent of drying paint), and eventually the process will finish.

You can now launch the toolkit from your Start | Programs menu. You should see the following screens appear:

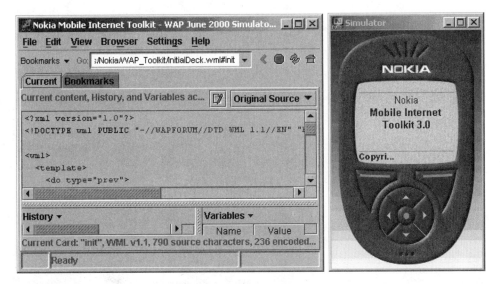

The simulator shown is the default simulator, but you can also download some additional simulators that mimic actual phones. These will all have varying capabilities, so it's useful to test your code on as many of these as possible for real-world applications.

To find these extra simulators, head back to the page on the Nokia site, where we downloaded the simulator, scroll down the page, and you'll see links to download additional simulators:

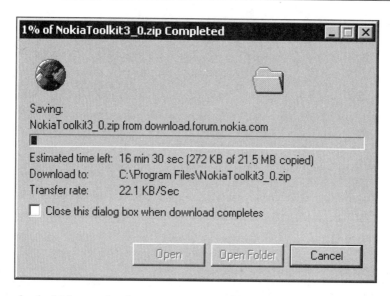

Feel free to download whichever simulators you require. Here are some examples of the available simulators:

This simulator comes as part of the default installation and is resizable.

This is the 6210 emulator

This is the 7110 emulator

All of these simulators are fairly easy to use. All you need to do is type the address for your test code into the control panel address bar in the same way as you would for normal browsing. The resulting pages appear in the phone simulator. The buttons on the phone behave in a similar way to real phones, so you'll have to pretend you're using a real phone to surf, and forget that you're on a computer.

Of course, there's a lot more browsers out there, so let's have a look at the Openwave offering:

The Openwave Simulators

The Openwave browser is employed on many different makes of handsets, and is subtly different from the Nokia browser. Let's take a look at how we can download some Openwave simulators.

First of all, let's head to the Openwave web site:

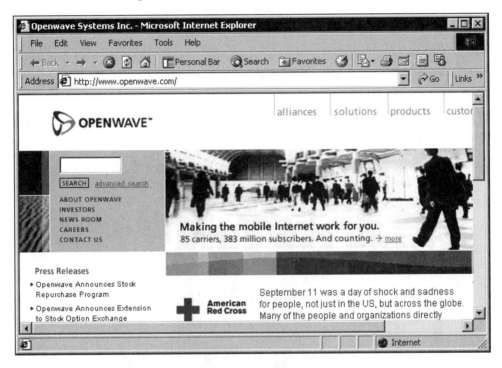

At the bottom of the page, you'll find a link to the new Openwave Software Development Kit (Version 5). Follow this link and you'll be taken to a page with a download link. From the link you're presented with some options. Version 5 of the SDK has only recently been released, and we haven't been able to test the code in this book against this tool.

The procedure for downloading is much the same as before – once downloaded, you can simply install it in the usual way. Make sure you read the terms and conditions carefully before proceeding:

If you've got the old Version 4 SDK, you'll see the following when you run the simulator:

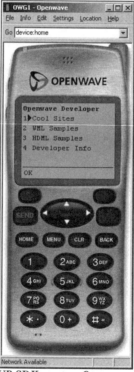

Image of UP.SDK courtesy Openwave Systems Inc.

If you've downloaded the newer Version 5 of the SDK, you are presented with a couple of options during installation. If you use the Typical installation and run the simulator, you'll be presented with something quite different from version 4:

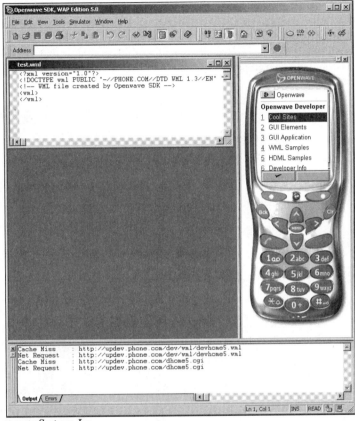

Image courtesy Openwave Systems Inc.

As you can see, you end up with a fairly interesting development environment. However, since it's designed for working with WML, cHTML, and so on, and not with the mobile controls, it's not a lot of use to us for the purposes of this book. We're only concerned with the phone simulator and the address bar.

The Microsoft Mobile Explorer

The Microsoft Mobile Explorer is a generic Pocket PC emulator, and is really useful for testing code to be viewed on PDA-style devices. It's a free download from Microsoft, and you can get it from the following location:

http://download.microsoft.com/download/VisualStudioNET/Install/3.0/NT45XP/
EN-US/MME30.exe

However, given that links to MSDN don't tend to last for long, you can navigate to the download via the main MSDN download site, http://msdn.microsoft.com/downloads/, then by clicking through the links on the left-hand side Windows Development | Mobility | Microsoft Mobile Explorer 3.0 (MME) Technology Preview.

If we click on the 'Download' link, we're transported to yet another license agreement. Again, as long as you're happy with the Terms and Conditions, you can carry on to download the emulator. If you have Visual Studio .NET installed, you can install a version of this emulator that integrates into the development environment, as well as the stand alone version. If you run the standalone version, you'll see the following:

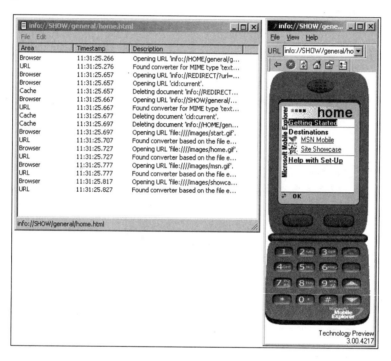

However, if you run the emulator within the Visual Studio .NET environment, you can dock the explorer window just like any other window:

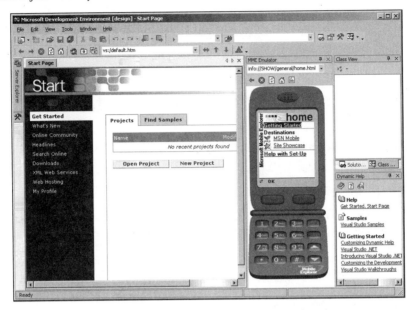

We'll learn more about using Visual Studio .NET to create mobile Web Form applications in Chapters 17 and 18.

The last browser we'll look at is actually part of the Pocket PC Software Development Kit, and as such is bundled as part of a very large download. Again, you can find it on the MSDN site, in the section on **Embedded Development**, as the **Talisker Emulation Edition Preview Beta 2**, which is the next version of Windows CE. Because this is a beta product, you'll need to have a passport to register for the beta, and you'll need to fill in a couple of fields. The download is a whopping 400MB, so you may want to leave it running overnight. Once downloaded, and installed, you'll see the following:

In order to access the browser on this device, you need to click on the Start menu in the top left corner, and then select the Pocket Internet Explorer browser. From then on you're on familiar territory.

Now we've got a fairly healthy range of devices that can be used to test our code, we need to take the plunge and set up our computer to actually get our code running. Let's move on to a brief recap of how we go about this.

Virtual Directories And Web Applications

In order to serve our mobile Web Forms via a web server, we need to set up a **virtual directory** for our code, so that it is processed by IIS and parsed by ASP.NET. For those of you unfamiliar with this process, or who are in need of a refresher, we'll explain this briefly.

What Is A Virtual Directory?

A virtual directory is the method used by IIS to indicate a folder that contains all of the code used in a particular **web application**. The actual directory that contains our code is referenced via an IIS console, and assigned a set of attributes that denote whether the application is to be read-only, whether the files in the application are able to be browsed, or whether you want to allow people to run executable code from within the application. These properties are all controlled from one dialog box.

Setting Up A Virtual Directory

Our first step is to open up the IIS manager. You can do this either by navigating from the Start menu:

❑ **Windows 2000**: Start | Settings | Control Panel | Administrative Tools | Internet Services Manager

❑ **Windows XP**: Start | Control Panel, then either switch to Classic View and select Administrative Tools then the Internet Services Manager, or select the Performance and Maintenance category, and select Administrative Tools, then Internet Services Manager.

If you're after a shortcut, I find the easiest way to launch the console is to hit Start | Run and type inetmgr into the box and hit return.

This console will eventually pop up:

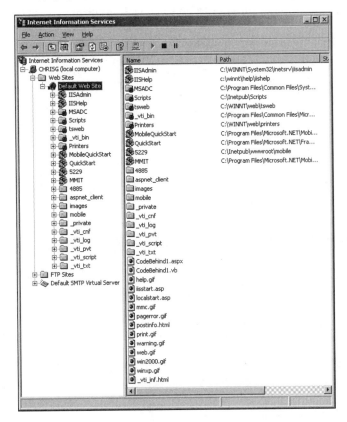

The left-hand pane in this window is where all the action happens. Expand the tree until you can see the contents of the **Default Web Site**. You'll see some icons appear – some look like folders, some look like folders with globes in the corner, and others look like bluey-green boxes with globes in them – these are our web applications, and are virtual directory representations of physical folders on our hard drive. Let's create our own virtual directory where we can store all of our code:

Try It Out – Creating A Virtual Directory

Let's start off by creating our physical directory:

1. Open up **My Computer** by double-clicking the icon on the desktop, then select the hard-drive of your choice (for this demonstration, we'll assume you're using the C: drive).

2. Right-click in the window and select **New | Folder**. Type in the name of your new folder – we'll call ours **Mobile**.

3. Double-click on your new **Mobile** folder to open it, and then create a text file, containing the following code, that we encountered in Chapter 1, inside it:

```
<%@ Page Inherits="System.Web.UI.MobileControls.MobilePage" Language="C#"%>
<%@Register TagPrefix="mobile" Namespace="System.Web.UI.MobileControls"
                                        Assembly="System.Web.Mobile" %>

 <mobile:Form id="Form1" runat="server">
   <mobile:Command id="Command1" runat="server">It Worked!</mobile:Command>
 </mobile:Form>
```

4. Save the file as `Example1.aspx` in your **Mobile** directory.

5. In the Internet Services Manager console, right-click on **Default Web Site**, and select **New | Virtual Directory**.

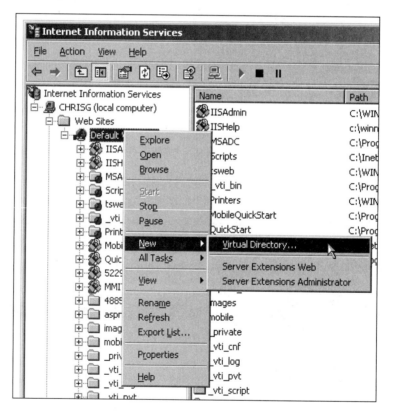

6. Click **Next** to move past the **Wizard** introduction screen, and on the next page, where you can type an alias for your site – for example, we'll use the last four digits of the ISBN of this book, so enter 5229 as the alias for your web site. We'll explain this in a moment in the *How It Works* section.

7. Now, enter the path to your directory (in our case, C:\mobile), then click Next again. In the final screen, make sure that only the top two permissions boxes are checked. Click Next and then Finish and we're done:

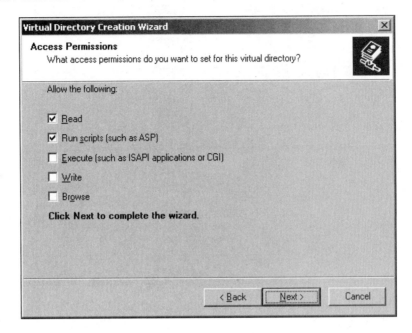

How It Works

We've created a physical directory called C:\Mobile, which is where we'll be storing our example code throughout this book. We then created a virtual directory called 5229, which is an alias for the physical directory. Now, whenever we want to test code, we can type the following into our browser:

http://localhost/5229/sample.aspx

This virtual alias will point towards the files stored in our c:\mobile folder, so that every time we enter the URL to run our ASPX pages, the web server will know where the files are stored and run them correctly.

So, what did all those permissions boxes mean?

Permissions In IIS

As we've just seen, we can assign permissions to a new directory as we create it, by using the options offered in the Virtual Directory Wizard. Alternatively, we can set permissions at any time, from the IIS admin tool in the MMC. To do this, right-click on the 5229 virtual directory in the IIS admin tool, and select Properties. You'll get the following dialog:

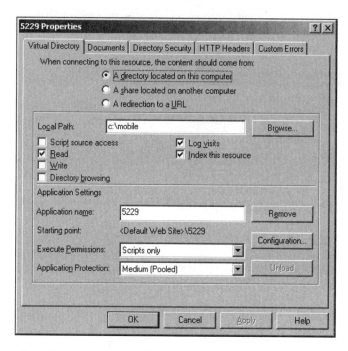

It's quite acomplicated, and it contains a lot of options – not all of which we wish to go into now. Let's break this down into sections:

Access Permissions

The four check-boxes on the left are of interest to us, as they govern the types of access for the given directory and dictate the permissions allowed on the files contained within that directory. Let's have a look at what each of these options means:

- **Script source access** – This permission enables users to access the sourcecode of an ASP.NET page. It's only possible to allow this permission if the Read or Write permission has already been assigned. But we generally don't want our users to be able to view our ASP.NET sourcecode, so we would usually leave this check-box unchecked for any directory that contains ASP.NET pages.

- **Read** – This permission enables browsers to read or download files stored in a home directory or virtual directory. If the browser requests a file from a directory that **doesn't** have the Read permission enabled, then the web server will simply return an error message.

- **Write** – If the Write permission on a virtual directory is enabled, then users will be able to create or modify files within the directory, and change the properties of these files. This is not normally turned on, for reasons of security and we don't recommend you alter it.

- **Directory browsing** – If you want to allow people to view the contents of the directory (that is, to see a list of all the files that are contained in that directory), then you can allow this by checking the Directory browsing option.

Execute Permissions

There's a dropdown list box near the foot of the Properties dialog, labeled Execute permissions – this specifies what level of program execution is permitted on pages contained in this directory. There are three possible values here – None, Scripts only, or Scripts and Executables:

❑ Setting Execute permissions to None means that users can only access static files, such as image files and HTML files. Any script-based files of other executables contained in this directory are inaccessible to users. If you tried to run an ASP.NET page, from a folder with this permission set to None, you would get an Execute Access Permission forbidden message in your page.

❑ Setting Execute permissions to Scripts Only means that users can also access any script-based pages, such as ASP.NET pages. So if the user requests an ASP.NET page that's contained in this directory, the web server will allow the ASP.NET code to be executed, and the resulting HTML to be sent to the browser.

❑ Setting Execute permissions to Scripts and Executables means that users can execute any type of file that's contained in the directory. It's generally a good idea to avoid using this setting, in order to prohibit users from executing potentially damaging applications on your web server.

> **For any directory containing ASP.NET files that you're publishing, the appropriate setting for the Execute permissions is Scripts Only.**

Now we're all set up, it's time to test our setup.

Testing Our Installation

Let's do a quick test to see if this worked. All we need to do is to enter the following address into the address bars of any of our browsers:

http://localhost/5229/example1.aspx

You should get results like those shown below:

Openwave Browsers:

Image courtesy Openwave Systems Inc.   Image of UP.SDK courtesy Openwave Systems Inc.

Nokia Browsers:

Pocket PC emulators:

Throughout the rest of this book we'll be showing results in just two clients per example – this book is about the controls, not the clients, so we'll leave it for you to have a play with any of these or other simulators. But, you should bear in mind that not all functionality is present in all of the clients. And, while we're talking about examples, here's something for you to make a note of:

> **All the code in this book is available for download from the Wrox web site, at http://www.wrox.com.**

Help – It's Not Working!

If something should go wrong at any stage, and the browsers aren't displaying the results as planned, the first and most obvious thing to do is retrace your steps and make sure you've set up the virtual directory correctly, and that the simulators are installed correctly. Try right-clicking on the virtual directory icon in the IIS console, and double-checking that the properties are set up as required. If you're still having trouble, don't forget that you can always ask questions on our Programmer to Programmer (P2P) lists at p2p.wrox.com. If you don't find the solution to your problem on those lists, then you can e-mail suppport@wrox.com as explained in the introduction to this book.

Summary

This has been a very quick overview of how to get our development environment set up correctly. We've managed to look at:

❑ Setting up the Microsoft Mobile Internet Toolkit

❑ Installing simulators for both mobile phones and handheld devices

❑ Configuring Web Applications and Virtual Directories

❑ Testing our installation

In the next chapter, we'll be moving on to examine the world of mobile communication, and how far it's come since WAP first came out about two years ago.

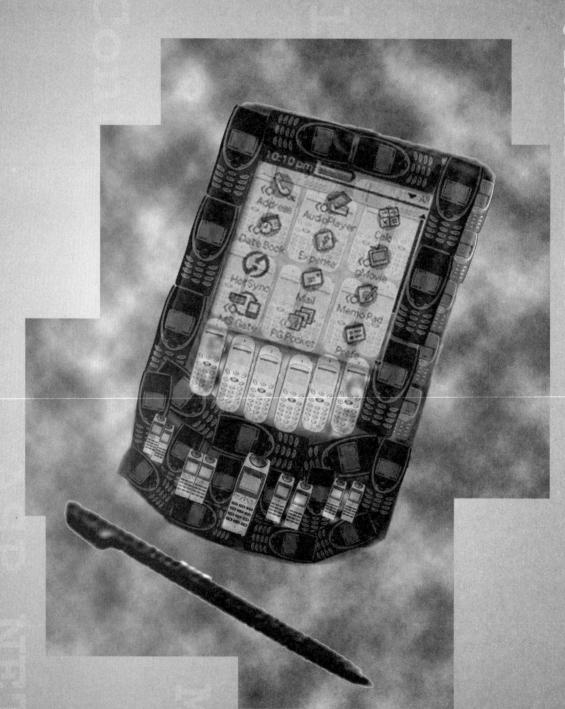

Mobile Communication

Communication between different mobile devices isn't that different a process to communication between desktop PCs. Information still travels using a standard protocol, and arrives in a format that the device can read. However, when you're using certain types of device, for example, a mobile phone, the standard protocols that we use day-to-day for transfer of information on PCs are simply too bulky to be used in low bandwidth situations, especially since the receiving device has much less functionality than a desktop machine. In many cases, these phones would access Internet data using WAP browsers, viewing sites designed to produce output compatible for these devices.

The aim of this chapter is to consider Mobile Communication in general, and the communication protocols employed. We'll begin by looking at wireless connectivity, and its benefits, before progressing to look at HTTP and WAP technology, and evaluating their impact to date and what the future may hold. By the end of this chapter, you should have gained a good foundation in the principles underlying mobile communication, which will be useful when learning about the mechanics of ASP.NET Mobile Forms.

Before we begin, a clear distinction should be made between the terms **mobile** and **wireless**. A mobile device is one that is portable, and can be used on the move – such as a laptop communicating through a telephone wire (wired communication). A wireless device, refers to communication over an 'air' network – a satellite dish would be an example of this. Some devices, such as cell-phones, can be both mobile **and** wireless, but one term does not necessarily imply the other. Because of their flexibility and tailored output ASP.NET Mobile Controls may provide the ideal solution for use with any of these platforms.

The Importance Of Being Mobile

It is becoming increasingly important for both businesses, and individuals, to be able to exchange information while on the move – regardless of time and place. This has seen a marked rise in the number of mobile devices in common use. In this next section, we'll briefly look at some of the factors that are behind that rise.

Mobile Is Better

Mobile devices are not simply a complement to wired-devices. They are rapidly providing better ways of solving problems in a changing technological world. There are two major types of information that a mobile solution can handle better than a static solution:

❑ **Locale Specific Data**, where elements, such as language and currency, will change in relation to where the information is accessed from

❑ **Volatile Information**, such as stock quotes or inventory listings, that are subject to rapid changes and to which you would ideally have access at all times

The challenge that now faces developers is to take the advances in mobile communication and apply them in a meaningful way to solve problems faced by business today. We'll look at this in the next section, which deals with the implications of the mobile revolution on the corporate world.

Mobile Business

Most businesses today are experiencing a trend towards office decentralization, with many employees either working from home, or from satellite offices. This approach brings many mutual benefits to both employer and employed:

❑ An opportunity to distribute load from company servers to home computers (if allowed by the applications used)

❑ Clearer measurement of tasks is made necessary by the (perceived) lack of direct supervision. This in turn forces higher management quality

❑ Increased employee motivation increases productivity

❑ Numerous social benefits (less traffic on the roads, lower pollution, and so on) encourage governments to support work-from-home schemes

There are many other benefits, of course, but the crux of the matter is that business is beginning to realize the potential of liberating its workforce. There is nothing to be gained from having workers at their desks if being on-site, or on the move, is more appropriate.

For example, imagine an engineering firm that had a mobile application allowing its engineers to submit information about the layout of the buildings they were surveying instantly, as they walked around the site, using a mobile client. This would remove the necessity of making notes by hand, and transporting them back to the office for input. Such an approach would have many advantages:

❑ Elimination of dead working time (traveling, waiting, and so on)

❑ Information only needs to be entered once, so the margin of error is reduced, while the efficiency of the process is simultaneously increased

❑ Queries and miscalculations can be spotted and rectified immediately on site

❑ Employees better understand their client's requirements through face to face communication

❑ Faster response to a client's queries and concerns as employees are always on hand

❑ Employees can build a more personal business relationship

Well-designed mobile applications can make the difference between the success or failure of a business. In the future it will become ever more important for successful companies to not rely on a single access medium. Rather, they will need to take advantage of many different methods of communication and select the one most suited to the task in hand. Furthermore, they will have less and less control over the kinds of client devices that will be trying to access their systems, so they will have to develop flexible methods of tailoring their information to these wide ranging clients. Put simply, rather than tailoring the task to the technology, we must now begin to tailor the technology to the task.

The WAP Experience

The Wireless Application Protocol (WAP) was developed by the WAP Forum (www.wapforum.org), and was widely anticipated as a wireless complement to the wired Internet. The requirements of this new information system were vastly different to that which had gone before – its client devices were very small, had little power, and had a limited capacity for color and sound. Worse still, data input was laborious, mistakes hard to rectify, and you couldn't rely on the quality or speed of your connection!

It was expected that the users of this new WAP system would be an entirely different breed from traditional Internet users, because they were coming from a different background. It was thought that they'd be much less tolerant of software errors (cell-phones don't crash!), more reluctant to explore and browse (phone options are only a couple of button presses away, and the user interface isn't conducive to browsing), and very impatient with anything that didn't work quickly and intuitively (you don't need a manual to operate the basic functions of your phone).

To make matters worse still, the wireless networks over which WAP had to operate were designed for mobile voice-calls, one of the most important features of which was to ensure that the connection was maintained as the client moved from one station's area of coverage to another. To do this, there was a constant overhead, above the communication, reporting if the reception quality was normal or whether a handover was required. This, and other invisible processes, inevitably degraded the bandwidth available for data transmission making speed and reliability a real problem, even though the call quality was still perfectly acceptable for voice-call transmission.

WAP needed to come up with a new way of transmitting information, as the techniques used by traditional HTTP Protocols were too bandwidth intensive for this environment. But before looking at this new Protocol here's a very quick refresher of the basics of HTTP to help you realize the differences.

The HTTP Protocol

Traditionally, wired Internet communication takes place using HTTP Protocols, which are very flexible and well suited to the distributed, web-like environment of the wired Internet, where information can be sent and received through a variety of different channels. The protocol copes with its flexible environment by attaching additional instructions to the packets of data that it sends to ensure that they can be sorted out and processed correctly when they get to the receiving server.

When a client communicates with a server over HTTP, to ask for a web page for example, there's a lot more involved than just sending the URL it wants. Every HTTP message assumes the same format (whether it's a client **Request** or a server **Response**). This format can be broken down into three sections:

- ❑ The Request/Response Line
- ❑ The HTTP Header
- ❑ The HTTP Body

The content of these three sections varies depending on whether the message is a Request or a Response, so we'll briefly outline each:

The HTTP Request

All HTTP Requests sent from the client to the server will contain the following three elements:

1. The Request Line
The first line of every HTTP request is the request line, containing three pieces of information:

- ❑ An HTTP command known as a **method**
- ❑ The path and filename of the resource the client is attempting to access
- ❑ The version of HTTP being used

Here's an example of a Request Line in this format

```
GET/Testpage.htm HTTP/1.1
```

2. The HTTP Header
The second section of information to be sent is the HTTP header. This contains information about the client, the information that it is sending, and the types of document that it will accept in return. It is divided into three categories:

- ❑ **General**: contains information about either the client or the server, but not specific to one or the other
- ❑ **Entity**: contains information about the data being sent between the client and the server
- ❑ **Request**: contains information about the client configuration and the different types of document that it is able to accept

An example HTTP header might look like this:

```
Accept: */*
Accept-Language: en-us
Connection: Keep-Alive
Host: www.wrox.com
Referer: http://webdev.wrox.co.uk/books/SampleList.aspx?bookcode=5040
User-Agent: Mozilla (X11; I; Linux 2.0.32 i586)
```

3. The HTTP Body
The HTTP Request body contains any data that is being sent to the server from the client, such as that collected by labels and textboxes.

The HTTP Response

The HTTP Response is sent back from the server to the client, and contains the same three basic elements as the Request:

1. **The Response Line**

The Response Line contains two pieces of information:

❑ The HTTP version number

❑ An HTTP status code that reports the success or failure of the request

Here's an example of this, showing that the Response is using HTTP 1.1, and the status code 200, meaning OK:

```
HTTP/1.1 200 OK
```

2. **The HTTP Header**

The HTTP Response header is similar to the HTTP Request header, and is divided into the same three parts:

❑ **General**: contains information about either the client or the server, but is not specific to one or the other

❑ **Entity**: contains information about the data being sent between the client and the server

❑ **Response**: Information about the server sending the response, and how it can deal with the response

Here's an example of what this header might look like:

```
HTTP/1.1 200 OK
Date: Mon, 1st Nov 1999, 16:12:23 GMT
Server: Microsoft-IIS/5.0
Last-modified: Fri, 29th Oct 1999, 12:08:03 GMT
```

3. **The HTTP Body**

If the Request was successful, then the HTTP Response Body will contain the requested HTML code, along with any script to be executed on the browser. Additional HTTP Requests will be used to download extra information, such as images and sound files, as dictated by the HTML code provided in the first request.

The WAP Protocol

The wireless world is a nightmare for HTTP Protocols, as the continuous back and forth flow of Requests and Responses, with their verbose style, will seriously degrade the bandwidth available for communication. For this reason, WAP is an attempt to produce a functional and efficient means of interacting in this environment. It consists of two principal parts:

❑ A new underlying **transmission protocol** that is efficient, robust, and secure

❑ A new **presentation format** that is user-friendly and minimizes the number of Requests and the amount of data transmitted

The Transmission Protocol

There are currently two WAP protocols; the widely adopted WAP 1.0 and the newly emerging WAP 2.0. Both of these are founded on something called the ISO-OSI model which defines a networking framework for implementing protocols over a series of seven layers, with control being passed, up and down, from one layer to another. At the sending station the information being transmitted is progressively simplified as it is passed down the layers, before eventually being transmitted. Then, on reaching the receiving station, it is progressively built back up again. The great advantage of this model is that it allows each level to be abstracted from those below it, and it is therefore possible for vendors products to easily interoperate.

> **The details of this model are outside the scope of this book, however, more information can be found on the ISO web site at www.iso.ch**

The Presentation Format

WAP's presentation uses a markup language known as WML (Wireless Markup Language). WML assumes that its clients will have a small screen and some method of data input, but requires nothing more of them. The language is an XML document format and has its roots in HDML (Handheld Device Markup Language).

Each WML document is called a **deck** and consists of one or more **cards**, each of which contains one screen-full of information. When the deck is accessed the first card is shown; then, based on the option selected, the user can navigate back and forth through the other cards. This produces a dialog-like interaction, without the constant need to make additional network requests, as the cards are already present on the client browser.

Operations, such as data validation and parsing, are conducted on the client-side through the use of WMLScript (Wireless Markup Language Script). This script, resembling JavaScript, has a variety of mathematical, string, and telephonic functions (WAP 2.0 also has some cryptographic functions built in).

We'll illustrate WAP's operation with a simple example, consisting of a single WML deck, containing two cards, that we will navigate between. The cards contain a combination of simple images and text to illustrate the basic capabilities of WAP. The code files for this example, along with the images used, can be downloaded from our web site at www.wrox.com.

Try It Out – Navigating Content On A Mobile Device

1. Create a new text file, and enter the following information :

```
<?xml version="1.0"?>
<!DOCTYPE wml PUBLIC "-//WAPFORUM//DTD WML 1.1//EN"
"http://www.wapforum.org/DTD/wml_1.1.xml">
<wml>

<!-- First card starts here -->
  <card id="init" newcontext="true">
  <p align="center">
  Welcome to Kosmos, discover your world!<br/>
  <img src="logo.wbmp" alt="Kosmos"/><br/>
  Get Info On Country:
  <input format="*M" name="NameC" title="Country:"/><br/>

  <do type="accept" label="Bring!">
    <go href="countryshttpscript.asp" method="post" >
      <postfield name="country" value="$(NameC)"/>
    </go>
  </do>

  <br/><br/><img src="advert.wbmp" alt="adbanner"/><br/>
  <a href="#nextcard">Please visit our sponsor</a><br/>
      </p>
  </card>

<!-- Second card starts here -->
  <card id="nextcard">
    <p align="center">
   When news happens, we are there to tell you all about it!<br/>
   Please visit our website for the latest in politics, sports and
entertainment.<br/>
   <img src="advert.wbmp" alt="adbanner"/><br/>

   <do type="accept" label="Go!">
     <go href="http://someotherwebsite.com" method="get" />
   </do>

   <do type="prev" label="Back">
     <prev/>
   </do>
   </p>
   </card>

</wml>
```

2. Save your file as Index.wml, and navigate to it from your client browser as
C:\WroxFiles\Index.wml:

Be sure to browse to the file across your file system (C:\ . . .), not via your web server (http://localhost/...). You will not be able to serve your WML files using a web server without a WAP Gateway, which does not come as a standard part of the Mobile Controls. See companies such as www.ccwap.com for more information about WAP Gateways.

3. Scroll to the bottom of the displayed card, and select the Please visit our sponsor link:

4. The next card in the deck is then shown:

How It Works

We've cut a significant corner to get this to work, in that we've not installed a WAP gateway on our machines, and hence we're viewing the pages directly, rather than through a web server. Since the focus of this book is the ASP.NET mobile controls (which don't require a gateway), we won't worry about this too much – we're more concerned with looking at how WML pages are structured.

Let's look quickly at the WML and see what is going on.

The file begins with an XML header that identifies the code as an XML 1.0-compliant document, and gives details of the WML specification to which it adheres (version 1.1 in this case):

```
<?xml version="1.0"?>
<!DOCTYPE wml PUBLIC "-//WAPFORUM//DTD WML 1.1//EN"
"http://www.wapforum.org/DTD/wml_1.1.xml">
```

Next, a `<wml>` tag identifies the start of the WML instructions . The WML document is broken up into two cards, the line `<card id="init" newcontext="true">` establishes the first of these. The code then goes on to display some greeting text and possibly an image (if the client can't support images, then the alternate text denoted by `alt` will be displayed instead):

```
<wml>
<!-- First card starts here -->
  <card id="init" newcontext="true">
  <p align="center">
  Welcome to Kosmos, discover your world!<br/>
  <img src="logo.wbmp" alt="Kosmos"/><br/>
  Get Info On Country:
  <input format="*M" name="NameC" title="Country:"/><br/>
```

Now the `<do>` tag is used to map actions to the left or right buttons of a cell-phone. `<do type="accept">` usually maps to the right button (positive action) and `<do type="prev">` to the left button (negative action):

```
<do type="accept" label="Bring!">
```

This correspondence may be reversed on some phones, especially those of European origin. This is the reason why WML denotes them as "`accept`" and "`prev`", rather than left and right.

Now the `<go>` tag serves the function of URL navigation. It has the added advantage of being able to contain a `<postfield>` element, which is equivalent to the `<input>` tag in HTML, making it useful for URL submission. In this case it is being used to navigate to a fictional ASPX page (`countryscript.aspx`) if the user selects the `Bring!` label:

```
    <go href="countryshttpscript.aspx" method="post" >
      <postfield name="country" value="$(NameC)"/>
    </go>
</do>
```

Next, after the linebreaks, the `advert.wbmp` image is displayed (or its alternate text), and an anchor is placed to `#nextcard`, which is the name of the second card in the deck. If users select this anchor in their client browser they will be transported to the second card:

```
<br/><br/><img src="advert.wbmp" alt="adbanner"/><br/>
<a href="#nextcard">Please visit our sponsor</a><br/>
   </p>
</card>
```

The second card is simpler than the first. After its initial `<card>` tag, some text is output to the client with central alignment, and an image (`advert.wbmp`) displayed after it. Finally, there are a pair of labels. The first, Go!, directs the browser to another (fictional) web site, while the other, Back, returns the user to the previous page. Finally, all open tags are closed, with the last, the `</wml>` tag, signaling the end of the WML document:

```
<!-- Second card starts here -->
  <card id="nextcard">
    <p align="center">
   When news happens, we are there to tell you all about it!<br/>
   Please visit our website for the latest in politics, sports and
entertainment.<br/>
    <img src="advert.wbmp" alt="adbanner"/><br/>

    <do type="accept" label="Go!">
      <go href="http://someotherwebsite.com" method="get" />
    </do>

    <do type="prev" label="Back">
      <prev/>
    </do>
    </p>
    </card>

</wml>
```

How Successful Is WAP Technically?

Let's side-step the consumer impressions of WAP for a moment (which haven't exactly been all that positive) and instead let's take a look at how successful the WAP 1.0 standard has been, and consider briefly how things are likely to change under the emerging WAP 2.0 standard.

A Good Protocol For Wireless Data

WAP does a good job in difficult circumstances. The heavy overheads of the HTTP connection mechanisms make them a difficult proposition for wireless communication. Furthermore, outside factors like sudden line-drops, losses of signal quality, and limited network coverage can make the situation worse. To deal with this, WAP dispenses with a lot of the 'administrative' functionality of HTTP – for example, HTTP expends bandwidth tracking out-of-order packets (packets sent to the client via several different roots won't necessarily arrive in the same order that they were transmitted). WAP dispenses with this, and only allows transmission by one route, so the packets cannot arrive out of order.

Removing some of the administrative overheads means WAP is losing some of HTTP-TCP/IP's ability to ensure all sent data is getting to its destination, but this must be balanced against the fact that the communication environment may cause HTTP to enter into retransmissions over extended periods of time, which may even result in loss of connection.

In the near future, we can expect to see an added improvement in the functionality offered by WAP, as WAP 2.0 begins to take over from WAP 1.0. Here are a few of the things we can look forward to:

- ❑ Reduction of packet size, by compiling WML pages into WMLC (a binary version)
- ❑ Optional translation of HTML pages into WML
- ❑ Checking of WML and WMLScript for errors
- ❑ Access control by allowing only specific mobile phone numbers to retrieve content

With these improvements taken into account, WAP reveals itself as a solid protocol for mobile communication, the only major flaw of which is its need to use a dedicated WAP Gateway, when HTTP does not. However, the most important aspect of WAP is that it took the idea of wireless data communications away from the proof-of-concept stage and made it into a commercial reality. As a direct result of this work, the founding principals of a wireless Internet have been created upon which more complex infrastructures can be built.

A Presentation Problem

Initial resistance to WAP came mainly from those who had just spent a fortune designing compelling HTML web sites, only to realize that this new medium would require a completely parallel design! To make matters worse this redesign wasn't just a matter of mechanically translating HTML in to WML, but required a great deal of thought about such matters as deck size, screen size, data entry, and lack of color. In short they were looking at spending a fortune all over again!

To make matters worse, the lack of any one dominant browser meant that the WMLScript, which offered local processing on the client, differed from phone to phone. Couple that with the fact that WML was rendered differently depending on the device and it was a consistency nightmare.

Also from an egalitarian point, many realized that the network operators had great control over the content viewed by their users. Normally phone users only change their default settings once, and never touch them again. So, when the operator supplied default gateways and homepages, they were rarely changed. As a result, space on an operator's home page went to the highest bidders – not exactly the equality that the Internet was famed for.

Lessons From WAP

A lot has already been learned about the implementation of wireless networks from WAP, and this has been reflected in the confidence with which operators have bid for extra bandwidth. It has become clear to companies that the network bottleneck needs to be removed before anyone can even contemplate commercial success.

WAP has done the following for developers:

- ❑ Started the process of bringing wireless information services to a consumer with different requirements to wired users

- ❑ Made it apparent that users will be attempting to connect to services from a wide variety of client browsers

- ❑ Reinforced the need for flexible web site design that can be viewed in a variety of different but complementary ways depending on the browser being used.

Summary

This chapter has given a quick tour of the world of mobile communications, and attempted to outline how mobile applications could soon become invaluable for handling certain kinds of data. We've looked at the implications of using HTTP and WAP, and discussed the strong and weak points of each. In the next chapter we will build on this knowledge to look at the mechanics of ASP.NET Mobile Controls.

Here's a reminder of the main points that we've covered in this chapter:

- ❑ A clarification of the distinction between the terms wireless and mobile

- ❑ Why a mobile solution can make better business sense in some situation

- ❑ A brief discussion of the Hyper Text Transfer Protocol (HTTP), Wireless Application Protocol (WAP), and Wireless Markup Language (WML)

- ❑ A simplified view of WAP's transmission protocol and presentation format, together with a simple example of how they work

- ❑ A look at how WAP has diverged from HTTP in an effort to maximize the use of its bandwidth

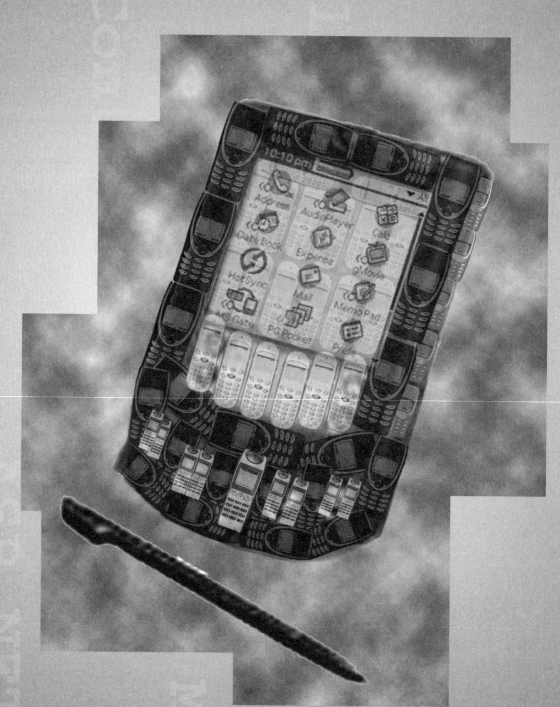

The Mechanics Of ASP.NET Mobile Forms

The ASP.NET mobile runtime is made up of controls, components, and tools that allow us to build web-based applications for many types of mobile devices. When a mobile form is called from a consuming application (such as a browser) on one of these devices, the mobile runtime located on the web server with the .NET Framework recognizes and provides the appropriate rendering for a .NET-compliant device. This ultimately shields us from having to write code that is tailored to one specific device (or set of devices), which often restricts us in the WML world.

How do mobile forms work? In this chapter, we'll see how mobile forms function within the context of the .NET Framework. We'll show what happens when an ASP.NET mobile web browser ASPX page is requested by a device, how the .NET environment knows how to display screens based on the device being used, what elements comprise a mobile form and, finally, how it compares with a standard Web Form.

Before we delve into the specific mechanics of ASP.NET mobile forms, let's begin with a brief review of the .NET Framework, so we can better understand how this fits in with the world of mobile devices.

.NET Framework Basics

The .NET Framework is comprised of two major areas:

- ❑ The Common Language Runtime (CLR)
- ❑ .NET Framework Class Library

We'll briefly talk about each of these topics as a basis for future discussion about its specific use with ASP.NET Mobile Controls.

> **For a more detailed discussion of the .NET Framework, please see *Professional ASP.NET* (ISBN 1-861004-88-5) from Wrox Press.**

The Common Language Runtime (CLR)

The Common Language Runtime provides an environment that manages code within the context of the .NET Framework.

It has these five distinct assets:

- ❑ **Cross-Language Support** – Languages compatible with the .NET Framework are equally supported. For instance, when C# sourcecode is compiled using the C# compiler, its Intermediate Language (IL) uses the same types and object references as the Intermediate Language generated by the compiler from, for example, VB.NET sourcecode. Therefore, programs created in one language can interact with programs written in another language. This provides developers with the option of coding in the language of their choice.

- ❑ **Memory Management** – The CLR handles 'Garbage Collection' by automatically destroying objects within the scope that are no longer used in an application during runtime. This keeps us from consuming unnecessary amounts of memory, which helps improve performance on our server.

- ❑ **Debugging** – Using parameters (such as Debug and Trace in the Page directive within an ASPX web page) and debugging capabilities such as Visual Studio .NET's watch and task windows (which we'll discuss later), we have a myriad of tools available to assist us in removing errors from our code. For instance, we have the ability to display variable values, see execution times, and if needed, interactively debug between application code written in different languages seamlessly.

- ❑ **Security** – Managed application code within the .NET environment has the ability to declare the security it requires and determine whether access has been granted to it. This allows us to control who can and cannot view or modify our code.

- ❑ **Versioning** – Another great thing about the .NET CLR is that we may run different versions of the same component at the same time, even on the same machine. CLR versioning enables applications that use this component to use the old component until they are able to move to the new one.

During runtime and development, the CLR is designed to improve performance flexibility over previous versions of ASP. Once we have created our sourcecode, we compile it using a language-specific compilation utility, which creates a common Intermediate Language (IL). Just before the code is to be executed, the CLR compiles this Intermediate Language code into machine code.

The CLR improves performance by taking advantage of a feature called Just-In-Time (JIT) compilation. When a page is initially requested, the code is compiled into Intermediate Language. Provided no changes have been made to the file, the JIT compiler will execute for each subsequent request and convert the Intermediate Language into native code. By using JIT compilation, all managed code can run in the native language of the system on which it is executing.

.NET Class Library

To provide a more **Object-Oriented** environment, greater consistency and ease of use, the .NET Class Library is available. The Class Library contains classes that provide the ability to handle common tasks such as string management, data collection, database connectivity, file access, and manipulation. We've had to use namespaces in our ASP.NET Web Forms, such as `System.IO` and `System.Web.UI`, for reading and writing to files and handling form controls, respectively. For those that are familiar with Java, the concept of .NET namespace such as these, is quite similar to a **package**. For those that are familiar with C++, this is also analogous to the concept of a **header file**.

If we happen to know the basic function of a class we wish to use, we can run the `WinCV Class Viewer` provided with the .NET Framework to explore its contents (normally found at C:\Program Files\Microsoft.NET\FrameworkSDK\bin\wincv.exe). Here, we simply insert a value in the Searching for field (for example, StreamReader). As we enter the class name, the list is dynamically populated to show which ones are available.

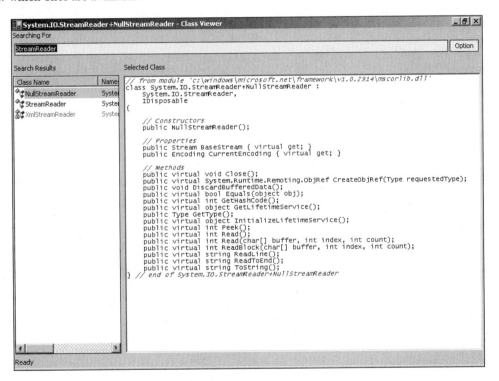

We'll see how making use of mobile controls will require that we use a new class in our page, `System.Web.Mobile`.

Now let's take a look at how a mobile web browser ASPX page behaves within the .NET Framework.

Lifecycle Of A Mobile Form

The first step in the life of a mobile web browser ASPX page is that we must create and save the file with an ASPX extension on a web server containing the .NET Framework. The next is that this mobile web browser ASPX page will be converted from a source language (such as C# or VB.NET) into an Intermediate Language and compiled. As other requests are made for this particular page, the JIT compiler turns the IL into machine code.

So, what kind of information is passed between a mobile device and a .NET web server during runtime? When a device requests a mobile web browser ASPX page from a web server, the data posted with the form is captured, retains the relevant values, and these object properties are made available for use in our code, provided they are defined with the appropriate scope (such as `public`, `friend`, etc.). This is very similar to the behavior that a Web Form possesses.

For instance, a mobile form may contain a textbox and a command button. If a user uses his wireless device to enter a value and clicks the button, a subroutine associated with the `onclick` event of the command button may take the user to a second form displaying the entered text.

To see one example of how a mobile form behaves during a request, we can see a HTTP `request/response` exchange below. The mobile form uses HTTP to establish the nexus with the HTTP exchange.

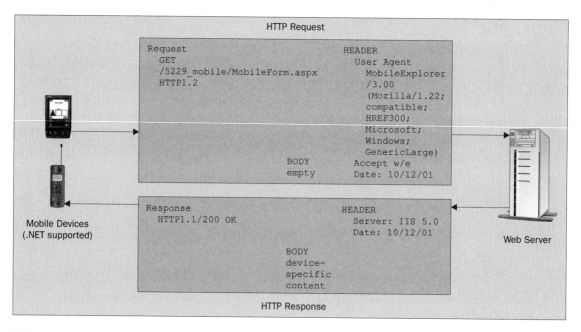

We'll use a utility available with the Microsoft Mobile Explorer 3.0 emulator (MME) to explain how this data exchange works. The MME can be downloaded free of charge from the Microsoft web site. There are two versions available: one is for Windows while the other is integrated within the Visual Studio .NET environment, which we'll see later in this book.

The MME Windows version has an accompanying utility that displays the HTTP activity when a mobile web browser ASPX page is browsed. This tool can be displayed by selecting View | Output when the MME is running. We can see the output produced when this address is entered in the MME:
http://localhost/5229_5/MobileForm.aspx.

HTTP	14:48:46.019	Sent: 'GET /5229_5/MobileForm.aspx HTTP/1.1'
HTTP	14:48:46.019	Sent: 'Host: localhost'
HTTP	14:48:46.029	Sent: 'User-Agent: MobileExplorer/3.00 (Mozilla/1.22; compatible; MMEF300; Microsoft; Windows; GenericLarge)'
HTTP	14:48:46.029	Sent: 'UA-color: color8'
HTTP	14:48:46.029	Sent: 'UA-pixels: 128x160'
HTTP	14:48:46.029	Sent: 'Accept: text/html, image/gif, image/jpeg, text/x-vcard, text/x-vcalendar, application/vnd.wap.wmlc, image/vnd.wap.wbmp, application/vnd.wap.wmlscriptc, text/vnd.wap.wml, text/vnd.wap.wmlscript, application/vnd.wap.connectivity-wbxml, text/vnd.wap.connectivity-xml, application/x-www-form-urlencoded, audio/*, x-audio/*'
HTTP	14:48:46.029	Sent: 'Accept-Encoding: chunked'
HTTP	14:48:46.039	Sent: 'Accept-Language: en, *'
HTTP	14:48:52.858	Response: 'HTTP/1.1 200 OK'
HTTP	14:48:52.858	Received: 'Server' = 'Microsoft-IIS/5.0'
HTTP	14:48:52.858	Received: 'Date' = 'Wed, 17 Oct 2001 14:48:52 GMT'
HTTP	14:48:52.858	Received: 'Set-Cookie' = 'ASP.NET_SessionId=zjmaf245ioranmi51xi2sc55; path=/'
Cookies	14:48:52.858	Started checking for expired cookies (time=1003330132).
Cookies	14:48:52.868	Finished checking for expired cookies.
Cookies	14:48:52.878	Adding new cookie: 'ASP.NET_SessionId'='zjmaf245ioranmi51xi2sc55' at '/' for 'localhost'.
HTTP	14:48:52.878	Received: 'Cache-Control' = 'private'
HTTP	14:48:52.889	Received: 'Content-Type' = 'text/vnd.wap.wml; charset=utf-8'
URL	14:48:52.899	Found converter based on the MIME type 'text/vnd.wap.wml; charset=utf-8'.
HTTP	14:48:52.899	Received: 'Content-Length' = '2058'

Table continued on following page

Compiler Status	14:48:52.909	Started WML compiler for data received from 'http://localhost/5229_5/MobileForm.aspx'. Document size is 2058 bytes.
Compiler Status	14:48:53.369	Finished compiling source document. Compiled size is 872 bytes.
Browser	14:48:53.519	Executing OnEnterForward action.
Cache	14:48:53.610	Deleting document 'info://SHOW/general/home.html'.

What's Happening In The Lifecycle

Assuming that this is the first time this mobile web browser ASPX page has been displayed, a new request will be made to the server. Based on the HTTP_USER_AGENT server variable in the HTTP Request Header, the device browser provides the appropriate Content Type. In this case, the Content Type is WML since the MME can support this markup language:

```
'Content-Type' = 'text/vnd.wap.wml; charset=utf-8'
```

The color capabilities and pixel resolution are also sent to the web server:

```
Sent: 'UA-color: color8'
Sent: 'UA-pixels: 128x160'
```

The Content Type is specific to the browser used. This variable is useful to describe the data contained in the body, so that the receiving user agent can choose an appropriate agent or mechanism to handle the data display and/or processing accordingly. For instance, if this mobile form had been viewed by Internet Explorer 5.5 or greater, the Content Type would have been HTML, instead of WML. Another mobile device may send yet another Content Type.

When the web server receives this request, the Internet Information Server (IIS) works in conjunction with the .NET Framework to accept the request and to identify and run the appropriate converter for the WML MIME types, based on the Content Type. MIME, which stands for Multipurpose Internet Mail Extensions, allows various type of content in message headers. With this MIME type, the converter is used to compile the mobile web browser ASPX page sourcecode into WML. The web server then sends the device-specific WML, the IITTP status and date, and the version of IIS that it is being run on the server (which is IIS 5.0 in this case).

This response is received by the Microsoft Mobile Emulator, and the markup is rendered on the device's screen. As events occur on the mobile web browser ASPX page (entering text, select options, clicking links), requests and responses are sent back and forth between the device and the web server via HTTP. Information is passed to the server about the mobile controls that exist on the mobile form, as well as their contents, with additional information. The web server takes this information, processes it and returns it the browser.

To continue with our discussion of ASP.NET mobile controls, it is important for us to address what happens when a mobile web browser ASPX page is processed on the server.

Mobile Form Processing

The stages of Mobile web browser ASPX page processing on the web server can be summarized into five stages:

❑   Initialization

❑   Event Handling

❑   Device Detection

❑   Rendering

❑   Cleanup

The Device Detection stage is a key to the Mobile Controls, since it's at this point when the user agent is identified and the content needed is returned. Let's take a look at each of these stages below.

Initialization

This is the first stage that occurs when a mobile web browser ASPX page is processed. Unless otherwise set, the first mobile form in the page flow is automatically made active. On subsequent postbacks, another mobile form may be made active by resetting the status of the `ActiveForm` property.

In addition, the page state is restored, followed by the execution of any actions within the **Page_Load** event. For example, the following lines in a mobile page set the text in a textbox when the page is first loaded:

```
<script runat="server">
  void Page_Load(object sender, System.EventArgs e)
  {
    txtTextBox.Text = "First time";
  }
</script>
```

In the code above, the textbox `txtTextBox` will contain the text 'First time'.

Following this, any previously stored values for controls and state are read and restored. Then the `IsPostBack` page property is checked to determine whether this is the first time the page has been processed.

```
<script runat="server">
  void Page_Load(object sender, System.EventArgs e)
  {
    if (IsPostBack)
    {
      lblCaption.Text = "I've been here before.";
    }
    else
    {
      lblCaption.Text = "I've NEVER been here before.";
    }
  }
</script>
```

In the code above, if this page has been visited for the first time by a user in a session, the text for a label control called lblCaption will appear as "I've NEVER been here before.". On any future visits to this page during the session, the lblCaption control will contain the following text: "I've been here before", unless programmatically changed elsewhere.

Data binding on controls is also performed for the first time the page is visited (as well as on subsequent round trips from the browser to the server). Finally, any new control properties are read, and their values are updated.

Event Handling

If our mobile web browser ASPX page is reloaded in response to an event (for example, onclick), the corresponding event-handling method in the page is called. For instance, if a command button control called btnGo will change the Text property of a label control to "Go was pressed" using the routine ChangeText:

```
<script runat="server">
  public void ChangeText(object sender, System.EventArgs e)
  {
    lblNewText.Text = "Go was pressed";
  }
</script>
<mobile:Command id="btnGo" text="Go" runat="server" onclick="ChangeText" />
```

In addition, cached control events are processed before the posting event. These are specified by the control's AutoPostBack property which allows the .NET environment to track whether or not the mobile web browser ASPX page has been previously visited.

If the page contains validation controls, we can check the IsValid property for the page or for individual validation controls. The state of global page variables that we are maintaining should be manually saved, as well as the controls that are dynamically added to the page.

Device Detection

Part of the power of ASP.NET mobile web browser ASPX pages lies in the fact that they are capable of rendering to a variety of supported mobile devices using one set of code. The mobile controls server runtime handles a lot of implicit formatting appropriate for display on a variety of device types. The .NET mobile runtime contains a register of compatible devices. These are matched up based on the Content Type within an HTTP request, as explained earlier.

However, as we'll learn, the mobile runtime will not allow rendering to occur such that it specifies one string as a label on one device and a different string in a textbox on another device. The developer must provide application code that sets the properties of the controls differently based upon the device. To customize this, we must define a set of device filters for the application and then specify the filter for each type of device. Again, we'll discuss this later in the book.

Rendering

Rendering is the process whereby the HTTP request header details are used to determine the appropriate page to produce or display to the requesting browser or device. In the case of a mobile page, once the web server has determined the markup language that can be handled by the calling device, a stream is returned via HTTP response to the device.

Cleanup

Once all HTML has been rendered, the .NET Framework goes through the process of managing resources (garbage collection) by eliminating unused objects.

The types of action that are performed during this stage include:

❑ Closing files

❑ Closing database connections

❑ Destroying objects within the application scope

It is important that resource-intensive items (such as database connections) be deliberately closed. Otherwise, they will remain open until the next garbage collection occurs. If the web server eventually accumulates enough of these unused objects, its memory can be quickly consumed, which normally results in poor performance.

Mobile Forms Versus Web Forms

So far, we've seen how a mobile form is requested and served to be displayed on a wireless device. We've also gone through each of the steps that are performed when a mobile web browser ASPX page is processed. In this section, we'll show some ways in which a mobile form compares with an ASP.NET Web Form.

❑ **Processing** – Web Forms render output in HTML once server-side compilation is complete. Mobile forms render output after being compiled in the markup language based on the Content Type of the supported device. Again, this occurs when the HTTP User Agent is received by the web server, and the converter is executed to return the correct output to the device.

❑ **Platform** – The only requirement for viewing Web Forms is a browser running on the client. The web server where the Web Form resides must be running the .NET Framework, but ASP.NET Web Forms can be run/accessed on any operating system (UNIX, Linux, Mac OS, or Windows, as they do not require the .NET Framework to be installed on the client) using a variety of browsers, such as Internet Explorer, Netscape, and Opera. Mobile Forms can output to a variety of .NET compatible mobile devices and browsers.

❑ **Images** – Any dynamic graphics require round trips to the server for updates within its server-side image control. However, with a Web Form, there is normally one file that is specified for a page image. A Mobile Form's Image control allows us to specify multiple image files for one page image, using multiple formats and the CLR chooses the correct image file based on device characteristics as we discussed earlier.

❑ **Performance** – Web Forms must run script on the server and return the output to the client browser or download the script to the client browser and then execute it. The responsiveness is limited by network bandwidth and data making trips between the client and server. Mobile Web Forms include controls that automatically paginate content according to the device (creating card-decks, for example) keeping the paged data on the server until requested by the user. However, it's still limited by server bandwidth at one point.

Since we're familiar with how a mobile web browser ASPX page is processed, let's take a look at what the code for a typical one looks like. .

Anatomy 101

So what does a mobile form look like? To start, let's clarify some concepts. Building a mobile application begins by first creating an ASPX page. This page contains some required declarations, followed by one or more mobile forms, which in turn contains one or more mobile controls, such as label, textbox or selection list.

This falls in line with our earlier discussion in Chapter 3 about WML, as the ASPX page is analogous to a deck and a mobile form to a card. As an application is accessed by multiple users via browsers, speed is optimized since all of the forms are contained in one file.

In order to get a sense of how this works, let's compare a mobile web browser ASPX page to a web browser ASPX page (both shown below in Microsoft Internet Explorer). A web browser ASPX page can contain only one Web Form. In comparison, a mobile web browser ASPX page contains one or more mobile forms.

In the figures below, the goal of both pages is to have the user enter a name and select an age from the appropriate controls. Once this is complete, the **Add** button is pressed and that person's information will be stored in an array list and displayed in a list control below the **Add** button.

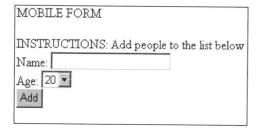
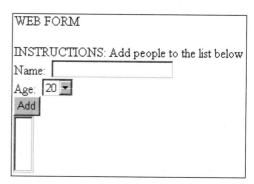

As we can see, in design mode, the mobile web browser ASPX page displays almost as if it is a web browser ASPX page. The advantage of the mobile form is that it can also be displayed during runtime just as easily on a .NET-supported mobile device as shown below:

Let's look at this web browser ASPX page line-by-line, followed by a discussion of the segments that make up the comparable mobile web browser ASPX page.

Web Page

Let's take a look at the web browser ASPX page. Its logic appears below:

```
<%@ Page Language="C#" %>
<script runat="server">
  ArrayList PersonList;
  protected void Page_Load(object sender, System.EventArgs e)
  {
    for (int i=20;i<=80;i++)
    {
    ddlAgeList.Items.Add("" + i + "");
    }
    if (Page.IsPostBack == true)
    {
      PersonList = (ArrayList) ViewState["Names"];
    }
    else
    {
      PersonList = new ArrayList();
      ViewState["Names"] = PersonList;
    }
  }
  public void AddPerson(object sender, System.EventArgs e)
  {
  string strPersonStats = txtName.Text + ", " +
  ddlAgeList.SelectedItem.ToString();
    PersonList.Add(strPersonStats);
    lstEnteredNames.DataSource = PersonList;
    lstEnteredNames.DataBind();
  }
</script>
```

```
<html>
<body>
<form id="frmWebForm" runat="server">
  WEB FORM<br><br>
  <asp:Label id="lblFormCaption" text="INSTRUCTIONS:
                      Add people to the list below" runat="server" /><br>
  Name: 
  <asp:Textbox id="txtName" runat="server" /><br>
  Age: 
  <asp:DropDownList id="ddlAgeList" runat="server" /><br>
  <asp:Button id="btnAdd" text="Add" runat="server"
                                      onclick="AddPerson" /><br>
   <asp:ListBox id="lstEnteredNames" runat="server" />
</form>

</body>
</html>
```

Page Directive

The first line of the web browser ASPX page is the Page directive. As we know, this furnishes the .NET Framework with certain parameters so that, when the page compiles, actions can be performed during processing.

```
<%@ Page Language="C#" %>
```

The first attribute is the Language attribute, which sets the language to be used on the web page, which in our case is C#.

Server-side Script

In order to have our two form versions work as desired, we must include scripting. As indicated in the Page directive, the scripting language is C#. In the web browser ASPX page, we have the following tag set:

```
<script runat="server">...</script>
```

As we know, this declares code within the tags as server side (as denoted by the runat-"server" attribute). The next line declares the variable PersonList as an array.

```
ArrayList PersonList;
```

This will contain the name and age combinations for each of the entries entered by the users.

The following routine is the initial logic executed when the page is requested.

```
protected void Page_Load(object sender, System.EventArgs e)
{
    for (int i=20;i<=80;i++)
    {
```

```
        ddlAgeList.Items.Add("" + i + "");
    }

    if (Page.IsPostBack == true)
      {
        PersonList = (ArrayList) ViewState["Names"];
      }
      else
      {
        PersonList = new ArrayList();
        ViewState["Names"] = PersonList;
      }

}
```

The `for` loop populates the `Age` dropdown list (`ddlAgeList`) for ages 20 to 80. Following that, we have a condition that checks to see if the form has been loaded previously using the `IsPostBack` property of the `Page` object. As we've learned, this boolean value is managed automatically by the .NET Framework and shields us from having to determine whether this is the first visit or the fiftieth.

If the page has not been visited, the `PersonList` arraylist is instantiated, and the `PersonList` is stored in the `Names` object. Once the user enters a name, selects his/her age and presses **Add**, these values will be stored in our defined `Names` arraylist, which we include in the `ViewState` collection to be passed to the page during each post action.

The next routine is executed when the **Add** button is pressed on the form.

```
    public void AddPerson(object sender, System.EventArgs e)
    {
        string strPersonStats = txtName.Text + ", " +
ddlAgeList.SelectedItem.ToString();
        PersonList.Add(strPersonStats);
        lstEnteredNames.DataSource = PersonList;
        lstEnteredNames.DataBind();
    }
</script>
```

A string (`strPersonStats`), containing the concatenation of the entered name and selected age, is added to the Items collection of the `PersonList` arraylist. To display this information in the listbox, we must specify `PersonList` as the data source and bind it to the listbox control. Finally, we have the HTML that renders the controls on the Web Form. The code shown below is quite standard:

```
<html>
<body>
<form id="frmWebForm" runat="server">
    WEB FORM<br><br>
    <asp:Label id="lblFormCaption"
      text="INSTRUCTIONS: Add people to the list below" runat="server" /><br>
    Name: 
    <asp:Textbox id="txtName" runat="server" /><br>
    Age: 
    <asp:DropDownList id="ddlAgeList" runat="server" /><br>
```

```
        <asp:Button id="btnAdd" text="Add" runat="server"
                                        onclick="AddPerson" /><br>
     <asp:ListBox id="lstEnteredNames" runat="server" />
   </form>
   </body>
   </html>
```

Within a Web Form, we must always use the `<html>` and `<body>` tags. Then we specify our form below with the ubiquitous `runat="server"` attribute and its id.

```
<form id="frmWebForm" runat="server">
```

The next control on this Web Form is the `<asp:label>`, which allows us to specify a control that contains only display text with no direct user interaction. However, this control has properties that may be altered programmatically.

```
<asp:Label id="lblFormCaption" text="INSTRUCTIONS: Add people to the list below"
runat="server" />
```

With the next line, the Web Form allows users to enter a name into a field:

```
<asp:Textbox id="txtName" runat="server" />
```

The Web Form `DropDownList` control provides us with the ability to select an age (within a given range based on our script):

```
<asp:DropDownList id="ddlAgeList" runat="server" />
```

Next, the **Add** button submits the values of our Web Form controls back to the page:

```
<asp:Button id="btnAdd" text="Add" runat="server" onclick="AddPerson" /><br>
```

Finally, we have the `asp:ListBox` control, which displays the new names and ages added to the `PersonList` arraylist:

```
<asp:ListBox id="lstEnteredNames" runat="server" />
```

Now, let's see how the mobile page handles its processing.

Mobile Page

This is the code for the comparable mobile form on the mobile web ASPX page. As we can see, there is only one mobile form within the page; however, we could insert additional mobile forms as needed.

```
<%@ Page Language="C#" Inherits="System.Web.UI.MobileControls.MobilePage" %>
<%@ Register TagPrefix="mobile" Namespace="System.Web.UI.MobileControls"
```

```
        Assembly="System.Web.Mobile" %>
<script runat="server">
  ArrayList PersonList;
  protected void Page_Load(object sender, System.EventArgs e)
  {
    for (int i=20;i<=80;i++)
      {
        slAgeList.Items.Add("" + i + "");
      }
    if (Page.IsPostBack == true)
    {
        PersonList = (ArrayList) ViewState["Names"];
    }
    else
    {
        PersonList = new ArrayList();
        ViewState["Names"] = PersonList;
    }
  }
  public void AddPerson(object sender, System.EventArgs e)
  {
    string strPersonStats = txtName.Text + ", " +
                                        slAgeList.Selection.Text;
    PersonList.Add(strPersonStats);
    lstEnteredNames.DataSource = PersonList;
    lstEnteredNames.DataBind();
  }
</script>

<mobile:Form runat="server" id="frmMobileForm">
  MOBILE FORM<br><br>
  <mobile:Label id="lblFormCaption"
    text="INSTRUCTIONS: Add people to the list below" runat="server" />
  Name: 
  <mobile:Textbox id="txtName" runat="server" /><br>
  Age: 
  <mobile:SelectionList id="slAgeList" runat="server" /><br>
  <mobile:Command id="btnAdd" text="Add" runat="server"
                                      onclick="AddPerson" /><br>
  <mobile:List id="lstEnteredNames" runat="server" />
</mobile:Form>
```

In the following sections, we'll take our understanding of web browser ASPX web page elements and apply it to mobile controls. We won't discuss the server-side script since almost all of the code is identical.

Page Directive

We can view the corresponding Page directive in the mobile web browser ASPX page counterpart:

```
<%@ Page Language="C#" Inherits="System.Web.UI.MobileControls.MobilePage" %>
```

Notice that this directive contains the `Inherits` attribute which references the `System.Web.UI.MobileControls.MobilePage` class. This is required for any ASP.NET mobile Web Form. `System.Web.UI.MobileControls` is the namespace in which the `MobilePage` class resides, and we reference this namespace in the next line, as described in the following section. A stand-alone mobile web browser ASPX page, such as this one, inherits directly from the `MobilePage` class, which is the base class for all mobile ASP.NET pages and provides access to the outermost-layer of all the containers available within a mobile application.

Register Directive

A second directive registers the namespace used by mobile controls with the prefix `mobile`.

```
<%@ Register TagPrefix="mobile" Namespace="System.Web.UI.MobileControls"
Assembly="System.Web.Mobile" %>
```

This allows us to declare mobile controls on the page using the `mobile` prefix. We can use any prefix we want; however, `mobile` is recommended for forward compatibility.

Server-side Controls

This is where the differences between the web browser ASPX page and the mobile page occur. Here, we encounter controls specific to ASP.NET mobile development.

Let's look at how the mobile presentation code differs (though the difference is often in name only):

```
<mobile:Form runat="server" id="frmMobileForm">
    MOBILE FORM<br><br>
    <mobile:Label id="lblFormCaption" text="INSTRUCTIONS: Add people to the list
below" runat="server" />
    Name: 
    <mobile:Textbox id="txtName" runat="server" /><br>
    Age: 
    <mobile:SelectionList id="slAgeList" runat="server" /><br>
    <mobile:Command id="btnAdd" text="Add" runat="server" onclick="AddPerson"
/><br>
    <mobile:List id="lstEnteredNames" runat="server" />
</mobile:Form>
```

With the mobile form, we have the following declaration for the mobile form:

```
<mobile:Form runat="server" id="frmMobileForm">
```

As we can see, the `mobile` prefix is used based on the `Register` compiler directive in the previous section. Within the `System.Web.UI.MobileControls` namespace, the `form` control serves as the foundation for the mobile web browser ASPX page. As stated earlier, we may have as many mobile forms within our page as we wish. We have the same attributes as the Web Form.

```
<mobile:Label id="lblFormCaption"
        text="INSTRUCTIONS: Add people to the list below" runat="server" />
```

The mobile form has a similar label control in `<mobile:label>`. This label is rendered the same way in HTML and WML; however, the style with which it's rendered may differ based on the device. The control renders the text of the label on its own line with the appropriate style attributes applied.

The mobile `textbox` control is similar to the Web Form control, and allows either a single-line text input:

```
<mobile:Textbox id="txtName" runat="server" />
```

or a two-tag approach, where we can specify some `innerText` between the two tags:

```
<mobile:Textbox id="txtName" runat="server">Some text here</mobile:Textbox>
```

The mobile controls offer us a similar function to the Web Form's `DropDownList` in the `SelectionList` control:

```
<mobile:SelectionList id="slAgeList" runat="server" />
```

The mobile `<mobile:Command>` control serves a similar purpose to that of the Web Form control `asp:button`. The fact that the button control is called a `command` button is a hold-over from the WML world.

```
<mobile:Command id="btnAdd" text="Add" runat="server"
                                      onclick="AddPerson" /><br>
```

Again, how this is rendered on the screen depends upon the device. Notice that the `onclick` attribute value is `AddPerson`, which is the name of the routine in our script block.

As we notice how this is displayed in the browser, the web browser ASPX page appears by default with a border. The equivalent mobile `mobile:List` control does not.

```
<mobile:List id="lstEnteredNames" runat="server" />
```

As we've seen, the differences between web browser ASPX pages and mobile web browser ASPX pages can be quite significant. However, mobile web browser ASPX page creation is an easy step up from ASPX page development.

Summary

We've covered a fair bit of ground in this chapter, and we'll be revisiting a lot of the issues and concepts raised here in later chapters. In this chapter, we've taken a look at:

❑ How devices communicate with web servers to view mobile ASPX pages

❑ How mobile Web Forms are constructed

❑ How they compare with traditional ASP.NET Web Forms

The next chapter will build upon the knowledge we've gained here, where we'll discuss how mobile forms work and apply this to structuring mobile ASPX pages.

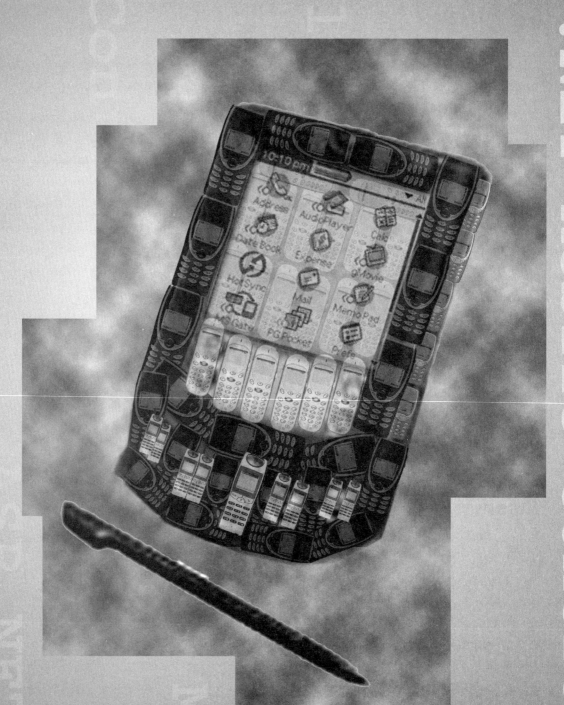

Structuring Mobile Web Form Pages

In Chapter 4 we looked at how the Mobile Internet Toolkit works with, and within, the .NET Framework. We saw that all Mobile Web Form controls are descendants of the `System.Mobile.UI.MobileControl` base class and we talked about the life cycle of a Mobile Web Form. We also discussed the Mobile Web Form Control's abilities to detect and render client-device specific markup code.

This chapter will discuss the container controls that developers can use as foundations for building their Mobile Pages.

Mobile Web Form Structure

Like ASP.NET Web Form controls, ASP.NET Mobile Web Form controls have containment rules. This means that a Mobile Web Form Control cannot exist outside of specific controls that are designated as containers. For example, if you try adding a `<mobile:Command>` to your page outside of a `<mobile:Form>` you will get an error in your browser:

System.Exception: MobileControl must be contained within a Form

Container controls "play host" to other controls, and allow developers an easy way to organize groups of controls on their pages – properties can be set for the parent container, and then inherited or overridden as desired in the child controls.

Currently, the only container controls are the `<mobile:Panel>` and the `<mobile:Form>`. You need to have the `<mobile:Form>` control on a page for any other mobile Web Form controls to work, since none of the functionality offered by the other controls is available outside of a `<mobile:Form>` tag set. The `<mobile:Panel>` control is also a container control, but this control must also be nested within a `<mobile:Form>`, and it is subjected to the same containment laws as the others.

As is the case with all Mobile Web Form controls, <mobile:Form> and <mobile:Panel> detect the client device (provided it's supported) and render the appropriate markup language. As we saw in Chapter 1, this can result in a wide variety of visual and structural representations depending on the client device. In later chapters, we will see how these controls restructure the presentation of content, and the method of navigation, depending on the client device used to access the content.

Now we'll look at the container controls individually.

The <mobile:Form>

A <mobile:Form> is analogous to a **card** in WML and is the outermost addressable grouping of controls within an ASP.NET MobilePage (we can also think of the MobilePage as the equivalent of a deck in WML). A <mobile:Form> can contain as many controls as the developer would like to use, but the display limitations of the client mean that in practice they should be used sparingly (if the client can only handle two or three controls at a time, as is the case with most mobile phones, then the excess controls will be buried in an Options menu). The run-time treats each <mobile:Form> as a separate unit and will not send more than one to the client at the same time. This means that where, in the past, we might have directed a user to another page in a wizard-like registration process, now we can programmatically direct the user to another <mobile:Form> **within** the same page:

```
ActiveForm = Form2;
```

This direction is transparent to the user, but makes life easier for developers, as they don't have to cope with large numbers of small pages; the downside to this is that it limits the reusability of your code.

The <mobile:Form> control works just like the ASP.NET <form> control. It has method and action attributes to dictate the form's behavior, and like ASP.NET's <form>, it also has a few of its own attributes to make things easier for the developer.

In addition to the base attributes that all Mobile Controls have, the <form> control has the following additional attributes:

- ❑ **Action** – this is just like the action attribute in an ASP.NET or HTML form where you designate a target page or URL.

- ❑ **Method** – again, like the ASP.NET or HTML equivalent, this sets or returns the type of HTTP method that will be used to submit the form (GET or POST, for example).

- ❑ **OnActivate** – this event handler is called when the form becomes active.

- ❑ **OnDeactivate** – this event handler is called when the form becomes inactive.

- ❑ **Paginate** – set this to true or false depending on whether you want pagination in effect. We will discuss pagination in Chapter 12.

- ❑ **Title** – this sets or returns the title of the form. In HTML the title will show up as a <title> tag within <head> tags. In WML it will show up as the title attribute in the <card> tag.

- ❑ **OnInit** – this event handler is called when the form is initialized.

We will be looking at numerous examples in this book that will show the `<mobile:Form>` control in many different situations, because it is such an integral part of the Mobile Controls, so we will only give a simple example of it here.

It is important to note that controls placed within a `<mobile:Form>` will inherit any of its style properties that have been set. For instance, suppose you have the following code:

```
<mobile:Form id="Form1" runat="server" Font-Bold="True">
    <mobile:Command id="Command1" runat="server">Command</mobile:Command>
    <mobile:Panel id="Panel1" runat="server">Test</mobile:Panel>
</mobile:Form>
```

The resulting text on the `<mobile:Command>` and `<mobile:Panel>` controls would be in bold because they are inheriting the Font-Bold="True" property of the `<mobile:Form>` control.

Let's look at an example of a `<mobile:Form>` in action (you can download this code from www.wrox.com):

Try It Out – The <mobile:Form> control

This example will demonstrate the use of a `<mobile:Form>` to host other controls and act as the catalyst to process the client-side events, and serve as an alternative to using a separate ASPX page in place of an additional `<mobile:Form>`:

1. Open your text editor and enter the following code:

```
<%@ Page Inherits="System.Web.UI.MobileControls.MobilePage" Language="C#"%>
<%@ Register TagPrefix="mobile" Namespace="System.Web.UI.MobileControls"
                                        Assembly="System.Web.Mobile" %>
<script runat="server">

private void Command1_Click(object sender, System.EventArgs e)
{
  Label1.Text = "You made it " + TextBox1.Text + "!";
  ActiveForm = Form2;
}

</script>

<mobile:Form id="Form1" runat="server">
Enter your name:
    <mobile:TextBox id="TextBox1"runat="server" />
    <mobile:Command id="Command1"runat="server" OnClick="Command1_Click">
    Go</mobile:Command>
</mobile:Form>

<mobile:Form id="Form2" runat="server">
  <mobile:Label id="Label1" runat="server" />
</mobile:Form>
```

2. Save it as `WroxMobileWebFormEx.aspx` in a virtual directory.

Browse to the page in your client browser and you should see something like the following:

Following through the process, we see:

How It Works

This example shows how `<mobile:Form>` controls can be used both as a container, and also as an additional page in the interaction process.

In the header of the page (`MobilePage`), we have the `@Page` and `@Register` directives, which you will remember from our example in Chapter 1:

```
<%@ Page Inherits="System.Web.UI.MobileControls.MobilePage" Language="C#"%>
<%@Register TagPrefix="mobile" Namespace="System.Web.UI.MobileControls"
Assembly="System.Web.Mobile" %>
```

Looking at the `Command1_Click` event handler (which comes next in the code) would be getting ahead of ourselves so, for now, let's look at the code within the first `<mobile:Form>`, and come back to it later. In the actual `<mobile:Form>` element itself, we set the `id` to `Form1` and include the `runat="server"` attribute that is mandatory for all ASP.NET Mobile Web Form Controls:

```
<mobile:Form id="Form1" runat="server">
```

Within the `<mobile:Form>` tag set we find two controls and text directing the user to enter their name. Remember that the above `<mobile:Form>` is acting as a **container** for these controls: they cannot be put directly into a `MobilePage`:

```
Enter your name:
  <mobile:TextBox id="TextBox1" runat="server" />
  <mobile:Command id="Command1" runat="server" OnClick="Command1_Click">
    Go</mobile: Command>
```

When `Command1` is clicked, the `Command1_Click` event handler is invoked, so now let's go back in the page's code to find that method. The first line of code in this method (after the method signature, itself) creates a string using the value from `TextBox1` (which should be your name) and assigning it to `Form2`'s `Label1` Text property. The user sees `Form2` after `ActiveForm` is set to `true` in the method's next line of code:

```
<script runat="server">
private void Command1_Click(object sender, System.EventArgs e)
{
  Label1.Text = "You made it " + TextBox1.Text + "!";
  ActiveForm = Form2;
}
</script>
```

Next, we see `Form2` with `Label1`, whose text we just saw set in the `Command1_Click` method above, residing within it. This form is being used as an alternative to directing the user to another page. It is much more tidy to add the second form to a page than to add another page in the applications directory:

```
<mobile:Form id="Form2" runat="server">
  <mobile:Label id="Label1" runat="server" />
</mobile:Form>
```

The <mobile:Panel>

The <mobile:Panel> control is very useful when you want to partition groups of controls within a <mobile:Form>. Using this control, you can easily assign common properties to a group of controls, or toggle the visibility of a group. This control has a huge amount of potential for developers who are seeking to organize the functionality of their user interfaces, for example, by creating tagged dialog boxes (or as close as you can come on a small screen).

When device specific behaviors are encountered, each individual control will apply the differences to the inherited properties, as happens with the <mobile:Form> control. Since this control is merely a stylistic and organizational container for other controls, the only attributes that the <mobile:Panel> has are the ones inherited from System.Mobile.UI.MobileControl (the base class for all ASP.NET Mobile Controls). The only required attribute is, as with all Mobile Web Form controls, runat="server". The <mobile:Panel> control can accept literal text in its inner text property and will accept five markup tags, they are:

- ❑   <p> – begins a new paragraph. You need to use it with an ending tag (</p>) so that it will put the inner text in an entirely separate paragraph.

- ❑
 – new line.

- ❑   ... – makes the inner text bold.

- ❑   <i>...</i> – renders the text in an italicized style.

- ❑   <a>...</a> – the inner text will be rendered as a hyperlink.

Just to make it clear what we are talking about, this is how the code would look if we wanted the inner text of a panel to be a link to Microsoft (you need to put this code inside a <mobile:Form> tag to try this out). The inner text property, with its markup tags, is highlighted:

```
<mobile:Panel id="Panel3" runat="server" Alignment="Right">
  <a href="http://www.microsoft.com">Microsoft</a>
</mobile:Panel>
```

The <mobile:Panel> has a containment rule that says it must always be seated in a <mobile:Form> but that it can hold other <mobile:Panel> controls. These additional controls inherit, or override, the properties from the parent container. For example, if you have Panel1, which has Alignment="Right", that contains Panel2, which has Alignment="Center", any control that resides within Panel1 (on the same level as Panel2) it will be subjected to the right alignment property setting. Any control that sits within Panel2 will align to the center due to Panel2 having its Alignment property set to Center, thus overriding its parent container.

Let's look at an example of this to make things clearer:

Try It Out – The <mobile:Panel>

This example will demonstrate controls inheriting properties from the <mobile:Panel> control, as well as an embedded <mobile:Panel> that will override its parent container.

1. Open your text editor and enter the following code:

```
<%@ Page Inherits="System.Web.UI.MobileControls.MobilePage" Language="c#"%>
<%@ Register TagPrefix="mobile" Namespace="System.Web.UI.MobileControls"
                                     Assembly="System.Web.Mobile" %>


<mobile:Form runat="server" ID="Form1">
  <mobile:Panel id="Panel1" runat="server"
                      Font-Size="Small" Font-Bold="true" Alignment="Right">
    <mobile:Label id="Label1" runat="server">
      GaryJ
    </mobile:Label>
    <mobile:Label id="Label2" runat="server">
      DaiseyK
    </mobile:Label>
  </mobile:Panel>

  <mobile:Panel id="Panel2" runat="server"
                              Font-Italic="true" Font-Size="large">
    <mobile:Label id="Label3" runat="server">
      AngeloK
    </mobile:Label>
    <mobile:Label id="Label4" runat="server">
      BradA
    </mobile:Label>
  </mobile:Panel>

  <mobile:Panel id="Panel3" runat="server"
                                  Alignment="Right" Font-Bold="True">
    <mobile:Label id="Label5" runat="server">
      On Panel 3
    </mobile:Label>

    <mobile:Panel id="Panel4" runat="server" Alignment="Center">
      <mobile:Label id="Label6" runat="server">
        On Panel 4
      </mobile:Label>
    </mobile:Panel>

  </mobile:Panel>
</mobile:Form>
```

2. Save it as `WroxPanelEx.aspx` in a virtual directory.

3. Navigate your emulator to the file. You'll probably have to scroll-down on cell-phone browsers to be able to see the whole page:

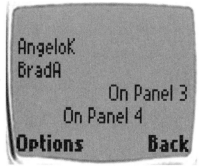

Note how the font effects and formatting differ slightly between the different browsers.

How It Works

We will skip over discussing the header directives, as they are the same as the last example, and instead we'll go directly to the `<mobile:Form>` control. Here we see a `<mobile:Form>` that contains two `<mobile:Panel>` controls. The first one is setting its font properties to `small` and `bold`, with the alignment property set to push everything to the right. These properties are inherited by the `<mobile:Label1>` and `<mobile:Label2>` controls that reside within it:

```
<mobile:Panel id="Panel1" runat="server"
                    Font-Size="Small" Font-Bold="true" Alignment="Right">
  <mobile:Label id="Label1" runat="server">
    GaryJ
  </mobile:Label>
  <mobile:Label id="Label2" runat="server">
    DaiseyK
  </mobile:Label>
</mobile:Panel>
```

`<mobile:Panel2>` is responsible for rendering the next two lines of text. We can see the two font properties are set to italicize the text and make it large. Again, these properties are inherited by the two `<mobile:Label>` controls that the panel contains:

```
<mobile:Panel id="Panel2" runat="server"
                            Font-Italic="true" Font-Size="large">
  <mobile:Label id="Label3" runat="server">
    AngeloK
  </mobile:Label>
  <mobile:Label id="Label4" runat="server">
    BradA
  </mobile:Label>
</mobile:Panel>
```

`<mobile:Panel3>` is where we begin to see how embedding a panel within another one will allow the child `<mobile:Panel>` to inherit properties from its parent. In this case we have `<mobile:Panel3>` with its alignment property set to right and its font set to bold. The panel contains `<mobile:Label5>`, whose text is affected by `<mobile:Panel3>`'s alignment and font property settings and as such is right justified, in bold:

```
<mobile:Panel id="Panel3" runat="server"
                            Alignment="Right" Font-Bold="True">
  <mobile:Label id="Label5" runat="server">
    On Panel 3
  </mobile:Label>
```

Still within `<mobile:Panel3>`, we come to `<mobile:Panel4>`. This control will inherit all of its parents' property settings and employ the ones that are not overridden. In this example we are overriding the Alignment property and setting it to `Center` instead of `Right`. Since we did not change the `Font-Bold` setting we have inherited that property from the parent panel, and our resulting display of the label is centered, and in bold:

```
<mobile:Panel id="Panel4" runat="server" Alignment="Center">
  <mobile:Label id="Label6" runat="server">
    On Panel 4
  </mobile:Label>
</mobile:Panel>
```

Finally, of course, we have our closing tags:

```
  </mobile:Panel>
</mobile:Form>
```

Summary

This chapter has looked at the two mobile container controls, which are controls that can host other controls within them for ease of organization. These controls are:

❏   `<mobile:Form>`

❏   `<mobile:Panel>`

We saw how the <mobile:Form> control is necessary for everything that is done with Mobile Web Forms, and that it is the most outwardly addressable control within the toolkit. Which is to say that you can't place any controls outside of the <mobile:Form> control. We also learned that <mobile:Panel> is great for grouping controls that need to inherit some of the same common properties, or need to be easily addressed as a programmatic cluster.

The next chapter will build upon these containers to begin interacting with users using four controls that facilitate the collection and display of data.

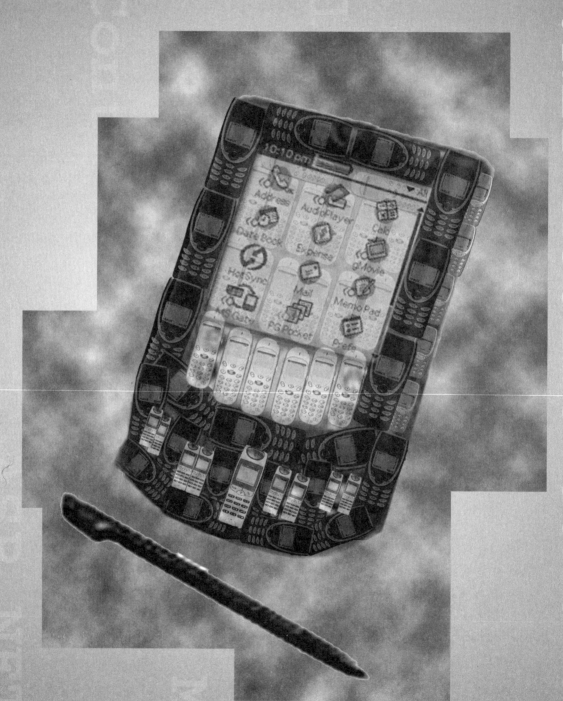

Interacting With Users

In the previous chapter we looked at the `Form` and `Panel` user controls that we can use to deliver functionality to the user. We saw that all other Mobile Web Form controls have containment rules that require them to reside within one of these two. In this chapter, we'll look at the controls provided for us to display information for the user (and in one case, collect information from the user). We will also talk about the movement of information or data from the user to the server, and consider a few of the things you should bear in mind when it gets there.

By the end of this chapter you will have a firm understanding of the basic foundations from which our Mobile Web Form applications interact with the user.

The User Experience

Most, if not all, business applications have some type of user interaction, this can be anything from showing the user a time and place for a secret business meeting, to asking for a password or directing the user to some other resource. This means that the user is most likely not going to be sitting idle while the content in the browser does a song and dance routine – users will most often have a specific purpose and will take actions within the application that will generate responses, the results of which will give them the information that they need to know. The Microsoft Mobile Internet Toolkit provides a set of controls that we'll use to do this. They have the same ease-of-use as the other controls we've seen so far (as do the other controls we will meet throughout the book) due to their tag-based programming model.

These controls are where we will start to put together the picture that makes up the application-user interaction experience. We are looking at them first, because displaying some sort of prompting content to the user is how almost all user-centric applications will initiate contact and set things into motion.

The controls we will discuss are:

❑ `<mobile:Call>` - Depending on the capabilities of the client device, this control allows the programmatic calling of a phone number through a UI presented to the user, or will display an alternative URL if the device does not support making a phone call through web content.

❑ `<mobile:Label>` - This is an output-only control whose sole purpose is to display text to the user.

❑   <mobile:TextBox> – This acts as both an input and an output control. It is the Text property of this control that corresponds to the text that is currently in the TextBox itself. The Text property of this control is both read and write and is set when the user enters something into the control or the developer sets it programmatically.

❑   <mobile:TextView> –This control is used for displaying formatted text and is an output-only control. It supports the use of markup tags embedded within the text to handle the formatting.

Now we'll go ahead and look at examples of each of these types of control.

The <mobile:Call> Control

There may be times when it would be nice to allow the user to place a phone call directly from our Mobile Web Form application. One example of where this would be useful is within an application that has a company directory as part of its functionality. Users could search for the name of the person they need to contact, get a list of potential matches back, and choose to dial the number of the one they want.

To provide this kind of functionality the Mobile Internet Toolkit gives us the <mobile:Call> control. Like the other controls we have seen, this control inherits from the base class System.Mobile.UI.MobileControl that provides us with properties such as Alignment, innerText, and Font (refer back to Chapter 4 where we explained this). In addition to these properties we have three additional basic properties there is some functionality specific to this control:

❑   AlternateFormat – This property formats the value contained in the text within the PhoneNumber property. This is only used if the client device is unable to make phone calls from web content. The default values are {0} and {1}. {0} is the Text (it will also work with the value of the innerText property) property and {1} is the value assigned to the PhoneNumber property. So, if we had AlternateFormat="{0} at {1}", the Text Property was set to Call Bob, and the PhoneNumber property was set to 305-555-1212, when this property was used in a rendering we would get a string that looked similar to this: Call Bob at 617-555-1212. We will look at this in more detail in the example.

❑   AlternateURL – This property is used with the previous one to compensate for clients that do not support making calls from web content. If this property has a value other than null, it will render the text in AlternateFormat as an anchor and if the anchor is activated the client browser will navigate to the URL specified in this property. Make sure you double-check the value you enter for this property to ensure that it is a valid URL or your client will be misdirected.

❑   PhoneNumber – This sets or returns a string representing a phone number. A phone number can consist of an optional country or region code (prefixed by a "+" sign) followed by any sequence of digits that make up the phone number. There are a few characters that can be used as delimiters, or decorators, that are permitted within the phone number to format it and make it more readable. They are ( ) - and {space}. These have no impact on how the <Call> control behaves, and are, in fact, ignored by it. A few examples of valid phone numbers are:

❑   (800) 873-9769

❑   +44 (0)121 687 4100

❑   +33)1(42.44 23 54

When you first look at the above examples of acceptable phone number formats you may notice what appears to be decorator character misuse, this is intentional to emphasize the point that they are ignored by the <Call> control and therefore will not inhibit its functionality. When deciding on the formatting for your own phone numbers, you may want to take into consideration the locale of the audience you are targeting with your application (you might also consider using CustomValidator to validate. We'll learn more about validation controls in Chapter 10).

By setting these properties we can dictate how our control behaves when it encounters clients that do and do not support making calls from web content. This means that a user with a browser that doesn't support this will be shown a link to alternate information while another user having a browser that does support it will be able to make the call. Clients that will support making calls from web content will be those armed with telephony capabilities. A detailed explanation of telephony in this context is far beyond the scope of this book, so for our purposes let's just say that it is the interaction between Internet and phone functionality.

Let's now look at an example of the <mobile:Call> control in action:

Try It Out – The <mobile:Call> Control

1. Enter the following code in your text editor:

```
<%@Page Inherits="System.Web.UI.MobileControls.MobilePage" Language="C#"%>
<%@Register TagPrefix="mobile" Namespace="System.Web.UI.MobileControls"
Assembly="System.Web.Mobile" %>
<mobile:Form id="Form1" runat="server">
  <mobile:Call
    id="Call1"
    runat="server"
    AlternateFormat="{0} at {1}"
    AlternateURL="OtherPage.aspx"
    PhoneNumber="617-555-1212">
    Call Bob
  </mobile:Call>
</mobile:Form>
```

2. Save this file, in a virtual directory, as WroxCallExample.aspx.

3. In a new file in your text editor, enter the following code:

```
<%@Register TagPrefix="mobile" Namespace="System.Web.UI.MobileControls"
Assembly="System.Web.Mobile" %>
<%@ Page Inherits="System.Web.UI.MobileControls.MobilePage" Language="C#"%>
<mobile:Form id="Form1" runat="server">
```

```
<mobile:Label id="Label1" runat="server">
  I was unable to make the call.
</mobile:Label>
</mobile:Form>
```

4. Save this file as `OtherPage.aspx` in the same virtual directory as the first.

5. Serve `WroxCallExample.aspx` in your emulator, and you should see something like the following:

6. If we choose to activate this anchor (that is to say, we try and run it) we are directed to `OtherPage.aspx` which gives the user the indication that the control was unable to make the requested phone call:

How It Works

In the first page of our example application (`WroxCallExample.aspx`) we have the typical header directives @Page and @Register that inherit the class necessary for Mobile Web Forms, set the language to be used, and register the mobile tag namespace:

```
<%@ Page Inherits="System.Web.UI.MobileControls.MobilePage" Language="C#"%>
<%@Register TagPrefix="mobile" Namespace="System.Web.UI.MobileControls"
Assembly="System.Web.Mobile" %>
```

Next, we see the <mobile:Call> control embedded in the <mobile:Form>. We can see that the id is set to Call1 and includes the necessary runat="server" property, but what warrants our attention here are the AlternateFormat, PhoneNumber, and AlternateURL properties:

```
<mobile:Form id="Form1" runat="server">
  <mobile:Call
    id="Call1"
    runat="server"
    AlternateFormat="{0} at {1}"
    PhoneNumber="617-555-1212"
    AlternateURL="OtherPage.aspx">
    Call Bob
  </mobile:Call>
</mobile:Form>
```

In the first screenshot above we see an anchor that reads (you might need to scroll right in order to see it all) Call Bob at 617-555-1212. The first thing to note is that this is displayed because our emulator does not support making phone calls from web content. Since this is the case, the property AlternateFormat springs into action to create an anchor to display to the user.

> Remember that the **AlternateFormat** property is the property that actually constructs the anchor for the user when the client device does not support telephony.

In the code for the <mobile:Call> control above, we can see hints of where this anchor may have been derived from, but let's go ahead and clarify this. In the string Call Bob at 617-555-1212 we see the innerText property value, Call Bob, and the PhoneNumber property value, 617-555-1212. We also see the word 'at'. The value for AlternateFormat causes the innerText value to be entered in place of the {0} and the value of PhoneNumber to be placed where {1} resides. Notice, the word 'at' is between the {0} and the {1}, which is why it is placed it gets between the values of these two properties (innerText and PhoneNumber) in the string Call Bob at 617-555-1212.

Here is the markup code that was rendered to my emulator. Within this you can see that the anchor is represented both as an item in the Options menu and as a regular link:

```
<card id="Form1">
  <do type="prev" label="Back">
    <prev/>
  </do>
  <p>
    <do type="accept" label="Call Bob at 617-555-1212">
      <go href="OtherPage.aspx"/>
```

```
      </do>
        <a href="OtherPage.aspx" title="Call Bob">
         Call Bob at 617-555-1212
        </a>
        <br/>
      </p>
    </card>
```

In the WML code that's produced by the controls, we have a <card> element that contains other elements for the Options menu (the <do> element) and the anchor (the <a> element) that both point to our OtherPage.aspx. (For further information on WAP/WML see *Professional WAP,* ISBN 1-861004-04-4 by Wrox Press). The label attribute in the <do> element is the text that the user sees as the item in the Options menu and the <go> element designates the page to seek when it is invoked. Within the <a> element we have the standard href attribute to specify the page to go to and the innerText property will dictate what is displayed.

If the link or Options menu item is activated, the browser navigates to OtherPage.aspx, which is just a basic page with a <mobile:Label> that lets the user know that the call could not be made. The destination could just as easily have been somewhere within your application or another site altogether. Here is a snippet of our destination page's code:

```
  . . .
  <mobile:Form id="Form1" runat="server">
    <mobile:Label id="Label1" runat="server">
      I was unable to make the call.
    </mobile:Label>
  </mobile:Form>
```

The <mobile:Label> Control

The <mobile:Label> control's sole purpose is to display text to the user, it is an 'output' only control, and does not actually define any of its own properties. Consistent with all other Mobile Web Form controls, it inherits from the base class System.Mobile.UI.MobileControl and inherits one property from System.Web.UI.MobileControls.TextControl, which is its Text property. Though it has an innerText property as well, this can only be set at design time. If we want to make any changes to the text that is displayed during the lifetime of the application, it will have to be done through the Text property, which will override the innerText settings that may exist (if both are set at design time, innerText takes precedence until Text is changed programmatically).

> **The innerText property cannot be set programmatically; it can only be set at design time.**

Common uses for the <mobile:Label> control are to prompt the user for the type of information that an input control might need, and to display a message that reports the outcome of some action that the user may have requested of the application. I'm sure that within a short interval of time, a number of creative ways to put this control to use will emerge.

Now, let's look at an example of the `<mobile:Label>` control in action, with text being set both at design time and programmatically:

Try It Out – The <mobile:Label> Control

1. Open your favorite text editor and enter the following code:

```
<%@ Page Inherits="System.Web.UI.MobileControls.MobilePage" Language="C#"
AutoEventWireup="true"%>
<%@Register TagPrefix="mobile" Namespace="System.Web.UI.MobileControls"
Assembly="System.Web.Mobile" %>
<script runat="server">
private void Command1_Click(object sender, System.EventArgs e)
{
  Label1.Text = TextBox1.Text;
}
</script>
<mobile:form id="Form1" runat="server">
  <mobile:Label id="Label1" runat="server">
    This is the default text. Enter your own and click the button:
  </mobile:Label>
  <mobile:TextBox id="TextBox1" runat="server">
  </mobile:TextBox>
  <mobile:Command id="Command1" onClick="Command1_Click" runat="server">
    Go!
  </mobile:Command>
</mobile:form>
```

2. Save the file as `WroxLabelExample.aspx` in your virtual directory.

3. Browse to the `WroxLabelExample.aspx` file and you should see a page that looks like this:

Enter the string "New Text!":

Click on Go! (this may be in the Options menu on some browsers):

4. We can see the text that we entered into the text box is now displaying on the <mobile:Label> as well (because of ASP.NET's ViewState the text is still in the text box, too. We will look at this further in Chapter 16). If you've entered the exact text of the example, you should see a screen similar to this:

How It Works

In this example we set the text to be displayed to the user at design time and then changed it programmatically in response to the user's action of 'clicking' the Go! Button.

The first screen we saw had a <mobile:Label> displaying text that was set through its innerText property along with a TextBox that the user was being prompted to enter text into and finally a Command button to submit the form:

```
<mobile:form id="Form1" runat="server">
  <mobile:Label id="Label1" runat="server">
    This is the default text. Enter your own and click the button:
  </mobile:Label>
  <mobile:TextBox id="TextBox1" runat="server">
  </mobile:TextBox>
  <mobile:Command id="Command1" onClick="Command1_Click" runat="server">
    Go!
  </mobile:Command>
</mobile:form>
```

Once the form is submitted and received on the server, an event handler for the <mobile:Command> button, Command1_Click, runs (don't worry too much about the method signature for now, we will go over it in the next chapter). This is because, in the above code, we set the onClick event for Command1 to run this method. The method only contains one line which sets the <mobile:Label> control's Text property to the value contained in TextBox1's Text property. This overrides the innerText property for the <mobile:Label> control that was set at design time and will be shown to the user upon return from the server:

```
<script runat="server">
private void Command1_Click(object sender, System.EventArgs e)
{
   Label1.Text = TextBox1.Text;
}
</script>
```

The <mobile:TextBox> Control

The <mobile:TextBox> control generates the single-line text boxes that we are used to seeing on registration forms and search engine UIs. This control is used to display or collect text, or mask characters to act as a password entry point.

Like <mobile:Label>, the <mobile:TextBox> inherits the base Mobile Control properties from System.Mobile.UI.MobileControl and its Text property from System.Web.UI.MobileControls.TextControl. It also supplies four of its own properties. Let's meet them now.

- ❑ **MaxLength** – This property sets or returns the maximum amount of characters allowed in the textbox. The default is zero (0), which means there is no limit to the number of characters.

- ❑ **Numeric** – This sets or returns True if the input should be only numeric. Not all client devices will support solely numeric input (for example HTML browsers weren't designed to cope with this type of input). The default value is False.

- ❑ **Password** – This sets or returns True if the user's entry should be treated as a password and masked with asterisks or hashes. The default value is False.

- ❑ **Size** – Set this to the length you would like the rendered <mobile:TextBox> to be. How this affects the rendering of the control depends on the client's support for it.

There is also an OnTextChanged property that is called when the text in a <mobile:TextBox> is changed and submitted back to the server, raising the override-able TextChanged event. If, for some reason, we have a method that needs to run when the Text property changes from its current state, we can set OnTextChanged to the name of that method and it will be called when the TextChanged event is raised. An example of this control, with that property set, looks like this:

```
<mobile:TextBox
   id="TextBox1"
   runat="server"
   OnTextChanged="ItChanged_OnTextChanged"
   Size="15"
   MaxLength="15">
</mobile:TextBox>
```

Note that controls like this can be created in two ways – the first is using a pair of tags, for example:

```
<mobile:TextBox attributes="example"> </mobile:TextBox>
```

The second style is to use an empty element:

```
<mobile:TextBox attributes="example" />
```

Both styles are perfectly legal and legitimate, the only difference being that if you use the two-tag syntax, you can enter default values for the text box in the space between the two tags, as we do for label controls.

Now that we have a grip on some of the details of this control, let's look at an example to clarify things a little more:

Try It Out – The <mobile:TextBox> Control

1. Open your favorite text editor and enter the following code:

```
<%@Register TagPrefix="mobile" Namespace="System.Web.UI.MobileControls"
                              Assembly="System.Web.Mobile" %>
<%@ Page Inherits="System.Web.UI.MobileControls.MobilePage" Language="C#"
                              AutoEventWireup="true"%>
<script runat="server">
private void ItChanged_OnTextChanged(Object sender, EventArgs args){
  Label1.Text = "Hello " + TextBox1.Text + "! Your fake password is " +
                                        TextBox2.Text;
}
</script>
<mobile:Form id="Form1" runat="server">
  <mobile:Label id="Label2" runat="server">
    Username:</mobile:Label>
  <mobile:TextBox id="TextBox1" runat="server"
    OnTextChanged="ItChanged_OnTextChanged" Size="15"
    MaxLength="15">
  </mobile:TextBox>
  <mobile:Label id="Label3" runat="server">
    Fake password:
  </mobile:Label>
  <mobile:TextBox
    id="TextBox2"
    runat="server"
    Size="5"
    MaxLength="5"
    Password="True">
  </mobile:TextBox>
  <mobile:Command id="Command1" runat="server">
    Go
  </mobile:Command>
  <mobile:Label id="Label1" runat="server">
  </mobile:Label>
</mobile:Form>
```

2. Save the file as `WroxTextBoxExample.aspx` in a virtual directory.

3. Navigate your browser to the `WroxTextBoxExample.aspx` file, and you should see something like this:

Enter a user name:

Then a password:

4. Finally, select Go! (This may be in an Options menu on some browsers), you should see something like this afterwards (you may have to scroll down):

How It Works

First we have the header directives, which are identical in syntax and behavior to the previous example's set:

```
<%@Register TagPrefix="mobile" Namespace="System.Web.UI.MobileControls"
                              Assembly="System.Web.Mobile" %>
<%@ Page Inherits="System.Web.UI.MobileControls.MobilePage" Language="C#"
                              AutoEventWireup="true"%>
```

Next, let's look into the core of the page and skip the ItChanged_OnTextChanged method for the moment. In this code we find three Label controls, two TextBox controls, and one Command control. The first Label control is prompting the user to enter a username into the TextBox that follows. That box, TextBox1, has three of its unique properties set. They are OnTextChanged, Size, and MaxLength. When the value of the Text property of this control changes we want to run the method called ItChanged_OnTextChanged, so we set the value of OnTextChanged property accordingly. We then set the Size property to try and influence the width of the rendered control (remember, the success of this depends on the client device's support for it):

```
<mobile:Form id="Form1" runat="server">
  <mobile:Label id="Label2" runat="server">
    Username:
  </mobile:Label>
  <mobile:TextBox
    id="TextBox1"
    runat="server"
    OnTextChanged="ItChanged_OnTextChanged"
    Size="15"
    MaxLength="15">
  </mobile:TextBox>
```

Next we have another Label control that is prompting the using to enter a "fake password" into the TextBox that follows (we don't want to take any chances with real ones). That TextBox, named TextBox2, has its Size property set to 5 that, again, may or may not affect the rendering depending on the device. We then see the MaxLength property set to 5, which will make sure that the user can't make an entry greater than 5 characters in length. Finally, the Password property is set to True so a user's entry will be masked with either asterisk (*) or hash (#) symbols, depending on the client device:

```
<mobile:Label id="Label3" runat="server">
  Fake password:
</mobile:Label>
<mobile:TextBox
  id="TextBox2"
  runat="server"
  Size="5"
  MaxLength="5"
  Password="True">
</mobile:TextBox>
<mobile:Command id="Command1" runat="server">
  Go
</mobile:Command>
```

Following this, we have the `Label` that our `ItChanged_OnTextChanged` method will alter and display, followed by the closing tag of the form:

```
<mobile:Label id="Label1" runat="server">
</mobile:Label>
</mobile:Form>
```

Finally, let's take a look at the method that is fired if the control detects that the text changed in the `TextBox`, this is called `ItChanged_OnTextChanged`. The single line in this method constructs a greeting string that consists of both literal strings and values extracted from the `TextBox` controls that the user will have populated. We can see that the syntax to access the `<mobile:TextBox>` controls `Text` property is `ControlID.Text`, where `ControlID` is the value of the `id` property that you are trying to access. We do this twice, once to get the username (`TextBox1.Text`), and again to get the fake password (`TextBox2.Text`). The `Text` property of `Label1` is populated with the result:

```
<script runat="server">
private void ItChanged_OnTextChanged(Object sender, EventArgs args){

    Label1.Text = "Hello " + TextBox1.Text + "! Your fake password is " +
    TextBox2.Text;

}
</script>
```

We have the `ItChanged_OnTextChanged` method being triggered from the text box that collects the username because we still want to greet a user that has no password.

The <mobile:TextView> Control

The `<mobile:TextView>` is a programmatically accessible control that allows us to display multi-lined text with support for the markup tags `<a>`, `<b>`, `<br>`, `<i>`, and `<p>`.

> **Though we can put literal text on a Mobile Web Form and format it with markup tags, we are unable to access it from within code to change or add to it.**

Aside from the properties it inherits from the base class, there is also a `Text` property. This is the one you will need to manipulate in order to set and change the text to be displayed. To set `Text` programmatically we would use the `SetText` method (notice that we can still wrap the text in markup tags):

```
TextView1.SetText("My New <b>Text</b>");
```

This control is great for working with any large chunk of text that might need to be formatted or changed through the course of its lifetime. For those times when there might be too much text for a particular client to display, it supports both internal and custom pagination (which we discuss in Chapter 12) that will break it into multiple pages and include a navigation system for the user to leaf through.

This control is very simple to implement, as this example will show:

Try It Out – The <mobile:TextView> Control

1. Open your text editor and enter the following code:

```
<%@ Page Inherits="System.Web.UI.MobileControls.MobilePage" Language="c#" %>
<%@ Register TagPrefix="mobile" Namespace="System.Web.UI.MobileControls"
Assembly="System.Web.Mobile"  %>
<mobile:Form id="Form1" runat="server">
  <mobile:TextView id="TextView1" runat="server">
    Hello! I am the <i>TextView</i> control!
</mobile:TextView>
</mobile:Form>
```

2. Save the file as WroxTextViewExample.aspx in a virtual directory.

3. Navigate to the file in your browser, and you should see something like the following:

Notice that the Nokia browser has been unable to render the italic text that we have requested. Further, in an attempt to do so it has actually removed the space between the words TreeView *and* "control"*!*

How It Works

Since we have discussed the basic structure of Mobile Web Forms so much in this chapter already, this time we'll go directly to the <mobile:TextView> control itself, and forego explanation of the surrounding code. The way this control works is by allowing us to write text in the space usually reserved for innerText:

```
<mobile:TextView id="TextView1" runat="server">
  Hello! I am the <i>TextView</i> control!
</mobile:TextView>
```

When the page is executed the `<mobile:TextView>` control renders the text and markup code found in its `Text` property. How this actually ends up looking in the client device is of course up to the capabilities and idiosyncratic differences found between client browsers.

Something Else To Take With You

Interacting with the user is obviously more than just displaying information in a client browser. It also includes collecting information input by the users and processing it into meaningful results that aid the users in whatever task they have undertaken.

In the rest of this book, you'll find a lot of information on user-interaction as your knowledge is built up chapter by chapter. Each chapter will bring into focus another part of the ASP.NET Mobile Internet Toolkit that aids in providing a beneficial experience for your users, whether the part it plays is in the foreground or background.

Throughout the rest of the book we will be discussing many different controls, each with duties that range from moving the user from one place to another within the application, to validating data collected from the user before processing it with our business logic. Those, combined with the controls we looked at in this chapter, add up to be the sum total of user interaction.

When you're reading each chapter and working through the examples, try to relate each control or example to an application that you may have already worked on. Chances are that the scenario in your head is more complex than the given examples. Try to conceptualize what would need to be done to the example for it to fit in with your specific situation. Doing this will trigger little epiphanies and it will start to clarify how the Mobile Web Form controls work together.

Summary

In this chapter we looked at the controls that the ASP.NET Mobile Internet Toolkit provides for us to display data to the user, giving us a foundation from which we can start to interact with the user. The controls we looked at are:

- ❏ `<mobile:Call>`
- ❏ `<mobile:Label>`
- ❏ `<mobile:TextBox>`
- ❏ `<mobile:TextView>`

In the next chapter we will look at different ways to navigate through an ASP.NET Mobile Web Form application, and, in doing so, acquire the next piece of the user interaction puzzle.

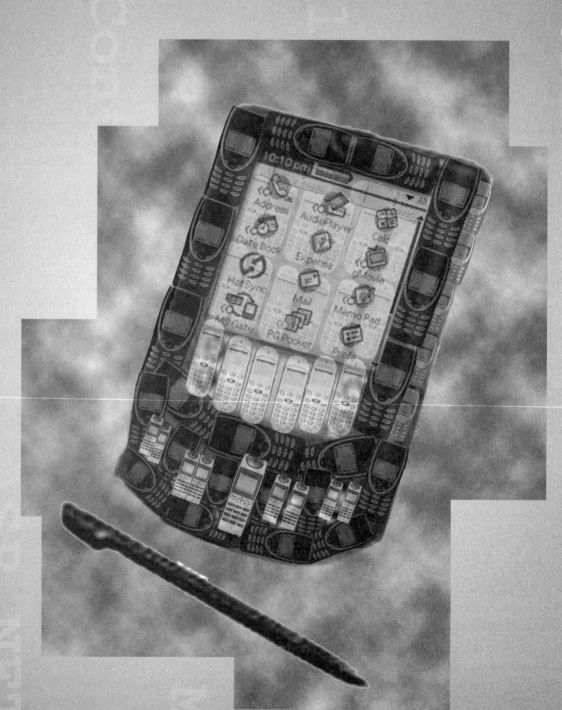

Navigating a Mobile Site

Building easily navigable web sites is not easy at the best of times, and becomes much more challenging when you have to build them for mobile devices with their small screen sizes and cumbersome methods of data entry.

In this chapter we'll look at how you can create navigation options for a mobile web site using the following ASP.NET Mobile Controls:

- ❑ `<mobile:Link>` control
- ❑ `<mobile:Command>` control
- ❑ `<mobile:Image>` control

We'll also be considering the different types of image that can be supported by different devices and how to render the appropriate image types to the target device. We'll begin our discussion with arguably the simplest form of navigation – hyperlinks.

Hyperlinks

At its heart all navigation relies on **hyperlinks** to link one resource to another. The target of a hyperlink can be part of the resource that you are currently working with, a resource located elsewhere on your server, or anywhere else on the Web. It really doesn't matter.

Hyperlinks are created using the `<anchor>` or `<a>` markup tags in languages like HTML, cHTML, xHTML and WML. These anchor tags cause a certain part of the user's display to take them to another destination when they are selected. In order to specify where an anchor tag will send the user **Uniform Resource Locators** (URLs) are used.

Uniform Resource Locators (URLs)

URL's are always specified in the same way:

```
Protocol://domainname/filename.extension
```

So, a web site could be defined with the following:

```
http://www.anysite.com/index.aspx
```

Beyond this level, we can access page **bookmarks** (if they exist) using the # symbol. If we wanted to jump to the "Books" bookmark on the index page, then we could use the following code:

```
http://www.anysite.com/index.aspx#Books
```

In a WAP-based environment web sites are arranged on cards. The same technique as we used for jumping to bookmarks can be used to jump between these cards. To go to the second card (in this example, "second" is the name of the card) of a WAP deck we could use the following:

```
http://www.anysite.com/index.wml#second
```

We can pass parameters with a URL by using a question mark at the end of the file name:

```
http://www.anysite.com/index.aspx?isbn=1861005229
```

In this example, the parameter isbn is being passed, containing the value 1861005229. Multiple parameters can be included by separating each of them with an ampersand character (&):

```
http://www.anysite.com/index.aspx?isbn=1861005229&type=Beginning
```

URLs can be defined in either **absolute** or **relative** terms. Absolute URLs include the domain name and the full path to the filename (as in our previous examples on this page), while relative URLs only hold the filename or sub-folder name, as shown here:

```
index.aspx?isbn=1861005229&type=BeginningASP.NETMobileControls
Books/index.aspx?isbn=1861005229&type=BeginningASP.NETMobileControls
```

When a relative URL is used and no is location included it is assumed that the file resides on the same server, in the root directory of the domain. For example:

```
http://www.anysite.com/books.aspx?isbn=1861005229&type=BeginningASP.NETMobileContr
ols
```

The <mobile:Link> Control

The <mobile:Link> control allows us to create text-based hyperlinks in mobile web forms. It has two main properties, a Text property, that defines what the text of the hyperlink will read, and a NavigateURL property, that defines the destination resource.

You can set the Text property by either setting it directly:

```
<mobile:Link runat="server" NavigateURL="#Welcome" Text="Hello World" />
```

or, when you have more complicated text (for example, text that includes its own control tags), including the hyperlink text within the control tags:

```
<mobile:Link runat="server" NavigateURL="#Welcome">Hello World</mobile:Link>
```

Now we're going to pull the concepts we've look at so far together and create a simple navigation site using mobile web controls:

Try It Out – Using The <mobile:Link> Control

1. Create a new file in your favorite text editor, and enter the following code:

```
<%@ Register TagPrefix="Mobile" Namespace="System.Web.UI.MobileControls"
                                 Assembly="System.Web.Mobile"%>
<%@ Page Inherits="System.Web.UI.MobileControls.MobilePage" %>

<mobile:Form id=Form1 runat="server">
  <mobile:Link runat="server" NavigateURL="#Welcome">
    Say Hello World
  </mobile:Link>
</mobile:Form>

<mobile:Form id="Welcome" runat="server">
  <mobile:Label id=Label1 runat="server">Hello, world!</mobile:Label>
</mobile:Form>
```

2. Save this file as Hello.aspx in your test directory (remember this must be a virtual directory for your code to be served).

3. Now open your mobile browser and browse to your saved code, you should see something like the following:

We've broken with the screenshot presentation convention of the rest of the book in this chapter, to stress the varied ways that a site can appear, and allow navigation, when viewed in different browsers.

OpenWave Browser

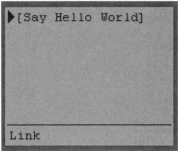

Image of UP.SDK courtesy Openwave Systems Inc.

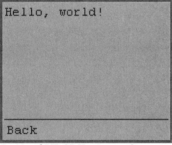

Image of UP.SDK courtesy Openwave Systems Inc.

Nokia Browser

Now, let's see the results for the same code when viewed on PDAs:

Pixo Simulator

Desk Pocket PC Simulator

Finally, let's see the output from the Ericsson R380s simulator.

Ericsson R380s

How It Works

Hopefully this example will have shown you how easy it is to create a cross-device mobile application. Now let's look at the code that has made this possible.

This code imports the mobile controls to the ASP.NET page, and registers them for use.

```
<%@ Page Inherits="System.Web.UI.MobileControls.MobilePage" %>
<%@ Register TagPrefix="Mobile" Namespace="System.Web.UI.MobileControls"
Assembly="System.Web.Mobile"%>
```

Next the mobile page is inherited into the current ASP.NET page.

```
<mobile:Form id=Form1 runat="server">
  <mobile:Link runat="server" NavigateURL="#Welcome">
    Say Hello World
  </mobile:Link>
</mobile:Form>
```

We define a mobile form control, with the ID of "Form1", and set it to run on the server. Within this `<mobile:Form>` control a `<mobile:Link>` control is defined. This has the title of "Say Hello World" and navigates to the next mobile form (called Welcome) using the # operator:

```
<mobile:Form id="Welcome" runat="server">
  <mobile:Label id=Label1 runat="server">Hello, world!</mobile:Label>
</mobile:Form>
```

Finally, we defined a mobile form with the ID of "Welcome", and within it placed a `<mobile:Label>` control to display the greeting "`Hello World!`"

When our ASPX page is requested by a browser, ASP.NET automatically detects the browser type and renders the correct markup language to it, whether that be HTML, cHTML, xHTML, or WML. No coding is required on the developer's part for this to happen.

Using The SoftKeyLabel Attribute

Many cell-phones have an extra shortcut navigation key called a **SoftKey** that is not present on other forms of mobile device. You can set the `SoftKeylabel` attribute of a mobile control to provide additional functionality for this key if it is present.

If a `SoftKey` is not present, then no information will be rendered.

We'll modify our previous Hello World example to illustrate this:

Try It Out – Using <mobile:Link> Control

1. Open the file `Hello.aspx`, that we created for the previous example.

2. Make the following changes to the code and save it as `Hello1.aspx`:

```
<%@ Register TagPrefix="Mobile" Namespace="System.Web.UI.MobileControls"
                                 Assembly="System.Web.Mobile"%>
<%@ Page Inherits="System.Web.UI.MobileControls.MobilePage" %>

<mobile:Form id=Form1 runat="server">
  <mobile:Link runat="server" SoftKeyLabel="Hello" NavigateURL="#Welcome">
    Say Hello World
  </mobile:Link>
</mobile:Form>

<mobile:Form id="Welcome" runat="server">
  <mobile:Label id=Label1 runat="server">Hello, world!</mobile:Label>
</mobile:Form>
```

3. Open a browser and view the ASPX file from your virtual directory. You will notice that while the OpenWave browser displays our `SoftKey` on its first screen the Nokia browsers, due to a difference in design, only display the `SoftKey` under their "**Options**" menu:

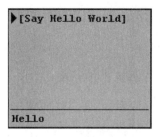

Image of UP.SDK courtesy Openwave
Systems Inc.

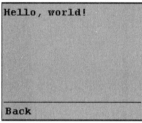

Image of UP.SDK courtesy Openwave
Systems Inc.

4. Finally, try displaying the page on a PDA, or other device that does not support SoftKeys at all. You will see that the rendering information for them is simply ignored:

How It Works

When a request is sent to the ASPX page ASP.NET automatically detects the browser type. Then when its compiler reaches the portion of code containing the SoftKey information it makes a decision as to whether this information should be provided to the browser.

> *Note, output caching still works with mobile web forms, and compilation will only occur when either the cached page expires, or a particular device needs it to.*

```
<mobile:Link runat="server" SoftKeyLabel="Hello" NavigateURL="#Welcome">
   Say Hello World
</mobile:Link>
```

If the code is included, then the browser will then render the SoftKey information to the screen in a manner dependent on its own design:

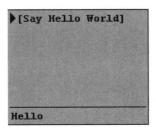

Image of UP.SDK courtesy Openwave Systems Inc.

Creating A Menu With The <mobile:Link> Control

Menus are powerful, easy to create, aids to site navigation. This is just as true of mobile web sites as it is of traditional web sites. The <mobile:Link> control is used to create menus, and can optionally include SoftKey information to increase functionality on those devices that can make use of them.

We'll illustrate this with an example that will display dummy financial information (highs, lows, and totals) for three major stock exchanges, the NYSE, AMEX, and NASDAQ:

Try It Out – Creating A Menu

1. Create a new file, and enter the following code:

```
<%@ Register TagPrefix="Mobile" Namespace="System.Web.UI.MobileControls"
Assembly="System.Web.Mobile"%>
<%@ Page Inherits="System.Web.UI.MobileControls.MobilePage" %>

<!-- Beginning Main Mobile Form -->
<mobile:Form id="MainMenu" runat="server">
  <mobile:Label id=Label1 runat="server">--Financial Data--</mobile:Label>
```

```
      <mobile:Link runat="server" SoftKeyLabel="NYSE" NavigateURL="#NYSE">
        NYSE Info
      </mobile:Link>
      <mobile:Link runat="server" SoftKeyLabel="AMEX" NavigateURL="#AMEX">
        AMEX Info
      </mobile:Link>
      <mobile:Link runat="server" SoftKeyLabel="NASDAQ" NavigateURL="#NASDAQ">
        NASDAQ Info
      </mobile:Link>
</mobile:Form>
<!-- Ending Main Mobile Form -->

<!-- Beginning NYSE Mobile Form -->
<mobile:Form id="NYSE" runat="server">
  <mobile:Label runat="server">--NYSE--</mobile:Label>
  <mobile:Label runat="server">Highs: 89</mobile:Label>
  <mobile:Label runat="server">Lows: 20</mobile:Label>
  <mobile:Label runat="server">Total Issues: 2,974</mobile:Label>
</mobile:Form>
<!-- Ending NYSE Mobile Form -->

<!-- Beginning AMEX Mobile Form -->
<mobile:Form id="AMEX" runat="server">
  <mobile:Label runat="server">--AMEX--</mobile:Label>
  <mobile:Label runat="server">Highs: 12</mobile:Label>
  <mobile:Label runat="server">Lows: 07</mobile:Label>
  <mobile:Label runat="server">Total Issues: 591</mobile:Label>
</mobile:Form>
<!-- Ending AMEX Mobile Form -->

<!-- Beginning NASDAQ Mobile Form -->
<mobile:Form id="NASDAQ" runat="server">
  <mobile:Label runat="server">--NASDAQ--</mobile:Label>
  <mobile:Label runat="server">Highs: 59</mobile:Label>
  <mobile:Label runat="server">Lows: 36</mobile:Label>
  <mobile:Label runat="server">Total Issues: 3,404</mobile:Label>
</mobile:Form>
<!-- Ending NASDAQ Mobile Form -->
```

2. Save this file as `FinInfo.aspx` in your test directory.

3. Open your browser and request the file. We've provided the output of several browsers here for comparison:

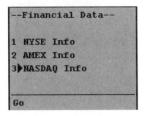

Image of UP.SDK courtesy
Openwave Systems Inc.

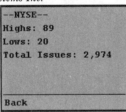

Image of UP.SDK courtesy
Openwave Systems Inc.

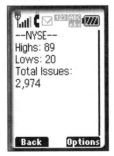

Browser Differences

Before discussing how the code for this works there is a very important difference in the browsers that needs highlighting. If you remember the previous example, with single SoftKey hyperlink implementation, the Openwave browser showed the SoftKey label on the SoftKey, and the Nokia browser showed the SoftKey label within the Options menu:

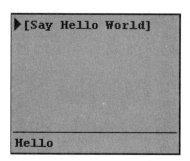

However, when multiple SoftKey labels are added the OpenWave browser no longer shows the SoftKey labels, and instead simply renders a SoftKey labeled "Go". while the Nokia browser shows the SoftKey name for each label as we browse the menu:

This is an important difference that we should remember when developing mobile applications.

How It Works

```
<%@ Register TagPrefix="Mobile" Namespace="System.Web.UI.MobileControls"
                              Assembly="System.Web.Mobile"%>
<%@ Page Inherits="System.Web.UI.MobileControls.MobilePage" %>
```

As in previous examples, the first few lines register the mobile controls and inherit the mobile page into the ASP.NET page.

```
<!-- Beginning Main Mobile Form -->
<mobile:Form id="MainMenu" runat="server">
<mobile:Label id=Label1 runat="server">--Financial Data--</mobile:Label>
  <mobile:Link runat="server" SoftKeyLabel="NYSE" NavigateURL="#NYSE">
    NYSE  Info
  </mobile:Link>
  <mobile:Link runat="server" SoftKeyLabel="AMEX" NavigateURL="#AMEX">
    AMEX Info
  </mobile:Link>
  <mobile:Link runat="server" SoftKeyLabel="NASDAQ" NavigateURL="#NASDAQ">
    NASDAQ Info
  </mobile:Link>
</mobile:Form>
<!-- Ending Main Mobile Form -->
```

The `<!-- Beginning Main Mobile Form -->` section defines the main mobile form to have an ID of "Main Menu" using a `<mobile:Label>` control. This label also gives it the title "--Financial Data--", as well. The menu itself is created using a set of mobile link controls with titles "NYSE Info", "AMEX Info", and "NASDAQ Info". These `<mobile:Link>` controls also contain SoftKey information.

```
<!-- Beginning NYSE Mobile Form -->
<mobile:Form id="NYSE" runat="server">
  <mobile:Label runat="server">--NYSE--</mobile:Label>
  <mobile:Label runat="server">Highs: 89</mobile:Label>
  <mobile:Label runat="server">Lows: 20</mobile:Label>
  <mobile:Label runat="server">Total Issues: 2,974</mobile:Label>
</mobile:Form>
<!-- Ending NYSE Mobile Form -->
```

Each of the `<mobile:Link>` controls point to a different `<mobile:Form>` on the same ASP.NET mobile page. For example, the "`NYSE Info`" link control hyperlinks to the mobile form with the ID of "`NYSE`". Inside the `NYSE` mobile form we've four different `<mobile:Label>` controls that display financial information and a header for the mobile page:

```
<!-- Beginning AMEX Mobile Form -->
<mobile:Form id="AMEX" runat="server">
<mobile:Label runat="server">--AMEX--</mobile:Label>
<mobile:Label runat="server">Highs: 12</mobile:Label>
<mobile:Label runat="server">Lows: 07</mobile:Label>
<mobile:Label runat="server">Total Issues: 591</mobile:Label>
</mobile:Form>
<!-- Ending AMEX Mobile Form -->

<!-- Beginning NASDAQ Mobile Form -->
<mobile:Form id="NASDAQ" runat="server">
<mobile:Label runat="server">--NASDAQ--</mobile:Label>
<mobile:Label runat="server">Highs: 59</mobile:Label>
<mobile:Label runat="server">Lows: 36</mobile:Label>
<mobile:Label runat="server">Total Issues: 3,404</mobile:Label>
</mobile:Form>
<!-- Ending NASDAQ Mobile Form -->
```

We've created two other, similar, forms to display financial information for the other exchanges.

When this code is requested ASP.NET determines the browser type and supplies it with the appropriate markup language to display.

Wiring The Mobile Site

Looking back to results displayed by the previous example you can see that the cell-phone-based browsers were displaying a "back" button to return the user to the main menu, while the PDA-based browsers were not. This discrepancy could cause navigational problems if you do not supply a means of returning to the previous menu for PDAs.

While some PDAs like the PocketPC provide an integral "back" button on their interfaces, this is not consistent across other devices and should not be relied upon.

For this reason, you should always provide a "back" option as a matter of course. We will see how to do this in our next example:

Try It Out – Creating A 'Back' Button

1. Open the `FinInfo.aspx` file that we created in the previous Try It Out, and make the following modifications:

```
<%@ Register TagPrefix="Mobile" Namespace="System.Web.UI.MobileControls"
Assembly="System.Web.Mobile"%>
<%@ Page Inherits="System.Web.UI.MobileControls.MobilePage" %>
```

```
<!-- Beginning Main Mobile Form -->
<mobile:Form id="MainMenu" runat="server">
  <mobile:Label id=Label1 runat="server">--Financial Data--</mobile:Label>
  <mobile:Link runat="server" SoftKeyLabel="NYSE" NavigateURL="#NYSE">
    NYSE Info
  </mobile:Link>
  <mobile:Link runat="server" SoftKeyLabel="AMEX" NavigateURL="#AMEX">
    AMEX Info
  </mobile:Link>
  <mobile:Link runat="server" SoftKeyLabel="NASDAQ" NavigateURL="#NASDAQ">
    NASDAQ Info
  </mobile:Link>
</mobile:Form>
<!-- Ending Main Mobile Form -->

<!-- Beginning NYSE Mobile Form -->
<mobile:Form id="NYSE" runat="server">
  <mobile:Label runat="server">--NYSE--</mobile:Label>
  <mobile:Label runat="server">Highs: 89</mobile:Label>
  <mobile:Label runat="server">Lows: 20</mobile:Label>
  <mobile:Label runat="server">Total Issues: 2,974</mobile:Label>
  <mobile:Link runat="server" SoftKeyLabel="Menu" NavigateURL="#MainMenu">
    Main Menu
  </mobile:Link>
</mobile:Form>
<!-- Ending NYSE Mobile Form -->

<!-- Beginning AMEX Mobile Form -->
<mobile:Form id="AMEX" runat="server">
  <mobile:Label runat="server">--AMEX--</mobile:Label>
  <mobile:Label runat="server">Highs: 12</mobile:Label>
  <mobile:Label runat="server">Lows: 07</mobile:Label>
  <mobile:Label runat="server">Total Issues: 591</mobile:Label>
  <mobile:Link runat="server" SoftKeyLabel="Menu" NavigateURL="#MainMenu">
    Main Menu
  </mobile:Link>
</mobile:Form>
<!-- Ending AMEX Mobile Form -->

<!-- Beginning NASDAQ Mobile Form -->
<mobile:Form id="NASDAQ" runat="server">
  <mobile:Label runat="server">--NASDAQ--</mobile:Label>
  <mobile:Label runat="server">Highs: 59</mobile:Label>
  <mobile:Label runat="server">Lows: 36</mobile:Label>
  <mobile:Label runat="server">Total Issues: 3,404</mobile:Label>
  <mobile:Link runat="server" SoftKeyLabel="Menu" NavigateURL="#MainMenu">
    Main Menu
  </mobile:Link>
</mobile:Form>
<!-- Ending NASDAQ Mobile Form -->
```

2. Save the file as `FinInfo1.aspx`.

3. Browse to the file and you will see that all the browsers, regardless of any integral back functionality that they may have, now have a "Main Menu" hyperlink, as well:

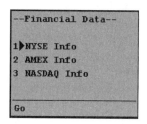

Image of UP.SDK courtesy Openwave Systems Inc.

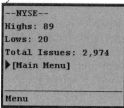

Image of UP.SDK courtesy Openwave Systems Inc.

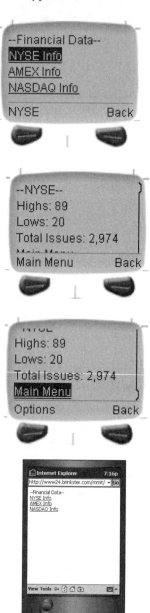

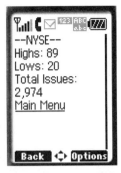

How It Works

In this example we modified our previous financial information mobile page a little to add hyperlinks pointing back to the main menu from the mobile forms.

The code hasn't changed a great deal. Only the small section, highlighted below, has been added to each of the forms below the main menu:

```
<!-- Beginning NYSE Mobile Form -->
<mobile:Form id="NYSE" runat="server">
  <mobile:Label runat="server">--NYSE--</mobile:Label>
  <mobile:Label runat="server">Highs: 89</mobile:Label>
  <mobile:Label runat="server">Lows: 20</mobile:Label>
```

```
   <mobile:Label runat="server">Total Issues: 2,974</mobile:Label>
   <mobile:Link runat="server" SoftKeyLabel="Menu" NavigateURL="#MainMenu">
     Main Menu
   </mobile:Link>
 </mobile:Form>
 <!-- Ending NYSE Mobile Form -->
```

This change ensures that our users will always be able to navigate back to the site's main menu, regardless of the existence, or absence, of integral "back" buttons on their client devices.

The <mobile:Command> Control

The <mobile:Command> control can be thought of as a more flexible version of <mobile:Link>. While <mobile:Link> holds the hyperlink destination hard-coded within itself, <mobile:Command> directs the user to the destination specified in its NavigateURL property. Further, unlike the link control, <mobile:Command> will call a server-side code block during its execution. This means that we can apply logic to where the user is directed.

<mobile:Link> is always rendered as a text-based hyperlink, while <mobile:Command> rendering is dependant on the capabilities of the client browser. On cell-phones it is usually rendered as a text-based link very similar to <mobile:Link>, while on more functional PDA browsers it is rendered in HTML.

To illustrate this, we'll create a simple ASPX page to greet the current user:

Try It Out – Using <Mobile:Command> Control

1. Create a new file, and enter the following code:

```
<%@ Register TagPrefix="Mobile" Namespace="System.Web.UI.MobileControls"
                                 Assembly="System.Web.Mobile"%>
<%@ Page Inherits="System.Web.UI.MobileControls.MobilePage" %>

<!-- Beginning C# Code Block -->
<script language="C#" runat="server">
public void Cmd_Click(Object sender, EventArgs e)
{
  //Say Hello to the user
  lblHello.Text = "Hello " + txtName.Text;

  //Change the active form to the frmHello
  this.ActiveForm = frmHello;
}
</script>
<!-- Ending C# Code Block -->

<!-- Beginning First Mobile Form -->
<mobile:Form id="frmWelcome" runat="server">
  <mobile:Label runat="server">Name:</mobile:Label>
  <mobile:TextBox runat="server" id="txtName" />
```

```
        <mobile:Command runat="server" id="CmdBtn" OnClick="Cmd_Click"
                                    >Say Hello</mobile:Command>
</mobile:Form>
<!-- Ending First Mobile Form -->

<!-- Beginning Second Mobile Form -->
<mobile:Form runat="server" id="frmHello">
  <mobile:Label runat="server" id="lblHello" />
  <mobile:Link runat="server" SoftKeyLabel="Home"
                     NavigateURL="#frmWelcome">Back to Home</mobile:Link>
</mobile:Form>
<!-- Ending Second Mobile Form -->
```

2. Save this file as `CmdSayHello_CS.aspx` in your test directory.

3. Open your browser and navigate to the file. You should see something resembling the following:

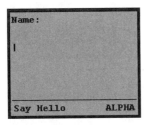

Image of UP.SDK courtesy Openwave Systems Inc.

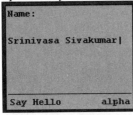

Image of UP.SDK courtesy Openwave Systems Inc.

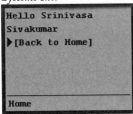

Image of UP.SDK courtesy Openwave Systems Inc.

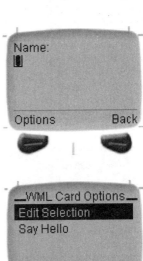

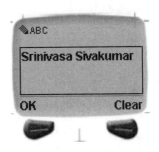

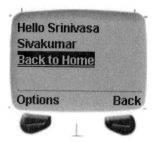

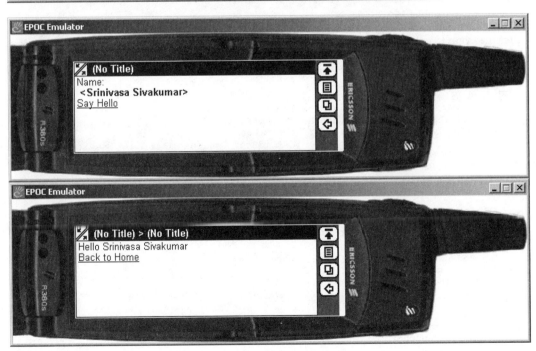

How It Works

We've created a mobile application based around the `<mobile:Command>` control. It accepts a name from the user and then produces a personalized greeting for them on the subsequent form.

In the first few lines we register the mobile controls and inherit the mobile page into the ASP.NET page:

```
<%@ Register TagPrefix="Mobile" Namespace="System.Web.UI.MobileControls"
Assembly="System.Web.Mobile"%>
<%@ Page Inherits="System.Web.UI.MobileControls.MobilePage" %>
```

Next comes a C# code block. The `Cmd_Click` event handler gets the name typed by the user from the `txtName` mobile textbox control (explained next) and concatenates the string "Hello" in front of it before assigning the value to the `lblHello` label control in the second `<mobile:Form>`:

```
<!-- Beginning C# Code Block -->
<script language="C#" runat="server">
public void Cmd_Click(Object sender, EventArgs e)
{
  //Say Hello to the user
  lblHello.Text = "Hello " + txtName.Text;

  //Change the active form to the frmHello
  this.ActiveForm = frmHello;
}
</script>
<!-- Ending C# Code Block -->
```

After the event handler code, we define the first mobile form. This form has a `<mobile:textbox>` control to collect the user's name and a `<mobile:command>` control to trigger a server-side event procedure using the "`Cmd_Click`" event handler:

```
<!-- Beginning First Mobile Form -->
<mobile:Form id="frmWelcome" runat="server">
  <mobile:Label runat="server">Name:</mobile:Label>
  <mobile:TextBox runat="server" id="txtName" />
  <mobile:Command runat="server" id="CmdBtn" OnClick="Cmd_Click">
    Say Hello
  </mobile:Command>
</mobile:Form>
<!-- Ending First Mobile Form -->
```

The second `<mobile:form>` contains a `<mobile:label>` control to display the tailored greeting, and a `<mobile:link>` control to return the user to the first `<mobile:form>`:

```
<!-- Beginning Second Mobile Form -->
<mobile:Form runat="server" id="frmHello">
  <mobile:Label runat="server" id="lblHello" />
  <mobile:Link runat="server" SoftKeyLabel="Home" NavigateURL="#frmWelcome">
    Back to Home
  </mobile:Link>
</mobile:Form>
<!-- Ending Second Mobile Form -->
```

Image Types

Not only is a picture worth a thousand words, it can also take up much less display space! Images do much more than make your site look pretty – judiciously used they can provide identity and continuity that is hard to do with words alone. Unfortunately they're not always applicable to all devices, and can take much longer to download. The majority of wireless connections are very slow when compared to their wired equivalents, and this needs to be taken into account when you are designing your sites. Image files can be stored in a wide variety of file formats, suitable to different hardware and software configurations. Below are listed a few of the most common ones:

❑ **GIF – Graphics Interchange Format**: The UNISYS Corp. and CompuServe (a commercial network), devised the Graphics Interchange Format (GIF), for use on their on-line service. GIFs are color-mapped files that can have anywhere from 2 to 256 colors. Most applications support both the 87a and 89a versions of the GIF standard. GIF files are always compressed and offer an efficient way to store large images. The default file extension for Graphics Interchange Format files is ".GIF". GIF files may contain multiple images to create an animation effect called **Animated GIFs**.

❑ **JPEG – Joint Photographic Experts Group**: JPEG is a standard created by the Joint Photographic Experts Group initially designed specifically for photographic images. The JPEG format uses a method of compression that reduces image file size by selectively reducing the amount of detail contained in the image and by transforming the image data into a format that is better suited for compression. JPEG images are either **true color, 256 colors,** or **grayscale** (256 shades of gray). The default file extension for JPEG files is ".JPG" or ".JPEG".

❑ **BMP – Bitmap**: The Windows Bitmap file format is the standard file format used by Microsoft Windows. Bitmap files can contain 2 (black and white), 16, 256 or 16.7 million colors. Windows uses a fixed color palette for BMP files, which cannot be changed, as doing so would make the screen and border colors change too. This means that transferring an image to the BMP format may result in some color shifts when BMP files are imported into Windows applications. The default file extension for Windows Bitmap files is ".BMP".

❑ **WBMP – Wireless Bitmap**: The WAP Forum has defined the WBMP format for WAP devices, which is optimized for effective transmission over low-bandwidth networks. This is a very simple picture format with no compression, which only supports black and white images. The default file extension for Wireless Bitmap files is ".WBMP".

Images Supported By Devices

The mobile devices support different types of markup languages like HTML, cHTML, xHTML, and WML. In the same way they also support different types of images based on the markup language that they support. For example if the device supports any of the HTML family of markup languages such as HTML, cHTML or xHTML, then the devices could support the JPG and GIF image formats. If the device supports WML markup languages, then the device will support the WBMP file format. Again, this is up to the device manufacturer and the browser manufacturer to decide, if they want to include the support for images. We can detect the type of the image format supported by the mobile device in the code and spool the appropriate image back to the device.

Many of the devices support images and they've an option in the browser to turn off the images. This option is left to the users to decide, an what they want to do with images. For example the Pixo browser provides the following image options:

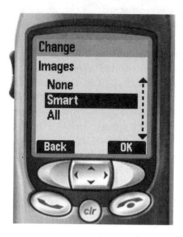

When we select the "Smart" option, small images will be downloaded to the page. When select the "All" option all the images will be downloaded to the device and "None" will not download any images into the device.

The <mobile:Image> Control

The `<mobile:Image>` control is used to embed images into mobile pages, and also to create image-based navigation for your site. The control has two main properties, `ImageURL` and `NavigateURL`. The `ImageURL` contains the source-image filename and `NavigateURL` contains the destination resource for the hyperlink (this is optional).

As we saw previously there are a plethora of different image formats for different devices, and not all devices support all formats. To deal with this ASP.NET provides the option to render different images to different devices, or even to display a textual substitute for your images if the client device is unable to handle them.

We'll build some simple image-based site navigation to demonstrate this:

Try It Out – Using The <mobile:Command> Control

1. Create a new file, and enter the following code:

```
<%@ Register TagPrefix="Mobile" Namespace="System.Web.UI.MobileControls"
                                 Assembly="System.Web.Mobile"%>
<%@ Page Inherits="System.Web.UI.MobileControls.MobilePage" %>

<!-- Beginning Main Mobile Form -->
<mobile:Form id="Main" runat=server>
```

```
    <mobile:Label runat="server">
      Click the here to visit Wrox Press:
    </mobile:Label>
    <mobile:Image runat="server" ImageURL="Images/Wrox.GIF"

NavigateURL="#Wrox" AlternateText="Wrox Press">
    <DeviceSpecific>
       <Choice Filter="isWML11" ImageURL="Images/Wrox.WBMP" />
       <Choice Filter="prefersWBMP" ImageURL="Images/Wrox.Wbmp" />
       <Choice Filter="prefersBMP" ImageURL="Images/Wrox.Bmp" />
    </DeviceSpecific>
    </mobile:Image>
</mobile:Form>
<!-- Ending Main Mobile Form -->

<!-- Beginning Wrox Mobile Form -->
<mobile:Form id="Wrox" runat="server">
  <mobile:Label runat="server">Welcome to Wrox Press!!!</mobile:Label>
  <mobile:Image runat="server" ImageURL="Images/Wrox.GIF"
                                    AlternateText="Wrox Press Logo">
    <DeviceSpecific>
      <Choice Filter="isWML11" ImageURL="Images/Wrox.WBMP" />
      <Choice Filter="prefersWBMP" ImageURL="Images/Wrox.Wbmp" />
      <Choice Filter="prefersBMP" ImageURL="Images/Wrox.Bmp" />
    </DeviceSpecific>
  </mobile:Image>
</mobile:Form>
<!-- Ending Wrox Mobile Form -->
```

2. Save this file as `image.aspx` in your test directory.

3. Create a second new file and enter the following code:

```
<configuration>
  <system.web>
    <customErrors mode="Off"/>
  </system.web>
  <system.web>
    <deviceFilters>
      <filter name="prefersWBMP" compare="preferredImageMIME"
                                    argument="image/vnd.wap.wbmp" />
      <filter name="prefersBMP" compare="preferredImageMIME"
                                    argument="image/bmp" />
    </deviceFilters>
  </system.web>
</configuration>
```

4. Save the file as `web.config` in your test directory.

5. Fire up your browser and you should see results similar to the following:

Image of UP.SDK courtesy Openwave Systems Inc.

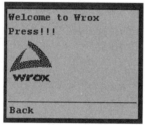

Image of UP.SDK courtesy Openwave Systems Inc.

How It Works

The example is a simple image-based navigation page that directs a user from one <mobile:Form> to another. It contains device-specific code to spool the appropriate image type from the image control.

Looking at the code in detail, we import the mobile controls in ASP.NET, and inherit the mobile page into the ASP.NET page:

```
<%@ Register TagPrefix="Mobile" Namespace="System.Web.UI.MobileControls"
Assembly="System.Web.Mobile"%>
<%@ Page Inherits="System.Web.UI.MobileControls.MobilePage" %>
```

We define a <mobile:form> control with the ID of "Main" within which we define a <mobile:label> with the title of "Click the image to visit Wrox Press":

```
<!-- Beginning Main Mobile Form -->
<mobile:Form id="Main" runat=server>
  <mobile:Label runat="server">
    Click the image to visit Wrox Press:
  </mobile:Label>
```

Next we create a <mobile:image> control with the imageURL property set to "Images/Wrox.GIF", the NavigateURL property set to "#Wrox", and the AlternateText property set to "Wrox Press":

```
<mobile:Image runat="server" ImageURL="Images/Wrox.GIF" NavigateURL="#Wrox"
                                          AlternateText="Wrox Press">
```

After the <mobile:image> control comes the <DeviceSpecific> section which adds conditions using the <Choice> statement. This statement has a filter property that matches the capabilities of the current device-type, and matches the appropriate image filename to it. In this case the conditions are very simple; if the device type is "prefersWBMP" then we're also spooling the WBMP file back to the device.

```
<DeviceSpecific>
   <Choice Filter="prefersWBMP" ImageURL="Images/Wrox.Wbmp" />
```

If the device type is "prefersBMP" then we spool a BMP file back to the device:

```
   <Choice Filter="prefersBMP" ImageURL="Images/Wrox.Bmp" />
 </DeviceSpecific>
</mobile:Image>
</mobile:Form>
<!-- Ending Main Mobile Form -->
```

Next, we create a second <mobile:form> with the ID of "Wrox", and within it place a <mobile:label> control, that displays the greeting "Welcome to Wrox Press!!!"

```
<!-- Beginning Wrox Mobile Form -->
<mobile:Form id="Wrox" runat="server">
  <mobile:Label runat="server">Welcome to Wrox Press!!!</mobile:Label>
```

Following the <mobile:Label> control we define a <mobile:Image> control with a <DeviceSpecific> section exactly as for the previous image control:

```
<mobile:Image runat="server" ImageURL="Images/Wrox.GIF"
                                  AlternateText="Wrox Press Logo">
  <DeviceSpecific>
    <Choice Filter="isWML11" ImageURL="Images/Wrox.WBMP" />
    <Choice Filter="prefersWBMP" ImageURL="Images/Wrox.Wbmp" />
    <Choice Filter="prefersBMP" ImageURL="Images/Wrox.Bmp" />
  </DeviceSpecific>
</mobile:Image>
</mobile:Form>
<!-- Ending Wrox Mobile Form -->
```

The only difference between this <mobile:Image> control and the previous one is that we've not included information for the NavigateURL property, as we do not wish the image to be used as a hyperlink.

Finally we create a separate `web.config` XML configuration file that maps the filters used in the `<DeviceSpecific>` section of the image control:

```
<configuration>
  <system.web>
```

The `"deviceFilters"` section provides namely access to the device capability. For example if you see the `"filter"` tag, we're comparing the MIME type supported by the MIME type value. For example, we're comparing the MIME (using the preferredImageMIME with the compare attribute) type supported by the device (using the `"image/vnd.wap.wbmp"` with the argument attribute) and we're giving it a meaningful name `"prefersWBMP"` that can be used from the mobile form:

```
    <deviceFilters>
      <filter name="prefersWBMP" compare="preferredImageMIME"
                                  argument="image/vnd.wap.wbmp" />
      <filter name="prefersBMP" compare="preferredImageMIME"
                                  argument="image/bmp" />
    </deviceFilters>
  </system.web>
</configuration>
```

When a device requests our ASP.NET mobile page, its `<DeviceSpecific>` section will detect the device's type with the help of the `web.config` mappings. Then the `<Choice>` statement's filter property will select the correct image to spool back to the device:

Our default image is a WBMP file, and this will be displayed in preference to any others. If this cannot be displayed and it is possible to display a BMP, then ASP.NET will do this. If it is not possible to display either of the images than the `AlternateText` property of the `<mobile:image>` control will be displayed.

On devices that support **labels** for images the `AlternateText` property will be displayed as the label:

The "Using Device Capabilities" section of Chapter 12 talks about device capabilities in greater detail.

Summary

This chapter has shown how to create navigable ASP.NET mobile pages, and has covered the following topics:

❑ **Hyperlink basics** – We say how to build different URLs like absolute URLs and relative URLs. We've also seen how to use the bookmarks in the URL.

❑ **Creating Hyperlinks** – We've seen how to use the `<mobile:link>` control to create hyperlinks in the mobile web form. And we've also seen how it is rendered differently on different devices.

❑ **Specifying SoftKey** – We've looked at how the `SoftKeyLabel` attribute is used in the `<mobile:link>` control to customize cell-phone displays.

❑ **Wiring the site** – We then saw how to wire the site with the "Back" buttons to ensure your sites work on a wide range of devices, and that the users will not get lost at the site at any point.

❑ **Mobile Command control** – We looked at the `<mobile:command>` control that allows you to use logic when determining which page to send a user to, and to tailor the content they will see there.

❑ **Adding image support** – Finally, we looked at the use of the `<mobile:image>` control to display images and image-based hyperlinks, including how to spool the specific image type supported by that device using the `<DeviceSpecific>` section.

In the next chapter we will look at how to collect and display data from data sources.

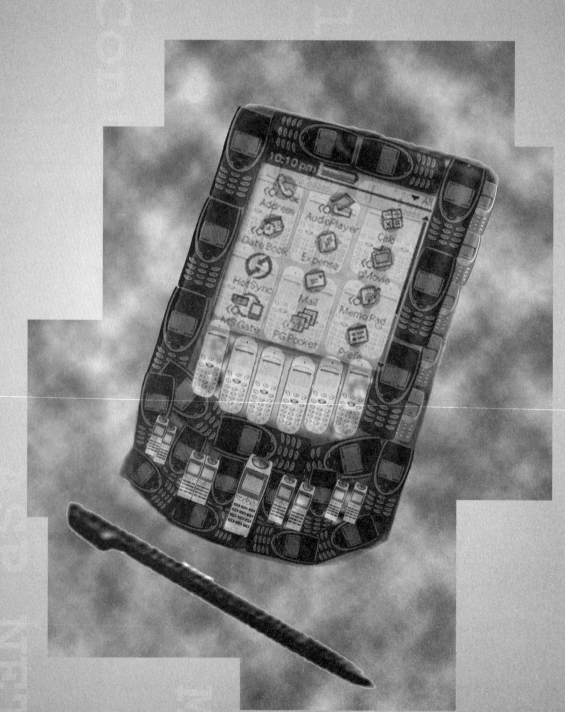

List Controls And Data Binding

As we all know, the majority of mobile devices are very limited in terms of their memory, screen size, data entry capability, and so on – it's not unusual for it to take several minutes to enter your name and contact information into a cell-phone browser, and this speed is not much improved when using a stylus on a PDA. This means that different methods of data entry need to be sought, to allow users to select the option that they want without having to do too much awkward typing. This chapter is devoted to this topic, and will cover the various options available using the ASP.NET Mobile Controls:

- ❑ <mobile:List> control
- ❑ <mobile:SelectionList> control
- ❑ A brief discussion about ADO.NET

We'll begin by looking at the <mobile:List> control.

The <mobile:List> Control

The <mobile:List> control can be used to present a simple list of options for users. It can be rendered as either a **static list** or an **interactive list**. A static mobile list just lists a few items on the screen and we can't interact with it like using the list control for navigation. An interactive list control can be selected and can be used for navigational purposes. The list controls also manage paging internally, based on the capability of the target device they limit the number of items that can be displayed on the screen and split the results into multiple pages.

Our first example is of a static list, with which the user cannot interact:

Try It Out – Using The <mobile:List> Control

1. Create a new file, and enter the following code:

```
<%@ Register TagPrefix="Mobile" Namespace="System.Web.UI.MobileControls"
                                    Assembly="System.Web.Mobile"%>
<%@ Page Inherits="System.Web.UI.MobileControls.MobilePage" %>

<mobile:Form id="Main" runat="server">
  <mobile:Label runat="server" Text="Traffic Info" />
  <mobile:List runat="server">
    <Item Text="I90 East: 50 Mins" />
    <Item Text="I90 West: 33 Mins" />
    <Item Text="I94 North: 70 Mins" />
    <Item Text="I94 South: 40 Mins" />
  </mobile:List>
</mobile:Form>
```

2. Save this file as `SimpleList.aspx` in your test directory.

3. Open the file in your browser. You should see something like the following, depending on your browser:

 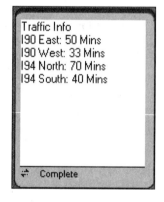

How It Works

This example created a simple static list using the `<mobile:list>` control that displays traffic information for highways near Chicago, USA.

It begins by importing the mobile controls to the ASP.NET page, and then inheriting them into the mobile page:

```
<%@ Register TagPrefix="Mobile" Namespace="System.Web.UI.MobileControls"
                                    Assembly="System.Web.Mobile"%>
<%@ Page Inherits="System.Web.UI.MobileControls.MobilePage" %>
```

Then a new Mobile Form is added, containing a `<mobile:Label>` control that displays the title of our page – "Traffic Info":

```
<mobile:Form "i.d=Main" runat="server">
  <mobile:Label runat="server" Text="Traffic Info" />
```

Next, a `<mobile:List>` control is added, containing predefined items that hold our traffic information. As you can see, we're using the `<Item>` tag to define list items.

```
<mobile:List runat="server">
  <Item Text="I90 East: 50 Mins" />
  <Item Text="I90 West: 33 Mins" />
  <Item Text="I94 North: 70 Mins" />
  <Item Text="I94 South: 40 Mins" />
</mobile:List>
</mobile:Form>
```

Our page is then ready to be served. As was mentioned in the previous chapter, exactly how it will be rendered depends on the capabilities of the client device, and is automatically taken care of by ASP.NET.

Interacting With The `<mobile:List>` Control

The mobile list is an excellent control to give a list of options for the users to select from. For example, we can use the mobile list control to render a menu of options or allow the users to select a state or country from the list of options.

In our previous example, we saw how to display a list of options for the user. The example was very basic, and did not allow the users any interaction with our information. In this next example we're going to go one step further and make our list interactive, by the use of the `OnItemCommand` property of the `<mobile:List>` control. This property points to an event procedure that will be executed when a user selects an item from the `<mobile:List>` control.

Our example will now respond to user selections, and display the travel time on a different mobile form:

Try It Out – Interacting With `<mobile:List>` Control

1. Create a new file, and enter the following code:

```
<%@ Register TagPrefix="Mobile" Namespace="System.Web.UI.MobileControls"
Assembly="System.Web.Mobile"%>
<%@ Page Inherits="System.Web.UI.MobileControls.MobilePage" %>

<!-- Beginning C# Code Block -->
<script runat="server" language="C#">
void OnItemSelection(Object s, ListCommandEventArgs e)
{
```

```
      lbl.Text = e.ListItem.Text + " : " + e.ListItem.Value;
      ActiveForm = Result;
}
</script>
<!-- Ending C# Code Block -->

<!-- Beginning First Mobile Form -->
<mobile:Form runat="server" id="Main">
   <mobile:Label runat="server" Text="Traffic Info" />
   <mobile:List runat="server" OnItemCommand="OnItemSelection">
      <Item Text="I90 East" Value="50 Mins" />
      <Item Text="I90 West" Value="33 Mins" />
      <Item Text="I94 North" Value="70 Mins" />
      <Item Text="I94 South" Value="40 Mins" />
   </mobile:List>
</mobile:Form>
<!-- Ending First Mobile Form -->

<!-- Beginning Second Mobile Form -->
<mobile:Form id="Result" runat="server">
   <mobile:Label runat="server" Text="Traffic Info" />
   <mobile:Label runat="server" id="lbl" />
   <mobile:Link runat="server" NavigateURL="#Main">Back</mobile:Link>
</mobile:Form>
<!-- Ending Second Mobile Form -->
```

2. Save this file as `SimpleList1_CS.aspx` in your test directory.

3. Request the file from your browser, and you should see something approximating the following – depending on your client device:

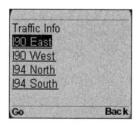

After selecting I90 East, we see the following screen:

How It Works

Since this example has built on the foundation we laid in the previous example, let's concentrate on the differences between this example and the previous one, and explain the new steps in the process.

We started by creating some C# event handler code which reads the list element that the user has selected:

```
<script runat="server" language="C#">
void OnItemSelection(Object s, ListCommandEventArgs e)
{
```

We then take the values of the text and corresponding value attributes, and place these in the text property of a label control. This label control resides in the second form, which is called Result (we'll look at the code for this form in a moment). We set the currently active form to be the Result form, then we close our <script> tags:

```
   lbl.Text = e.ListItem.Text + " : " + e.ListItem.Value;
   ActiveForm = Result;
}
</script>
```

Now we come to the first of our two Mobile Forms. It contains a <mobile:Label> control that displays the title "Traffic Info" on our page.

```
<mobile:Form id="Main" runat="server">
  <mobile:Label runat="server" Text="Traffic Info" />
```

Below this comes another <mobile:List> control, containing preloaded information about the highway name in its text property, and travel time in its value property (this is the information that is accessed by our C# code to produce the output).

```
    <mobile:List runat="server" OnItemCommand="OnItemSelection">
      <Item Text="I90 East" Value="50 Mins" />
      <Item Text="I90 West" Value="33 Mins" />
      <Item Text="I94 North" Value="70 Mins" />
      <Item Text="I94 South" Value="40 Mins" />
    </mobile:List>
  </mobile:Form>
```

We've added the `OnItemCommand` property to the mobile list control and we've called the server-side event handler "OnItemSelection". The `OnItemSelection` event procedure will be triggered when the user makes a selection on the mobile list control. The `OnItemSelection` event procedure passes two arguments to the procedure. The first argument is, as usual, "`Object s`" and the second argument is "`ListCommandEventArgs e`". The `ListCommandEventArgs` object supports the `ListItem` property and we're using the `ListItem` property to read the selected list item name and the value in the C# event handler and displaying it on the label control.

Finally, we have our second mobile form that displays the `<mobile:Label>` with the ID of `lbl`. This displays the information created in our C# code to the user.

```
<mobile:Form id="Result" runat="server">
  <mobile:Label runat="server" Text="Traffic Info" />
  <mobile:Label runat="server" id="lbl" />
  <mobile:Link runat="server" NavigateURL="#Main">Back</mobile:Link>
</mobile:Form>
```

Navigation And Style With <mobile:List>

The `<mobile:List>` control can be rendered in three styles; plain text, a bulleted list, or a numbered list. This additional formatting can be very useful for making the information that you're presenting as clear as possible to the user.

This next application takes advantage of interactive lists to create a system of navigation for your site:

Try It Out – <mobile:List> Control Navigation And Style

1. Create a new file, and enter the following code:

```
<%@ Register TagPrefix="Mobile" Namespace="System.Web.UI.MobileControls"
Assembly="System.Web.Mobile"%>
<%@ Page Inherits="System.Web.UI.MobileControls.MobilePage" %>

<!-- Beginning C# Code Block -->
<script runat="server" language="C#">
void OnItemSelection(Object s, ListCommandEventArgs e)
{
  if (e.ListItem.Value == "1")
    ActiveForm = Bulleted;
```

```
    else if (e.ListItem.Value == "2")
      ActiveForm = Numbered;
    else if (e.ListItem.Value == "3")
      ActiveForm = None;
}
</script>
<!-- Ending C# Code Block -->

<!-- Beginning First Mobile Form -->
<mobile:Form id="Main" runat="server">
  <mobile:Label runat="server" Text="Traffic Info" />
  <mobile:List runat="server" OnItemCommand="OnItemSelection">
    <Item Text="View Bulleted List" Value="1" />
    <Item Text="View Numbered List" Value="2" />
    <Item Text="View Normal List" Value="3" />
  </mobile:List>
</mobile:Form>
<!-- Ending First Mobile Form -->

<!-- Beginning Bulleted Mobile Form -->
<mobile:Form id="Bulleted" runat="server">
  <mobile:Label runat="server" Text="Traffic Info - Bulleted Style" />
  <mobile:List runat="server" Decoration="Bulleted">
    <Item Text="I90 East: 50 Mins" />
    <Item Text="I90 West: 33 Mins" />
    <Item Text="I94 North: 70 Mins" />
    <Item Text="I94 South: 40 Mins" />
  </mobile:List>
  <mobile:Link runat="server" NavigateURL="#Main">Main Menu</mobile:Link>
</mobile:Form>
<!-- Ending Bulleted Mobile Form -->

<!-- Beginning Numbered Mobile Form -->
<mobile:Form id="Numbered" runat="server">
  <mobile:Label runat="server" Text="Traffic Info - Numbered Style" />
  <mobile:List runat="server" Decoration="Numbered">
    <Item Text="I90 East: 50 Mins" />
    <Item Text="I90 West: 33 Mins" />
    <Item Text="I94 North: 70 Mins" />
    <Item Text="I94 South: 40 Mins" />
  </mobile:List>
  <mobile:Link runat="server" NavigateURL="#Main">Main Menu</mobile:Link>
</mobile:Form>
<!-- Ending Numbered Mobile Form -->

<!-- Beginning None Mobile Form -->
<mobile:Form id="None" runat="server">
  <mobile:Label runat="server" Text="Traffic Info - No Style" />
  <mobile:List runat="server" Decoration="None">
    <Item Text="I90 East: 50 Mins" />
    <Item Text="I90 West: 33 Mins" />
    <Item Text="I94 North: 70 Mins" />
    <Item Text="I94 South: 40 Mins" />
  </mobile:List>
  <mobile:Link runat="server" NavigateURL="#Main">Main Menu</mobile:Link>
</mobile:Form>
<!-- Ending None Mobile Form -->
```

2. Save this file as `simpleList2_CS.aspx` in your test directory.

3. Open the file in your browser and you will see something resembling the following (dependent on the client):

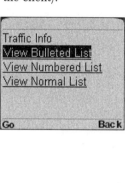

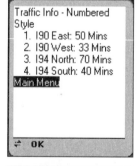

How It Works

We created a mobile list-based navigation application with three options that link with three other mobile pages. Then we created three separate mobile forms with three mobile list controls that have predefined traffic data and decoration property to be rendered differently.

Let's take a look at the code we've just entered. Once again, we'll highlight the unique aspects of this example:

We created a block of C# code containing an event handler in a similar manner to the previous example. This event handler reads the selected list item from the menu and provides navigation information to a second Mobile Form. Navigation is determined by the value of the item selected. If it is '1', then the user is transferred to the `Bulleted` mobile form, if it is '2' they are transferred to the `Numbered` mobile form, and if '3' to the `None` mobile form:

```
<script runat="server" language="C#">
void OnItemSelection(Object s, ListCommandEventArgs e)
{
  if (e.ListItem.Value == "1")
    ActiveForm = Bulleted;
  else if (e.ListItem.Value == "2")
    ActiveForm = Numbered;
  else if (e.ListItem.Value == "3")
    ActiveForm = None;
}
</script>
```

Next, we define the first Mobile Form, containing a `<mobile:Label>` control to display the title, and a `<mobile:List>` control to display the list. The `<mobile:List>` control contains three `Item` controls. Each of these has a `Text` element that contains the text displayed to the user, and a `Value` which will determine where the user is directed.

```
<mobile:Form id="Main" runat="server">
  <mobile:Label runat="server" Text="Traffic Info" />
  <mobile:List runat="server" OnItemCommand="OnItemSelection">
    <Item Text="View Bulleted List" Value="1" />
    <Item Text="View Numbered List" Value="2" />
    <Item Text="View Normal List" Value="3" />
  </mobile:List>
</mobile:Form>
```

Then we define the second mobile form with the ID "`Bulleted`". This mobile form has a label to display the title and a mobile list control to display the traffic information. This list control is pretty much same as the one we used previously; the only difference is the decoration property of the list control is set to "Bulleted" meaning the list will be rendered as a bulleted list if the target device supports it.

```
<mobile:Form id="Bulleted" runat="server">
  <mobile:Label runat="server" Text="Traffic Info - Bulleted Style" />
  <mobile:List runat="server" Decoration="Bulleted">
    <Item Text="I90 East: 50 Mins" />
    <Item Text="I90 West: 33 Mins" />
    <Item Text="I94 North: 70 Mins" />
    <Item Text="I94 South: 40 Mins" />
  </mobile:List>
  <mobile:Link runat="server" NavigateURL="#Main">Main Menu</mobile:Link>
</mobile:Form>
```

Then we defined the third and fourth mobile forms, which are very similar to the second form. The only differences are the decoration properties on the fourth line, which are shown below:

```
<mobile:List runat="server" Decoration="Numbered">
<mobile:List runat="server" Decoration="None">
```

When the user requests the page from the device, the output will be rendered according to the capabilities of the device.

> The HTML–and cHTML–based emulators utilized the decoration property of the
> <mobile:List> control and rendered the output accordingly. The WML-based
> emulators didn't show any differences between the decoration properties. This is
> because the HTML–and cHTML–based emulators will render the list as "<OL> ...
> </OL>" for a numbered list and "<UL> ... </UL>" for bulleted list. In WML there
> is no concept of ordered or unordered list controls, so the output will be rendered as a
> "<select>" tag and the decoration property will be omitted.

In the previous section we've seen how to use the mobile list control with some examples that display the simple mobile list, the interactive list, and finally we've added style to the list mobile control. The mobile list control is a great way to present a list of options to the users for display or to make selections.

The <mobile:SelectionList> Control

The <mobile:SelectionList> control differs slightly from the mobile list control. Before going further, let's go through the differences between the mobile list control and the mobile Selectionlist control.

❑   The mobile SelectionList control doesn't support internal paging, whereas the mobile list control supports internal paging so that the content of the mobile list control will be rendered into multiple pages based on the devices limitations.

❑   The mobile SelectionList control supports multiple selection options and the mobile list control doesn't support this option.

❑ The mobile `SelectionList` control can be rendered as listbox, multi-selection listbox, Combo box, etc. and the mobile `list` control doesn't support these options.

When the user makes a selection on the mobile `SelectionList` control, it won't trigger an event on the server-side – to see the selections made by the user we've got to submit the mobile Web Form using a command control. This is not the case with the mobile `list` control.

To conclude, the `SelectionList` control is a good option:

❑ If you want to render a small list of options to choose from

❑ If you want a multiple selection list option

❑ If you want to render the list as any list box or multiple selection list box or check box list, etc.

Let's create a new example for the `SelectionList` controls. We'll add a list of software companies to the `SelectionList` control and display the selected company names and their stock ticker symbols.

Try It Out – The <mobile:SelectionList> Control

1. Create a new file, and enter the following code:

```
<%@ Register TagPrefix="Mobile" Namespace="System.Web.UI.MobileControls"
Assembly="System.Web.Mobile"%>
<%@ Page Inherits="System.Web.UI.MobileControls.MobilePage" %>

<script runat="server" language="CS">
void OnCompanySelect(Object sender, EventArgs e)
{
  string strResult = "";

  //Loop through all the items in the
  //selection list
  foreach (MobileListItem mItem in SelLst.Items)
  {
    //If the current item is selected then
    if (mItem.Selected)
    {
      //Add it to the result string
      strResult += mItem.Text;
    }
  }

  //If something is selected
  if (strResult.Length > 0)
  {
    //Display the result
    lblResult.Text = strResult;
  }
  else
  {
    //Display the result
    lblResult.Text = "Nothing is selected!";
  }
```

```
  //Change the Active Form
      this.ActiveForm = Result;
}

</script>

<mobile:Form runat="server" id="Main">
  <mobile:Label runat="server" Text="Select a Company:" />
  <mobile:SelectionList runat="server" id="SelLst">
    <Item Text="Microsoft Corp.: MSFT" />
    <Item Text="Sun Micro Systems: SUNW" />
    <Item Text="Oracle Corp: ORCL" />
    <Item Text="i2 Corp: ITWO" />
  </mobile:SelectionList>
  <mobile:Command runat="server" OnClick="OnCompanySelect" Text="Go!" />
</mobile:Form>

<mobile:Form id="Result" runat="server">
  Chosen Company: <mobile:Label runat="server" id="lblResult" />
  <mobile:Link runat="server" NavigateURL="#Main">Back</mobile:Link>
</mobile:Form>
```

2. Save this file as `SelectionList_CS.aspx` in your test directory.

3. Open the file in your browser and you will see something resembling the following (dependent on the client):

How It Works

We've created a `<mobile:SelectionList>`-based application with four options that display the company names and their stock ticker symbols based on the selections.

Let's talk about the code briefly:

We've created a C# code block with an event handler (`OnCompanySelect`) that is similar to the previous example.

```
<script runat="server" language="CS">
void OnCompanySelect(Object sender, EventArgs e)
{
  string strResult = "";
```

The event handler code reads all the items in the mobile `SelectionList` using the `foreach` loop and checks if the current item is selected using the `Selected` property.

```
//Loop through all the items in the
//selection list
foreach (MobileListItem mItem in SelLst.Items)
{
  //If the current item is selected then
  if (mItem.Selected)
  {
```

If the current item is selected then we're adding the name of the selected item into the string variable `strResult`.

```
    //Add it to the result string
    strResult += mItem.Text;
  }
}
```

We then check the length of the string variable and if it's greater than zero we display the selected items in the `lblResult` mobile label control, otherwise we display the message "Nothing is selected!" and change the `ActiveForm` to `Result`.

```
//If something is selected
if (strResult.Length > 0)
{
  //Display the result
  lblResult.Text = strResult;
}
else
{
  //Display the result
  lblResult.Text = "Nothing is selected!";
}

//Change the Active Form
    this.ActiveForm = Result;
}
</script>
```

153

We defined our first mobile form with the ID as "Main" and a label control to display the title. Then we added a `SelectionList` control with a predefined set of information.

```
<mobile:Form runat="server" id="Main">
  <mobile:Label runat="server" Text="Select a Company:" />
  <mobile:SelectionList runat="server" id="SelLst">
    <Item Text="Microsoft Corp.: MSFT" />
    <Item Text="Sun Micro Systems: SUNW" />
    <Item Text="Oracle Corp: ORCL" />
    <Item Text="i2 Corp: ITWO" />
  </mobile:SelectionList>
```

We added a command control and called the C# event handling code (`OnCompanySelect`) from the `OnClick` event.

```
    <mobile:Command runat="server" OnClick="OnCompanySelect" Text="Go!" />
  </mobile:Form>
```

Then we defined the next mobile form with a mobile label control and mobile link control. We're using the label control to display the result from the first mobile form.

```
<mobile:Form id="Result" runat="server">
  Chosen Company: <mobile:Label runat="server" id="lblResult" />
  <mobile:Link runat="server" NavigateURL="#Main">Back</mobile:Link>
</mobile:Form>
```

The <mobile:SelectionList> Control – Radio Button List

We can also render `SelectionList` list as a radio buttoned list. The radio button list is also like the dropdown list that allows single selection among the list of options. When you consider the real estate occupied by these two controls, the dropdown list control takes less space and the radio button list takes more space. When it comes to the readability, with the radio button list, all the options in the page are visible and with the dropdown list the user has to get the list by selecting the dropdown menu.

All it takes for this is to set the `SelectType` to `Radio`. Let's modify the previous example and make it as a radio buttoned list.

Try It Out – Radio Button List

1. Open the `selectionList_CS.aspx` file and make the following highlighted change to it.

```
</script>
<mobile:Form runat="server" id="Main">
    <mobile:Label runat="server" Text="Select a Company:" />
    <mobile:SelectionList runat="server" id="SelLst" SelectType="Radio">
        <Item Text="Microsoft Corp.: MSFT" />
        <Item Text="Sun Micro Systems: SUNW" />
        <Item Text="Oracle Corp: ORCL" />
        <Item Text="i2 Corp: ITWO" />
    </mobile:SelectionList>
    <mobile:Command runat="server" OnClick="OnCompanySelect" Text="Go!" />
</mobile:Form>
```

2. Save this file as `SelectionList1_CS.aspx` in your test directory.

3. Open the file in your browser and you will see something resembling the following (dependent on the client):

If we click 'OK' on either browser, we're taken to the following screens:

All of the device emulators emulated the radio button list, with the exception of the Openwave emulator, which emulates the radio button list as a numbered list.

How It Works

We've created a `<mobile:SelectionList>`-based application that is very similar to the previous example. In this example we've set the `SelectType` property to "Radio". The remaining code stays the same, therefore we don't need to go into too much detail on this occasion.

In this mobile form we've set the `SelectType` property of the `SelectionList` control to "Radio".

```
<mobile:Form runat="server" id="Main">
  <mobile:Label runat="server" Text="Select a Company:" />
  <mobile:SelectionList runat="server" id="SelLst" SelectType="Radio">
    <Item Text="Microsoft Corp.: MSFT" />
    <Item Text="Sun Micro Systems: SUNW" />
    <Item Text="Oracle Corp: ORCL" />
    <Item Text="i2 Corp: ITWO" />
```

```
    </mobile:SelectionList>
    <mobile:Command runat="server" OnClick="OnCompanySelect" Text="Go!" />
</mobile:Form>
```

As you can see, the change in the code is minimal compared to the previous example. With a minimal change in the code, we can render the `<mobile:SelectionList>` in a number of different ways, including a check box list, a `listbox`, and a multi selection `listbox`.

As the code is so similar, we won't run through it in any great detail, we'll just discuss the changes to the `<mobile:SelectionList>` radio button example.

The *<mobile:SelectionList>* Control – Check Box List

We can also render `SelectionList` as a check-boxed list. The check box list provides multiple selection options to the list control. All it takes for this is to set the `SelectType` to `CheckBox`. Let's modify the previous example and make it as a check-boxed list.

Try It Out – Check Box List

1. Open the `selectionList1_CS.aspx` file and make the following highlighted changes to it.

```
{
    //If the current item is selected then
    if (mItem.Selected)
    {
        //Add it to the result string
        strResult += mItem.Text + ", ";
    }
}

<mobile:Form runat="server" id="Main">
    <mobile:Label runat="server" Text="Select a Company:" />
    <mobile:SelectionList runat="server" id="SelLst" SelectType="CheckBox">
        <Item Text="Microsoft Corp.: MSFT" />
        <Item Text="Sun Micro Systems: SUNW" />
```

2. Save this file as `selectionList2_CS.aspx` in your test directory.

3. Open the file in your browser and you will see something resembling the following (dependent on the client). As you can see, the Nokia emulator doesn't provide for a different view from the last example, whereas the MME certainly does:

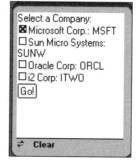

How It Works

We've created a mobile `SelectionList`-based application that is very similar to the previous example. In this example we've changed the `SelectType` property from "Radio" to "CheckBox" :

```
<mobile:SelectionList runat="server" id="SelLst" SelectType="CheckBox">
```

It's a simple change, and it really does highlight how simple it is to produce powerful output with ASP.NET. Let's move on now to examine another option for our `SelectionList` control – the single-selection `listbox`.

The <mobile:SelectionList> Control – List Box

We can also render `SelectionList` list as a `Listbox`. All it takes for this is to set the `SelectType` to `ListBox`. This will create a single selection list box control where it is supported. Let's modify the previous example and make it as a ListBox.

Try It Out - ListBox

1. Open the `selectionList1_CS.aspx` file (not the `selectionList2_CS.aspx` file) and make the following highlighted change to it.

```
<mobile:Label runat="server" Text="Select a Company:" />
<mobile:SelectionList runat="server" id="SelLst" SelectType="ListBox">
    <Item Text="Microsoft Corp.: MSFT" />
```

2. Save this file as `selectionList3_CS.aspx` in your test directory.

3. Open the file in your browser and you will see something resembling the following (dependent on the client):

How It Works

Again, we've merely modified the previous example to change the checkbox-based list to a single selection-based list box. For this we've changed the `SelectType` property from "CheckBox" to "ListBox".

```
<mobile:SelectionList runat="server" id="SelLst" SelectType="ListBox">
```

The remaining code stays the same as in the previous examples.

We're not limited to single-selection lists – with very little coding on our part, we can render a multiple selection `Listbox`.

The `<mobile:SelectionList>` Control – Multi Select List Box

It's also possible to render `SelectionList` list as `MultiSelectListBox`. Like the check box list, the multi select `listbox` control also allows users to select multiple selections on the list of options.

All it takes for this is to set the `SelectType` to `MultiSelectListBox`. This will create a multiple selection list box control where it is supported.

Try It Out –MultiSelectListBox

1. Open the `selectionList2_CS.aspx` file (not the `selectionList3_CS.aspx` file) and make the following highlighted change to it:

```
<mobile:Label runat="server" Text="Select a company:" />
<mobile:SelectionList runat="server" id="SelLst"
                                      SelectType="MultiSelectListBox">
    <Item Text="Microsoft Corp.: MSFT" />
```

2. Save this file as `selectionList4_CS.aspx` in your test directory.

3. Open the file in your browser and you will see something resembling the following (dependent on the client):

How It Works

As we've modified a previous example (`selectionList2_cs.aspx`) to change the single selection list box-based list to a multiple selection list box, the only change relates to the `SelectType` property changing from "`ListBox`" to "`MultiSelectListBox`".

```
<mobile:SelectionList runat="server" id="SelLst"
                                SelectType="MultiSelectListBox">
```

Again, there's no change to the rest of the code on our page.

Let's change gear and take a look at data access in ASP.NET, and how we can connect to a data source with the aim of displaying data on our mobile devices.

Data Access

Data access is inevitable in dynamic web applications. When it comes to wireless web applications, dynamic data is the key to winning customers. The .NET Framework includes a set of data access namespaces and classes called ADO.NET. When it comes to accessing data, ADO.NET makes our life easier by providing easy-to-use objects and methods that allow us to connect to the data source and manipulate the data, even in the disconnected mode.

Getting Started

Every successful application that uses the database starts with a good data modeling. Data modeling is nothing more than conceiving a perfect way to store the data in one or more tables and defining the relationship between them.

> For more information about the data modeling, check out the *Data Models* section of the chapter *Reading From A Data Source* in *Beginning ASP.NET with C#* (ISBN: 1-861006-15-2).

ADO.NET is a group of classes and objects provided by the .NET Framework that allow selecting, modifying, and deleting data from the data source. The data source can be:

❑   Small-scale databases such as MS Access, Dbase, and so on

❑   Large scale databases such as MS SQL Server, Oracle, IBM DB/2, and so on

❑   Formatted text files such as comma-separated text files, and so on

❑   XML documents

❑   Mail servers (such as MS Exchange)

ADO.NET connects to data sources using a managed provider, which is a little like the OLEDB provider or the ODBC driver that we used in the past. The managed provider translates the conversations between the data source and the application that consumes the data source.

ADO.NET Classes

ADO.NET includes classes to connect, retrieve, manipulate, and save the data. The heart of the data access starts with the connection object. The connection class uses a managed provider and sends the connection parameters such as the data source name, location, username, and password to connect to the database.

Once a connection to the data source has been established we can use the command class to retrieve the data for manipulation. We can use either `DataSet` or `DataReader` classes to retrieve the data using the command object and present the data to the users.

Types Of Provider

ADO.NET can use the SQL Server managed provider or the OleDb managed provider to connect to the data source. The SQL Server managed provider can be used to connect to the MS SQL Server database, and for other data sources, such as MS Access, the generic implementation OleDb managed provider can be used.

The following figure describes the relationship between all the objects.

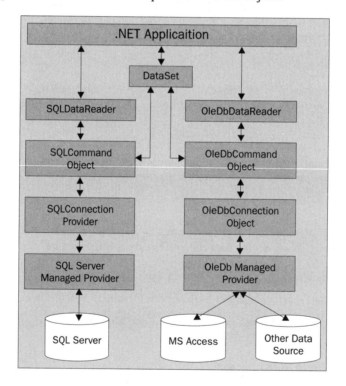

Connecting To The Data Source

To be able to connect to a data source we need the following information:

- ❑ Data source type

- ❑ Data source location

- ❑ Credentials (if any)

To open a connection to the data source we need to build a connection string, and with the above information, we can build a connection string to connect to the data source. Then we can pass the connection string to the Open() method of the connection object to establish a connection to the data source.

Command And DataReader Classes

Simply opening a connection to the data source will not allow us to retrieve data from the data source. We need to use the command object to retrieve the data from the data source and use the DataReader to manipulate the data. We can do this by defining a SQL statement which will be passed to the data source to retrieve the data. Then we can use the ExecuteReader method of the command object to create a DataReader object to retrieve the data.

Traffic Database

Let's create an access database with a single table that holds the traffic information that we've used in our first examples.

This database will be available for download from the Wrox website, at http://www.wrox.com/, so don't worry if you don't have a copy of Access installed to create the database. All that you need to understand is the structure of the data in the database.

Create an Access Database

Start the MS Access application. You'll see a new dialog box like this. Select the 'Blank Access database' radio button and click the OK button.

In the new dialog box, type "C:\Traffic.mdb" and click the 'OK' button.

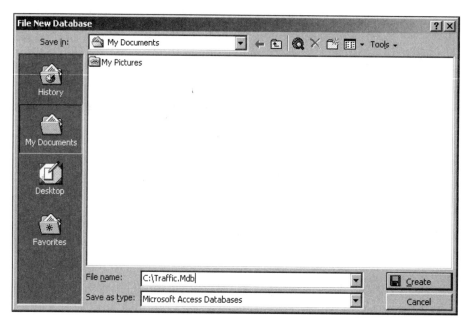

You'll see a new screen. Click the new button on the top after the 'Tables' option is selected on the left side bar. You'll see a new dialog box like this. Select 'Design View' and click the OK button.

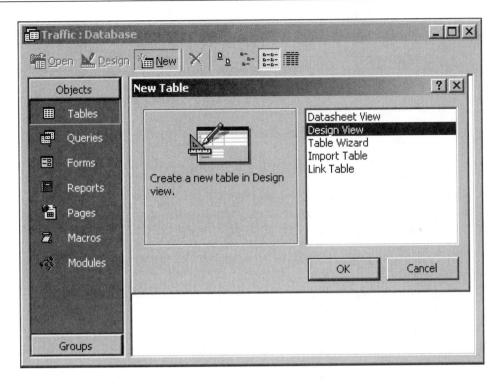

In the table design view dialog box create a new table with the following structure.

Field Name	Data Type	Field Size	Required	Indexed
HighwayName	Text	50	No	No
TravelTime	Text	50	No	No

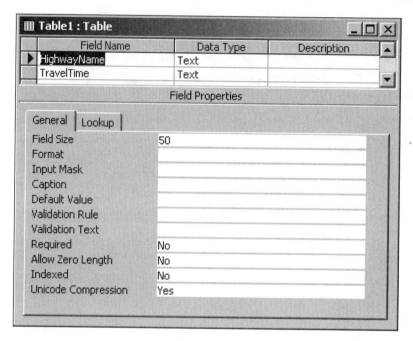

Save the new table as "TrafficInfo".

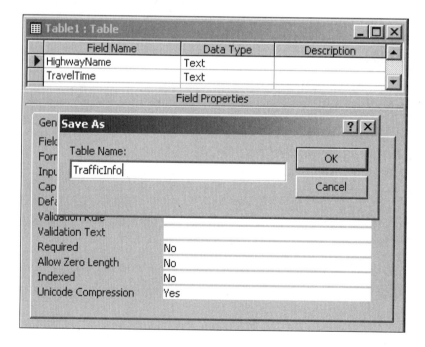

Now you'll see the new table name in the table's collection.

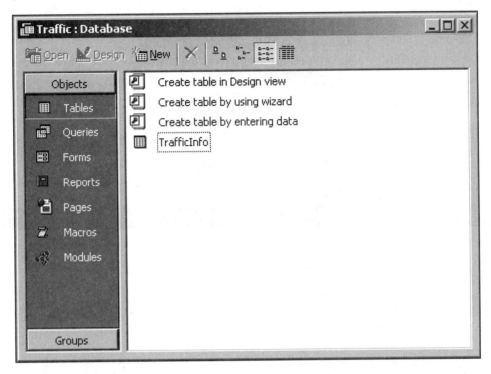

Now select the "TrafficInfo" table and click the "Open" button on the top of the dialog box. You'll see a blank dialog box like this.

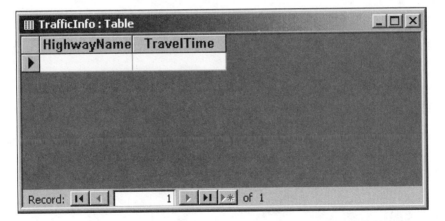

Let's insert four rows of data into the table. We're using some of the data we used in one of our previous examples.

HighwayName	TravelTime
I90 East	50 Mins
I90 West	33 Mins
I94 North	70 Mins
I94 South	40 Mins

TrafficInfo : Table

Now the database is ready to use.

Try It Out – Reading From A Data Source

1. Create a new file, and enter the following code:

```
<%@ Register TagPrefix="Mobile" Namespace="System.Web.UI.MobileControls"
Assembly="System.Web.Mobile"%>
<%@ Page Inherits="System.Web.UI.MobileControls.MobilePage" %>
<%@ Import Namespace="System.Data" %>
<%@ Import Namespace="System.Data.OleDb" %>

<!-- Beginning C# Code Block -->
<script runat="server" language="C#">
void Page_Load(Object sender, EventArgs e)
{
  if (!IsPostBack)
  {

    //Create a connection string
    string strConn = "PROVIDER=Microsoft.Jet.OLEDB.4.0;DATA SOURCE=" +
      "C:\\ Traffic.mdb;";

    //Create the SQL Statement
    string strSQL = "select * from TrafficInfo";

    //Create a Connection object
        OleDbConnection Conn = new OleDbConnection(strConn);

        //Create a command object using the connection object
        OleDbCommand Cmd  = new OleDbCommand(strSQL,Conn);

        //Open the DB connection
        Conn.Open();

    //String for output
    string strOutput = "";
```

```
        //Create a OleDbDataReader object
        OleDbDataReader Rdr;

        //Execute the command object's ExecuteReader method to
        //create a new DataReader object
        Rdr = Cmd.ExecuteReader(CommandBehavior.CloseConnection);

        // Read all the data in the DataReader object using a while loop
        while (Rdr.Read()) {
          //Create the output string object
                strOutput += Rdr["HighwayName"] + " - " +
           Rdr["TravelTime"] + ", ";
           }

        //Display the result
        Output.Text = strOutput;

           // always call Close when done reading.
           Rdr.Close();

        // Close the connection when done with it.
        Conn.Close();
     }
}
</script>
<!-- Ending C# Code Block -->

<!-- Beginning First Mobile Form -->
<mobile:Form id="Main" runat="server">
  <mobile:Label runat="server" Text="Traffic Info" />
  <mobile:Label id="Output" runat="server" />
</mobile:Form>
<!-- Ending First Mobile Form -->
```

> **Make sure you change the path of the database connection string to point to where your database is stored. The relevant line to change is highlighted in bold.**

2. Save this file as `DataAccess_CS.aspx` in your test directory.

3. Open your browser, and you should see a result similar to those shown below:

How It Works

We created a simple ASP.NET mobile page that reads data from an Access database. To connect to the MS Access database, we've used the `OleDb` managed provider and we've used the `OleDbDataReader` to read the data and display it in the label control.

Let's talk about the code briefly. The first two lines of the ASP.NET mobile code imports the mobile controls to the ASP.NET page and inherits the mobile page. Then we've included two namespaces "`System.Data`" and "`System.Data.OleDb`" to access the data from the mobile ASP.NET page. The "`System.Data`" namespace provides access to the common data access objects and the "`System.Data.OleDb`" namespace provides access to the data access objects such as `OleDbConnection`, `OleDbDataReader`, etc.

```
<%@ Import Namespace="System.Data" %>
<%@ Import Namespace="System.Data.OleDb" %>
```

We then created a C# code block with `Page_Load` event handler. Then we checked if the page is being posted back to the server. If this is the first time we are accessing our page, the result of this test is False, so we included the data access code.

```
<script runat="server" language="C#">
void Page_Load(Object sender, EventArgs e)
{
  if (!IsPostBack)
  {
```

We don't need to re-create this on subsequent trips to the server, which is why it's a good idea to include this clause in your code to reduce overhead.

Our next step was to create a connection string that connects to the Access database, `Traffic.mdb`, which, for the purposes of this example, is located on the root C drive of the machine – if your machine is set up differently, you may want to change this path. In this section, we also specified the OLEDB provider name to be "`Microsoft.Jet.OLEDB.4.0`", referring to the fact that Microsoft Access databases require the `Jet` provider to access their data, since this is the underlying protocol.

```
//Create a connection string
string strConn = "PROVIDER=Microsoft.Jet.OLEDB.4.0;DATA
   SOURCE=C:\\Traffic.mdb;";
```

We defined a SQL statement that fetched all of the rows from the table "`TrafficInfo`".

```
//Create the SQL Statement
string strSQL = "select * from TrafficInfo";
```

Our next step was to create a new `OleDbConnection` object, and pass the connection string to it.

```
//Create a Connection object
    OleDbConnection Conn = new OleDbConnection(strConn);
```

We then created an `OleDbCommand` object and passed the SQL statement and the `OleDbConnection` object to it as parameters. Next, we opened the database connection by calling the `Open()` method of the `OleDbConnection` object.

```
//Create a command object using the connection object
OleDbCommand Cmd = new OleDbCommand(strSQL,Conn);

//Open the DB connection
Conn.Open();
```

We created a string variable to generate the output string, and we also created an `OleDbDataReader` object to read the data from the `OleDbCommand` object.

```
//String for output
string strOutput = "";

//Create a OleDbDataReader object
OleDbDataReader Rdr;
```

The next step was to call the `ExecuteReader` method of the `OleDbCommand` object. The `ExecuteReader` method returns an `OleDbDataReader` object and we assigned the return in the `OleDbDataReader` object. We also passed the `CommandBehavior.CloseConnection` to the `ExecuteReader` method and this will close the database connection when all the data is read from the data source.

```
//Execute the command object's ExecuteReader method to
//create a new DataReader object
Rdr = Cmd.ExecuteReader(CommandBehavior.CloseConnection);
```

Using a `while` loop, we read the data we required from the database using the `DataReader` object, in this case, we're after the `HighwayName` and `TravelTime` fields. The resulting data is passed into an output string:

```
// Read all the data in the DataReader object using a while loop
while (Rdr.Read()) {
  //Create the output string object
    strOutput += Rdr["HighwayName"] + " - " +
  Rdr["TravelTime"] + ", ";
  }
```

We can then display the output in the label control and close the `DataReader` object.

```
//Display the result
Output.Text = strOutput;

  // always call Close when done reading.
  Rdr.Close();
}
}
</script>
```

The last part of our code is where we define our form, which has two label controls on it. The first label is used to display the title for the mobile form, and the next one is used to display the output from the database.

```
<mobile:Form id="Main" runat="server">
  <mobile:Label runat="server" Text="Traffic Info" />
  <mobile:Label id="Output" runat="server" />
</mobile:Form>
```

Summary

In this chapter, we've looked at the list controls available as part of the ASP.NET Mobile Controls, including the mobile `list`, and `SelectionList` controls. We started this chapter with the mobile `list` control, and we looked at displaying static and interactive lists that displayed data as a list of options, and that took action when the user made a selection. We've also seen how to render the mobile `list` control as bulleted, numbered, and plain lists. We then moved on to looking at how to use the list control to help in navigating your site.

The next section in this chapter dealt with the mobile `SelectionList` control, and we looked at how different the mobile `SelectionList` control is from the mobile `list` control. We discussed how to render the mobile `SelectionList` control as:

❑   A Dropdown list

❑   A Radio button list

❑   A Check box list

❑   A Single selection list box

❑   A Multiple selection list box

We finished the chapter by learning how we could access data from mobile ASP.NET pages using ADO.NET. We looked at the basic concepts involved in data access, and we looked at reading data using the `DataReader` object. For our test purposes, we created an Access database with a single table that holds sample traffic information. We then read sample data from this database and displayed it on the client.

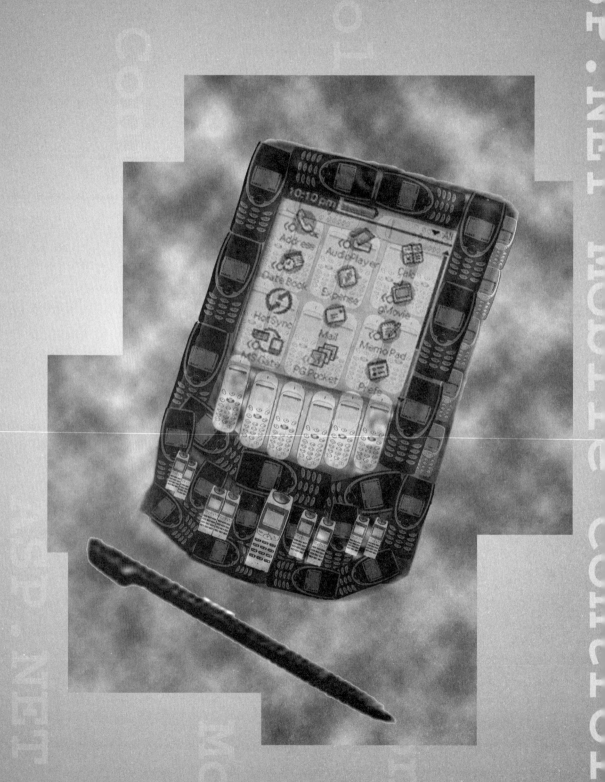

Data Binding

Data binding is arguably one of the most useful features of Mobile Controls. It hides all the complexities of reading data from data sources, and inserting them into server controls, leaving the developer free to concentrate on more pertinent coding issues.

In this chapter, we'll learn how to data bind `<mobile:List>` controls to a database, and look at how to use collections such as the `ArrayList` object. We'll also learn how to use the `<mobile:ObjectList>` control.

What Is Data Binding?

Data binding is a process that binds a mobile control with a data source. The process takes care of the following:

❑　Retrieving data from the data source

❑　Looping through the data source's records

❑　Formatting and presenting the data to the Mobile Control

In the previous chapter we saw an example that read data from a database using an `OleDbDataReader` object, then looped through the records, and displayed the result on a `<mobile:Label>` control. To achieve this same effect using data binding, all we have to do is specify the data source as `OleDbDataReader` and let the data binding process take care of the rest.

To data bind a mobile server control to a data source, we need to provide two pieces of information:

❑　A **Data source**, such as a `DataReader` object, or a collection object such as an `ArrayList`.

❑　Then we need to identify the **Data Text** field and the **Data Value** field in the data source. Data stored in the Data Text field will be shown in the **content** of the list and data stored in the Data Value filed will be added in the **supporting data**.

Data Binding A <mobile:List> Control With An ArrayList Object

To clarify this a little, let's look at an example that will data bind an `ArrayList` to a mobile control. We're going to define a custom class to add traffic-specific information to an `ArrayList` object:

Try It Out – Data Binding With ArrayList

1. Create a new file, and enter the following code (or download the samples from www.wrox.com):

```
<%@ Register TagPrefix="Mobile" Namespace="System.Web.UI.MobileControls"
Assembly="System.Web.Mobile"%>
<%@ Page Inherits="System.Web.UI.MobileControls.MobilePage" %>

<!-- Beginning C# Code Block -->
<script runat="server" language="C#">

//Private Class declaration to
//expose traffic related properties
private class Traffic
{
  //Private members of the class
  string strHighway, strTravelTime;

  //Default constructor
  public Traffic(string HighWay, string TravelTime)
  {
    this.strHighway = HighWay;
    this.strTravelTime = TravelTime;
  }

  //HighwayName read only property
  public string HighwayName
  {
    get
    {
      return this.strHighway;
    }
  }

  //TravelTime read only property
  public string TravelTime
  {
    get
    {
      return this.strTravelTime;
    }
  }
}

void Page_Load(Object sender, EventArgs e)
{
  if (!IsPostBack)
  {
    //Declare a new ArrayList object
    ArrayList aryTraffic = new ArrayList();
```

```
        //Add some traffic data to the array object
        //in the form of the Traffic object.
        aryTraffic.Add(new Traffic("I90 East", "50 Mins"));
        aryTraffic.Add(new Traffic("I90 West", "33 Mins"));
        aryTraffic.Add(new Traffic("I94 North", "70 Mins"));
        aryTraffic.Add(new Traffic("I94 South", "40 Mins"));

        //Data bind the Array List object
        //into the List control
        lst.DataSource = aryTraffic;
        lst.DataBind();
    }
}
</script>
<!-- Ending C# Code Block -->

<!-- Beginning First Mobile Form -->
<mobile:Form id="Main" runat="server">
  <mobile:Label runat="server" Text="Traffic Info " />
  <mobile:List id="lst" runat="server"
  DataTextField="HighwayName" DataValueField="TravelTime" />
</mobile:Form>
<!-- Ending First Mobile Form -->
```

2. Save this file as `DataBinding_CS.aspx` in a virtual directory.

3. Navigate to it in your browser, and you should see something like this:

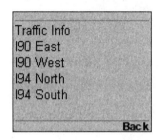

How It Works

We've created an ASP.NET mobile page that data binds an `ArrayList` object to a `<mobile:List>` control. Let's talk about the code briefly. The first two lines import the mobile controls to the ASP.NET page and inherit the mobile page:

```
<%@ Register TagPrefix="Mobile" Namespace="System.Web.UI.MobileControls"
Assembly="System.Web.Mobile" %>
<%@ Page Inherits="System.Web.UI.MobileControls.MobilePage" %>
```

Then we've defined a custom C# class with two private variables. As was mentioned earlier, we're defining the custom class so that we can name the `DataTextField` and `DataTextValueField` names. If we didn't do this there'd be no way we could define the `DataTextField` and `DataTextValueField` names, and our example would be unable to function:

```
//Private Class declaration to
//expose traffic related properties
private class Traffic
{
  //Private members of the class
  string strHighway, strTravelTime;
```

Next we've defined a constructor function with two parameters and we're assigning the values to the private variables. When we create an object using a default constructor the variables `strHighway` and `strTravelTime` will be initialized:

```
//Default constructor
public Traffic(string HighWay, string TravelTime)
{
  this.strHighway = HighWay;
  this.strTravelTime = TravelTime;
}
```

Then we've defined the `HighwayName` property that returns the `strHighwayName` private variable:

```
//HighwayName read only property
public string HighwayName
{
  get
  {
    return this.strHighway;
  }
}
```

Next, we've defined the `TravelTime` property that returns the `strTravelTime` private variable:

```
//TravelTime read only property
public string TravelTime
{
  get
  {
    return this.strTravelTime;
  }
}
}
```

Then we've declared the `Page_Load` event and checked to see if the current event is occurring due to a `Postback`. Since the mobile server controls maintain state, we have to check if the page has been posted back. If it has, we'll want to avoid binding the data, again, as this will create redundant information:

```
void Page_Load(Object sender, EventArgs e)
{
  if (!IsPostBack)
  {
```

Now we declare a new `ArrayList` object:

```
//Declare a new ArrayList object
ArrayList aryTraffic = new ArrayList();
```

We use the `Add` method of the `ArrayList` object to add a new instance of the custom-defined `Traffic` object to the `ArrayList`:

```
//Add some traffic data to the array object
//in the form of the Traffic object.
aryTraffic.Add(new Traffic("I90 East", "50 Mins"));
aryTraffic.Add(new Traffic("I90 West", "33 Mins"));
aryTraffic.Add(new Traffic("I94 North", "70 Mins"));
aryTraffic.Add(new Traffic("I94 South", "40 Mins"));
```

Then, we assign the `ArrayList` object to the `DataSource` property of the `<mobile:List>` control, and call its `DataBind` method to perform the data binding operation:

```
//Data bind the Array List object
//into the List control
lst.DataSource = aryTraffic;
lst.DataBind();
  }
}
```

So far, we've defined a custom class that can store traffic-specific information. In the `Page_Load` event, we've created four objects of the `Traffic` class, and added them to the `ArrayList` object, and we've bound the `ArrayList` object to the mobile server control:

Next, we define a new `<mobile:Form>` containing a `<mobile:Label>` control. This is used to display the title for the `<mobile:Form>`:

```
<mobile:Form id="Main" runat="server">
    <mobile:Label runat="server" Text="Traffic Info" />
```

Then we define a `<mobile:List>` control and set the `DataTextField` property to `HighwayName` and `DataValueField` property to `TravelTime`:

```
<mobile:List id="lst" runat="server"
    DataTextField="HighwayName" DataValueField="TravelTime" />
</mobile:Form>
```

Let's move on now to looking at how we bind data from a database to our mobile controls.

177

Data Binding The <mobile:List> Control With A DataReader

In the previous example we bound an `ArrayList` to a `<mobile:List>` control. But we can bind data from other sources, such as databases, in the same manner. In the previous chapter we saw an example demonstrating how to connect to an Access database and read its data using a `DataReader` object. Now we're going to see how we can bind the `DataReader` object using a `<mobile:List>` control.

Note that the Access database for this example was discussed in a bit more detail in the previous chapter. It is also available to download from http://www.wrox.com/.

Try It Out – Data Binding With A DataReader

1. Create a new file and enter the following code:

```
<%@ Register TagPrefix="Mobile" Namespace="System.Web.UI.MobileControls"
Assembly="System.Web.Mobile"%>
<%@ Page Inherits="System.Web.UI.MobileControls.MobilePage" %>
<%@ Import Namespace="System.Data" %>
<%@ Import Namespace="System.Data.OleDb" %>

<!-- Beginning C# Code Block -->
<script runat="server" language="C#">
void Page_Load(Object sender, EventArgs e)
{
  if (!IsPostBack)
  {
    //Create a connection string
    string strConn = "PROVIDER=Microsoft.Jet.OLEDB.4.0;DATA SOURCE=" +
        "C:\\Traffic.mdb;";

    //Create the SQL Statement
    string strSQL = "SELECT * FROM TrafficInfo";

    //Create a Connection object
        OleDbConnection Conn = new OleDbConnection(strConn);

        //Create a command object using the connection object
        OleDbCommand Cmd  = new OleDbCommand(strSQL,Conn);

        //Open the DB connection
        Conn.Open();

    //Data bind the DataReader object
    //into the List control
    lst.DataSource = Cmd.ExecuteReader(CommandBehavior.CloseConnection);
    lst.DataBind();
  }
}
</script>
<!-- Ending C# Code Block -->
```

```
<!-- Beginning First Mobile Form -->
<mobile:Form id="Main" runat="server">
    <mobile:Label runat="server" Text="Traffic Info" />
    <mobile:List id="lst" runat="server"
    DataTextField="HighwayName"
    DataValueField="TravelTime" />
</mobile:Form>
<!-- Ending First Mobile Form -->
```

2. Save this file as `DataBinding1_CS` in a virtual directory:

> **Make sure you change the path of the database connection string to point to where your database is stored. The relevant line to change is highlighted in bold.**

3. When you navigate to the file in your browser you should see something like this:

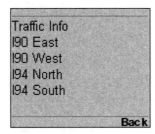
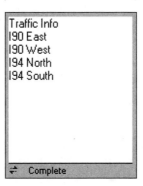

If you compare the results from this Try It Out with the previous one, you will not see any difference in the browser output. This is because they are both using the same controls. The only difference lies in the way that we are binding the data, behind the scenes, within the code. In the previous example, we bound an `ArrayList` to the `<mobile:List>` control, and in this example we've bound a `DataReader` object to the `<mobile:List>` control, instead.

How It Works

We've created a simple ASP.NET mobile page that consumes a MS Access database. To connect to the database, we've used the OleDB Managed Provider with the `OleDbDataReader` object to read the data. Then we're binding the `OleDbDataReader` object to the `<mobile:List>` control.

Because the `OleDbDataReader` object only provides read-only access to the data source, it doesn't have the overheads that its cousin, the `DataSet` object, does, making it the fastest way to bind a data source with a `<mobile:List>` control.

Now, let's talk briefly about the code. The first two lines import the mobile controls to the ASP.NET page and inherit the mobile page:

```
<%@ Register TagPrefix="Mobile" Namespace="System.Web.UI.MobileControls"
Assembly="System.Web.Mobile"%>
<%@ Page Inherits="System.Web.UI.MobileControls.MobilePage" %>
```

Then we include the data access namespaces:

```
<%@ Import Namespace="System.Data" %>
<%@ Import Namespace="System.Data.OleDb" %>
```

Next we create a C# code block with the Page_Load event handler which is similar to the previous data access code example. The only change you'll see in this code is that we're not running a loop to read all the rows from the DataReader object. Instead we're binding it to the <mobile:List> control:

```
<script runat="server" language="C#">
void Page_Load(Object sender, EventArgs e)
{
  if (!IsPostBack)
  {
```

Next we create a connection string that connects to the access database Traffic.mdb located in the C:\ directory (which you'll need to amend according to how your machine is set up). We're also specifying the OleDB provider name as "Microsoft.Jet.OLEDB.4.0":

```
//Create a connection string
string strConn = "PROVIDER=Microsoft.Jet.OLEDB.4.0;DATA
    SOURCE=C:\\Traffic.mdb;";
```

Then we define the SQL statement to get all the rows from the TrafficInfo table:

```
//Create the SQL Statement
string strSQL = "SELECT * FROM TrafficInfo";
```

Next, we create a new OleDbConnection object and pass the connection string to it:

```
//Create a Connection object
    OleDbConnection Conn = new OleDbConnection(strConn);
```

Then we instantiate an OleDbCommand object and pass the SQL statement and the OleDbConnection object to it, before opening a database connection by calling the Open() method of the OleDbConnection object:

```
//Create a command object using the connection object
OleDbCommand Cmd  = new OleDbCommand(strSQL,Conn);

//Open the DB connection
Conn.Open();
```

Now, we call the ExecuteReader method of the OleDbDataReader object. This method returns an OleDbDataReader object and we're assigning this object to the <mobile:List> control's DataSource property, before calling the DataBind() method of the <mobile:List> control to perform the data binding operation:

```
        //Data bind the DataReader object
        //into the List control
        lst.DataSource = Cmd.ExecuteReader(CommandBehavior.CloseConnection);
        lst.DataBind();
    }
}
</script>
```

Finally, we define a <mobile:Form> control containing <mobile:Label> and <mobile:List> controls. The <mobile:Label> is used to display the title for the <mobile:Form> and the <mobile:List> control is used to bind the data from the Access database. We've defined the <mobile:List> control and set the DataTextField property to HighwayName and the DataValueField property to TravelTime. This assignment will be used to place the database fields in the proper position when data binding is performed:

```
<mobile:Form id="Main" runat="server">
    <mobile:Label runat="server" Text="Traffic Info" />
    <mobile:List id="lst" runat="server"
    DataTextField="HighwayName" DataValueField="TravelTime" />
</mobile:Form>
```

Data Binding the <mobile:SelectionList> Control

The <mobile:SelectionList> control also supports data binding. Let's see a simple example of this now:

Try It Out – Data Binding with the <mobile:SelectionList> Control

1. Open the DataBinding1_CS.aspx file, that we created in the previous example, and make the following small highlighted changes to it:

```
<%@ Register TagPrefix="Mobile" Namespace="System.Web.UI.MobileControls"
Assembly="System.Web.Mobile"%>
<%@ Page Inherits="System.Web.UI.MobileControls.MobilePage" %>
<%@ Import Namespace="System.Data" %>
<%@ Import Namespace="System.Data.OleDb" %>

<!-- Beginning C# Code Block -->
<script runat="server" language="CS">
void Page_Load(Object sender, EventArgs e)
{
  if (!IsPostBack)
  {
    string strConn = "PROVIDER=Microsoft.Jet.OLEDB.4.0;DATA SOURCE=" +
    "C:\\Traffic.mdb;";
    string strSQL = "select * from TrafficInfo";
        OleDbConnection Conn = new OleDbConnection(strConn);
        OleDbCommand Cmd  = new OleDbCommand(strSQL,Conn);
        Conn.Open();
```

```
        //Data bind the DataReader object
        //into the List control
        SelLst.DataSource = Cmd.ExecuteReader(CommandBehavior.CloseConnection);
        SelLst.DataBind();
    }
}
</script>
<!-- Ending C# Code Block -->

<mobile:Form runat="server" id="Main">
    <mobile:Label runat="server" Text="Select a Highway:" />
    <mobile:SelectionList runat="server" id="SelLst" SelectType="CheckBox"
    DataTextField="HighwayName" DataValueField="TravelTime" />
</mobile:Form>
```

2. Save this file as `DataBinding2_CS.aspx` in a virtual directory.

3. Navigate to it in your browser of choice, and you should see something like this:

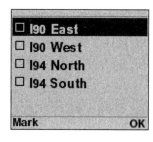
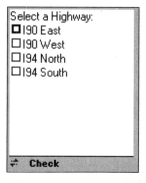

How It Works

We've modified the `<mobile:List>` data binding example code and replaced the `<mobile:List>` control with a `<mobile:SelectionList>` control. The rest of the code in this example remains the same.

In the first change, we're calling the `ExecuteReader` method of the `OleDbDataReader` object. This method returns an `OleDbDataReader` object and we're assigning this returned object to the `<mobile:SelectionList>` control's `DataSource` property. Then we call the `DataBind()` method of the `<mobile:SelectionList>` control to perform the data binding operation:

```
        //Data bind the DataReader object
        //into the SelectionList control
        SelLst.DataSource = Cmd.ExecuteReader(CommandBehavior.CloseConnection);
        SelLst.DataBind();
    }
}
</script>
```

In the second alteration to the code, we've defined a `<mobile:Form>`, as before, but this time the `<mobile:SelectionList>` control is being used to bind the data from the Access database:

```
<mobile:Form runat="server" id="Main">
    <mobile:Label runat="server" Text="Select a Highway:" />
    <mobile:SelectionList runat="server" id="SelLst" SelectType="CheckBox"
    DataTextField="HighwayName" DataValueField="TravelTime" />
</mobile:Form>
```

Data Binding The `<mobile:ObjectList>` Control

Anyone who has done any development with traditional ASP.NET Web Forms will be familiar with the `DataGrid` control. The `<mobile:ObjectList>` control is its counterpart in the world of Mobile Web Forms, it is similar to the `<mobile:List>` and `<mobile:SelectionList>` controls, but with a couple of important differences:

Where the `<mobile:List>` control can only deliver one field of information for the client to display at a time, the `<mobile:ObjectList>` control can display multiple fields (like a table) based on the targeted device's capability. Secondly, unlike a `<mobile:List>` or `<mobile:SelectionList>`, we cannot add **static** data to an `ObjectList` control using an `Add()` method – the only way to get data into it is by data binding.

To explore the `<mobile:ObjectList>` control in more detail, let's see a simple example that binds the `<mobile:ObjectList>` control to our Access database:

Try It Out – Data Binding with the `<mobile:ObjectList>` Control

1. Open the `DataBinding2_CS.aspx` file that we created earlier and make the following highlighted change to it:

```
<%@ Register TagPrefix="Mobile" Namespace="System.Web.UI.MobileControls"
Assembly="System.Web.Mobile"%>
<%@ Page Inherits="System.Web.UI.MobileControls.MobilePage" %>
<%@ Import Namespace="System.Data" %>
<%@ Import Namespace="System.Data.OleDb" %>

<!-- Beginning C# Code Block -->
<script runat="server" language="CS">
void Page_Load(Object sender, EventArgs e)
{
  if (!IsPostBack)
  {
    //Create a connection string
    string strConn = "PROVIDER=Microsoft.Jet.OLEDB.4.0;DATA" +
      " SOURCE=C:\\Traffic.mdb;";

    //Create the SQL Statement
    string strSQL = "select * from TrafficInfo";

    //Create a Connection object
        OleDbConnection Conn = new OleDbConnection(strConn);
```

```
                    //Create a command object using the connection object
                    OleDbCommand Cmd  = new OleDbCommand(strSQL,Conn);

                    //Open the DB connection
                    Conn.Open();

            //Data bind the DataReader object
            //into the List control
            objlst.DataSource = Cmd.ExecuteReader(CommandBehavior.CloseConnection);
            objlst.DataBind();
        }
    }
</script>
<!-- Ending C# Code Block -->

<!-- Beginning First Mobile Form -->
<mobile:Form runat="server" id="Main">
    <mobile:Label runat="server" Text="Select a Highway:" />
    <mobile:ObjectList runat="server" id="objlst" AutoGenerateFields="True" />
</mobile:Form>
<!-- Ending First Mobile Form -->
```

2. Save this file as `DataBinding3_CS.aspx` in a virtual directory.

3. Open it in your browser, and you should see something similar to the following, when you click a link to follow through:

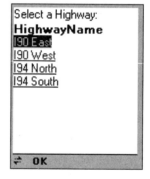

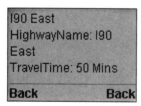

How It Works

We've modified the <mobile:SelectionList> data binding example code and replaced the <mobile:ObjectList> with a <mobile:SelectionList> control. The rest of the code remains unchanged.

Because this example is very similar to the previous one, we'll only discuss the few lines of code that have changed, as the rest of the code operates in exactly the same way.

In the changed section, we're calling the ExecuteReader method of the OleDbDataReader object. This method returns a populated OleDbDataReader object and we're assigning this returned object to the <mobile:ObjectList> control's DataSource property. Then we simply call the DataBind() method of the <mobile:List> control to perform the data binding operation:

```
    //Data bind the DataReader object
    //into the ObjectList control
    objlst.DataSource = Cmd.ExecuteReader(CommandBehavior.CloseConnection);
    objlst.DataBind();
  }
}
</script>
<!-- Ending C# Code Block -->
```

Summary

This chapter addressed the question of how we could data bind information using the ASP.NET Mobile Controls. In exploring this we've looked at examples of the following:

❑   Data binding a <mobile:List> control with an ArrayObject by defining a custom class

❑   Data binding a <mobile:List> control using an OleDBDataReader object

❑   Data binding a <mobile:SelectionList> control using an OleDBDataReader object

❑   Data binding a <mobile:ObjectList> control using an OleDBDataReader object

We'll end this chapter with a brief summary table that illustrates the respective strengths and weaknesses of the three controls that we've considered:

Control	Pros	Cons
`<mobile:List>`: A great control if you want to build a static or interactive list	❑ Can accept predefined data ❑ Can use an `Add()` method to add data at runtime ❑ Supports data binding ❑ Supports internal page for large lists	❑ Can't render a list as specific list controls such as list box or combo box ❑ Can't display multiple columns
`<mobile:SelectionList>`: Good for displaying a small list or selection	❑ Can accept static data ❑ Supports data binding ❑ Supports multiple list rendering options such as list box, check box list, and so on	❑ Doesn't support internal paging ❑ Only good for small numbers of records ❑ Can't display multiple columns
`<mobile:ObjectList>`: The most versatile control in the list control family, ideal for displaying tables	❑ Can display multiple columns ❑ Supports internal paging for large lists ❑ Supports automatic header file generation	❑ Only supports data binding and static data is not supported

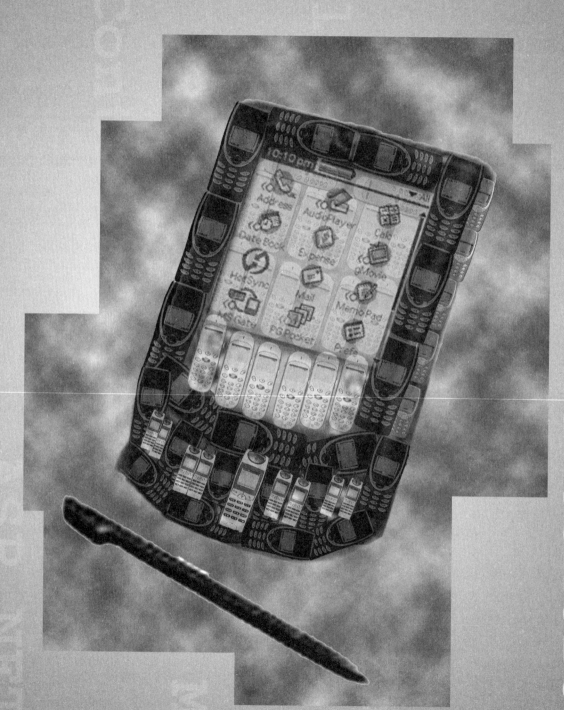

Validation Controls

In the last chapter we looked at how ASP.NET Mobile Web Forms interact with, and collect data from, the user. We looked at how data is packaged and sent to the server and the ways we can retrieve and process that data. In most cases, our code is going to expect to receive data of a certain type or format in order for it to be processed correctly, for example, if asked for a user's date of birth, we expect the user to type in a date. But what format do we want that date in? Say we preferred our date to be in the form of mm/dd/yy, but our user typed in a long date, for example, July 20 1969? If our code wasn't designed to accept dates in any format other than mm/dd/yy, we could end up with some nasty error messages. To protect against this we add a step between the time the data is collected and when it is sent into our business logic that tests to make sure that the information entered is valid in every respect. This step is called **data validation**.

In the past, validating data collected from mobile devices was limited to a hybrid combination of the `format` attribute and WMLScript. This was not very powerful due to the limitations of WMLScript and low client memory resources. Ultimately, the majority of data validation in mobile web applications took place on the server. These limitations made validating user input a laborious task.

Luckily the Microsoft Mobile Internet Toolkit provides us with features that make this easy. ASP.NET generalizes Web Form validation into logical groups and provides us with **validation controls**. These controls automatically validate the data of the control it is assigned to, and if the data does not pass validation, it displays a customizable error message to the user.

If you are already familiar with validation in Web Forms, then you will be right at home here, because we use validation controls in exactly the same way as we do in ASP.NET – by adding the control to a form, assigning it a control to validate, and setting a few properties (such as the validation criteria).

In this chapter, we will look at the different types of validation controls available and learn how to use them in our mobile Web Form applications.

There are several different types of validation controls:

❑ **CompareValidator** – Compares the value of one control to the value of another control or a fixed value using a comparison operator, for example, to check that a password is entered exactly the same way twice on a registration page.

❑ **RangeValidator** – Tests to make sure that the user enters data that falls between two values. The minimum and maximum values can be provided directly or by referencing another control. For example, a numerical representation of a month must fall between 1 and 12 inclusive.

❑ **RegularExpressionValidator** – This control ensures that the value of another control matches a specified pattern, for example, for a date, we could ensure that our date consists of three sets of two numbers, separated by a forward slash character. In this situation, 07/20/69 would be accepted, but 7.20.1969 would not.

❑ **RequiredFieldValidator** – This control ensures that the required field has data entered into it, and is not left blank.

❑ **CustomValidator** – This control allows the developer to write a method to handle the validation of the data in the control that the `CustomValidator` is assigned to. This allows the developer to break out of the box and design a control more specific to the task, instead of using a built-in control, for example, testing that an ISBN or a credit card number is valid by using a checksum.

❑ **ValidationSummary** – This control displays a 'report' of all of the validation errors that occurred within a mobile Web Form page, and can be used in conjunction with any of the validation controls.

We'll be looking at each of the validation controls that the MMIT provides for us in action in a bit. Let's start off by learning a bit more about how they work, before understanding how to integrate them into our mobile pages.

How Do Validation Controls Work?

Validation controls are server control that provide the functionality needed to easily check data received by a user interface control on either a normal Web Form or mobile Web Form. Their tag attribute-based structure makes them very easy and fast to use. Later in this section we will look at the base class that all of the validation controls in the MMIT inherit from and what it provides them with.

> All validation controls must be contained within a `Form` or `Panel`.

In the same way that the other controls contained in the MMIT detect the client type and send appropriate markup code, validation controls will detect the client browser, and if it supports DHTML will send validation code to the browser to handle the task on the client. If the browser does not support DHTML, then all of the validation is done on the server and a response sent back to the user with the details of any failed validation so they can correct their input. The interesting thing to note is that even if the browser **does** support DHTML, the validation is performed again if a page is then round-tripped to the server.

Mobile validation controls display the same behaviors as their standard ASP.NET cousins.

When a form is submitted, the user's input is passed to the correct validation control, or controls, which test it for validity and move to complete the remaining part of the process on the server. Depending on the outcome, the validation control's IsValid property is then set to true or false, to indicate if the user's entry has passed or failed the required tests. Once all of the validation controls have completed this task, the Page.IsValid property is set. If any of the individual controls have had their IsValid property set to false, then the Page.IsValid property is also set to false and an error message will be returned to the user indicating the fields that were invalid.

> For validation to occur on a mobile Web Form, the control that triggers the submission of the form must have its **CausesValidation** property set to **true**. (Currently, the only control that this applies to is the **Command** button, and its **CausesValidation** property defaults to **true** anyway.)

Common Properties

As we mentioned earlier, all mobile validation controls inherit from a base class called System.Web.UI.MobileControls.BaseValidator and as a result share a set of common properties. The following table describes those properties.

Properties	Description
ControlToValidate	This sets or returns the ID of the control to validate. It defaults to " ", and cannot be left blank.
Display	This toggles the visibility of the validation control. It defaults to true.
ErrorMessage	The text that will be used in the ValidationSummary control. If the control does not have the Text property set, it returns the value in this property.
IsValid	Sets or returns a Boolean value property that indicates whether the data passed to the control is valid or not.

In order to work, a validation control needs to be assigned to an input control that resides in the same form. This is done by setting the ControlToValidate property of the validation control to the id of the input control:

Currently, the only controls that support validation are the SelectionList and the TextBox.

```
<mobile:RequiredFieldValidator id=RequiredFieldValidator1 runat="server"
  ControlToValidate="TextBox1">
```

Validation controls also inherit `System.Web.UI.MobileControls.MobileControl`, which is the base class common to all Mobile Controls. There's no need to recap all of its functionality here, but we do need to mention its `Text` and `innerText` properties. These properties are used by the validation controls to deliver their error messages. All of the validation controls, with the exception of the `ValidationSummary` control, use the `innerText` property. This property is set when you enclose text with tags, like this:

```
<mobile:RequiredFieldValidator
id=RequiredFieldValidator1
runat="server"
ControlToValidate="TextBox1">
A value in TextBox1 is required!
</mobile:RequiredFieldValidator>
```

If the validation fails, this text will be displayed on the screen for the user. In addition to the `innerText` property, we also have a `text` property available to us, which we can set like this:

```
<mobile:RequiredFieldValidator
id=RequiredFieldValidator1
runat="server"
ControlToValidate="TextBox1"
Text = "Validation failed.">
A value in TextBox1 is required!
</mobile:RequiredFieldValidator>
```

The `innerText` value takes priority over the `text` property, so if both are set, as is the case above, the text that appears on the screen for the user is the value of the `innerText` property, not the Text property. However, if the `Text` property is set programmatically, then the newly-set Text property will be displayed instead:

```
RequiredFieldValidator1.Text = "Validation has bombed!"
```

In this case, the `innerText` property will be overridden by the newly-set `Text` property, which will be displayed instead.

Control-Specific Properties

In addition to the base properties that each control inherits, there will be additional properties for each control that are dictated by the control's functionality. For instance, `CompareValidator` will have a `minimum` and `maximum` value attribute, whereas the `RegularExpressionValidator` will have a `ValidationExpression` attribute. We'll be looking at each of these properties when we look at each type of validation control.

Device-Specific Behavior

When any of the validation controls are rendered they're shown the same way that the device displays the `Label` control. The difference is that the `StyleReference` property is initially set to `Error`. The controls will use the error style in the page's style sheet; if there isn't one then it will use the system default.

Putting Validation Controls to Work

We will now work through a series of examples to show how the different validation controls work. I encourage you to experiment with these examples, rather than just run them. Whenever you are looking at a new technology, try to find something that it **can't** do, rather than just reading what it **can** do. This will lead to a deeper understanding of its usefulness and how it can be employed.

> **If your validation controls display unexpected behavior (such as showing an error message that you were not expecting, or duplicate reporting of errors), your property settings should be the first place you'll look.**

Now, let's have a look at a validation control at work using the `CompareValidator`:

The CompareValidator

The `CompareValidator` provides an easy way to validate user input against a static value, or the value of another control. In this way, this control is ideal for checking when a user has entered a password on a registration form, where you'll likely ask the user to enter their password twice to ensure that the correct password has been entered. In this situation, you're comparing the values of two controls. Alternatively, you might also want to use this tool to check that a user-supplied value is less than a given number, and as such, you're comparing the value of a control against a static value.

The functionality provided by this tool is based on the standard comparison operators of less than, greater than, equal to (>, <, =), and so on.

Properties

The `CompareValidator` exposes a flexible set of properties through which we can direct the control's behavior. With these we can set the comparison operation to be done and also set the data type that the control should expect using the `Type` property. This is where the flexibility comes in; we can compare numbers, currency, dates, and strings.

The `CompareValidator` has the following unique properties:

Property	Description
ControlToCompare	Set this to the id of the control that you want to compare `ControlToValidate` with. If you are comparing it to a static value you should leave this property blank.
Operator	This sets or returns the type of comparison to be done during validation; the default is `Equal`. The comparison operators are: ❑ DataTypeCheck ❑ Equal ❑ GreaterThan ❑ GreaterThanEqual ❑ LessThan ❑ LessThanEqual ❑ NotEqual
Type	This is the data type that the validation will be done on. The default is `string`. The types are: ❑ Currency ❑ Date ❑ Double ❑ Integer ❑ String
ValueToCompare	Sets or returns a static value that is used in the validation. If both the `ValueToCompare` and `ControlToCompare` properties are present, it defaults to the value in `ControlToCompare`.

Let's go ahead and test the `CompareValidator` in a mobile Web Form. Since this is our first validation control, we are going to let some of the properties remain in their default state.

Try It Out – The CompareValidator

1. Open your text editor and enter the following code:

```
<%@ Page Inherits="System.Web.UI.MobileControls.MobilePage" Language="C#"%>
<%@Register TagPrefix="mobile" Namespace="System.Web.UI.MobileControls"
Assembly="System.Web.Mobile" %>

<mobile:Form id="Form1" runat="server">

  Value 1:<mobile:TextBox id="TextBox1" runat="server"></mobile:TextBox>
  Value 2:<mobile:TextBox id="TextBox2" runat="server"></mobile:TextBox>
  <mobile:Command id="Command1" runat="server">Command</mobile:Command>

  <mobile:CompareValidator id="CompareValidator1" runat="server"
    ControlToValidate="TextBox1"
    ControlToCompare="TextBox2">
    Not Equal
  </mobile:CompareValidator>

</mobile:Form>
```

2. Save it to your `WroxCompareValidator.aspx` in a virtual directory.

3. Browse to the file and you will see the following:

 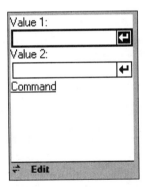

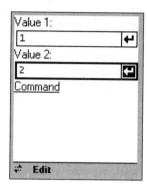

How It Works

The first section of our page should be familiar by now as we set up our basic page features. Let's take a look at our form:

```
<mobile:Form id="Form1" runat="server">

    Value 1:<mobile:TextBox id="TextBox1" runat="server"></mobile:TextBox>
    Value 2:<mobile:TextBox id="TextBox2" runat="server"></mobile:TextBox>
    <mobile:Command id="Command1" runat="server">Command</mobile:Command>
```

We're creating two text boxes and a command button to provide the basic functionality on our form. Then we move on to the validation control:

First, we set the validation control in our form and gave it a unique id and included the mandatory runat="server" attribute:

```
<mobile:CompareValidator id="CompareValidator1" runat="server"
```

Then we indicated the control to validate by setting our ControlToValidate property to the id of the desired control (in this case TextBox1):

```
ControlToValidate="TextBox1"
```

Then, by setting the `ControlToCompare` property to "TextBox2", we set it to compare the value in `TextBox1` to the value in `TextBox2`, thereby validating `TextBox1`:

```
ControlToCompare="TextBox2">
```

Next we set the `innerText` property (the message that is returned to the user if the data does not validate):

```
Not Equal
</mobile:CompareValidator>
```

Remember that the default value for the `Operator` property is `Equal`, but if you would like to test for an inequality between values, you can change it to any of the options we outlined in the table, earlier in this section.

The RangeValidator Control

We use the `RangeValidator` control to make sure that a value contained in another controls falls within a certain range. This would be useful, for instance, if your site is offering discounts on travel during a certain time of the year and you wanted your application to monitor and apply the discounts automatically.

Since we know that the `RangeValidator` inherits from `BaseValidator`, it already has the base properties available to it, as we saw earlier. Let's look at the properties unique to this control:

Property	Description
MinimumValue	The value of the control that you are validating must be greater than or equal to this value.
MaximumValue	The value of the control that you are validating cannot be greater than this value, though it can be equal to it.
Type	Use this property to set the data type of the value you are going to check. Valid types are: ❑ Currency ❑ Date ❑ Double ❑ Integer ❑ String

Let's build a quick illustrative example to validate a user's entry between two dates:

Try It Out – The RangeValidator Control

1. Open your text editor and enter the following code:

```
<%@ Page Inherits="System.Web.UI.MobileControls.MobilePage" Language="C#"%>
<%@Register TagPrefix="mobile" Namespace="System.Web.UI.MobileControls"
Assembly="System.Web.Mobile" %>

<mobile:Form id="Form1" runat="server">

   Enter a date between 1/01/2001 and 1/01/2002:
   <mobile:TextBox id="TextBox1" runat="server"></mobile:TextBox>
   <mobile:Command id="Command1" runat="server">Command</mobile:Command>

   <mobile:RangeValidator id="RangeValidator1" runat="server"
     Type="Date"
     MaximumValue="1/01/2002"
     MinimumValue="1/01/2001"
     ControlToValidate="TextBox1">
     Out of Range
   </mobile:RangeValidator>

</mobile:Form>
```

2. Save it as `WroxRangeValidator.aspx` in a virtual directory.

3. Navigate your browser to the file, and you should see something like this:

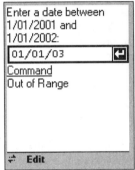

How It Works

Using this control is fairly straightforward. Making sure that we have the mandatory headers and form tags, we put a mobile text box and a command button in our form:

```
<mobile:TextBox id="TextBox1" runat="server"></mobile:TextBox>
<mobile:Command id="Command1" runat="server">Command</mobile:Command>
```

Now we add the validation control code. Since we're going to validate a date we set the Type property to Date:

```
<mobile:RangeValidator id=RangeValidator1 runat="server"
   Type="Date"
```

We then set the MaximumValue and the MinimumValue properties on our control to encapsulate our range:

```
MinimumValue="1/01/2001"
MaximumValue="1/01/2002"
```

We set the ControlToValidate property to Textbox1:

```
ControlToValidate="TextBox1">
```

We then put the text message that we want the user to see in case of validation failure in the `innerText` property space:

```
    Out of Range
</mobile:RangeValidator>
```

Once the form is posted to the server, the value that is in `TextBox1` is passed into the `RangeValidator`. At that point it is tested to see if it agrees with the `Type` property. If it does, then the data is tested against the range. Again, if the validation fails, the `IsValid` property is set to `False`. This is the `RangeValidator's` 'vote' that the page should not be considered valid.

> If the user does not enter a value for the control, it will pass validation. If you want to ensure that the user enters a value, use this control in conjunction with the `RequiredFieldValidator` control.

The RegularExpressionValidator

Trying to remember syntax for regular expressions is tricky if you don't use them often, yet they're some of the most powerful tools available to programmers. So, what's a regular expression?

Let's start our explanation with an example. Here's a regular expression for a US zip code:

```
\d{5}(-\d{4})?
```

To the untrained eye, this may appear to be a string of random gibberish produced by an errant kitten and a keyboard, but there's actually some logic in here. Let's break it down piece by piece.

The first part of our expression, `\d`, matches any digit character. Adding `{5}` next to this means that we're actually looking for five digit characters. The second part of our expression is enclosed in normal brackets, a bit like a formula, indicating that everything within that set of brackets is to have the `?` applied to it, meaning that the second part of the expression is optional. Within the brackets, we have a hyphen - , which means nothing more than the fact that if anything exists after the initial 5 digits, then the following sequence must begin with a hyphen. If there is a hyphen in the second part of the sequence, the `\d{4}` is telling us that we need four more digits after the hyphen. In this way, acceptable values would be:

```
12345-6789
12345
```

but the following would not pass validation:

```
12345-67
12345-
```

It's a little tricky to get your head around at first, but breaking these expressions down into smaller groupings in your head should help you to translate the expression into what you're expecting, and vice versa.

If you are using Visual Studio .NET, you have access to many common (and some not so common) regular expression phrases as part of the package. If you are not using Visual Studio .NET, you will still have to write your own regular expression code, but this control makes it easy to put the code to use.

> **If the user does not enter a value for the control, it will pass validation. If you want to ensure that the user enters a value, use this control in conjunction with the `RequiredFieldValidator` control.**

The `RegularExpressionValidator` has only one property that is unique to it, called `ValidationExpression`. You set this property to the regular expression that you want to use to validate. For example, to implement our US zip code expression, you would set the property like this:

`ValidationExpression="\d{5}(-\d{4})?".`

Or if you wanted to validate an e-mail address you could use:

`ValidationExpression="\w+([-+.]\w+)*@\w+([-.]\w+)*\.\w+([-.]\w+)*".`

Here's a quick rundown of what some of the above regular expression code means:

Character	Description
\w	Matches any word character including an underscore.
+	Matches the preceding character or sub expression one or more times. For example Mo+ would match the Mo in Monkey and Moose.
*	Matches the preceding character or sub expression zero or more times.
.	Matches any single character except \n (which is an octal escape).
\d	Matches a digit character.
?	Marks the preceding section as optional.
{X}	X is a non-negative integer and matches the preceding expression exactly X times. For example: e{2} matches the *ee* in *fleet* but not the *e* in *bet*.

Since there are many more types of element that you can use, for a complete reference on regular expression syntax, you may wish to refer to http://msdn.microsoft.com and search for Regular Expression Syntax.

Let's see this in action with a simple example:

Try It Out – The RegularExpressionValidator

1. Open your text editor and enter the following code:

```
<%@ Page Inherits="System.Web.UI.MobileControls.MobilePage" Language="C#"%>
<%@Register TagPrefix="mobile" Namespace="System.Web.UI.MobileControls"
Assembly="System.Web.Mobile" %>

<mobile:Form id="Form1" runat="server">

  Enter a web address (http://www.example.com):
  <mobile:TextBox id="TextBox1" runat="server"></mobile:TextBox>
  <mobile:Command id="Command1" runat="server">Command</mobile:Command>

  <mobile:RegularExpressionValidator id="RegularExpressionValidator1"
    runat="server"
    ValidationExpression="http://([\w-]+\.)+[\w-]+(/[\w- ./?%&=]*)?"
    ControlToValidate="TextBox1">
    Validation Failed
  </mobile:RegularExpressionValidator>

</mobile:Form>
```

2. Save it in a virtual directory as `WroxRegularExpressionValidator.aspx`.

3. Browse to the file and you should see something like this:

How It Works

In this example, it was a simple mistake that caused our input to fail validation – we omitted the http:// from the beginning of the URL. Let's take a look at the code then we'll see how our regular expression was created.

We started off our form with some plain text, a text box and a command button:

```
Enter a web address (http://www.example.com):
<mobile:TextBox id="TextBox1" runat="server"></mobile:TextBox>
<mobile:Command id="Command1" runat="server">Command</mobile:Command>
```

Next we come to our validation control. Firstly, we populate the ValidationExpression property with the regular expression code that we want to use:

```
<mobile:RegularExpressionValidator
    id="RegularExpressionValidator1" runat="server"
    ValidationExpression="http://([\w-]+\.)+[\w-]+(/[\w- ./?%&=]*)?"
```

Note that if your regular expression syntax is malformed, ValidationExpression throws an HttpException, without any additional effort on your part. This control works in the same way as the rest of the validation controls; it is placed in the form that contains the control to be validated. In our case, we're validating the content of TextBox1:

203

```
    ControlToValidate="TextBox1">
    Validation Failed
  </mobile:RegularExpressionValidator>
```

Aside from the complexity of the regular expressions themselves, this is actually a fairly simple control.
Getting used to using regular expressions takes time and practice, so have a play with this control and
see how different expression elements affect the outcome.

The RequiredFieldValidator

It is not uncommon to have some fields on a Web Form that must be completed and others that are
optional. For the fields that are required, the old ways of doing things would have us handcraft a script
that would make sure the user filled them in. However, now that we have ASP.NET, we can use the
`RequiredFieldValidator` control, which packages this functionality for us and makes it relatively
trivial to implement.

It tests the value of the control designated by `ControlToValidate` against its own `InitialValue`
property. If the two values are different, the `RequiredFieldValidator` assumes that the user
entered a value. It is best to leave the default value of `null` for the `InitialValue` property when you
are validating a `TextBox`. If you change it to something like `"myInitialValue"` and the user enters
anything **other** than that, their response will be validated, even if they do not enter anything at all.

If you happen to be validating a `SelectionList` control, you would most likely set the
`InitialValue` property to the default-selected item in the `SelectionList`.

This validation control is used the same way the other validation controls are used; the control is placed
within the `Form` or `Panel` that the `ControlToValidate` resides in and is assigned to it.

Let's run through a quick example, that checks to see whether the user has entered a value. If they
haven't, the validation fails.

Try It Out – The RequiredFieldValidator

1. Open your text editor and enter the following code:

```
<%@ Page Inherits="System.Web.UI.MobileControls.MobilePage" Language="C#"%>
<%@Register TagPrefix="mobile" Namespace="System.Web.UI.MobileControls"
Assembly="System.Web.Mobile" %>

<mobile:Form id="Form1" runat="server">Enter a value:
  <mobile:TextBox id="TextBox1" runat="server"></mobile:TextBox>
  <mobile:Command id="Command1" onclick=Command1_Click runat="server">
    Command
  </mobile:Command>
  <mobile:RequiredFieldValidator
```

```
      id="RequiredFieldValidator1"
      runat="server" ControlToValidate="TextBox1">
      A value in TextBox1 is required!
    </mobile:RequiredFieldValidator>
  </mobile:Form>

  <mobile:Form id="Form2" runat="server">
    <mobile:Label id="Label1" runat="server">
      Passed Validation
    </mobile:Label>
  </mobile:Form>

  <script runat="server">
    private void Command1_Click(Object sender, EventArgs e)
    {
      if (Page.IsValid)
      {
        ActiveForm = Form2;
      }
    }
  </script>
```

2. Save it in a virtual directory as `WroxRequiredFieldValidator.aspx`.

3. When you navigate to the file in your browser you should see something like this:

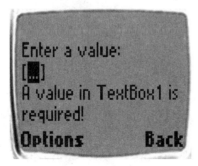

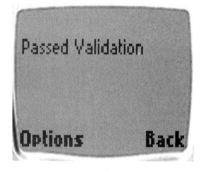

How It Works

Our control is using `null` as the `InitialValue` property, so we can enter anything we like in the text box in order for the page to pass validation.

Let's take a quick look at `Form1`:

```
<mobile:Form id="Form1" runat="server">Enter a value:
  <mobile:TextBox id="TextBox1" runat="server"></mobile:TextBox>
  <mobile:Command id="Command1" onclick=Command1_Click runat="server">
    Command
  </mobile:Command>
  <mobile:RequiredFieldValidator
    id="RequiredFieldValidator1"
    runat="server" ControlToValidate="TextBox1">
    A value in TextBox1 is required!
  </mobile:RequiredFieldValidator>
</mobile:Form>
```

In our example, we added the `RequiredFieldValidator` to our form and set the `ControlToValidate` property to `TextBox1`. We wanted to test for a `null` value, so we left the `InitialValue` at its default.

Let's move to the script block. In the `Click` event handler for `Command1`, we test the `Page.IsValid` property to test whether the page has passed validation or not:

```
<script runat="server">
  private void Command1_Click(Object sender, EventArgs e)
  {
    if (Page.IsValid)
    {
```

If it reads `True` (the page is valid), we set the `ActiveForm` to `Form2`:

```
      ActiveForm = Form2;
    }
  }
</script>
```

`Form2` then gives the all clear by showing `Label1`'s `innerText`:

```
<mobile:Form id="Form2" runat="server">
  mobile:Label id="Label1" runat="server">Passed Validation</mobile:Label>
</mobile:Form>
```

However, if validation fails, the user is shown the `RequiredFieldValidator`'s `innerText` property:

```
<mobile:RequiredFieldValidator
  id="RequiredFieldValidator1"
  runat="server" ControlToValidate="TextBox1">
  A value in TextBox1 is required!
</mobile:RequiredFieldValidator>
```

One thing to note about this control is that it will not ensure that the data entered by the user is of a specific type. To handle that, you can do a bit of creative tweaking with the `CompareValidator` *to accomplish your end.*

The CustomValidator

The other validation controls do a great job in specific situations, but they handle a finite level of complexity. What if you find yourself taking credit card numbers (which I suspect that you would not do from a mobile Web Form just yet) and wanted to validate them with the LUHN algorithm (formula for calculating a check digit on credit card numbers) before sending it into your business objects? For that we would use the `CustomValidator`. There is no other combination of validation controls that would do this for you. The `CustomValidator` allows you to write your own method that will perform the validation when it is called into action.

The `CustomValidator` does its job with the aid of the `OnServerValidate` property and `ServerValidate` event. The `ServerValidate` event calls any method that is registered with it when the value of the `ControlToValidate` property is validated by the `CustomValidator` control. We set `OnServerValidate` to the name of our custom validation method, which responds to the `ServerValidate` event raised when the `ControlToValidate` property is validated.

> *Conceptually, the `CustomValidator` is a delegate method that late-binds to your validation code. A delegate method acts as a 'hub' and redirects calls to the appropriate method.*

Now, we'll go through a slightly more simplistic example than a credit card number validator – we're testing for whether a number entered is an even number.

Try It Out – The CustomValidator Control

This example takes a numeric entry and tests to see if it is an even number or not, an even number being a valid entry, and an odd number being invalid.

1. Open your text editor and enter the following (rather large) piece of code:

```
<%@ Page Inherits="System.Web.UI.MobileControls.MobilePage" Language="C#"%>
<%@Register TagPrefix="mobile" Namespace="System.Web.UI.MobileControls"
Assembly="System.Web.Mobile" %>

<mobile:Form id="Form1" runat="server">
  Enter a number:
  <mobile:TextBox id="TextBox1" runat="server">
  </mobile:TextBox>
  <mobile:Command id="Command1" onclick="Command1_Click" runat="server">
    Command</mobile:Command>
  <mobile:CustomValidator id="CustomValidator1" runat="server"
    ControlToValidate="TextBox1"
    OnServerValidate="CheckEven">
    Failed
  </mobile:CustomValidator>
</mobile:Form>

<mobile:Form id="Form2" runat="server">
  <mobile:Label id="Label" runat="server">
  Passed!</mobile:Label>
</mobile:Form>

<script language="C#" runat="server">
  protected void CheckEven(Object source, ServerValidateEventArgs args)
  {
    String UserVal = args.Value;
    int tempVal = 0;

    try
    {
      tempVal = int.Parse(UserVal);
    }
```

```
    catch (System.Exception err)
    {
      CustomValidator1.Text = err.Message;
      args.IsValid = false;
      return;
    }

    if (tempVal % 2 == 0)
    {
      args.IsValid = true;
    }
    else
    {
      args.IsValid = false;
    }
  }

  private void Command1_Click(Object sender, EventArgs e)
  {
    if (Page.IsValid)
    {
      ActiveForm = Form2;
    }
  }
}
</script>
```

2. Save it in a virtual directory as `WroxCustomValidator.aspx`.

3. Browse to the file, and you should see something like this:

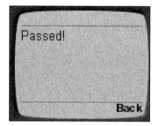

How It Works

Let's start our examination of the code with a look through `Form1`:

```
<mobile:Form id="Form1" runat="server">
  Enter a number:
  <mobile:TextBox id="TextBox1" runat="server">
  </mobile:TextBox>
  <mobile:Command id="Command1" onclick="Command1_Click" runat="server">
    Command</mobile:Command>
```

As is the case with all other mobile web controls you will see the `runat` and `id` attributes being set. Then, we assign our `CustomValidator` control `TextBox1` to validate using the `ControlToValidate` property:

```
<mobile:CustomValidator id="CustomValidator1" runat="server"
  ControlToValidate="TextBox1"
```

Next, we set the `OnServerValidate` property to the name of our custom validation method. In this case our validation method is called `CheckEven`:

```
OnServerValidate="CheckEven">
```

We then finish off our form with some `innerText` and closing tags:

```
      Failed
   </mobile:CustomValidator>
</mobile:Form>
```

When validation is done it raises the `ServerValidate` event. The method designated by the `OnServerValidate` property responds to this event, which we set to the `CheckEven` method. Let's look at this method in detail.

Within this routine we do a basic test on the value passed in to see if it is evenly divisible by two. The `CheckEven` method signature looks like this:

```
<script language="C#" runat="server">
  protected void CheckEven(Object source, ServerValidateEventArgs args)
  {
    ...
  }
```

The variable `source` is a reference to the calling `CustomValidator` instance, which we don't use in this code. The `args` variable represents an instance of `System.Web.UI.WebControls.ServerValidateEventArgs` being passed in (although we don't need to include `System.Web.UI.WebControls` in our declaration, since this namespace is imported by default). It carries two properties with it; `Value`, which is the value contained in the control to validate, and `IsValid`, which we set to `True` or `False` depending on the outcome of our validation routine.

Note that the variable names `args` and `source` can change to whatever suits your needs, but the type cannot.

```
      String UserVal = args.Value;
      int tempVal = 0;
```

We now move on to declare a couple of values. The first, UserVal, stores the number that the user input initially. The second is going to come in useful in a moment.

```
      try
      {
        tempVal = int.Parse(UserVal);
      }
```

The default type of the value of a textbox is a string, and we can't do mathematical operations on a string, so this next block takes the value entered by the user, and calls a method `int.parse` on the value to convert the string into an integer, and stores this value in the `tempVal` integer.

```
      catch (System.Exception err)
      {
        CustomValidator1.Text = err.Message;
        args.IsValid = false;
        return;
      }
```

If for some reason, the user entered a text string in the text box, for example "abc", then we won't be able to parse the value and turn it into an integer, so this `catch` block exists to trap that kind of error. It outputs an error message to the user, and causes the validation to fail:

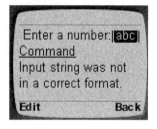
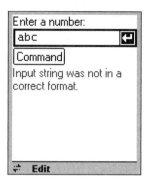

```
if (tempVal % 2 == 0)
{
   args.IsValid = true;
}
else
{
   args.IsValid = false;
}
```

Here's where the action happens. We divide `tempVal` by 2 and if the modulus is zero (0) then we give the all-clear by setting `args.IsValid` to `True`. The validation control is giving its 'vote' that the page should be considered validated. However, if validation fails, we go to the `else` statement, and set the `IsValid` property to `false`.

When the `Click` event for the `command` button is handled, the `Page.IsValid` property is used as the expression in a control block. If the control failed validation, this property will read `False` and the sub will exit without doing anything. If the control contained valid data, then `True` is returned and execution falls through to set the active form to `Form2`:

```
private void Command1_Click(Object sender, EventArgs e)
{
   if (Page.IsValid)
   {
      ActiveForm = Form2;
   }
}
</script>
```

If the data passes validation, `Form2` is set to be the active form, and the user is shown the label text which simply says **Passed!**.

```
<mobile:Form id="Form2" runat="server">
  <mobile:Label id="Label" runat="server">
  Passed!</mobile:Label>
</mobile:Form>
```

In an abstract way, the mechanisms that validation controls use resemble transactions.

If the data does not validate, then the user is shown the string contained in the `Text` property of the `CustomValidator` in `Form1` and given the chance to reenter the data:

```
<mobile:CustomValidator ... >
  Failed
</mobile:CustomValidator>
```

The ValidationSummary

The `ValidationSummary` will give a bit of added flexibility to displaying the text associated with each validation failure. With this control, you can show the user a separate error page summarizing the problems with their input.

The `ValidationSummary` displays the string that is contained in the `ErrorMessage` property for each of the controls that failed validation. You can choose to display the individual validation controls along with the summary or just the summary itself.

In our discussion at the beginning of this chapter about the `Text` and `innerText` properties that are available in all validation controls, we discussed how the `innerText` property will take precedence over the `Text` property if they are both set as attributes for the control, however, if the Text property of the control is set later on in the code, it will then take over and become visible in place of the `innerText` property.

If you are using a `ValidationSummary` control, then you'll need to place some text in the validation control's `ErrorMessage` property, and you'll need to rethink what you put in the `innerText` or `Text` properties. You will also need to consider how to set your `Display` property. When using a `ValidationSummary` control, we may not want each validation control showing at the same time that the `ValidationSummary` is showing, for example, when you want to show all of the errors in one place instead of scattered throughout the page. For that purpose, we would set the `Display` property to `None`. Setting `Display` to `Static` or `Dynamic` will make the validation control visible.

Properties

Unlike the actual validation controls, the `ValidationSummary` inherits directly from `System.Web.UI.MobileControls.MobileControl`. It has three crucial properties:

Property	Description
`BackLabel`	This is the text that the 'try again' link will show on the summary page. The default is **Back**.
`FormToValidate`	A valid `id` of the form that you want to validate.
`HeaderText`	Header text for the summary control. Default is `null`.

Let's work through a quick example to show this control in action.

Try It Out – The ValidationSummary

This example displays two `TextBox` controls; one is a required field, the other tests to see if the value entered is less than five.

1. Open your text editor and enter the following code:

```
<%@ Page Inherits="System.Web.UI.MobileControls.MobilePage" Language="C#"%>
<%@Register TagPrefix="mobile" Namespace="System.Web.UI.MobileControls"
Assembly="System.Web.Mobile" %>
```

```
<mobile:form id="Form1" runat="server">
  Required Field:
  <mobile:TextBox id="TextBox1" runat="server">
  </mobile:TextBox>
  Enter number less than 5:
  <mobile:TextBox id="TextBox2" runat="server">
  </mobile:TextBox>
  <mobile:RequiredFieldValidator id="RequiredFieldValidator1"runat="server"
    Display="None"
    ErrorMessage="Field is required"
    ControlToValidate="TextBox1">
  </mobile:RequiredFieldValidator>
  <mobile:CompareValidator id="CompareValidator1" runat="server"
    Display="None"
    ErrorMessage="Compare Failed"
    ControlToValidate="TextBox2"
    ValueToCompare="5"
    Operator="LessThan">
  </mobile:CompareValidator>
  <mobile:Command id="Command1" onclick="Command1_Click" runat="server">
    Command
  </mobile:Command>
</mobile:form>

<mobile:form id="Form2" runat="server">
```

```
  <mobile:Label id="Label1" runat="server" Visible="true">
    If your data had errors they will be listed below:
  </mobile:Label>
  <mobile:ValidationSummary id="ValidationSummary1" runat="server"
    FormToValidate="Form1"
    BackLabel="Try Again">
  </mobile:ValidationSummary>
</mobile:form>

<script runat="server">
  private void Command1_Click(Object sender, EventArgs e)
  {
    ActiveForm = Form2;
  }
</script>
```

2. Save it in a virtual directory as WroxValidationSummary.aspx.

3. When you navigate to it in your browser, you should see something like this:

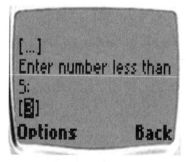

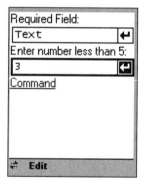

How It Works

The first thing we do is put a `TextBox` in our form named `TextBox1` and another called `TextBox2`. `TextBox1` will be a required field and `TextBox2` will need a number less than five so we add text that says this:

```
Required Field:
<mobile:TextBox id=TextBox1 runat="server"></mobile:TextBox>
Enter number less than 5:
<mobile:TextBox id=TextBox2 runat="server"></mobile:TextBox>
```

Next, we add the `RequiredFieldValidator` to the form and 'hook it up' to `TextBox1`. We set the display property `Display` to `None` so we can let the `ValidationSummary` handle all of the error reporting. Notice that we have not used the `innerText` or `Text` property, but instead put our error message in the `ErrorMessage` property. This is where the `ValidationSummary` looks to find the text it should display for the error:

```
<mobile:RequiredFieldValidator id="RequiredFieldValidator1" runat="server"
  Display="None"
  ErrorMessage="Field is required"
  ControlToValidate="TextBox1">
</mobile:RequiredFieldValidator>
```

Next comes the `CompareValidator`. For this control we have set the `ControlToValidate` property to `TextBox2`, the `Operator` property to `LessThan`, the `ValueToCompare` to 5, and `Display` to `None`:

```
<mobile:CompareValidator id="CompareValidator1" runat="server"
  Display="None"
  ErrorMessage="Compare Failed"
  ControlToValidate="TextBox2"
  ValueToCompare="5"
  Operator="LessThan">
</mobile:CompareValidator>
```

Next, we have the server-side event handler for our command button, which sends the user to `Form2` when it is invoked:

```
private void Command1_Click(Object sender, EventArgs e)
{
  ActiveForm = Form2;
}
```

Here is the second form that contains the `ValidationSummary` control. We set the `FormToValidate` property to `Form1`, which contains the controls that we want to validate. When our control is invoked, it looks to `Form1` to see if there is a collection of errors that we need to handle. We then set the `BackLabel` property to the text that we want the `ValidationSummary` control to display in its **Back** line:

```
<mobile:form id="Form2" runat="server">
  <mobile:Label id="Label1" runat="server" Visible="true">
    If your data had errors they will be listed below:
  </mobile:Label>
  <mobile:ValidationSummary id="ValidationSummary1" runat="server"
    FormToValidate="Form1"
    BackLabel="Try Again">
  </mobile:ValidationSummary>
</mobile:form>
```

Summary

In this chapter, we've thought a bit about what it used to be like to validate data collected from the Web and some of the related inefficiencies. We then saw how the validation controls, provided in the Microsoft Mobile Internet Toolkit, help to make Mobile Web Form validation a less tiresome task.

We saw examples of:

- ❑ CompareValidator
- ❑ CustomValidator
- ❑ RangeValidator
- ❑ RegularExpressionValidator
- ❑ RequiredFieldValidator
- ❑ ValidationSummary

As you develop mobile Web Forms applications, you'll probably find that these controls come in very handy indeed when working with user input. In our next chapter we will look at the Rich Controls that are a part of the Mobile Internet Toolkit.

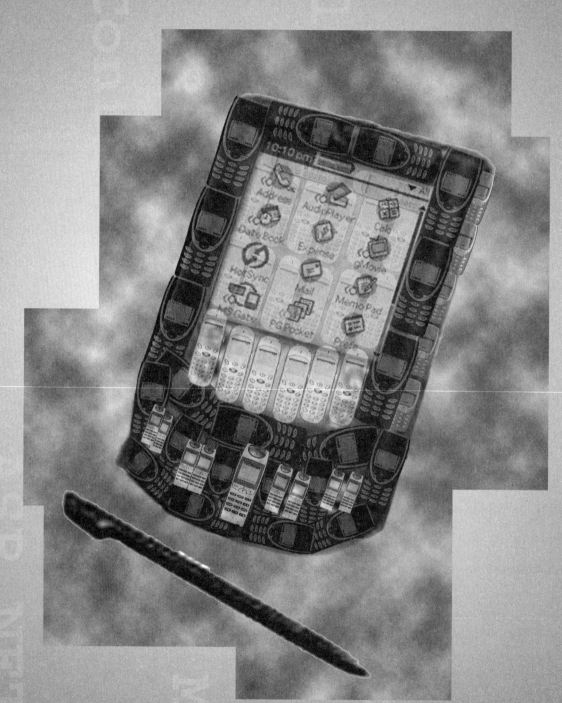

Working With Rich Controls

In the last chapter we looked at the validation controls that are shipped with the Microsoft Mobile Internet Toolkit. That completed our look at the controls that aid in gathering validated data from users and processing it in our server code, but there are still two controls left that pack a very useful punch.

Those controls are:

- ❑ The **AdRotator** Control
- ❑ The **Calendar** Control

These controls are great in certain situations: Need to deliver targeted content? Do you sell ad space on your site to multiple clients and need to rotate ad banners based on who bought the most time? The **AdRotator** will be indispensable for showing advertisements on-the-fly with a display rate whose proportion is configurable by the programmer. Are you gathering date-based data from the user that would necessitate the developer needing to code a makeshift HTML or ActiveX representation of a calendar? Most likely the **Calendar** control will be of great help in that situation with the smart features it brings with it.

The power-packed functionality that these controls are equipped with has earned them the title of **Rich Controls**. We will look at these controls and describe some of the implementation details while working through the examples. By the end of the chapter you should expect to have a strong understanding of how these two controls work and when to use them.

Using the Rich Controls

Implementing these controls is just as easy as using the other mobile Web Forms. Using the same tag-based structure that you have with the other controls, we can set properties that govern the styling of the display and the details of its behavior.

The `AdRotator` and `Calendar` controls both have the same containment rules that all other Mobile Web Form Controls have; they must be contained within a `Form` or `Panel`.

> You can refer back to Chapter 6 for details on the `Form` and `Panel` controls.

Let's start with AdRotator:

The AdRotator

The **AdRotator** component, available to us on installation of the MMIT, has the same behavior as its ASP.NET Web Form cousin (also called `AdRotator`), but there are a few extra features to handle rendering for different devices. Implementation of this control takes two parts:

❑   Instantiating and setting properties of the `AdRotator` in your page

❑   Correctly creating and configuring the **AdvertisementFile** XML file

Below we have the basic syntax needed to implement this control:

```
<mobile:AdRotator
    id="AdRotator1"
    runat="server"
    AdvertisementFile="Adv.xml">
    ...
</mobile:AdRotator>
```

The second and third lines show us setting the `id` attribute and including the necessary `runat` attribute. It is in the fourth line that we run into the first attribute specific to this control, and that is the `AdvertisementFile` attribute, which tells the `AdRotator` the name of the file where it will find the image names and rotation configuration information. We will look at this property and more in the next section:

Properties

The `AdRotator`'s properties are set in two different places, the Mobile Web Form and an XML file called the `AdvertisementFile` (Adv.xml in this case). The `AdRotator` inherits from the `System.Mobile.UI.MobileControl` class so it has the same base properties that all of the other Mobile Web Form controls have (`Font-Name`, `Font-Size`, and so on). In addition to this, the `AdRotator` has eight properties, one method, and one event:

Attribute	Description
AdvertisementFile	This is the path to the XML file that contains advertisement data such as the image file names and location. The default is empty.
imageKey	This sets the name of the element that contains the image URL that is retrieved from the `AdvertisementFile`.
KeywordFilter	This allows the developer to specify category/keywords to allow easy filtering of ads from the `AdvertisementFile`.
OnAdCreated	This is an event/method that allows the developer to run logic on each creation/display of an ad.

As we mentioned above, there are two parts to the implementation of this control. One is the mobile Web Form page and the other is the `AdvertisementFile`. The mobile Web Form page is where the tag-set code itself will reside. Within this code, as implied by the `AdvertisementFile` attribute definition in the table above, is where a reference is set to an XML file that contains configuration data for the `AdRotator` control to carry out its duties.

Let's look into the code that will reside in the mobile Web Form page:

Properties Set In The Mobile Page

The properties that are set in the `AdRotator` tag-set in the mobile Web Form page for this control are minimal, most of the action happens in the `AdvertisementFile`. But what does happen in the page code is still very important to the success of using this control, because without it, the `AdRotator` would have no idea where to find the information it needs to create the advertisements to display. The properties set in the code found within the mobile Web Form are the `AdvertisementFile` and `ImageKey`.

The `AdvertisementFile` property points to where the physical advertisement file is. This is how it is able to load this file on the fly, when the control is instantiated, which also means that you can name it whatever you need to, as long as this property is set with the path and the name of the file.

The `ImageKey` property corresponds to the name of an element in the `AdvertisementFile` that has the name and path of the ad's graphic. For instance if we have:

```
<mobile:AdRotator id=AdRotator1 runat="server"
AdvertisementFile="Adv.xml"
ImageKey = "ImageUrl"/>
```

then, in your AdvertisementFile, you might have an entry that looks like this:

```
<Ad>
    <ImageUrl>mslogo.gif</ImageUrl>
    <BmpImageUrl>mslogo.bmp</BmpImageUrl>
    <NavigateUrl>http://www.microsoft.com/</NavigateUrl>
    <AlternateText>.NET, yet?</AlternateText>
    <Keyword>Software</Keyword>
    <Impressions>15</Impressions>
</Ad>
```

Notice that the first element is `<ImageUrl>`; if you had `ImageKey` in the ASPX page set to another value, like `myGraphic`, you would need an element called `<myGraphic>` that contained the name and path of your ad's graphic. In that case, you would not have the `<ImageUrl>` element.

There can be a `Keyword` element for each ad entity in the `AdvertisementFile`; this is how you are able to designate a category from which to draw your advertisements. The `KeywordFilter` in the tag-set (residing in the mobile Web Form) is where you designate the category of advertisements to be pulled. Let's say, in the `AdvertisementFile`, you have ten ads; five with the `Keyword` element set to `Books` and five with the `Keyword` element set to `Software`. Then, in the mobile Web Form page, you have the `Keyword` attribute in the `<mobile:AdRotator>` set to `Books`. The only advertisements that would be considered for display would be the five that have the `Keyword` element set to `Books` – the others would be ignored.

AdvertisementFile

The `AdvertisementFile` is an XML configuration file where the properties are set for each ad entity. This file is parsed by the `AdRotator` control to determine a number of different things about the ad that should be served to the client. These properties include the relative 'weight' or rotation schedule for the advertisement, the URL to the image file, a property that supplies the URL to navigate to if the image is clicked on by the user, and a few others that we will go over in this section.

The Elements

We will go through each of the inherent elements of the AdvertisementFile and put them to use when we implement the AdRotator control.

The property elements in this file are:

❑   `<Advertisements>`.

❑   `<Ad>` - This is the element that encloses each advertisement property/element set.

❑   `<ImageUrl>` – This element contains the name and path of an image file for the advertisement. The name of this element is the default value of the ImageKey property found in the AdRotator code in the `.aspx` page. If the `ImageKey` property is not left at its default, you must make sure that the AdvertisementFile contains a custom element named whatever you changed the `ImageKey` property to. The new element should also contain the same information that the default tag would have had; the name and path to the image file. In our example, we leave ours at the default so as to not confuse things.

❑   `<MonoImageUrl>` – This element will contain a URL to a monochromatic image file, if there is one.

❑   `<NavigateUrl>` – This element will have the URL to navigate to when the user clicks on the advertisement, if it is indeed clickable.

❑   `<AlternateText>` – This element has the text that will be displayed as the graphic is loading, after it has loaded as the alternate text (like a tool-tip found in desktop applications), and when the graphic can't be displayed. The ALT attribute for the image tag in the resulting markup language is provided from this element.

❑   `<Keyword>` - This allows you to associate a keyword with the advertisement to enable filtering of the ads.

❑   `<Impressions>` - This element allows you to set the relative proportion of the rotation of the ads, one ad to another.

Things to Consider When Building an Advertisement File

❑   The advertisement file is an XML document and must be well formed. This means that the elements within the document must adhere to a strict and specific structure in order for the XML parser (the little engine that reads in the XML and translates it into something that the application can understand and use) to be able to read it. This is as opposed to HTML, which is more forgiving when it comes to the structure of the code. You can put what should otherwise be child elements (having containment rules) into a bare HTML page and see it rendered within a browser.

- ❏ There can only be one `<Advertisements>` element. The AdRotator will only parse the first one in the advertisement file.

- ❏ In the Microsoft documentation it says that the `<imageUrl>` is required. This is true to an extent. What is required is an element that has a name that matches the value contained in the ImageKey property.

- ❏ The sum of all of the numbers contained in the `<Impressions>` element cannot be over 2,048,000,000–1; this means if you add up all of the numbers contained in the `<Impressions>` elements within the AdvertisementFile, the sum cannot be larger than that number. If it is, the AdRotator throws an ArgumentOutOfRangeException exception.

Let's go through an example.

Try it Out - The AdRotator

This example will be a simple demonstration of the AdRotator control. For this example you should download the code from the Wrox site to acquire the images used. If you use your own images you will have to change the image names in the code to match yours.

1. Open your text editor and enter the following code:

```
<%@ Page Inherits="System.Web.UI.MobileControls.MobilePage" Language="C#"%>
<%@Register TagPrefix="mobile" Namespace="System.Web.UI.MobileControls"
Assembly="System.Web.Mobile" %>

<mobile:form id=Form1 runat="server">
        <mobile:AdRotator id=AdRotator1 runat="server"
        AdvertisementFile="Adv.xml"
        ImageKey = "ImageUrl"
        >
        <DeviceSpecific>
            <Choice Filter="isPocketIE" ImageKey="BmpImageUrl"/>
            <Choice Filter="isNokia7110" ImageKey="ImageUrl"/>
        </DeviceSpecific>
    </mobile:AdRotator>
</mobile:form>
```

2. Save it to your virtual directory as WroxAdRotator.aspx.

3. Open your editor again and enter the following code:

```
<?xml version="1.0" ?>
<Advertisements>
  <Ad>
    <ImageUrl> wroxImages/WroxLogo.gif</ImageUrl>
    <BmpImageUrl>wroxImages/WroxLogo.bmp</BmpImageUrl>
    <NavigateUrl>http://www.wrox.com/</NavigateUrl>
    <AlternateText>You'd be off your Wroxer to buy any other book!</AlternateText>
    <Keyword>Books</Keyword>
    <Impressions>70</Impressions>
  </Ad>
```

```
  <Ad>
    <ImageUrl>wroxImages/mslogo.gif</ImageUrl>
    <BmpImageUrl>wroxImages/mslogo.bmp</BmpImageUrl>
    <NavigateUrl>http://www.microsoft.com/</NavigateUrl>
    <AlternateText>.NET, yet?</AlternateText>
    <Keyword>Software</Keyword>
    <Impressions>30</Impressions>
  </Ad>
</Advertisements>
```

4. Save it to your virtual directory as `Adv.xml`.

5. Your virtual directory may already have a file called `web.config` in it – if it has, add the following code to the file. If you don't already have a `web.config` file, type in the code below and save it as `web.config`.

```xml
<?xml version="1.0" encoding="utf-8" ?>
<configuration>
  <system.web>
  <compilation defaultLanguage="c#" debug="true"/>
  <customErrors mode="Off"/>
  <deviceFilters>
    <!-- Markup Languages -->
    <filter name="isHTML32" compare="preferredRenderingType"
                                            argument="html32" />
    <filter name="isWML11" compare="preferredRenderingType"
                                            argument="wml11" />
    <filter name="isCHTML10" compare="preferredRenderingType"
                                            argument="chtml10" />
    <!-- Device Browsers -->
    <filter name="isGoAmerica" compare="browser" argument="Go.Web" />
    <filter name="isMME" compare="browser"
                               argument="Microsoft Mobile Explorer" />
    <filter name="isMyPalm" compare="browser" argument="MyPalm" />
    <filter name="isPocketIE" compare="browser" argument="Pocket IE" />
    <filter name="isUP3x" compare="type" argument="Phone.com 3.x Browser" />
    <filter name="isUP4x" compare="type" argument="Phone.com 4.x Browser" />
    <!-- Specific Devices -->
    <filter name="isEricssonR380" compare="type" argument="Ericsson R380" />
    <filter name="isNokia7110" compare="type" argument="Nokia 7110" />
    <!-- Device Capabilities -->
    <filter name="prefersGIF" compare="preferredImageMIME"
                                            argument="image/gif" />
    <filter name="prefersWBMP" compare="preferredImageMIME"
                                       argument="image/vnd.wap.wbmp" />
    <filter name="supportsColor" compare="isColor" argument="true" />
    <filter name="supportsCookies" compare="cookies" argument="true" />
    <filter name="supportsJavaScript" compare="javascript"
                                            argument="true" />
    <filter name="supportsVoiceCalls" compare="canInitiateVoiceCall"
                                            argument="true" />
```

```
    </deviceFilters>
   </system.web>
</configuration>
```

6. Make sure the images named in the advertisement are in the /Your-Application-Directory/wroxImages folder. You can get these with the downloadable code from the Wrox site (`mslogo.bmp`, `mslogo.gif`, `WroxLogo.bmp`, `WroxLogo.gif`).

7. Navigate your emulator to http://localhost/Your-Application-Directory/WroxAdRotator.aspx. Here we see it from the Nokia 6210 emulator and then the Microsoft Mobile Emulator (MME):

> If you refresh your emulators you will notice that the graphics that you named in your advertisement file are rotated in proportion to the value we put for the <Impressions> property.

How It Works

The first thing we did was put an AdRotator control in our mobile Web Form with this code:

```
<mobile:AdRotator id=AdRotator1 runat="server"
AdvertisementFile="Adv.xml"
ImageKey = "ImageUrl"
>
   ...
</mobile:AdRotator>
```

As you can see in the code above we set the `AdvertisementFile` property to the name of our advertisement file, `Adv.xml`, and the `ImageKey` property is at its default.

In case our code encounters a client device of type Pocket IE, Nokia 7110 or Nokia 6210, we want to show it a specific graphic. For that we have the device specific constructs between the AdRotator tags. When one of these is triggered, it tells the `AdRotator` to override the `ImageKey` property and use the new value as the name of the element from which to garner the image url for the advertisement. If the device is not listed in the `<DeviceSpecific>` construct then the ImageKey property set in the AdRotator tag is used:

227

```
<mobile:AdRotator id=AdRotator1 runat="server"
AdvertisementFile="Adv.xml"
ImageKey = "ImageUrl"
>
    <DeviceSpecific>
        <Choice Filter="isPocketIE" ImageKey="BmpImageUrl"/>
        <Choice Filter="isNokia7110" ImageKey="ImageUrl"/>
    </DeviceSpecific>
</mobile:AdRotator>
```

When the <Choice Filter> criteria are met the ImageKey property is overridden and changed to the appropriate value (we will explain device capabilities in detail in the next chapter, for now don't worry about the implementation details of it).

That's all that we needed for the ASPX file. The next file we create is the advertisement file. I will go over one entry from that file that should give you enough of an idea how it works to figure out the other entry or create your own. This will put the information we discussed prior to the example into perspective by showing it in practice.

Initially we have the declaration of the xml version:

```
<?xml version="1.0" ?>
```

The <Advertisements> element houses the individual <Ad> entities:

```
<Advertisements>
  <Ad>
```

The <ImageUrl> element gives us the name and path of our image file. This element is what is referred to in the ImageKey property for the AdRotator control code that is our .aspx page:

```
<ImageUrl>wroxImages/WroxLogo.gif</ImageUrl>
```

Here we have the <BmpImageUrl> element. This element is sought when directed by the <DeviceSpecific> construct. And you can see that it, too, has a name and path for an image file:

```
<BmpImageUrl>wroxImages/WroxLogo.bmp</BmpImageUrl>
```

The next element under the <Ad> element's hierarchy is the <NavigateUrl>. This element provides the URL that the user will be sent to if they click on the ad banner. This is an optional element. If it is not used, then no HREF property is rendered in the <Anchor> tag for the ad:

```
<NavigateUrl>http://www.wrox.com/</NavigateUrl>
```

Next is the <AlternateText> element. The value contained in this element is the value that will ultimately be found in the ALT attribute for the image that is rendered:

```
        <AlternateText>You'd be off your Wroxer to buy any other
    book!</AlternateText>
```

The next element is the `<Keyword>` which, for this ad we set to 'Books'.

```
    <Keyword>Books</Keyword>
```

The next element sets our impression ratio (I reloaded the page 20 times with these results; the Microsoft logo was loaded 8 times and the Wrox logo was loaded 12 times):

```
    <Impressions>20</Impressions>
```

Then we close the `<Ad>` and `<Advertisements>` elements:

```
    </Ad>
    </Advertisements>
```

Again, we only went over the first entry in the advertisement file.

Remember that we also created or changed a `Web.Config` file. We did this to demonstrate how to override the `ImageKey` property using the `<DeviceSpecific>` tags.

The part that we were most concerned about was where it made reference to the PocketIE browser:

```
    <filter name="isPocketIE" compare="browser" argument="Pocket IE" />
```

This entry registers the `isPocketIE` filter for use with the `<DeviceSpecific>` tags. Each one of the `<Choice>` tags are evaluated against the collection of `<filter>`s declared in the `Web.Config` file. The first `<Choice>` to match is the one used.

The `AdRotator` (in some form or another) has been around for quite a while. In its earlier incarnations there was not much need to give consideration to what type of client devices it would render to. With mobile computing becoming more prominent, this requirement has changed to the level of almost being mandatory. The need for the ability to serve the same advertisement in different ways to disparate clients is a common one now, and the `AdRotator` components that ship with ASP.NET in the Mobile Internet Toolkit meet that need nicely.

At this point you should have a good understanding of what it takes to implement the `AdRotator` control on mobile Web Forms and some of what it can do. Now let's look at the `Calendar` control.

The Calendar Control

The `Calendar` control is very useful when gathering or keeping track of date-based data. You can find uses for it in applications such as monthly planners, mortgage applications, or booking reservations. It has the same built-in functionality that its Web Form cousin has, the difference being that it renders on mobile devices.

The `Calendar` control has seven properties that allow you to dictate its behavior. These properties allow you to set things ranging from the initial selected date to whether or not to show the days of the week across the top of the control.

The `Calendar` control's properties are:

- **FirstDayOfWeek** – This property sets the date that you want to be shown in the first column. The default is the first day of the week of the server's locale. The value that is given must be of type `System.Web.UI.WebControls.FirstDayOfWeek`. Values that we have to work with are:

  - **Default**
  - **Sunday**
  - **Monday**
  - **Tuesday**
  - **Wednesday**
  - **Thursday**
  - **Friday**
  - **Saturday**

- **OnSelectionChanged** – We set this property to the name of the method that will handle the event that is raised when the user selects a date from the `Calendar` control

- **SelectedDate** – Sets a `System.DateTime` object to the selected date. The default is today's date.

- **SelectedDates** – Collection of `System.DateTime` objects that represent the currently selected dates.

- **SelectionMode** – This allows you set the scope of the user's selection ability. The modes are:

  - **Day** – This setting allows movement from month to month and the selection of individual days
  - **DayWeek** – This setting allows the select of individual days or entire week blocks
  - **DayWeekMonth** – This setting allows selection of month, day, or week
  - **None** – This effectively renders a read-only calendar view

- **ShowDayHeader** – `True` or `False` will toggle days of the week header on and off. The default is `true`.

- **VisibleDate** – The month that this value falls in will be the month that is displayed in the calendar rendering. The default is `System.DateTime.Empty`. The date can be any within the month.

- **WebCalendar** – This property returns the `Calendar` control.

In a way similar to the `CustomValidator` control that we saw in the last chapter, this control uses a delegate method to handle the `SelectionChanged` event. We set the `OnSelectionChanged` property in our page to the name of the method that we want to handle the event. The method that handles the event must accept a specific argument list (again, just like the `CustomValidator`), as we will see in the following example.

Try It Out – The Calendar Control

This example will demonstrate how to use the Calendar control to allow the user to view any month and choose a date.

1. Open your text editor and enter the following code:

```
<%@ Page Inherits="System.Web.UI.MobileControls.MobilePage" Language="C#"%>
<%@Register TagPrefix="mobile" Namespace="System.Web.UI.MobileControls"
Assembly="System.Web.Mobile" %>

<mobile:Form id=Form1 runat="server">
   <mobile:Calendar id="Calendar1" runat="server"
     OnSelectionChanged="Changed" SelectionMode="Day">
   </mobile:Calendar>
</mobile:Form>

<mobile:Form id="Form2" runat="server">
   <mobile:Label id="Label1" runat="server">
   </mobile:Label>
</mobile:Form>

<script language="c#" runat="server">
  protected void Changed(Object sender, EventArgs e)
  {
     Label1.Text = "You chose " + Calendar1.SelectedDate;
     ActiveForm = Form2;
  }
</script>
```

2. Save it to your folder as WroxCalendarControl.aspx.

3. Navigate your emulator to http://localhost/Your-Application-Directory/WroxCalendarControl.aspx.

Using the Nokia emulator and the MME we have two separate paths through the process of selecting a date. We'll look at both the Nokia emulator and the MME equivalent side by side in just a moment. Before that, however, let's firstly see the CalendarControl.aspx rendered on IE:

The first pages we see on the Nokia mobile emulator and the MME are quite similar:

From this screen we choose Options, or OK in the case of the MME. We are then shown the following screen, on both the Nokia MIT and the MME:

We have the option to Type a date or Choose a date. If we select Type a date, then we see the following:

We can either type in a date directly, or select OK – we're then presented with this screenshot.

Alternately, we can select Type a date, which leads us to this screenshot.

As you can see from the screenshots above, we have decided to choose Dec 2001 for the Nokia and we settled on Mar 2002 for the MME (there's no significant reason why we did that – it was an arbitrary choice!)

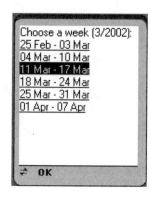

Upon choosing a month, we are asked to choose a week – in the Nokia case, we chose the first week of December, and with the MME, we decided upon the second week in March (again – no important reason why!)

After choosing the month, and then the week, we are simply left with choosing the day – the choices we made are shown above, with the results shown in the screenshot below.

How It Works

Our page contains two mobile Web Forms. The first one is to hold our `Calendar` control and the second one displays, in text form, the date that the user selected. Here is our `Form1` containing our `Calendar` control:

```
<mobile:Form id=Form1 runat="server">
   <mobile:Calendar
      id=Calendar1
      runat="server"
      OnSelectionChanged="Changed"
      SelectionMode=Day>
   </mobile:Calendar>
</mobile:Form>
```

Notice in the code above that we have set the `OnSelectionChanged` to the name of our event handler; `Changed`. This will be the name of the method that will handle the event.

Also in the code above we set the `SelectionMode` to `Day`, which is the default. This will allow the user to click through the months and choose individual days by clicking on them.

When the user chooses a date the `OnSelectionChanged` method is called and it, in turn, calls our method. Here is our method shown in C#

```
protected void Changed(Object sender, EventArgs e)
{
   Label1.Text = "You chose " + Calendar1.SelectedDate;
   ActiveForm = Form2;
}
```

As you can see, the code set the `Label1.Text` property to the message that includes the date the user chose using the `Calendar1.SelectedDate` property read. Then it sets the active form to `Form2`, which presents the label text to the user:

```
<mobile:Form id=Form2 runat="server">
   <mobile:Label id=Label1 runat="server">
   </mobile:Label>
</mobile:Form>
```

That is all it takes to get the basic functionality from the Calendar control. Take the time to experiment with this control and see what you can come up with.

Summary

In this chapter we looked at the Mobile Internet Toolkits Rich Controls:

❑   The AdRotator control

❑   The Calendar control

Both of these controls provide robust functionality right out of the box. We saw both of these controls in action in a couple of emulators and were able to observe their behavior on each.

We saw that the AdRotator expanded upon the older version, as it is equipped to detect client type and render advertisements using different images, depending on the <Choice> element attributes. We saw the Calendar controls useful, adaptive UI provide many types of calendar functionality without making the developer's life harder.

In the next chapter we will dig into device capabilities (we touched on them briefly here), styling, templates, and pagination.

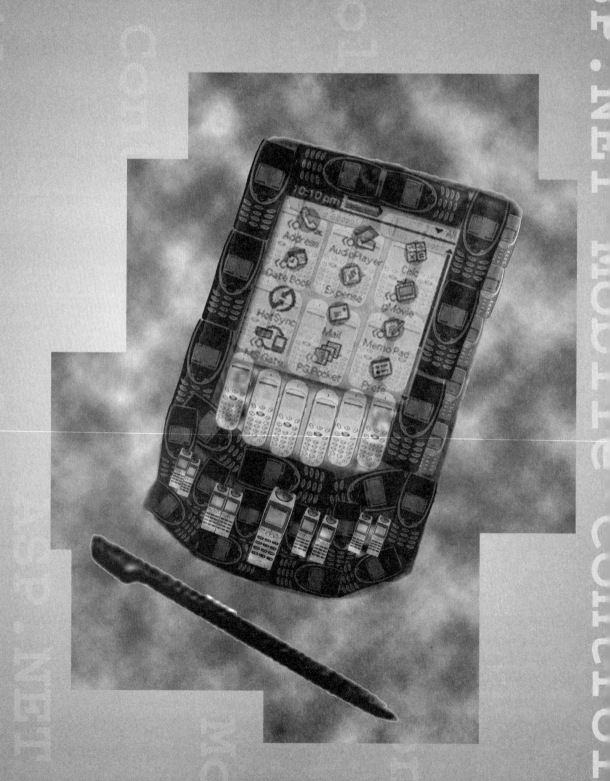

Styling Page Output

In previous chapters we've seen that a single page can render on multiple devices by using mobile controls. But what about controlling the appearance of the output to include style information? Can we take advantage of the capabilities of the requesting device to provide a richer experience for users?

In this chapter we will discuss modifying the page output. This includes two main areas:

❑   Setting the style of a control to affect its output

❑   Dynamically modifying the page, based on the characteristics of the requesting device

The first area refers to applying stylistic properties to controls which are then rendered appropriately for devices that support it. For example, we can set the style of a <mobile:Label> control to appear bold, then on devices where bold appearance is supported, the markup generated by the mobile controls run-time will produce bold text.

The second area we'll discuss is controlling the output based on the capabilities of the requesting device. This includes modifying control attributes, adding controls, or even specifying markup explicitly by using a template and filter construct to determine the capabilities of the device and react accordingly. This allows us to customize the output for the richer devices without sacrificing functionality on those with more basic capabilities. It also allows us to keep pieces of presentation and application logic centralized without sacrificing rich presentation.

As we explore styling page output, we are confronted directly with the fact that the devices supported by the Mobile Internet Toolkit possess very different sets of capabilities. As an application developer, it is important to consider this fact and design for the target audience. A form where we place many controls may render fine on a PDA, but become difficult for the user to deal with on a small cell-phone display. It may be better to write two forms and let the user navigate between them. Text labels and descriptions may need to be written with the small device in mind, and then overridden on devices where there is more screen real estate. Remember, the user is mobile, so the application should provide the functionality that the mobile user needs without necessarily attempting to replace a desktop application.

In this chapter we will talk about how and when you can use the following features of the Mobile Internet Toolkit:

❑ Style Attributes

❑ Style Properties

❑ Stylesheets

❑ Device Capabilities

❑ Pagination

❑ Device Specific Rendering

Style Attributes

The mobile controls support a set of style attributes that can be declared as part of the control element within a page. Developers don't need to be concerned with which devices support which styles, instead they can specify the style, and it will be rendered for devices with corresponding support using the appropriate markup.

This is the collection of style properties exposed in this way on the Mobile Controls:

Property Name	Default Value
Font-Bold	Boolean.NotSet
Font-Italic	Boolean.NotSet
Font-Name	String.Empty
Font-Size	FontSize.NotSet
ForeColor	Color.Empty
Alignment	Alignment.NotSet
Wrapping	Wrapping.NotSet

While you can see that the properties generally default to a NotSet value, the behavior of the NotSet value should be understood as corresponding to a control's inherited value. If Font-Bold is NotSet for a control but it is set for the parent, then the parent's value will be used. This actually extends to any ancestor, so long as the value of the parent is NotSet, the Mobile Controls runtime will look at the next parent until the root form is reached or a value is found. This allows us to set a style property once for a container control and have the setting affect all controls under it. If the value is not set for the control or any of its parents, then no markup will be sent to the client for that style, and the text will appear as default text for the browser. When the alignment is not specified, most browsers follow the convention for the Country/Region in which they are being used.

It's important to remember that not all of these style properties are supported on all mobile devices. On the most basic clients you may see almost no formatting change, even though richer clients will see dramatic differences.

Try It Out – Setting The Style

1. Create a new file with the following:

```
<%@ Page Inherits="System.Web.UI.MobileControls.MobilePage" Language="CS" %>
<%@ Register TagPrefix="Mobile" Namespace="System.Web.UI.MobileControls"
Assembly="System.Web.Mobile" %>
<Mobile:Form runat="server" Font-Bold="true" >
<Mobile:Label runat="server" Text="Hello bold world" />
<Mobile:Label runat="server" Font-Bold="false" Text="Wrox Press Welcomes You" />
</Mobile:Form>
```

2. Save the file as `bold.aspx` in a virtual directory.

3. Request `bold.aspx` in a web browser or device emulator:

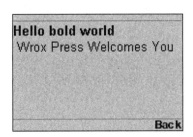

How It Works

As we have seen already, the first two commands establish this page as inheriting from the
`MobilePage` of the Mobile Internet Toolkit and set up the keyword `mobile` as a prefix for elements to
correspond to the Mobile Controls:

```
<%@ Page Inherits="System.Web.UI.MobileControls.MobilePage"
                                    Language="CS" %>
<%@ Register TagPrefix="Mobile" Namespace="System.Web.UI.MobileControls"
                            Assembly="System.Web.Mobile" %>
```

Next, in the mobile form `Font-Bold` is set to `true`, so all child controls will inherit this value, and the
first `<mobile:Label>` specifies that "**Hello bold world**" be rendered:

```
<mobile:Form runat=server>
<mobile:Label runat=server Font-Bold=true Text="Hello bold world" />
```

The second `<mobile:Label>` sets `Font-Bold` to `false`, indicating that its appearance should appear without the added emphasis. It is necessary to explicitly set `Font-Bold` on the second label because, if we did not, its default `NotSet` value would be overridden by the value set for its parent.

Every style property has a default value so that there is no need to specify it unless the desired output differs:

```
<Mobile:Label runat=server Font-Bold=false
                            Text="Wrox Press Welcomes You" />
</Mobile:Form>
```

Style Properties

The style properties can be set declaratively, as we have seen, as attributes on a control. Additionally, these properties can be accessed programmatically. The differences between setting the styles declaratively and programmatically is not difficult, it just requires an understanding that the names are not identical. Suppose we have a control with an `id` of `MyControl`. Here's a table that shows how the declarative syntax corresponds to object properties:

Declarative Access	Programmatic Access
Font-Bold	MyControl.Font.Bold
Font-Italic	MyControl.Font.Italic
Font-Name	MyControlFont.Name
Font-Size	MyControl.Font.Size
ForeColor	MyControl.ForeColor
Alignment	MyControl.Alignment
Wrapping	MyControl.Wrapping

This might still seem a bit complicated, so we'll illustrate what we're talking about with an example:

Try It Out – Setting Styles Programmatically

1. Create a new file and enter the following:

```
<%@ Page Inherits="System.Web.UI.MobileControls.MobilePage"
                                    Language="CS" %>
<%@ Register TagPrefix="Mobile" Namespace="System.Web.UI.MobileControls"
                                    Assembly="System.Web.Mobile" %>
<script runat="server">
protected void Page_Load(Object o, EventArgs e)
{
```

```
labelA.Font.Bold = BooleanOption.True;
labelA.Font.Size = System.Web.UI.MobileControls.FontSize.Large;
labelA.ForeColor = System.Drawing.Color.Red;
}
</script>
<Mobile:Form runat="server" Font-Bold="true" >
  <Mobile:Label runat="server" id="labelA" Text="Large, Bold and Red" />
</Mobile:Form>
```

2. Save the file as `programmatic.aspx` in a virtual directory.

3. Request the file using a web browser or device emulator:

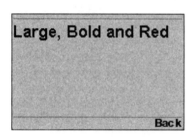

How It Works

We'll skip over the introductory portion of the form, which should be familiar by now, and just look at the section relevant to this example.

The form contains just one `<mobile:Label>` with no style attributes specified:

```
<Mobile:Form runat="server" Font-Bold="true" >
<Mobile:Label runat="server" id="labelA" Text="Large, Bold and Red" />
</Mobile:Form>
```

The style properties are then set during the `Page_Load` method, which is executed for each page rendering:

```
<script runat="server">
protected void Page_Load(Object o, EventArgs e)
{
 labelA.Font.Bold = BooleanOption.True;
 labelA.Font.Size = System.Web.UI.MobileControls.FontSize.Large;
 labelA.ForeColor = System.Drawing.Color.Red;

}
</script>
```

Setting the style attributes programmatically for a control is not complex, but it does necessitate remembering that the attribute names may vary from the corresponding property names.

The advantage of being able to set styles programmatically is in being able to react to conditions during the execution of the request. For example, suppose that you were displaying a list of stock quotes to your user. If the value of a stock had changed at least two percent, you might want to make it appear bold. You could set the font to red if the equity were declining, and blue if it were on the rise.

It is important to remember when designing these features that the application must present the information appropriately for the target device. In mobile development, style attributes may be used to improve the display of an application but they can't be relied upon as the only means of communicating information. For example, we couldn't rely exclusively on a color attribute to tell the user whether a stock price was up or down unless we know for sure that the client device supports a color display – on a grayscale device, the application would fail to communicate correctly. We'll talk more about this in the section about *Device Specific Rendering* later in the chapter.

Stylesheets

HTML developers will be familiar with using **cascading stylesheets** to achieve a desired appearance in a web browser. The Microsoft Mobile Internet Toolkit provides a similar concept. **Server stylesheets** can be established in separate files to allow style settings to be re-used by multiple pages. These stylesheets support inheritance, and the controls can make selective use of a particular stylesheet through use of the `StyleReference` property, allowing the developer to pick and choose what styles to use and where.

Here's a quick example of this:

Try It Out – Using A Server Stylesheet

1. Create a new file and enter the following:

```
<%@ Page Inherits="System.Web.UI.MobileControls.MobilePage"
                                    Language="CS" %>
<%@ Register TagPrefix="Mobile" Namespace="System.Web.UI.MobileControls"
                                    Assembly="System.Web.Mobile" %>
<Mobile:Stylesheet runat="server" >
  <Style Name="Emphasize" Font-Size="Large" Font-Bold="true" />
  <Style Name="DeEmphasize" Font-Size="Small" Font-Bold="false" />
</Mobile:Stylesheet>
<Mobile:Form runat="server">
<Mobile:Label runat="server"
  StyleReference="Emphasize"
  Text="Important Text" />
<Mobile:Label runat="server"
  StyleReference="DeEmphasize"
  Text="UnImportant Text" />
</Mobile:Form>
```

2. Save the file as `InlineStylesheet.aspx` in a virtual directory.

3. Request the file in a web browser or device emulator:

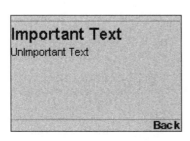

How It Works

Again, we'll just focus on the lines relevant to this example, as the others have been discussed in previous chapters. The first of these is where the stylesheet element occurs:

```
<Mobile:Stylesheet runat="server">
```

Inside the stylesheet, we set up two styles, Emphasize and DeEmphasize:

```
<Style Name="Emphasize" Font-Size="Large" Font-Bold="true" />
<Style Name="DeEmphasize Font-Size="Small" Font-Bold="false" />
```

The Emphasize style specifies a bold, oversized font, while the DeEmphasize style is a small font that is specifically not bold. The two <mobile:Label> controls in the form then use these styles by setting their StyleReference properties:

```
<Mobile:Label runat="server"
  StyleReference="Emphasize"
  Text="Important Text" />
<Mobile:Label runat="server"
  StyleReference="DeEmphasize"
  Text="UnImportant Text" />
```

This code sets the first label to be rendered as oversized bold on devices that support it. While the second, using the DeEmphasize style will appear, where supported, as non-bold small text.

Server stylesheets provide the ability to inherit settings and extend them where appropriate. Suppose that some text should take on the attributes set in the Emphasize style, but that we would also like to make the text appear red to denote an error. There's no need to specify the settings again. Instead, the new EmphasizeError style can refer to the already established style:

```
<Mobile:Stylesheet runat="server" >
  <Style Name="Emphasize" Font-Size="Large" Font-Bold="true" />
  <Style Name="DeEmphasize" Font-Size="Small" Font-Bold="false" />
```

```
        <Style Name="EmphasizeError" Font-Color="Red"
                                    StyleReference="Emphasize" />
    </Mobile:Stylesheet>
    <Mobile:Form runat="server" >
      <Mobile:Label runat="server"
        StyleReference="EmphasizeError"
        Text="Error Text" />
    </Mobile:Form>
```

Here the `EmphasizeError` style makes use of the settings in the `Emphasize style and adds` to it. The `<mobile:Label>` that uses the `EmphasizeError` style will then render with a large, bold, red font.

Stylesheets are probably most useful when they can be re-used across multiple files. This allows us to define a set of styles common to an entire web application and then simply set the `StyleReference` to one of those defined in the central location.

Here's an example of how we'd go about doing this:

Try It Out – Including A Stylesheet File

1. Create a new file and enter the following:

```
<Mobile:Stylesheet runat="server" >
  <Style Name="Emphasize" Font-Size="Large" Font-Bold="true" />
  <Style Name="DeEmphasize" Font-Size="Small" Font-Bold="false" />
</Mobile:Stylesheet>
```

2. Save the file as `MyStylesheet.aspx`.

3. Create another file and enter this code:

```
<%@ Page Inherits="System.Web.UI.MobileControls.MobilePage"
                                    Language="CS" %>
<%@ Register TagPrefix="Mobile" Namespace="System.Web.UI.MobileControls"
                              Assembly="System.Web.Mobile" %>

<!--#include file="MyStylesheet.aspx" -->
<Mobile:Form runat="server" >
<Mobile:Label runat="server"
  StyleReference="Emphasize"
  Text="Important Text" />
<Mobile:Label runat="server"
  StyleReference="DeEmphasize"
  Text="UnImportant Text" />
</Mobile:Form>
```

4. Save the file as `IncludeStylesheet.aspx`.

5. Request the `IncludeStyleSheet.aspx` file in a web browser or device simulator:

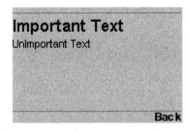

How It Works

When the page is assembled for compilation, the include directive causes the contents of the MyStylesheet.aspx file to be pulled in to the page for compilation. In essence, the include statement:

```
<!--#include file="MyStylesheet.aspx" -->
```

is being replaced with the contents of the file that it names:

```
<Mobile:Stylesheet runat="server" >
  <Style Name="Emphasize" Font-Size="Large" Font-Bold="true" />
  <Style Name="DeEmphasize Font-Size="Small" Font-Bold="false" />
</Mobile:Stylesheet>
```

This approach is very useful when you're trying to have consistent presentation across a web application. Because all your styles are stored in one place, you only need to update that one, centralized, resource to have the changes applied throughout all your pages.

Device Capabilities

Not all devices support all the styles that can be set on a control. For example, many mobile devices do not support color. But, if you set the ForeColor for a control it will render correctly even when the requesting device lacks color support. This is because the **Mobile Controls Runtime** assesses the capabilities of the device and does not render style markup where it can not be used. This saves the developer from having to constantly try and keep track of which tags are supported by which devices.

Different tags may be sent to different devices to achieve the same style setting. For example, a control specifying large font:

```
<Mobile:Label runat=server Font-Size=Large Text="some large text" />
```

may render like this on one device:

```
<font size="+1">some large text</font>
```

but like this on another:

```
<big>some large text</big>
```

This adaptive quality is key to development using the Mobile Internet Toolkit. Because a functional rendering can be provided from a single ASPX page to a large number of different client devices.

> **It is important to remember that the exact appearance of a page will vary between devices, so what you see on one device may not be what is seen by a user on another device:**

It is possible to programmatically assess a client to determine what extended capabilities it has. This is done by casting an `HttpBrowserCapabilities` object to a `MobileCapabilities` object:

```
MobileCapabilities capabilities =
                 (System.Web.Mobile.MobileCapabilities)Request.Browser;
```

Once this is done the `MobileCapabilities` object can then be used to look up information about the requesting device as determined by the Mobile Controls runtime:

```
bool isColor = capabilities.IsColor;
```

A device's capabilities are determined by matching data it sends when a request is made to information held about it in the mobile controls. The mobile control architecture is flexible, and provides us with the ability to extend the support if we discover new information about an existing device or wish to configure support for new devices. We'll be covering this in more detail in the later chapter on New Device Support.

Pagination

Content can be broken up across multiple pages automatically by the Mobile Controls Runtime. This can be advantageous in several ways. First, less memory is required to deal with a succession of small pages, than with a few large ones. This is also true of the download times across the typically slow wireless networks.

The slowest wired-modems used today are still several times faster than the majority of the mobile device networks. Many kilobytes of data can be sent to a desktop browser without difficulty, whereas most mobile devices can not accept page renderings of more than a few thousand **bytes**. Limiting the amount of data transmitted to the device at once accommodates these restrictions, and shortens the wait for data to be received.

An additional consideration is that the cost of accessing the Web from a desktop browser is currently much less than rates charged for mobile web requests. With some networks charging by the packet, mobile users will have a much cheaper, faster, and better experience when page sizes are limited. Pagination can help us in achieving this.

Pagination is best suited for handling lists and pieces of text, with the data being viewed by the user in chunks appropriately sized for their device. In these circumstances pagination gives faster responses and prevents clients from being given large amounts of data that they do not need.

Pagination is not ideal for user input forms The user may miss a required input and end up paging through fields that have already been entered trying to return to the field in error. This can be particularly frustrating when mixed with the output from validation controls.

The developer can control many aspects of pagination. The <mobile:Panel> control, and the <mobile:Form> control that it inherits from it, both expose a Paginate property for enabling and disabling pagination. When set to true for a panel, the controls contained within that panel can be split across multiple pages based on the size of the requesting device. The default value is false. In our next example, we create a list of one hundred items. When Paginate is set to true, only part of the list is rendered along with links for moving through pages of the content:

Try It Out – Using Pagination

1. Create a new file containing the following:

```
<%@ Page Inherits="System.Web.UI.MobileControls.MobilePage" Language="CS" %>
<%@ Register TagPrefix="Mobile" Namespace="System.Web.UI.MobileControls"
Assembly="System.Web.Mobile" %>
<script language="CS" runat="server" >
protected void MyList_OnLoadItems(Object sender, LoadItemsEventArgs args)
{
   //clear the current contents of the list
   MyList.Items.Clear();
   //populate the list with the items requested
   for(int i = args.ItemIndex; i < args.ItemIndex + args.ItemCount; i++)
   {
     MyList.Items.Add(new MobileListItem("item # " + i.ToString()));
   }
}
</script>
<Mobile:Form runat="server" Paginate="true">
<Mobile:List runat="server"
  id="MyList"
  ItemCount=100
  OnLoadItems="MyList_OnLoadItems" />
</Mobile:Form>
```

2. Save it as pagination.aspx in a virtual directory.

3. Request the file using a web browser or device emulator:

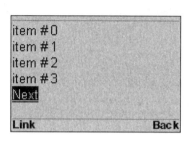

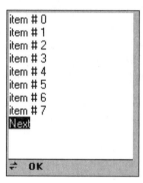

As we can see from the example screenshots, on a cell phone with a small screen, the list will automatically be broken into multiple pages with a subset of the list on each page. While on a device with a larger screen, the list will be broken into fewer pages containing more items on each page.

How It Works

The list element defines the number of items with the `ItemCount` attribute and an event handler for the `OnLoadItems` event:

```
<Mobile:List runat="server"
  id="MyList"
  ItemCount=100
  OnLoadItems="MyList_OnLoadItems" />
```

The Mobile Controls runtime performs its analysis of what items should be sent to the page. For a small device, just a few items may be needed. On a device with a larger screen, more items will be loaded. The event handler is told what items are needed for this page through the `LoadItemsEventArgs` argument:

```
protected void MyList_OnLoadItems(Object sender, LoadItemsEventArgs args)
```

Next, we clear whatever items are currently part of the list. This is important since the viewstate may be holding outdated information:

```
MyList.Items.Clear();
```

Then we enter a loop where we populate the list with the currently requested device. The `ItemIndex` property of `LoadItemsEventArgs` is the first item for this page:

```
for(int i = args.ItemIndex; i < args.ItemIndex + args.ItemCount; i++)
{
  MyList.Items.Add(new MobileListItem("item # " + i.ToString()));
}
```

It is important to remember that Paginate *is* false *by default and is dependent on the setting of the containing panel. So, for a panel to paginate, the paginate property must be* true *and the* <mobile:Form> *or* <mobile:Panel> *that contains it must also have paginate set to* true. *This is very useful when designing the appearance of a mobile page. As a developer can group controls within a* <mobile:Panel> *to prevent them from being split across page boundaries while still allowing other controls to be paginated.*

The <mobile:Form> also provides the ability to leave pagination turned off generally while specifying a single control, and its children, to be considered for pagination. The ControlToPaginate property can be set programmatically to override the pagination settings and inheritance to allow a subset of controls to paginate. For this to work the <mobile:Form> itself does not need to have pagination enabled. This is particularly useful when you are designing a page where you don't want the contents to be paginated, but find that you'd like to include a single list or text element that should be allowed to split across multiple rendered pages. Here's a small section of example code to illustrate this:

```CS
<script language="CS">
protected void Page_Load(Object sender, EventArgs args)
{
    //clear the current contents of the list
    theForm.ControlToPaginate = panel1;
}
</script>
<Mobile:Form runat="server" Paginate="false" >
<Mobile:Panel id="panel1" runat="server" >
</Mobile:Panel>
</Mobile:Form>
```

Any controls outside the <Mobile:Panel>would not be eligible for pagination, and even though paginate is false for the <Mobile:Form>, the panel contents would still be considered. We say that controls are eligible for pagination because the decision to split content across page boundaries is made by the Mobile Controls Runtime based on the characteristics of the requesting device, so it may not always occur.

A Word Of Caution

Pagination can be extremely useful, but it can tempt you to make design decisions that may not be appropriate. Sure, pagination allows you to data bind a list of a thousand people from a customer database and let the user page through it. But, even with the relatively large screen of a PDA, the user is not likely to suffer through page after page of data looking for the one specific entry in which they are interested. In this case, it's probably better to ask the user for some input to narrow the scope of the search.

Even in our example of just 100 items in a list it would be nearly impossible to navigate on a small cell phone where just a few items at a time are displayed. A list this size should be ordered according to how we expect the user to find the item they are after. If we really want the user to have access to the whole list, it would be better here to do a little extra work and present the user with an index of the items to let them narrow the scope of their search. Perhaps an index page could be provided that allows the user to choose from four subsets and then you could paginate those subsets? On a device that can present 25 items at a time, no extra paging would be required while a user of a small device would be subjected to three or four pages at most.

*The important thing to remember is that pagination **helps** in developing for mobile devices, but it doesn't replace the need to **design** for the mobile devices.*

Device Specific Rendering

The `deviceSpecific` element allows customization based on `deviceFilters`. These are configured as part of the application configuration. They are based on the capabilities of the requesting device and can range from very simple declarative checks to complex programmatic decisions. Does the device use WML or HTML? Is it color or black and white? What version is the browser? Who is the manufacturer?

This ability to customize the output more explicitly allows the developer to take advantage of features of a particular device while still maintaining support for a wide array of devices in a single file. In some application development, you may find that the adaptations, although varying from device to device, is adequate. Sometimes, you may be targeting a specific device for an internal application where you know that the majority of the users will all be using the same device. This is common when a company standardizes on a device. In this case, it may be necessary to provide extensive customization for that device. Often, you may be somewhere in the middle, where you need to maintain support for a broad array of devices, but want to improve the user interface beyond what is provided by the mobile controls runtime.

Here's a quick example of how you can employ this technique:

Try It Out – Device Specific Filters

1. Create a new `web.config` file in the virtual directory you are using for testing:

```
<configuration>
<system.web>
  <deviceFilters>
    <filter name="CheckHtml" compare="PreferredRenderingType" argument="html32" />
    <filter name="CheckWml" compare="PreferredRenderingType" argument="wml11" />
  </deviceFilters>
</system.web>
</configuration>
```

2. Create another new file containing the following code:

```
<%@ Page Inherits="System.Web.UI.MobileControls.MobilePage"
                                        Language="CS" %>
<%@ Register TagPrefix="Mobile" Namespace="System.Web.UI.MobileControls"
                                        Assembly="System.Web.Mobile" %>

<Mobile:Form runat="server" >
<deviceSpecific>
  <choice filter="CheckWml">
    <headerTemplate>
      <Mobile:Label runat="server" Text="Wrox" />
```

```
          </headerTemplate>
        </choice>
        <choice filter="CheckHtml">
          <headerTemplate>
            <Mobile:Label runat="server"
                          Text="Wrox Press : Programmer to Programmer" />
          </headerTemplate>
        </choice>
        <choice>
          <headerTemplate>
            <Mobile:Label runat="server" Text="Wrox Press" />
          </headerTemplate>
        </choice>
      </deviceSpecific>
    </Mobile:Form>
```

3. Save the file as `headerTemplate.aspx` in the test web application directory.

4. Request the file in both a WML-based web browser and an HTML-based device emulator:

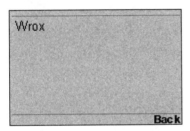

The HTML browser will get a page that says 'Wrox Press : Programmer to Programmer' while the WML browser will get simply 'Wrox.'

How It Works

Filters can be created declaratively using the application configuration files or programmatically by providing filter code. Here, in the `web.config` file, we establish two filters using the `deviceFilters` region. If the `PreferredRenderingType` is `html32`, then the `CheckHtml` filter will evaluate to true when used. The `CheckWml` filter checks for a `PreferredRenderingtype` of `wml11` in the same manner:

```
<deviceFilters>
  <filter name="CheckHtml" compare="PreferredRenderingType" argument="html32" />
  <filter name="CheckWml" compare="PreferredRenderingType" argument="wml11" />
</deviceFilters>
```

We then use the `<deviceSpecific>` region in the mobile page to customize the output based on the requesting device matching a filter:

```
<deviceSpecific>
  <choice filter="CheckWml">
    <headerTemplate>
      <Mobile:Label runat="server" Text="Wrox" />
    </headerTemplate>
  </choice>
  <choice filter="CheckHtml">
    <headerTemplate>
      <Mobile:Label runat=server
                    Text="Wrox Press : Programmer to Programmer" />
    </headerTemplate>
```

The choice elements are evaluated in the order that they appear until one that evaluates to `true` is found. Suppose that a request is made by an HTML-based device where the `PreferredRenderingType` is configured as `html32`. First, the `CheckWml` filter is evaluated and will return `false`. Next, the `CheckHtml` filter will be evaluated. When it returns `true`, the evaluations stop and the choice is selected. The `headerTemplate` contents for that choice are then included in the page. A choice element with no filter can be provided last and will be selected if none of the previous filters evaluate to True:

```
<choice>
    <headerTemplate>
      <Mobile:Label runat="server" Text="Wrox Press" />
    </headerTemplate>
  </choice>
```

It is not always necessary to include this last `choice` element which contains no filters.

Summary

In this chapter we have looked at how to control the appearance of the mobile controls by using **Style properties**. These can be set both declaratively, or programmatically with your programming language of choice. Pagination allows us to include sets of controls, lists or pieces of text that can be automatically split across several pages to suit the requesting device. The appearance of a page can be controlled further based on the characteristics of the requesting device by using `deviceFilters`. These filters are then used in `choice` elements in the `deviceSpecific` region and allow us to achieve fine-grained control over the appearance of the mobile page and take advantage of the unique capabilities of many different devices.

Here's a summary of the features we've looked at in this chapter:

- ❏ Style Attributes
- ❏ Style Properties
- ❏ Stylesheets
- ❏ Device Capabilities
- ❏ Pagination
- ❏ Device Specific Rendering

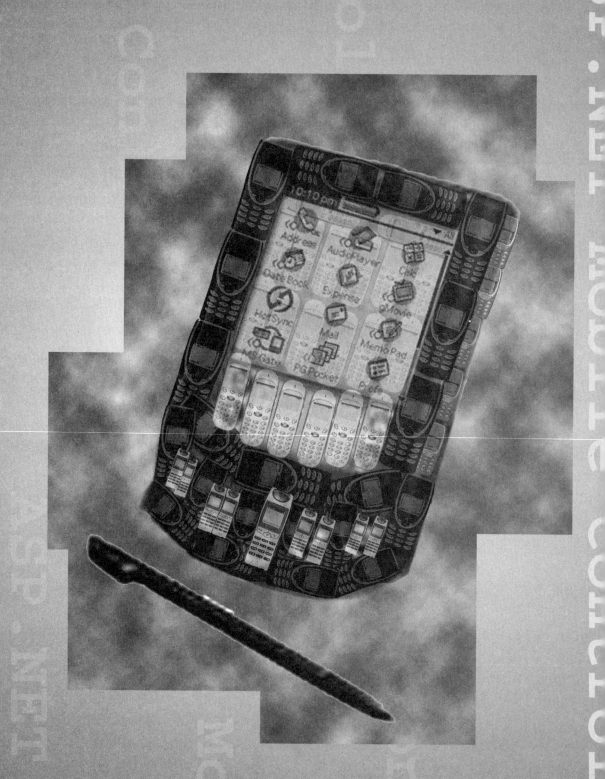

Writing Controls

The controls available as part of the Microsoft Mobile Internet Toolkit provide the building blocks for creating flexible web applications that render on a wide variety of devices. However, as you develop mobile-enabled web applications, you may discover situations where it would be beneficial to customize the behavior of a control or develop a new control. The Microsoft Mobile Internet Toolkit is built on ASP.NET, which provides ways for developing your own controls to accomplish this customized rendering. In this chapter, we will look at how to develop our own controls. This can be accomplished by extending an existing control, developing a control from scratch, or piecing together controls into a new control. The ability to create new controls allows us to improve the development process by creating controls that encapsulate behavior for re-use and develop more exacting behavior through customization.

There are two principal types of control that we can develop: **User Controls** and **Custom Controls**. A user control is built in much the same way that a mobile page is put together. The declarative tags are converted into code and compiled on-demand at runtime. A custom control is authored in an ASP.NET supported language and is compiled beforehand. Both types of control provide a method for grouping and re-using functional application pieces. The choice as to which type of user control to create really depends on what you are trying to accomplish. In this chapter, we will cover:

- ❑ Developing and using a user control
- ❑ Developing and using a custom control

User Control

Writing a user control is an easy way to encapsulate a set of controls or a piece of logic separate from the ASPX page. This can be advantageous in separating a functional application piece from the page in which it is used. This essentially makes a portion of a page into a component piece that is re-usable in many pages of an application. The user control file, which uses an ASCX extension, is very similar to an ASPX page, except that it extends the control object instead of the page object. When we write an ASPX page, it becomes a class of the Page type. The ASCX page becomes a class of the control type, which can then be used in a page. The ASCX page can contain declarative control tags, just like an ASPX page, as well as methods written in any language supported by ASP.NET. The user control behaves like a built-in control, allowing properties to be set and retrieved by using attributes of the control tag.

Suppose that, in an application, we wanted to list the contents of a directory on the web server. We could place the controls for displaying this information and the logic for populating those controls directly in the page. Now, suppose that we wanted to provide this same listing on several different pages within the application. We don't want to copy that code into many different pages. Instead, we want to be able to simply re-use the logic in many different places. This scenario appears ideally suited for employing a user control.

Try It Out – Creating a User Control

1. Create a new text file with your favorite editor called `UserControl.ascx`, and enter the following code. We can not request an ASCX file directly. Instead, it defines a control for use within an ASPX page.

```
<%@ Control Inherits="System.Web.UI.UserControl" Language="cs" %>
<%@ Register TagPrefix="Mobile" Namespace="System.Web.UI.MobileControls"
Assembly="System.Web.Mobile" %>
<%@ Import Namespace="System.IO" %>

<script runat="server">
private string _directoryName;
public string DirectoryName {
    get {
        return _directoryName;
    }
    set {
        _directoryName = value;
    }
}
protected void Page_Load(object o, EventArgs e) {
    if((DirectoryName != null) && (DirectoryName != String.Empty)) {
        directoryLabel.Text = DirectoryName;
        DirectoryInfo dir = new DirectoryInfo(DirectoryName);
        foreach(FileSystemInfo fsi in dir.GetFileSystemInfos()) {
            MobileListItem item = new MobileListItem(fsi.Name);
            fileList.Items.Add(item);
        }
    }
}
</script>

<Mobile:Label id="directoryLabel" runat="server" Text="" Font-Bold="true" />
<Mobile:List id="fileList" runat="server" />
```

2. Save the file as `UserControl.ascx` in a test web application directory.

How It Works

The first line of the page establishes this as a user control.

```
<%@ Control Inherits="System.Web.UI.UserControl" Language="cs" %>
```

In a typical ASPX mobile page, we would include a line declaring that the code is extending a page. A page is composed of a set of controls. Here, we are creating a control itself for use within a page, so we include this line. This control is extending the base `UserControl` class. The base control definition is already established, just as the mobile page is already available as part of the Microsoft Mobile Internet Toolkit. We are simply extending the control by defining what features we want it to encapsulate and expose.

Next, we include a register directive so that we can use Mobile Controls in our control.

```
<%@ Register TagPrefix="Mobile" Namespace="System.Web.UI.MobileControls"
Assembly="System.Web.Mobile" %>
```

This makes the word `"mobile"` a tag prefix identifier. Any controls prefixed with mobile will be retrieved from the `System.Web.UI.MobileControls` namespace in the `System.Web.Mobile` assembly.

Next, we give ourselves access to the input and output classes available as part of the base class libraries by importing that namespace.

```
<%@ Import Namespace="System.IO" %>
```

The IO classes are used to gain access to the file system and for reading and writing files. Without it, we would not be able to make our user control list the contents of a directory.

In the script section of the page, we declare a string for the name of the directory the control will list and provide property accessors for it. The accessors allow the `DirectoryName` to be assigned and retrieved programmatically when using the control.

```
private string _directoryName;
public string DirectoryName {
    get {
        return _directoryName;
    }
    set {
        _directoryName = value;
    }
}
```

After the script section of the page, we have placed our declaration of the controls that are part of this user control.

```
<Mobile:Label id= directoryLabel runat="server" Text="" Font-Bold="true" />
<Mobile:List id="fileList" runat="server" />
```

We have included a label and a list. We haven't set any default values for these controls. Instead, we will populate them in code based on the value of the `DirectoryName` property. The control will receive the events we are used to using in a regular mobile page, so we can provide a `Page_Load` method to create the directory listing. We do this so that our control can list any directory. Remember, we want to re-use this in our application and probably don't want to limit ourselves to a hard-coded default. In this example, we want to use that opportunity to set the text for display. We make an assumption that the `DirectoryName` property will be set to something useful and valid since we do not initialize it, its value will be Null. Notice that we first check that the `DirectoryName` property has been set to something.

259

```
protected void Page_Load(object o, EventArgs e) {
    if((DirectoryName != null) && (DirectoryName != String.Empty)) {
        directoryLabel.Text = DirectoryName;
        DirectoryInfo dir = new DirectoryInfo(DirectoryName);
        foreach(FileSystemInfo fsi in dir.GetFileSystemInfos()) {
            MobileListItem item = new MobileListItem(fsi.Name);
            fileList.Items.Add(item);
        }
    }
}
```

The label text is set to the value of the DirectoryName property, and the list is filled with the names of the directory contents by looping through the collection provided by a call to GetFileSystemInfos. The DirectoryInfo object is provided as part of the .NET Framework in the System.IO namespace we made available earlier. We call the GetFileSystemInfos method to get a collection of FileSystemInfo objects. Then, we loop through that collection and add the name of each file to the list for display.

The user control by itself is not very useful. In fact, ASP.NET will return an error message explaining that the file extension is prohibited from being served if we request it from a browser

The user control is designed for use from an ASPX page. The public properties of the control are accessible, and the methods exposed by the control can be called from any ASPX page in which the control is used.

Try It Out – Using A User Control

1. Create an ASPX file with your favorite text editor containing the following:

```
<%@ Page Inherits="System.Web.UI.MobileControls.MobilePage" Language="cs" %>
<%@ Register TagPrefix="Mobile" Namespace="System.Web.UI.MobileControls"
Assembly="System.Web.Mobile" %>
<%@ Register TagPrefix="Sample" TagName="Directory" Src="UserControl.ascx" %>

<script runat="server">
public void Page_Load(object o, EventArgs e) {
    MyControl.DirectoryName = "C:\\Inetpub\\wwwroot";
}
</script>
<Mobile:Form runat="server" Paginate="true" >
<Sample:Directory id="MyControl" runat="server" />
</Mobile:Form>
```

2. Save the file as UserControl.aspx in the same directory where we saved the UserControl.ascx file previously.

3. Request the file using a browser or device simulator, and you should see something similar to this:

How It Works

After the first two lines, where we establish the page as being a Mobile page and register the `Mobile` tag prefix, we register a tag prefix for our user control:

```
<%@ Register TagPrefix="Sample" TagName="Directory" Src="UserControl.ascx" %>
```

The `TagPrefix` is coupled with the `TagName` to identify our associated control declaratively in the page. Our `Register` declaration establishes that controls with the `'Sample'` prefix and `'Directory'` for the tag name correspond to a user control. That user control is contained in the file specified with the `Src` attribute, which we set to `UserControl.ascx` where we already saved our sample user control.

```
<Sample:Directory id="MyControl" runat=" server"/>
```

This marks the point in the ASPX page where the output from the user control will appear in the page rendering. The directory listing is produced by the user control. The directory it lists is the `DirectoryName` property, which we set in the ASPX page during the `Page_Load` method.

```
MyControl.DirectoryName = "C:\\Inetpub\\wwwroot";
```

The user control is compiled on-demand when it is needed. It can contain multiple controls and complex logic. The encapsulation model provides an easy method for re-use across multiple pages, or for simply keeping pieces of a single page compartmentalized. The model leverages what we are already familiar with in the ASPX page and provides for simple development and debugging. Just like with an ASPX page, if we make a typing mistake while writing our user control, ASP.NET can help us to identify the source of the error. When we request the page on the local machine, we will get a description of the compilation problem, and a pointer to where in the ASCX file the error occurs.

User controls provide a convenient means for encapsulating a piece of logic for re-use in multiple pages. They are also convenient for compartmentalizing work. In this example, we could use the basic directory listing in many pages of the application and upgrade it seamlessly. Suppose we wanted to improve the rendering by providing a more complex user control. We could work on a separate control to add context coloring or formatting. We could make all .EXE files listed appear in bold and all .DLL files render in italicized print. Of course this is subject to the device supporting this formatting. Refer to the previous chapter on 'Styling Page Output' for a more detailed discussion. When we were satisfied with the results of the new user control, we could simply replace the existing UserControl.ascx file with the new one, and the application would be upgraded without any additional configuration work.

Custom Controls

The flexibility of writing your own control jumps to another level when developing custom controls. You can simply inherit from an existing control to customize it for a particular application. Authoring custom controls also allows us to create a new control that is composed of multiple existing controls. Beyond this, the mobile controls run-time supports extending the framework further through the use of custom device adapters. This is explained more in the next chapter.

Every mobile control is associated with a set of device adapters that provide the low-level rendering support for that class of devices. In this example, we will duplicate the behavior that was shown in the first example, but using the custom control model for developing a new control. When deploying a user control, the code is placed directly on the web server. If you are placing a web application on a machine and would like to avoid including the code, the custom control offers this capability. Suppose that you are working as an outside consultant on a web application. You would most likely like to provide the functionality without giving away the code. Opting for a custom control over a user control can be particularly useful when you are working on a large project where you want to avoid the likelihood that another developer might modify the code of a user control, resulting in hours of code review to restore functionality. Ultimately, when dealing with complex design requirements, you will probably opt for the custom control in order to deal directly with issues like databinding, viewstate, or concerns of device specific rendering.

Try It Out – Extend A Control

1. Create a CS file with the following code:

```
using System;
using System.IO;
using System.Web.UI;
using System.Web.UI.MobileControls;

namespace Sample {
public class CustomCompositeControlClass : MobileControl, INamingContainer {

    private string _directoryName;
    public string DirectoryName {
        get {
            return _directoryName;
        }
        set {
```

```
            _directoryName = value;
        }
    }

    protected override void OnDataBinding(EventArgs e)
    {
        ClearChildViewState();
        Controls.Clear();
        CreateChildControls();
    }

    protected override void CreateChildControls()
    {
        Label label = new Label();
        label.Text = DirectoryName;
        List list = new List();
        DirectoryInfo dir = new DirectoryInfo(DirectoryName);
        foreach(FileSystemInfo fsi in dir.GetFileSystemInfos())
        {
            MobileListItem item = new MobileListItem(fsi.Name);
            list.Items.Add(item);
        }

        Controls.Add(label);
        Controls.Add(list);

        ChildControlsCreated = true;
    }
}
}
```

2. Save the file as `CustomCompositeControl.cs` in the test web application directory.

3. We now need to compile our control. One of the easiest ways of doing this is to create a batch file. Open your text editor, enter the following code, and save the file as `MakeCustomControl.bat`:

```
set indir=c:\inetpub\wwwroot\mobile\c13code\customcompositecontrol.cs
set outdir=c:\inetpub\wwwroot\bin\customcompositecontrol.dll
set assemblies=System.dll,System.Web.Mobile.dll,System.Web.dll

csc /t:library /out:%outdir% %indir% /r:%assemblies%
```

Note that you'll probably have to change the paths in this file to be applicable to your system, but saving this into a file makes it easy to make changes like that without having to type it all in fresh each time.

csc.exe is the c-sharp compiler, installed as part of the .NET Framework SDK and Visual Studio .NET.

Compile the control by opening up a command prompt window, navigate to the folder with your BAT file, and type `MakeCustomControl`. You should see the following:

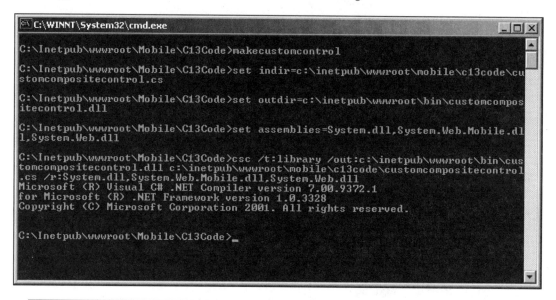

> If you have trouble getting this to run, then one possible point of failure is that your environment variables haven't been configured for command line compilation (as is the default case if you install Visual Studio .NET). To solve this problem, see Appendix A, *Configuring Environment Variables*, for more details.

4. Create a new ASPX file containing the following code:

```
<%@ Page Inherits="System.Web.UI.MobileControls.MobilePage" Language="cs" %>
<%@ Register TagPrefix="Mobile" Namespace="System.Web.UI.MobileControls"
Assembly="System.Web.Mobile" %>
<%@ Register TagPrefix="Sample" Namespace="Sample"
                           Assembly ="CustomCompositeControl" %>

<Mobile:Form runat="server" Paginate="true" >
<Sample:CustomCompositeControlClass id="MyControl" runat="server"
                                  DirectoryName="C:\Inetpub\wwwroot" />
</Mobile:Form>
```

5. Save it as `UseCustomControl.aspx`.

6. Request it using a browser or device simulator, and you should see something similar to this:

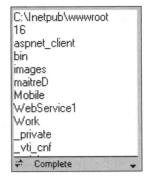

How It Works

The `CustomCompositeControl` extends the `MobileControl` implementation provided as part of the Mobile Internet Toolkit.

```
public class CompositeControl : MobileControl, INamingContainer {
```

We also implement the `INamingContainer` interface. We don't provide explicit code for the `INamingContainer` interface, as it is only used to indicate to ASP.NET that we're creating our own namespace hierarchy in the Page control hierarchy.

As in the previous example, we declare a variable to hold the name of the directory we will list and accessor methods to get and set that value:

```
private string _directoryName;
public string DirectoryName {
    get {
        return _directoryName;
    }
    set {
        _directoryName = value;
    }
}
```

Next, we provide an override of the `OnDataBinding` method to handle databinding of the `DirectoryName` property:

```
protected override void OnDataBinding(EventArgs e)
{
    ClearChildViewState();
    Controls.Clear();
    CreateChildControls();
}
```

The viewstate of our new control tree is cleared to remove existing data when the databinding to a new directory occurs. The collection of children controls is cleared with the `Controls.Clear` method and then re-created with a call to `CreateChildControls`.

In the `CreateChildControls` method we create a new Label control and set its text property to the name of the directory whose contents are being displayed:

```
Label label = new Label();
label.Text = DirectoryName;
```

Next, we create a list control and add items to it for each object in the collection returned by a call to `GetFileSystemInfos`.

```
List list = new List();
DirectoryInfo dir = new DirectoryInfo(DirectoryName);
foreach(FileSystemInfo fsi in dir.GetFileSystemInfos())
{
    MobileListItem item = new MobileListItem(fsi.Name);
    list.Items.Add(item);
}
```

Then, we must add the label and list control to the controls collection. Because we have established our own control tree by using the `INamingContainer` interface, we can add to it and count on the collection of controls being rendered.

```
Controls.Add(label);
Controls.Add(list);
```

Finally, we set the property for `ChildControlsCreated` to `True` to indicate that the control hierarchy has been populated.

```
ChildControlsCreated = true;
```

The fact that we had to pre-compile this code into a dll in the bin directory of the application is a key difference between the custom control and the user control. The user control is compiled on demand while the custom control must be pre-compiled. We have very fine-grained control over the behavior of the custom control. We don't have the opportunity to include controls using the declarative syntax we are used to from the ASPX page. Instead, all decisions about the behavior of our new control are controlled programmatically in the code that we provide and compile ahead of time.

The DLL is loaded from the \bin directory of the application when the page is requested. The correspondence between the **tagname** and the assembly is established in the directive at the beginning of the ASPX page:

```
<%@ Register TagPrefix="Sample" Namespace="Sample"
                             Assembly ="Sample.InheritControl" %>
```

We have just provided a specialization of the mobile list control to give it a specific behavior, again encapsulating the code outside of the ASPX page. Next, we will take a look at what is required to implement a custom control by extending the mobile control base class. We will again develop a control that provides information about a directory listing, but we will provide our own low-level rendering. This is a more complex undertaking that is larger than what it might at first seem. The Mobile Internet Toolkit provides multiple adapters for each control, whose output is customized based on the device capabilities of the particular devices. We'll establish what it takes to create and configure a custom control "from scratch" but you should note that it takes extra effort to test and customize with a wide variety of devices.

Summary

Web application development presents many opportunities for developing your own controls. The need to re-use pieces of presentation and logic across pages or across web applications can be dealt with efficiently by authoring new controls. The user control model allows us to leverage the familiar mechanism of providing declarative tags along with custom methods. They are compiled on-demand and provide easy debugging of compilation problems. The custom control model requires that the code be pre-compiled, but allows us to deploy just the dll containing the assembly instead of the code itself. The custom control is often used to author more complex pieces of code. In this chapter, we discussed and had examples for writing our own controls.

❑   Developing and using a user control

❑   Developing and using a custom control

In the next chapter, we will look at authoring new device adapters.

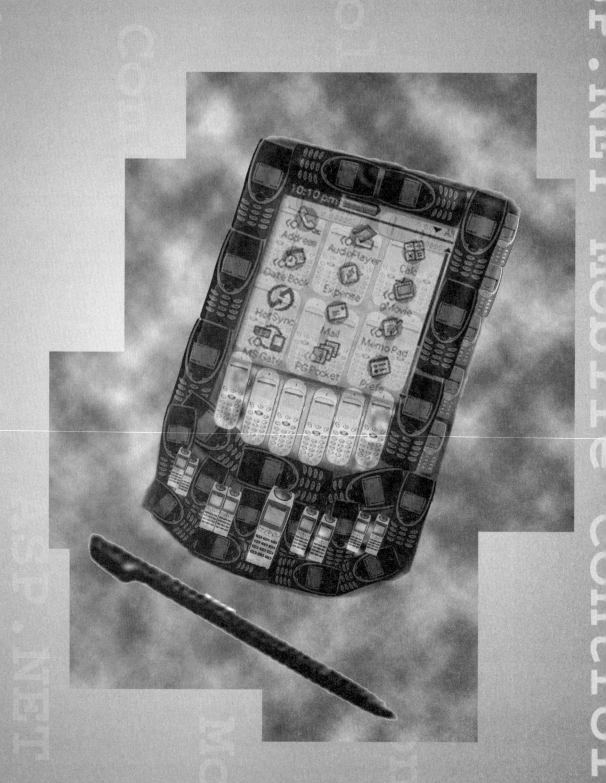

New Device Support

One of the features of the Microsoft Mobile Internet Toolkit is the ability to support new devices. This includes both new devices that do not differ significantly from existing devices, as well as those that offer dramatic new features. When a page is requested, the mobile controls runtime selects a set of device adapters to render output for the device. It does this by examining the HTTP headers sent as part of the request. Even devices that are not communicating directly with HTTP result in these headers being communicated to the device, as the request is proxied by a gateway on their behalf. This is the key to how a single page can render different markup for different devices. Each mobile control has an associated set of objects, called adapters. Each adapter generates a different type of markup. There are actually multiple adapters that generate the same base markup, HTML for example, with fine-grain differences to satisfy the requirements of the device. Some HTML-based mobile browsers do not support client-side script, while others do, so for a single mobile control, the MMIT provides different adapters that generate both. When you'd like the Mobile Internet Toolkit to take advantage of unique capabilities of a new device which are not part of the default configuration, modifying the configuration is a simple way to add support.

The first option for enabling a new device is to add an entry for it to the configuration to use an existing device adapter set. It is certainly not necessary to add new entries for each new device as it becomes available. The mobile controls runtime is configured to recognize the basic capabilities of a device and will render functional markup for it. However, as new devices continue to add capabilities, you may find that you want to fine tune the configuration before updated configuration information is made available either by Microsoft or the device manufacturers. Because this book didn't come with a dramatically improved new device for experimentation, we will modify the configuration for an existing device to get a feel for how this part of the Mobile Internet Tookit works.

The second option is more complicated. It involves providing new adapters for the mobile controls in order to take advantage of new features of the device. As new devices come to market, third parties may supply adapters that provide this extended functionality. Each mobile control must be mapped to a set of device adapters that will render the different markup for it. It is obviously a more involved undertaking to develop a new set of adapters. The Mobile Internet Toolkit comes with code for the device adapters that run as part of the installation. This makes it easier to see how certain behaviors are accomplished should you decide to write your own device adapter.

We can't begin to cover this topic in depth here, but we will walk through an example so that you gain a better understanding for the architecture of the Microsoft Mobile Internet Toolkit and see the steps involved in compiling and configuring a new device adapter. Although it is unlikely that you will immediately begin to write complete device adapter sets for new devices. We leave that to the device manufacturers to help us better utilize the capabilities they are adding. What is more likely is that you will write custom controls and want to control more precisely what is rendered. In this scenario, you could also develop your own device adapters.

We will write a custom control and associated adapters for it. This will give us a useful look into how the architecture of the Mobile Internet Toolkit works and how we can take advantage of it.

In this chapter we will:

❑   Modify the rendering behavior for an existing device through the configuration.

❑   Develop a custom control and control adapters.

❑   Install our custom control adapters into the application configuration.

Configuring a Device

When the MMIT is installed, it adds new entries to the `machine.config` file. By default, this file is installed in \WINNT\Microsoft.NET\Framework_version_\CONFIG. The _version_ portion of the path will correspond to the version of the Framework you have installed. For example, if using the release candidate, given to delegates at the Microsoft PDC 2002, the directory would be v1.0.3328. One of the `system.web` sections in the configuration file is used to define the capabilities of mobile devices. By matching data sent in by the device, the device can be identified, and its capabilities made available to the mobile page. Requests arrive at the web server using the HTTP protocol, which provides for a set of headers that provide information about the request. Although not all mobile devices support HTTP directly, the device will connect to the network through a provider gateway that will make the HTTP request on behalf of the phone and include the appropriate headers. The browsers send a wide variety of information about their capabilities in the HTTP headers. The configuration section where these headers are matched and capabilities about the device are determined is called the `browserCaps` section (short for browser capabilities) and begins with the following:

```
<system.web>
  <browserCaps>
    <result type="System.Web.Mobile.MobileCapabilities, System.Web.Mobile,
    Version=1.0.3300.0, Culture=neutral, PublicKeyToken=b03f5f7f11d50a3a"/>
```

The `browserCaps` section defines the result type that will be populated for the executing page as a `MobileCapabilities` object. The result type is the type of the capabilities object that will be created by matching the sections contained within the `browserCaps` section. It also specifies that the definition of the `MobileCapabilities` object is in the `System.Web.Mobile` assembly. Immediately following this is a set of default values. These values are then overridden when filters match data sent by the mobile device. Filters check a particular piece of header information to ascertain specific capabilities about the requesting device. The filters are contained within use sections. The `use` section identifies what information is being matched against the filters. For example, the defaults are contained within the use section for the user agent string.

```
<use var="HTTP_USER_AGENT" />
```

If no filters match, then none of the default values will be overridden. Therefore, the defaults would be used as the base when determining what type of rendering to provide for an unknown device. These are specifically selected to provide the most widely useful rendering. They target a fairly simple HTML-based browser without support for client-side script or color. Notice that the default values are selected to be a best guess at a generic mobile form factor with values that make it easy to tell if a particular entry has not been overridden.

```
<!-- Default values -->
mobileDeviceManufacturer = "Unknown"
mobileDeviceModel = "Unknown"
gatewayVersion = "None"
gatewayMajorVersion = "0"
gatewayMinorVersion = "0"
preferredRenderingType = "html32"
preferredRenderingMime = "text/html"
preferredImageMime = "image/gif"
```

At present, new devices are hitting the market with great frequency. Many of these new devices do not offer dramatically different feature sets and provide no need to be concerned with developing or installing new device adapters.

In this example, we will create a mobile page which sets some style preferences, which we know are supported on the desktop browser. We will then modify the configuration and view the change in the output. This will demonstrate that the configuration can control the behavior of the adapters to produce markup that corresponds to the reported capabilities of the requesting device. Although in practice we wouldn't typically change the configuration for an existing device, we would add a specialization to recognize a new set of devices in order to specify increasing client capabilities.

Try It Out – Modify Device Configuration

1. Create a new ASPX file with the following:

```
<%@ Page Inherits="System.Web.UI.MobileControls.MobilePage" Language="cs" %>
<%@ Register TagPrefix="Mobile" Namespace="System.Web.UI.MobileControls"
Assembly="System.Web.Mobile" %>

<Mobile:Form runat="server">
  <Mobile:Label runat="server"
    Text="Mobile Internet Toolkit"
    Font-Size="Large"
    Font-Bold="true"
    Font-Italic="true" />
</Mobile:Form>
```

2. Save the file as ModifiedDevice.aspx in your test application directory.

3. Request the file using your desktop browser. What you will see will be the page rendered using the default configuration for this device. We will then modify the configuration that is used for the desktop browser and observe that the rendering changes. We will not change the page itself.

4. Open the `machine.config` file in a text editor. The `machine.config` file is typically found in the Framework configuration directory `\WINNT\Microsoft.NET\Framework\_version_\Config`. (The _version_ portion of the path will correspond to the version or the Common Language Runtime you have installed. For the release candidate, that was v1.0.3328.) I recommend making a backup copy of your `machine.config` so that if you can't easily locate a change that was made to undo it, you can always replace the file with the original. Search for the following entry:

`supportsBold= "true"` – It should be included in a section that looks like this:

```
<filter>
  <case
    match="Mozilla/(?'major'\d+)">
    <filter>
      <case
        match="[^0-3]"
        with="${major}">
        supportsCss = "true"
        supportsImageSubmit = "true"
        supportsBold = "true"
        supportsItalic = "true"
        supportsFontSize = "true"
        supportsFontName = "true"
        supportsFontColor = "true"
        supportsBodyColor = "true"
```

```
                supportsDivAlign = "true"
                supportsDivNoWrap = "true"
            </case>
        </filter>
    </case>
</filter>
```

5. Change the entries for `supportsBold`, `supportsItalic`, and `supportsFontSize` from `true` to `false` and save the file. Now request the file again and notice the change in output:

How It Works

The `ModifiedDevice.aspx` file contains a label where we indicate that the rendering should take advantage of bold, large italicized font on devices where it is supported.

```
<Mobile:Label runat="server"
    Text="Mobile Internet Toolkit"
    Font-Size="Large"
    Font-Bold="true"
    Font-Italic="true" />
```

Before we modify the configuration, the HTML adapter renders markup that includes markup for the styles we specified. We then modify the configuration to indicate that the device doesn't support `Bold`, `Italicized` or `Font-Size` markup.

```
        supportsBold = "false"
        supportsItalic = "false"
        supportsFontSize = "false"
```

The filter section that we are modifying is checking the User-Agent header and matching Mozilla compatible versions of the browser. The vast majority of desktop browsers use this convention and report themselves as Mozilla compatible. After we change the configuration, when we make a subsequent request with the same device, the mobile controls runtime informs the adapter that the device no longer possesses these capabilities. Therefore, it renders no tags for our style settings.

Request Headers

As we can see from the previous chapter 15 "example", the device configuration information is easily accessible. We can simply match the unique device information sent as part of the request and set the browser capabilities appropriately. To view a listing of the headers sent by a device, create an ASPX page called RequestHeaders.aspx with the following code, and save it in your test directory:

```cs
<%@ Page Inherits="System.Web.UI.MobileControls.MobilePage" Language="cs" %>
<%@ Register TagPrefix="Mobile" Namespace="System.Web.UI.MobileControls"
Assembly="System.Web.Mobile" %>

<script runat="server" language="cs">
  protected void Page_Load(object o, EventArgs e)
  {
    string allHeaders = Request.ServerVariables["ALL_RAW"];
    string[] headers = allHeaders.Split(new Char[] {'\r'});
    foreach(string header in headers)
    {
        MobileListItem item = new MobileListItem(header);
        headersList.Items.Add(item);
    }
  }
</script>

<Mobile:Form runat="server">
  <Mobile:List runat="server" id="headersList" />
</Mobile:Form>
```

This page gets the header values from the Request.ServerVariables collection. It splits them up into separate lines as they were sent by the browser and added to the list of our mobile page. It is worthwhile to spend a few minutes requesting this page from a few mobile devices or device simulators to get a better feeling for the wide array of headers that are sent to indicate unique characteristics and capabilities of the mobile devices.

Many new devices will be recognized by the default configuration without needing to make any changes. The headers sent by new devices may already be recognized and the device and browser capabilities set to appropriate values. If you want to add support for a new device that sends a set of headers that are not currently recognized, you can add another filter section like the one that you just modified and set the capabilities. Although many of the headers sent by different devices are identical, there is, typically, something in the user-agent string that differentiates it from other similar devices.

Note that the default browser capability settings are for an html-based device without support for tables, frames, cookies, or client-side script.

When configuring a new device, locate the section for a device similar to the new one, and add a specialization for the capabilities that differ from the defaults. You don't need to worry about new devices coming to market – the mobile controls runtime will generally recognize the general requirements of markup that needs to be produced. The more likely scenario for wanting to modify the configuration is when a particular capability that you want to customize for is not registering. This may happen when producing an application targeting a user group that is standardizing on a particular device, giving you the opportunity to provide device specific customizations and work on producing even richer output on that device.

You will also notice that the configuration sections inherit the settings in a hierarchical fashion. A filter section may match one of the headers and then add another filter within that to check another header in order to make a further specialization. This is common for different versions of browsers from a single manufacturer. For example, suppose that one manufacturer sells two models of the same phone, one that is color, and one that is not. Although the user-agent string may be the same for both types of device, the filter that recognizes that user-agent string would probably contain an additional filter to check for a separate header to find out if the device supports color. All other things being the same in the two devices, they can share a common piece of configuration. There's no need to duplicate all of that configuration section when adding a small addition to a single section will determine which of the two types of that model is making a request.

Custom Control Adapters

There are several reasons why you might want to write your own control adapter. The first is that you want to create a custom control and provide rendering that's even more customized than what's available through specialization of an existing control, or through providing a composite control.

> **For more discussion on developing new controls, see Chapter 13 on *Writing Controls***

A new control can be configured to use custom device adapters, essentially extending the installed adapter sets to include support for the new control. For example, suppose you wanted to make use of a markup tag or attribute that isn't rendered by the existing controls, like the ability to make text blink in browsers that support it. Should you really want that kind of markup to be produced, you would need to provide your own control adapter. You would probably want to provide a new custom control for this instead of changing the behavior of existing controls, unless you wanted to make all of the text from label controls blink, which wouldn't make you all that popular with your customers.

Another reason to develop custom control adapters is to provide a new adapter set that provides rendering for the existing set of mobile controls. Suppose that a new mobile device were introduced with improved support for formatting and layout through the use of cascading stylesheets. If you wanted your existing web pages to take advantage of this new capability you would need to install a set of device adapters that would render markup with cascading stylesheets for the existing mobile controls.

In this example, we will provide an implementation of the directory listing sample used in the previous chapter on writing controls. In it, we created a control to list the contents of a directory. Here, we will do the same, but we will customize the behavior of the control depending on what type of markup we are generating. Suppose that we have been using our custom control to provide directory listings but have found that on WML-based devices, the listings are too long. Instead of providing the list, we want to provide just the name of the directory and a count of the number of files. For HTML-based devices, we still want to display the directory contents.

> **Note that we could accomplish this same result through the use of device specific rendering, which is discussed in Chapter 12.**

This example serves to demonstrate another method for providing customized output and extending the capabilities of the mobile internet toolkit. In practice, you wouldn't be likely to take on this extra complication unless you really needed output that was difficult to achieve with the existing controls, or you wanted to use markup not generated by the controls if adapters for that markup were not yet available from another party.

Try It Out – Custom Control Adapters

1. Create a CS file with your favorite editor containing the following code:

```
using System;
using System.Web.UI.MobileControls;
```

```csharp
using System.Web.UI.MobileControls.Adapters;
using System.IO;

namespace Sample
{
  public class DirectoryList : MobileControl
  {
    private string _directoryName;
    private DirectoryInfo _dirInfo;
    public string DirectoryName
    {
      get
      {
        return _directoryName;
      }
      set
      {
        _directoryName = value;
        _dirInfo = new DirectoryInfo(_directoryName);
      }
    }
    public DirectoryInfo DirectoryInfo
    {
      get
      {
        return _dirInfo;
      }
    }
  }

  public class HtmlDirectoryListAdapter : HtmlControlAdapter
  {
    public override void Render(HtmlMobileTextWriter writer)
    {
      writer.EnterStyle(this.Style);
      writer.Write(Control.DirectoryName);
      writer.WriteBreak();
      writer.ExitStyle(this.Style, false);
      foreach(FileSystemInfo fsi in
                      Control.DirectoryInfo.GetFileSystemInfos())
      {
        writer.Write(fsi.Name);
        writer.WriteBreak();
      }
    }

    protected new DirectoryList Control
    {
      get
      {
        return (DirectoryList)base.Control;
      }
```

```
        }
    }

    public class WmlDirectoryListAdapter : WmlControlAdapter
    {
        public override void Render(WmlMobileTextWriter writer)
        {
            writer.RenderText(Control.DirectoryName, true);
            writer.RenderText(Control.DirectoryInfo.GetFiles().Length.ToString() +
                                            " items", true);
        }

        protected new DirectoryList Control
        {
            get
            {
                return (DirectoryList)base.Control;
            }
        }
    }
} //end of sample namespace
```

2. Save the file as `DirectoryList.cs` in your test web application directory.

Open a command prompt and change to your test application directory. Compile the `DirectoryList.cs` file by typing the following command into the command prompt:

```
csc /out:bin\Sample.DirectoryList.dll /t:library
 /r:System.dll,System.Web.Mobile.dll DirectoryList.cs
```

To allow for debugging, add the debug flag and define trace and debug variables.

```
csc /debug+ /d:"TRACE,DEBUG" /out:bin\Sample.DirectoryList.dll /t:library
 /r:System.dll,System.Web.Mobile.dll DirectoryList.cs
```

When the compilation is successful, the bin subdirectory of your application directory will contain a file called `Sample.DirectoryList.dll`.

3. In that same directory, create a `web.config` file with the following code in it:

```
<configuration>
<system.web>
 <mobileControls>
  <device name="HtmlDeviceAdaptersCustom" inheritsFrom="HtmlDeviceAdapters">
   <control name="Sample.DirectoryList, Sample.DirectoryList"
         adapter="Sample.HtmlDirectoryListAdapter,Sample.DirectoryList" />
  </device>
  <device name="ChtmlDeviceAdaptersCustom"
                                     inheritsFrom="ChtmlDeviceAdapters">
```

```
      <control name="Sample.DirectoryList, Sample.DirectoryList"
              adapter="Sample.HtmlDirectoryListAdapter,Sample.DirectoryList" />
    </device>
    <device name="WmlDeviceAdaptersCustom" inheritsFrom="WmlDeviceAdapters">
      <control name="Sample.DirectoryList, Sample.DirectoryList"
              adapter="Sample.WmlDirectoryListAdapter,Sample.DirectoryList" />
    </device>
    <device name="UpWmlDeviceAdaptersCustom"
                                        inheritsFrom="UpWmlDeviceAdapters">
      <control name="Sample.DirectoryList, Sample.DirectoryList"
              adapter="Sample.WmlDirectoryListAdapter,Sample.DirectoryList" />
    </device>
  </mobileControls>
 </system.web>
</configuration>
```

4. Create an ASPX file called `DirectoryList.aspx` in your application directory, and enter the following code:

```
<%@ Page Inherits="System.Web.UI.MobileControls.MobilePage" Language="cs" %>
        <%@ Register TagPrefix="Mobile" Namespace="System.Web.UI.MobileControls"
                                        Assembly="System.Web.Mobile" %>
<%@ Register TagPrefix="Sample" Namespace="Sample" Assembly="Sample.DirectoryList"
%>
<Mobile:Form runat=server>
  <Sample:DirectoryList runat="server" DirectoryName="C:\Inetpub\wwwroot" Font-
Bold="true" />
  </Mobile:Form>
```

5. Request the `DirectoryList.aspx` in both an HTML-based and a WML-based browser or device simulator to view the differences.

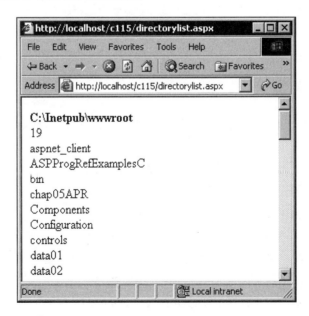

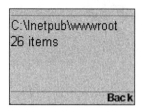

How It Works

The `DirectoryList.cs` file contains the code for our custom control and the device adapters for it. The `DirectoryList` control inherits directly from the `MobileControl` base class.

```
public class DirectoryList : MobileControl
{
```

The control specializes the `MobileControl` base class implementation only by adding two properties: a string for the `DirectoryName`, and a `DirectoryInfo` that retrieves the `DirectoryInfo` object for that directory.

```
public string DirectoryName
{
  get
  {
    return _directoryName;
  }
  set
  {
    _directoryName = value;
    _dirInfo = new DirectoryInfo(_directoryName);
  }
}

public DirectoryInfo DirectoryInfo
{
  get
  {
    return _dirInfo;
  }
}
```

When the `DirectoryName` is set, the `DirectoryInfo` object is created so that it's up to date and ready to be retrieved using the `get` property accessor. The `DirectoryInfo` object is accessed through the `System.IO` classes which provide support for working with the file system. All of the other behaviors of our new mobile control rely on the underlying `MobileControl` base class.

The new markup we want to provide is handled by our new adapter classes. We provide two adapters, one that produces HTML, and one that produces WML. They inherit from the `HtmlControlAdapter` and `WmlControlAdapter` respectively.

```
public class HtmlDirectoryListAdapter : HtmlControlAdapter {
public class WmlDirectoryListAdapter : WmlControlAdapter {
```

Both of these classes provide a `get` accessor which casts the base control for which they are doing the rendering as a `DirectoryList` object. This makes the assumption that the only control that will be configured to use the new adapters will be of the `DirectoryList` type.

```
protected new DirectoryList Control {
  get
  {
    return (DirectoryList)base.Control;
  }
}
```

We are safe to do this, since we are providing that configuration information in the `web.config`.

This allows us to use the `Control` property to access the `DirectoryName` and `DirectoryInfo` object of the `DirectoryList` control for which we are doing the rendering. The central piece of our new adapters is the overrides of the `Render` method. Here, we use the methods exposed by the writer object that is passed into the adapter. The writer we passed into our HTML-based adapter is an `HtmlMobileTextWriter` and the WML-based adapter receives a `WmlMobileTextWriter`. These writers have very similar behaviors, but are customized to generate the appropriate markup.

First, we'll look at the `Render` method of our `HtmlDirectoryListAdapter`. For the HTML output, we first write the name of the directory, using the styles specified in the ASPX page. We use that style by calling `EnterStyle` before we pass the `DirectoryName` to the Write method and `ExitStyle` after we are through with it. The second parameter to `ExitStyle` is a boolean indicating that we want a break after the directory name. Then, we loop through the contents of the directory and write out the name for each `FileSystemInfo` object in the collection returned by calling `GetFileSystemInfos` on the `DirectoryInfo` object. This lists just the files in that directory, not any directories it contains.

```
public override void Render(HtmlMobileTextWriter writer)
{
  writer.EnterStyle(this.Style);
  writer.Write(Control.DirectoryName),
  writer.ExitStyle(this.Style, false);
  foreach(FileSystemInfo fsi in
                        Control.DirectoryInfo.GetFileSystemInfos())
  {
      writer.Write(fsi.Name);
      writer.WriteBreak();
  }
}
```

For WML, the goal of our custom adapter was to minimize the amount of output, so we simply write the directory name and the number of files it contains. The second parameter to the `RenderText` method is a boolean indicating whether or not a break should be rendered after the text.

```
public override void Render(WmlMobileTextWriter writer)
{
  writer.RenderText(Control.DirectoryName, true);
  writer.RenderText(Control.DirectoryInfo.GetFiles().Length.ToString() +
                                        " items", true);
}
```

As we've already discussed, even simple custom adapters require more work. We haven't discussed yet how the page makes use of the custom control or how we configure the application to use the custom adapters being provided. First, we'll look at how the page uses our custom control. The page establishes a correspondence between the "Sample" tag prefix and our compiled assembly which was compiled into the bin subdirectory of our test web application:

```
<%@ Register TagPrefix="Sample" Namespace="Sample" Assembly="Sample.DirectoryList"
%>
```

When we include a tag with the `Sample` prefix, the assembly is searched for a control with a name corresponding to the tag suffix.

```
<Sample:DirectoryList runat="server" DirectoryName="C:\Inetput\wwwroot" Font-
Bold="true" />
```

The `DirectoryName` is set as an attribute in the control declaration making use of the set property accessor we provided as part of the `DirectoryList` control.

The final piece of the puzzle in this example is how the page requests map the rendering of our custom control, to our render control adapter implementations. We only provided HTML and WML renderings, but the Microsoft Mobile Internet Toolkit has more adapters to provide more granular adaptations. The `web.config` file includes these classes of adapters and maps them to our best fitting implementation. We declare a name for the device adapter and specify which adapter it extends. Inside the device tag, we list our controls and specify which adapter type will be used to provide the low-level rendering:

```
<device name="HtmlDeviceAdaptersCustom" inheritsFrom="HtmlDeviceAdapters">
   <control name="Sample.DirectoryList, Sample.DirectoryList"
       adapter="Sample.HtmlDirectoryListAdapter,Sample.DirectoryList" />
</device>
```

As you can see, there are several areas that must be brought together to make use of a custom device adapter. This example gives you a taste of what work is involved. The sample adapter code provided with the MMIT goes much further to demonstrate the complexities of authoring a new device adapter set. The more common scenario for the individual developer is to customize an existing adapter to obtain an application-specific behavior, or to take advantage of specific feature enhancements of new devices.

Summary

In this chapter, we have looked at how to modify the mobile web application configuration to accommodate new mobile devices. Most new devices will not require any intervention, rather the headers sent in a request from that device will map them correctly to a good fit to produce content adapter for their capabilities. The markup produced by the mobile controls run-time may not take advantage of the newest features introduced by the device manufacturer.

In this chapter we have:

❑ Modified the rendering behavior for an existing device through the configuration.

❑ Developed a custom control and control adapters.

❑ Installed our custom control adapters into the application configuration.

We also examined what is involved in producing custom adapters to take advantage of specific device features. This approach also improves our flexibility in authoring custom controls by allowing us to directly control the control adapter rendering. Additionally, new markup languages can be supported by providing new adapter sets for the existing mobile controls.

These two approaches for supporting new devices are very different, ranging from the very simply approach of modifying the configuration files to the much more involved method of providing code to generate markup that is incorporated into the mobile controls run-time. You may find that little is required for your mobile web applications to support new devices as they come into the mainstream. It is nice to understand how these features of the Microsoft Mobile Internet Toolkit enable adapting to the changing world of mobile devices.

It is a key concept, when we consider the range of possibilities available to extend the MMIT, that the fundamental principle lies in being able to centralize web development for a broad range of devices. The support is far-reaching which allows us to focus our efforts on the web application itself. We can write custom controls and custom device adapters to better utilize the capabilities of specific devices and device classes. As the mobile market continues to evolve, there will inevitably be changes in the types of markup supported in the devices. The open and extensible nature of the Mobile Internet Toolkit makes it possible to continue adding support so that the applications we write continue working for the end user, on whatever mobile device they may be using.

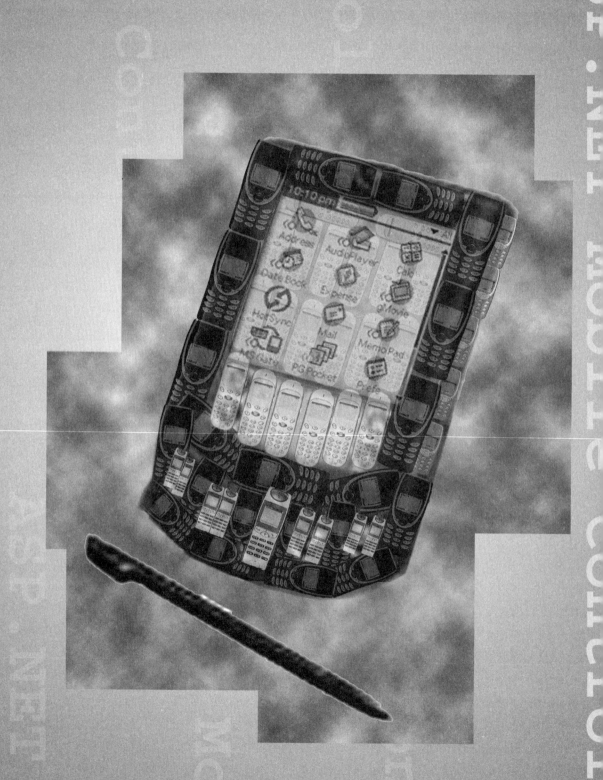

Web Services

This chapter is meant to serve as a quick refresher of your knowledge of Web Services, and to show how you can consume a Web Service from a Mobile Web Form, it is not meant to be a comprehensive introduction.

> **For a more in-depth look at Web Services, you may want to read** *Professional ASP.NET Web Services* **by Wrox Press, ISBN 1-861005-45-8.**

By the end of this chapter you will have the knowledge you need to build a basic Web Service and consume it from a mobile Web Form. We'll also be introducing Microsoft's idea of **Smart Devices**.

It is interesting to note that the paradigm by which Web Services work is not a new one – people have been accessing business logic over the Internet for years now. This has primarily been achieved through the use of either DCOM or CORBA, neither of which was ideally suited to the task. Both were fiddly to use, DCOM was proprietary, and CORBA implementations unique to each vendor (read incompatible with versions from other vendors).

Web Services Refresher

Using the aforementioned technologies it became obvious that what we needed was a universal way to access programmatic logic across the Internet. This needed to be done without the developer having to worry about the complexities of the remote logic implementation, such as the language it was written in, and with a relatively shallow learning curve. Part of the dream was also to eliminate some of the client dependencies that were incurred when using DCOM or CORBA. We finally got this when the .NET Framework shipped with Web Services bundled as part of ASP.NET.

Web Services make using remote objects as easy as using local ones. The Framework provides tools to help bridge the gap between the client application and the Web Service server, by creating proxy classes for the client application to use when accessing the Web Service. The .NET Framework also takes care of generating the WSDL (Web Service Description Language) for the Web Service.

All of the communication between the Web Service and the client application is done using the Web's lowest common denominator of HTTP. Whether you are sending parameters to the Web Service using HTTP POST or HTTP GET, or sending SOAP (Simple Object Access Protocol) packets, the Web Service is universally accessible:

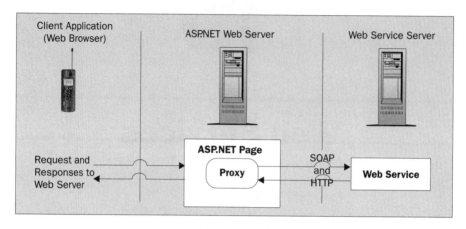

SOAP is the result of combining HTTP and XML for use as a means to transport data across the Internet (though there are other protocols that SOAP can be used with). SOAP uses HTTP POST or the HTTP extension framework (M-POST) to send method names and parameters across the Internet to invoke the remote objects that Web Services expose.

> **There are no special steps that the developer needs to take in order for the Web Service to handle the different invocation protocols (POST, GET, SOAP); the .NET Framework will handle this for you.**

Technically speaking, Web Services are programmable business logic that can be accessed using standard web protocols (they can be accessed by any system that supports XML, which these days is pretty much all of them). This definition, while comprehensive, is a little obscure. Another way to conceptualize this is to think of Web Services as providing an interface to the Internet for applications, in the same way that browsers provide an interface to the Internet for humans. This approach allows one application to act as a dedicated interface while another, across the Internet, does the hard work of processing the business logic. Not only does this allow us to make use of distributed application logic, but it also allows us to distribute processor load and even make performance gains by having each part of an application handle its own load by distributing the application on separate pieces of hardware. All of this has the potential to increase both the ease with which we can create applications, and also the ease with which we can make them available to others.

Now we've said all this, let's go ahead and build a simple Web Service, so we can look at how we go about consuming it from a Mobile Web Form:

Try It Out – Building And Consuming A Web Service

This example is in two parts. This first part deals with creating a simple Web Service that takes two integers and returns the sum. It will be consumed by a mobile Web Form in the second example.

1. Open your text editor and enter the following C# code, which will form the basis of your Web Service:

```
<%@ WebService Language="C#" Class="WroxWebServiceExample" %>
using System;
using System.Web.Services;

public class WroxWebServiceExample : WebService {

  [WebMethod] public int Add(int a, int b) {
    return a + b;
  }
}
```

2. Save this as `WroxWebServiceExample.asmx` in a virtual directory, configured as an application.

3. Go to the command prompt, and navigate across the file system to the virtual directory where your ASMX file resides.

4. Enter the following command and hit *Enter*:

```
wsdl http://localhost/WroxWebServiceExample.asmx?WSDL
```

You should see the following:

Be sure to adjust the path you enter here to correspond to the virtual directory you're using, if necessary.

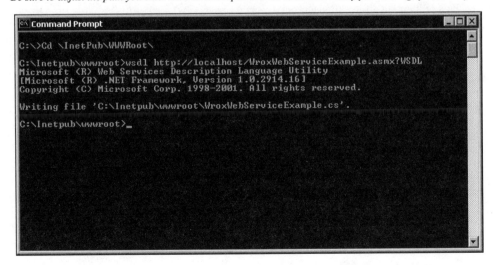

287

This action creates the **proxy source file** for your Web Service. **The file is created in the same directory that you have run the tool from.**

If wsdl.exe does not run, your machine probably doesn't recognize its path, in which case you may need to add it to the path statement in your environment variables. You can find it C:\Program Files\Microsoft.NET\FrameworkSDK\bin – see Appendix A for information on how to add information to the path statement in your environment variables.

5. Next, you need to compile your proxy code. At the command prompt, in the directory where your C# file resides, type the following and hit *Enter*:

```
csc /t:library /out:WroxWebServiceExample.dll WroxWebServiceExample.cs
```

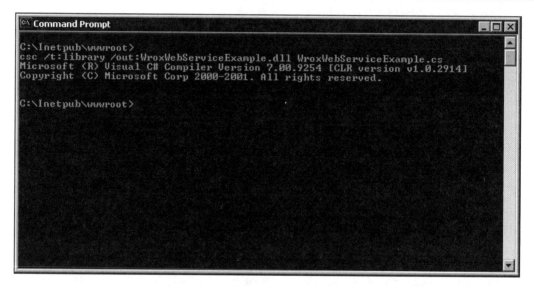

This will create a file called WroxWebServiceExample.dll in the same directory as the sourcecode that produced it.

If you have trouble running this, you may need to configure your environment variables – see Appendix A for details.

6. Place the newly created DLL within a \bin directory in your main virtual directory.

This concludes the creation of the Web Service, next we will create the Mobile Web Form client to consume it.

7. Enter the following code in a new file:

```
<%@ Page Inherits="System.Web.UI.MobileControls.MobilePage" Language="C#"%>
<%@Register TagPrefix="mobile" Namespace="System.Web.UI.MobileControls"
                              Assembly="System.Web.Mobile" %>
<script runat=server>
int a = 0;
```

```
int b = 0;

public void Command1_Click(object s, EventArgs e )
{
  string RetVal;
//variable to hold the value returned from the Web Service

  a = Int32.Parse(TextBox1.Text);
//variable that will have the value from TextBox1.
//This will be passed to the Web Service

  b = Int32.Parse(TextBox2.Text);
//variable that will have the value from TextBox2.
//This will be passed to the Web Service

  WroxWebServiceExample TestService = new WroxWebServiceExample();
  //Create instance of client proxy

  RetVal = TestService.Add(a, b).ToString();
//call method Add() from the instance of the client proxy

  TextResult.Text = RetVal;
//Set the Text property of TextResult in Form2
  ActiveForm = Form2;
//make Form2 the ActiveForm.  This is what the user will see.

}
</script>

<Mobile:Form id=Form1 runat=server>
  First Number
  <Mobile:textbox id=TextBox1 runat=server />
  Second Number
  <Mobile:textbox id=TextBox2 runat=server />
  <Mobile:Command id=Command1 onClick=Command1_Click Text=Submit
  runat=server />
</Mobile:Form>
<Mobile:Form id=Form2 runat=server>
  The sum is:
  <Mobile:TextBox id=TextResult runat=server />
</Mobile:Form>
```

8. Save this file as WroxWebServiceExample.aspx in your virtual directory.

9. Browse to this ASPX file in your emulator. It should look something like this:

10. Enter some values into the textboxes, in our example we've chosen 1 and 2:

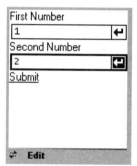

11. Submit the form (on some devices this may be in an **Options** menu):

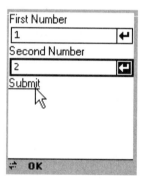

12. Your answer will be displayed to you on a new page:

How It Works

The scope of this book does not allow for comprehensive coverage of Web Services and the command line tools that we use to create them, so we will just deal with the rudimentary aspects of the tools we've used to create this example.

> Note that unlike ASP.NET Web Forms, Mobile ASP.NET Web Forms *cannot* be exposed as a Web Service.

We'll work through all the elements that go into creating and consuming a Web Service in turn:

The Web Service

The first file we created was `WroxWebServiceExample.asmx`, and this is where we put the logic for our Web Service:

Firstly we have the `WebService` directive. The syntax for this is the same as for standard ASP.NET pages. It contains a single directive, which may have multiple attributes, and is declared within `<%@ %>` tags. In the case of our example we use it to declare our language preference as C#, and to name our class, `WroxWebServiceExample` (both, incidentally, are required attributes of the `WebService` directive):

```
<%@ WebService Language="C#" Class="WroxWebServiceExample" %>
```

Next we import the base classes that we need to build a Web Service:

```
using System;
using System.Web.Services;
```

Now we define the class that we will be using as a Web Service. It needs to be made `public` in order to be accessible from outside. The class inherits `System.Web.Services` directly:

```
public class WroxWebServiceExample : WebService {
```

Next, we create the `method` that will be exposed for remote clients to implement. Coding a `method` to be exposed from a Web Service is exactly the same as coding a regular `public method`, with the exception that a `[WebMethod]` attribute is added at the beginning of the line. This tells the compiler that the method will be called over the Web:

```
[WebMethod] public int Add(int a, int b) {
    return a + b;
}
```

As a quick aside, one of the really cool things about .NET is some of the enhancements that have been made to the debugging and testing experience, and Web Services are no exception to this. If you navigate your web browser directly to your ASMX file you will receive a page that summarizes all of the `methods` the file exposes. You will also be able to both invoke them (by clicking their hyperlink and then entering your test values) and view their WSDL (by clicking the **Service Description** hyperlink). Here's what this page looks like for our Web Service:

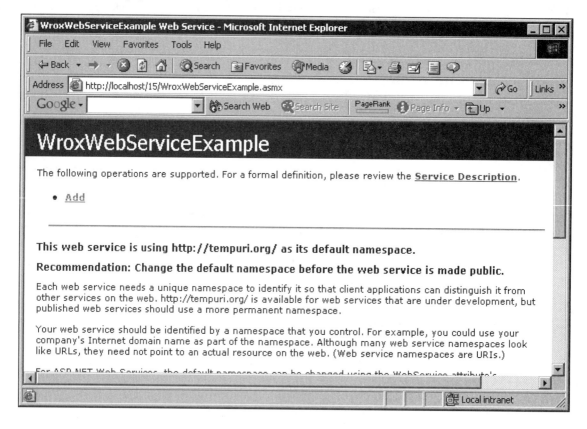

The Client Proxy Class

Now that we've coded our Web Service, and seen how to test it. We need to consume it from a Mobile Web Form. For that we will need to build a **proxy class** that will broker the dealings between our Mobile Web Form code and the server containing our Web Service code. We've done this using a command-line tool called wsdl.exe. We ran this tool from the command-line passing in the URL of the Web Service that we needed a proxy class for:

```
wsdl http://localhost/WroxWebServiceExample.asmx?WSDL
```

By appending the ?WSDL argument to the URL, we caused the Web Service to return it's WSDL, which the tool then used to create the proxy class for our client to use.The tool then output a called WroxWebServiceExample.cs file into the same directory that we were working from.

This C# file is then compiled by issuing the following command line entry:

```
csc /t:library /out:WroxWebServiceExample.dll WroxWebServiceExample.cs
```

The /t: switch tells the compiler to expect to build a DLL file. The /out: switch gives the full name of the file that the compiler should produce, and the final argument is the source file to build from.

After compiling, the file WroxWebServiceExample.dll will appear in the same directory as your source code. We then moved this into the \bin directory of your virtual application, so ASP.NET can find it when the client tries to instantiate it.

The Mobile Web Form Client

Finally, we created the Mobile Web Form that was to consume the Web Service. You will remember that there was nothing unusual about the code that the page was comprised of, it was just standard ASP.NET fare. The reason for this is that Web Services have been specifically designed so that developers can use them with the same ease as they would any other object. Looking at the script block of our page, we can see that this is, indeed, the case:

```
<script runat=server>
int a = 0;
int b = 0;
public void Command1_Click(object s, EventArgs e )
{
    string RetVal;
    a = Int32.Parse(TextBox1.Text);
    b = Int32.Parse(TextBox2.Text);
    WroxWebServiceExample TestService = new WroxWebServiceExample();
    RetVal = TestService.Add(a, b).ToString();
    TextResult.Text = RetVal;
    ActiveForm = Form2;
}
</script>
```

We simply create an instance of the proxy class and call our methods through it (this is highlighted in gray). When ASP.NET is told that we want an instance of this object, it looks in the application's \bin directory for the library that contains it.

The remainder of the ASPX file is very similar to the others shown throughout this book, and does not warrant further discussion. However, one question that may arise is this: What happens if the Web Service is not on the same box as the client, how do I handle it then? The key to this is to think back to when we were using the wsdl tool to generate the source file for the proxy. We issued a command that looked like this:

```
wsdl http://localhost/WroxWebServiceExample.asmx?WSDL
```

To consume Web Services on other servers, simply enter the URL where they lie. For example, to create a proxy for a mythical Web Service called StockTicker on the web server at www.wrox.com, we would issue this command:

```
wsdl http://www.wrox.com/StockTicker.asmx?WSDL
```

This would produce sourcecode capable of handling communication between our web server, and the web server where the Web Service resides.

Smart Devices

Microsoft's vision for Web Services technology is a key part of what they have termed **Smart Devices**. A Smart Device is anything from a desktop workstation to a handheld PDA, a game console, cell-phone, or laptop that keeps track of your personal data to provide you with a more personalized Internet experience. In the future, this could be taken a step further to include appliances in the home or the environment in your car. Personally, I can envisage a time when it will be common to have sensors on the body that will cause our cars to set our favorite radio station, the preferred temperature (for that time of year), seat position, mirrors, and maybe even fumigate with a fragrance when we get in! Perhaps a little further in the future the car could access a Web Service at the mechanic's shop to schedule maintenance, and send you a confirmation e-mail (of course you would have to provide strict parameters to the program so as to not conflict with your normal schedule).

A Smart Device is also aware of the environment that it lives in. It can sense when there may be bandwidth limitations and intelligently adjust the amount and type of information that it handles, while at the same time keeping you connected to any data that you need, from anywhere. They are also mutually aware of other devices that enter and depart their network.

Currently Microsoft is working on two embedded operating systems that Smart Devices will put to great use. They are **Talisker** and **Windows XP Embedded**. Talisker builds upon the components from the Windows CE kernel to create an OS that will be used to program things such as industrial automation or controlling a ship's steering system. Windows XP Embedded is the successor to Windows NT 4.0 Embedded, and is, in Microsoft's own words, "*based on the same binaries as Windows XP Professional*", so we can expect to have quite a bit of power at our disposal when using it. Windows XP Embedded is designed to be able to selectively install only those components that are needed, which will greatly aid in maintaining the low memory footprint that mobile devices demand and the kind of response that real-time systems need.

Clearly Microsoft is taking mobile and embedded computing very seriously and devoting serious resources to making sure that the company is a main contender in the race. It make sense for it do so, because, as time goes on, we will see more and more things controlled, configured, and liberated by the Internet. Smart Devices? Before long it will be Genius Devices.

Summary

In this chapter we refreshed our memory of Web Services, barely skimming the surface of the vast subject that it is, but nonetheless achieving our goal of consuming one from a Mobile Web Form.

We looked at:

- ❑ Creating the ASMX file that houses our Web Service code
- ❑ The two-step process of building a Proxy Class for a client application
  - ❑ Using the `wsdl.exe` command-line tool to create a source file based on the WSDL from our Web Service
  - ❑ Compiling the resulting sourcecode into a library DLL and relocating the file to the proper directory
- ❑ How to consume the Web Service from a mobile Web Form using the same syntax used to access local objects
- ❑ A quick overview of Microsoft's vision of Smart Devices and two of the powerful operating systems that they are developing for them

In the next chapter we'll be looking at how to secure ASP.NET Mobile Web Form applications, as well as how to use cookies and handle State Management.

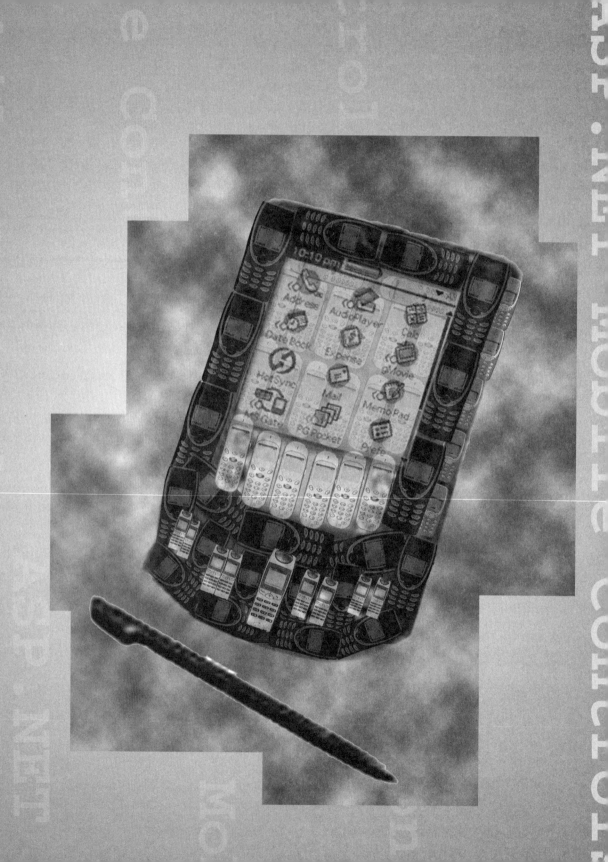

Security, Cookies, and State Management

It may seem a bit odd that these three subjects should be lumped together in one chapter, but by the end of it you will hopefully see the natural correlation between the three and have enough knowledge to effectively use each of them out of this particular context.

Briefly put, **security** refers to the process of allowing users to enter a login, and then validating their credentials to determine if they should be allowed access to your resources, or not. These resources can be anything from an entire system to a single file or application. Once a user has satisfied your validation procedures, and been granted access to your system, you need a way to keep track of them, without needing them to constantly login after every action they take. This is where **state management** comes in. Finally **cookies** can be employed to record information about a user so that you can recognize them when they visit your system again, and you can therefore forego the validation logic. There's not much scope for the use of cookies in Mobile Web Forms, so we'll be considering alternatives that can be employed in their place, as well.

> **A cookie is a temporary file stored on the client machine that contains key-value pairs that the server or developer has stored. This is passed between the client and the server in the HTTP headers as a text-only string.**

One of the questions that might be bubbling to the forefront of your mind is "What about all of the things that I might need to do with a cookie that has nothing to do with authentication?" (Such as recording the date of a user's last visit or data to aid in the personalization of your site.) Well, unfortunately, in most situations involving mobile devices and applications, you will not have the option to use cookies at all due to the limitation of the WAP Gateway or the client devices.

The material in this chapter is not meant to be an exhaustive thesis on security and state management in ASP.NET, it is included to give you some perspective on how mobile Web Forms are able to implement some of the security and state management features that ASP.NET provides and also talk about some of the issues that you may run into. This topic area is covered in more detail in *Professional ASP.NET*, ISBN 1-861004-88-5, if you want to look into it further.

.NET Security Overview

In the past two years we've seen a deluge of reports of web crime. This is mainly due to the exponential increase in connected users, and the proportionally increased opportunity for criminal gain. Knowing that criminals are opportunists, we have to take measures to minimize their potential entry points.

Entry points can include:

- **Vender oversight** – these are a few of the ways that this can manifest itself:

  - **Flawed vendor examples** – a well-known one was the ShowCode.asp file that was a part of previous versions of IIS examples. This file displayed the sourcecode to any other file whose name was passed as an argument. It was quickly learned that this example should **not** be installed on machines that were exposed to the Internet.

  - **Applications that work too well** – an example of this was a Microsoft Index Server 'feature' that would allow anyone with a web browser to read any file on the web server. That included the Global.asa file (which sometimes holds database passwords) among others.

  - **Default application settings** – there are times when the default installation of a product (database, web server, or OS) has settings that would allow anonymous access to resources that may be sensitive. The most notable within the past couple of years was the SQL Server "sa, no password" blunder. For those who are not familiar with this; SQL Server 7.0 installed with a default administrator account enabled with no password. This allowed full access to SQL Server, which ultimately led to full control over the machine (using the extended stored procedure xp_cmdshell one could run all sorts of DOS tools).

- **Programmer error** – some common mistakes can be:

  - **Hidden field misuse** – an example of this would be using a hidden form variable to submit the price of a catalog item. A rogue user could reconstruct the form that contains this field on their own machine, setting the price of a $200 item to $0.83 and subsequently make the purchase for that amount.

  - **Unchecked buffers** – Buffers are reserved clusters of memory that our variables point to and store their contents in. An unchecked buffer is one that has no code to validate the integrity of incoming data.

  - **Failing to check for script that is embedded in data sent to the web server** – an example of this type of problem could manifest itself in a threaded discussion application. A user could submit a posting with some JavaScript that opened 100 windows, or worse (I have seen a few examples of the 'worse' variety).

At every hour of the day there are people in the world trying to find the latest exploitable hole in every conceivable type of software. Their findings are most often unchecked buffers. To have an unchecked buffer means that the person doing the coding did not check the size of the data being passed in to the method as an argument. The danger in this is that malicious code can be attached to the end of the argument that the target server, in certain circumstances, will execute as native code. This does not mean that you can append your "ChangeHomePageToMyLovePoemToSally()" ASP script to the end of a "too-long" string and have it work its magic. The appended data must be passed in a HEX format. To illustrate this further, here is an example of some code from a character array taken from an old IIS 4.0 exploit (understand that this is only part of the *data* that is blasted at the server, it is part of a bigger program that does the work):

```
"\x21\x88\x86\x95\x89\x90\x94\x95\x83\x9a\x8f\x82"
"\x8e\x86\x21\x90\x98\x8f\x4f\x86\x99\x86\x21"
```

Initially we may think to ourselves "this isn't much of a threat, who is going to take the time and go to those lengths to distil their evil code into HEX to target *my* web site? It's far too complex." Not really. It only takes one person or "crew" to release a tool that any 12 year old can run against your site. Then consider that web site defacement has become a sort of mating ritual in some adolescent circles and you *do* have something to worry about, and this is a best-case scenario. Worst cases can range from nefarious individuals stealing credit cards to sell on the black market to other companies engaging in industrial espionage.

A system can be secure as long as everyone involved takes his or her part seriously. That includes everyone from users to developers to upper management. As developers it is our job to make sure that we do everything we can to lock down our code; double checking arguments, validating data size, and so on. From that point we can start to lock down the application from a more macro level.

Some of the key security concepts that are put to use when securing an application are:

❑ **Authentication** – this is the process of discovering or confirming the identity of the user and is generally encountered in the username/password context, though there are many other ways this can be done in the 'outside world' (fingerprints, drivers licenses, voice recognition, and so on).

❑ **Authorization** – this is the act of confirming that the user has permission to use the resource they have requested.

❑ **Impersonation** – this describes a situation where the ASP.NET application accesses a resource under a different identity on the user's behalf. Impersonation is disabled by default at the computer level.

❑ **Code Access Security** – this makes sure that the code that is requesting to be run has the correct permissions to do so and will not cause damage to the system.

❑ **Role Based Security** – conceptually similar to Windows Groups and Roles. This can be actual Windows accounts and groups, or a custom set of identities that are completely unrelated to any Windows accounts.

❑ **ASP.NET Application Security** – these are the provisions that .NET has put into place to allow developers to lock down specific areas of web applications, it is configurable in the `web.config` file. This is what we will be primarily dealing with in this chapter.

Due to the specific nature of what we will be dealing with when securing a Mobile Web Form Application, there are a couple of the salient points that I would like to refresh your memory of before moving into the meat of our subject:

Code Access Security

In the past few years we have seen new malevolent code entities released into the wild, almost quarterly, with payloads that do varying degrees of damage to unknowing users. Now, even mom gets hacked. Viruses and worms attached to an e-mail or buried in a macro can give millions of users plenty of grief and potentially cost businesses millions of dollars in wasted time and resources. Educated users have been curtailing some of the damage, but even the most astute will let one slip by every now and then. At that point it is up to the virus protection software or the e-mail client to handle it. If the virus is exploiting newly discovered vulnerabilities in the client software, you may be in trouble. Now, the approach to creating these digital diseases has evolved to the point that the user does not even need to open an e-mail to breach a server – the malicious work can be undertaken through a vulnerable web server.

> *A worm is a program that replicates itself and moves through a network by sending copies of itself via e-mail. A virus is a program that attacks a specific part of your computer (hardware or software) with the intent to cause some sort of damage.*

Before .NET, viral code could run amok on user's computers with impunity, but now you have something verifying that every single piece of code that runs is safe. This is not meant to imply that .NET has built-in virus protection functionality, rather to say it provides as much functionality as it can to assist the steps that we take as developers to protect our environment. This functionality is called **Code Access Security** and used correctly it ensures that no rogue code can be run within, or against, your application and cause damage.

> **This will not take care of e-mail viruses unless your e-mail client is running under .NET.**

Code access security is designed to prevent less trusted code from calling trusted code and using it to perform unauthorized tasks. Some of the functionality that it uses to achieve this goal is:

❑ Defines permissions and permission sets that represent access levels to certain system resources

❑ Restricts code at runtime by comparing the permission credentials of every caller on the stack to the permissions that callers are required to have

❑ Enables code to demand that its callers have certain permissions

Role-Based Security

Role-based application security is often used to designate groups of users that are under the same security policy and share the same access rights. This can be permissions for file systems, databases, or the web site code itself. For example, a medical application may have a Clinician role and a Patient role that both have very different functions and permissions. The Clinician role will probably have access to the information of many patients and other information pertinent to the internal business, while the Patient role will most likely only have limited access to their own information.

.NET has its own spin on this. It provides what it calls a **Principal** object. This object acts on behalf of the user, presenting the users, permissions upon being challenged over a requested resource. It does this by housing an **Identity** object and the user's group or role memberships. From a high-level view, the `Identity` object contains a name and an authentication type. The name that it contains can be the user name or the name of a Windows account. The authentication type can be one of the intrinsically supported login protocols (NTLM, for example) or a custom value. The `Principal` object provides a property to retrieve the user's identity as well as determine if the user is in a particular role. The `Principal` object represents the current security context.

We won't be going too deeply into this, as it would take up a book on its own, but you are encouraged to read the .NET Security information on MSDN.

Security In The Mobile Internet Toolkit

Securing a Mobile Web Form is very, very similar to securing an ASP.NET Web Form. The same entries are made in the `web.config` file and the same mindset is employed when writing the code. The differences can be found in the way that the authenticated state is maintained during the user's session. This is due to limitations in the way that some WAP gateways and certain devices handle cookies.

As you may know if you've studied standard ASP.NET, ASP.NET security 'does three things for a living', and they are **Authenticate**, **Authorize**, and **Impersonate**. It is through these three actions that your ASP.NET application's security is handled, as well as the security for your mobile Web Application.

Authentication

In a web application, when a user makes a request to access a protected resource or perform a questionable action, ASP.NET will challenge users to present some sort of credentials, thus authenticating them.

This is where we will put to use role-based security, authentication, and authorization. Microsoft Mobile Internet Toolkit security supports:

❑ **Windows Authentication** – initial challenge is handled by through one of IIS Basic, Digest, or Integrated Windows authentication. IIS then uses this account to access the requested resources. The accounts and their access to specific areas of the application are configurable through the `web.config` file.

❑ **Passport** – this is a subscription service that offers a single centralized web-based authentication service and profile functionality provided by Microsoft to subscribers.

❑ **Forms Authentication** – this is done through an HTML form page. If a user requests a protected resource and they are not authenticated they are redirected to an HTML login form. Once the user has logged in, ASP.NET will set a client-side cookie that will either have the user's identity stored in it or a key to retrieve it.

❑ **Default /Anonymous** – the level of access given to users that request resources will be determined by the security settings in IIS.

Windows Authentication

Using Windows authentication requires that the user has a valid user account on the target computer. This account can have its own specific permissions set, or it can be a member of a Group or Role. Windows authentication is well suited applications where you will have a finite amount of users and are prepared to add new ones manually. Since ASP.NET Mobile applications are IIS-centric, we will look at how IIS implements these mechanisms.

The types that IIS supports are:

❑ **Basic Authentication** – Least secure but most flexible (in its support for different client browsers) of the authentication types. Send client credentials in plain text. It does encrypt the information using Base-64 encoding, but, with a little effort, it can be cracked.

❑ **Digest Authentication** – Digest authentication is a very secure choice, as it shares much of the same functionality as the Windows Integrated authentication type, but it only works with Web Services and Internet Explorer.

❑ **Windows Integrated Authentication** – Very secure authentication type. Uses a hash code algorithm to encrypt the transported client credentials. Windows Integrated Authentication will not work through most proxy servers and some routers, so using it for the Internet would not be advisable, though I have seen it used successfully within intranet applications.

Try It Out – Setting Up Basic Authentication

For our first Mobile Web Form example we are going to use Basic Authentication so before we can begin, we need to set Basic Authentication up in IIS:

1. Open Internet Services Manager (Administrative Tools | Internet Services Manager in the Start menu) then right-click on the web site directory you want to secure, and choose Properties:

2. Select the Directory Security tab, and under Anonymous access and authentication control click the Edit button:

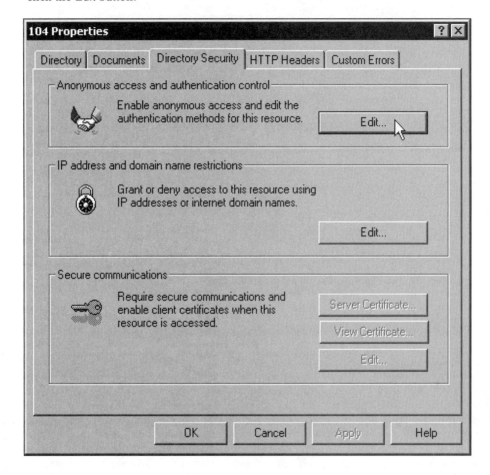

3. You will see the screen below. Make sure that the Basic authentication (password is sent in clear text) box is checked:

4. Your directory is now set up with Basic authentication activated.

During setup, you'll have received a warning that the password is sent in **clear text** (though it is encrypted using Base64 encoding). This means that the packets that are sent from the client to the server are not encrypted. Someone with a packet sniffer (a program that sits between the client and the server to collect passing IP packets) set up in the right place could glean the flimsily encrypted login credentials to the user's account, which could then be cracked with some ease. The decision of whether this is an acceptable risk is up to the developer and their company, but it is not advisable to use on high-security sites. You could think about maybe combining Basic Authentication with SSL to increase security, SSL will provide an encrypted channel between the client browser and the server. If the attacker is able to acquire any packets, they will have to go to great lengths to decrypt them.

> If increased security is needed and the application is within a Windows-only environment, use **Windows Integrated Authentication**. This uses a hash algorithm to encode and decode the client's username and password. It can be activated from the same panel as Basic Authentication.

Note that if anonymous access is disabled in IIS and all of the other types are enabled, IIS will attempt to use Integrated Windows authentication working its way back to the least secure, Basic Authentication.

It is very easy to implement Windows authentication for mobile Web Forms, now that we have set up IIS to use Basic Authentication, let's have a look at an example:

Try It Out – Windows Authentication

Firstly we're going to create a new user account to login under to test the example:

1. Open the Computer Management applet (Start | Programs | Administrative Tools | Computer Management) and expand the Local Users and Groups tree:

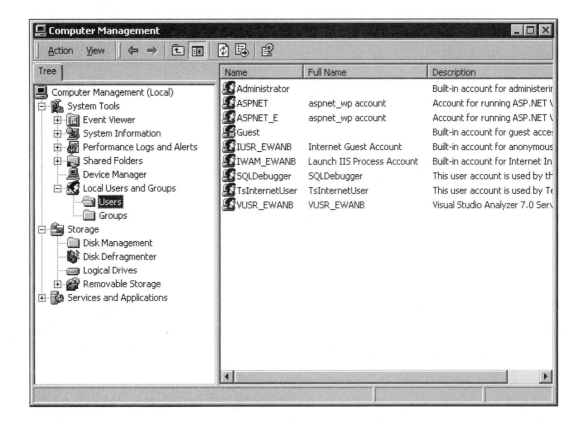

2. Right-click on Users and choose New User... then enter wrox for the username, add a password and make sure that the check boxes on your entry match the ones in the screen shot. Finally click Close, and close the Computer Management applet:

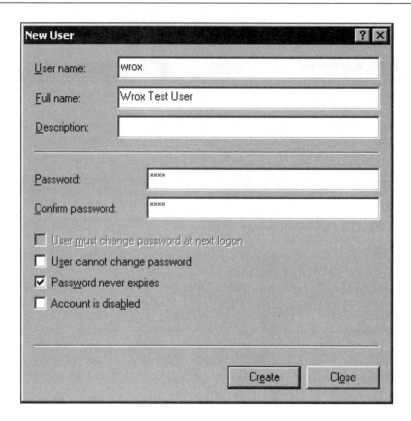

Now that we've setup our user, we'll create the code:

3. We now need to make some changes to your web.config file (which should be stored in your application root – if you don't have a web.config file in your application root, create a new one with the following code). Open your web.config in your editor and enter the following code:

```
<?xml version="1.0" encoding="utf-8" ?>
<configuration>
  <system.web>
    <compilation defaultLanguage="c#" debug="true" />
    <authentication mode="Windows"></authentication>
    <authorization>
      <allow users="Wrox" roles="Power Users" />
      <deny users="YOURDOMAIN\Administrator,?" />
    </authorization>
  </system.web>
</configuration>
```

4. Save the file in the root of your web application.

> **Make sure you change the YOURDOMAIN placeholder to the domain that you are working on.**

5. Create a new ASPX file and enter the following code:

```
<%@ Register TagPrefix="mobile" Namespace="System.Web.UI.MobileControls"
Assembly="System.Web.Mobile" %>
<%@ Page language="c#" AutoEventWireup="false" %>

<mobile:Form id="Form1" runat="server">
  <mobile:Link id="Link1" runat="server"
    NavigateURL="SecretPage.aspx"
    SoftkeyLabel="GO!">
    Go to the Secret Page!
  </mobile:Link>
</mobile:Form>
```

6. Save this file as `menu.aspx` in the same directory as your `web.config` file.

7. Create another new ASPX file and enter this code:

```
<%@Register TagPrefix="mobile" Namespace="System.Web.UI.MobileControls"
Assembly="System.Web.Mobile"%>
<%@Page language="c#" AutoEventWireup="false"%>

<mobile:Form id="Form1" runat="server">
  <mobile:Label id="Label1" runat="server">
  </mobile:Label>
</mobile:Form>

<script runat="server">
  private void Page_Load(object sender, System.EventArgs e)
  {
    if (User.Identity.IsAuthenticated){
      Label1.Text = "Hello " + User.Identity.Name +
            " you made it to the special *Secret Page* using the " +
            User.Identity.AuthenticationType + " authentication type";
    }
  }
}
</script>
```

8. Save this page as `SecretPage.aspx`, in the same directory as the others.

9. We'll use IE to browse the document first, so we can get a clear idea of what is going on. When you request the `main.aspx` file, you will be presented with a login box like this:

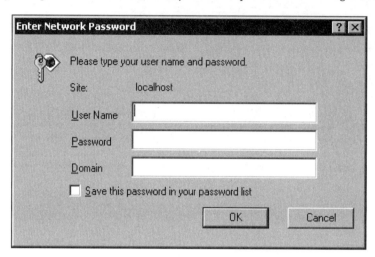

Not all systems will display the Domain textbox, if it is displayed you should enter the domain under which you are operating.

10. Enter the username and password that we set up earlier, along with a domain if required. If you get it right, you'll see the following page:

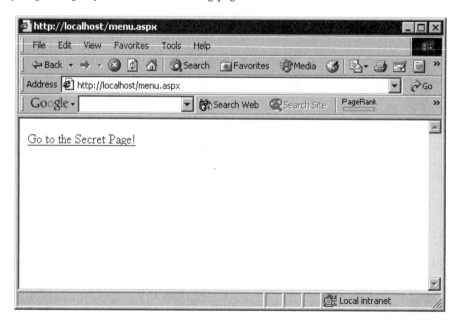

11. Clicking on the hyperlink will take you to `SecretPage.aspx`, which greets you by name (and domain) and tells you the type of authentication that you came in on.

12. Finally, now that you've seen the whole process in IE, and know what is going on, here's what it looks like if you try this from other devices:

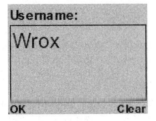

The Microsoft MME was unable to support Basic authentication in our tests.

How It Works

The crux of this example is the web.config file. The first thing we did was set the authentication mode to Windows:

```
<authentication mode="Windows"></authentication>
```

Then within our <authorization> elements we used two more tags, <allow> and <deny>. Both requiring at least a roles or a users attribute (there is an optional verb attribute which configures access to HTTP verbs (POST, GET, HEAD).

With the <allow> element we designated which users we wanted to give permission to. We allowed the Windows wrox account and the entire group Power Users (we can add additional users and roles by separating each entry with a comma):

```
<allow users="Wrox" roles="Power Users" />
```

Then we set forth to deny other users. We denied the administrator account (under which many people are logged in on test machines) and any anonymous request's that might happen by:

```
<deny users=\"YOURDOMAIN\Administrator,?" />
```

There are two special characters that are allowed in `<allow>` and `<deny>` elements. They are the question mark (?) and the asterisk (*). The question mark (?) means anonymous access (in this context that means the account set up for IIS use) and can only be used with the `users` attribute. The asterisk (*) means "all" `users`, `roles`, or `verbs`, depending on which attribute it is associated with.

That was all it took to set up our security. The `menu.aspx` page was nothing more than a Mobile Web Form with a link to our `SecretPage.aspx`, and doesn't bear mentioning, as you've seen it dozens of times before by now.

The `SecretPage.aspx` page is little more complicated. Briefly its `Page_Load` method first checks to see if the user is already authenticated through the `User` object:

```
If (User.Identity.IsAuthenticated)
```

Then, if they pass, it constructs a welcome string populating it with data from the `User` object:

```
Label1.Text = "Hello " + User.Identity.Name +
            " you made it to the special *Secret Page* using the " +
            User.Identity.AuthenticationType + " authentication type";
```

It's as easy as that. You can choose either Basic or Integrated Windows Authentication from IIS, and let ASP.NET take the strain of validating your users. Next, we're going to look at a slightly more complicated, but far more flexible method of securing your resources.

Forms Authentication

This authentication type will be familiar to traditional ASP developers. It uses an HTML form to have users log in with and plants a cookie, or token, to maintain the user's authenticated state. .NET has taken on most of the mundane coding tasks for you – the developer sets the cookie name and path, login page, user credentials, and allow/deny lists in the `web.config` file, and .NET does the rest. When a user requests a page, ASP.NET automatically checks for a validation cookie or token, if the user does not have it they are redirected to the login page.

There is a helper class that provides static methods to help manage the process of authentication by forms and it is called `FormsAuthentication` (unsurprisingly). This class exposes eleven methods, but in our example we will only be working with two of them. For the sake of reference, here are the eleven methods:

Method	Description
Authenticate	Takes supplied credentials and makes an attempt to validate them against a credential store.
Decrypt	This decrypts an encrypted authentication ticket from a cookie and returns an instance of the `FormsAuthenticationTicket` class. An authentication ticket represents the information contained in an authentication cookie.

Table continued on following page

Method	Description
Encrypt	This method produces an encrypted authentication ticket for use in a cookie when passed a `FormsAuthenticationTicket`.
GetAuthCookie	Creates an authentication cookie for a username passed to it.
GetRedirectUrl	This returns the URL that was originally requested before the user was redirected to the login page.
HashPasswordForStoringInConfigFile	Pass this method a password and string indicating the desired hash type and it will produce a hash password for use in the `web.config` file. Default is `autogenerate`, which uses a computer-specific key, so the code cannot be shared between computers. Our example will not use this.
Initialize	Initializes `FormsAuthentication` by loading the configuration from the `web.config` file and getting the cookie values and encryption keys for the application.
RedirectFromLoginPage	Redirects the user to the page they originally requested before being redirected to the login page.
RenewTicketIfOld	Updates the authentication ticket if it meets developer-defined criteria.
SetAuthCookie	Creates an authentication ticket for a username passed into it and attaches it to the cookie collection of the servers outgoing response.
SignOut	Deletes the authentication ticket by doing a `SetForms` with an empty value when passed an authenticated user. This will get rid of durable and session cookies.

> **If you would like to read further about the additional methods and forms, or authentication in general, please refer to *Professional ASP.NET*, by Wrox Press, ISBN 1 -86100-4-88-5**

Our example is similar to the Windows authentication example that we have just completed. Once again we will be trying to access the contents of our Secret Page, but in order to do so will have to get round the security features ....

Try It Out – Forms Authentication

1. Open your text editor and enter the following code:

```
<%@ Page language="c#" Inherits="WroxFormsAuthentication.MobileWebForm1"
AutoEventWireup="true" %>
<%@ Register TagPrefix="mobile" Namespace="System.Web.UI.MobileControls"
Assembly="System.Web.Mobile" %>

<mobile:Form id="Form1" runat="server">
  UserName
  <mobile:TextBox id="txtUserName" runat="server">
  </mobile:TextBox>
  Password
  <mobile:TextBox id="txtPWD" runat="server" Password="True">
  </mobile:TextBox>
  <mobile:Label id="Label1" runat="server">
  </mobile:Label>
  <mobile:Command id="Command1" runat="server" onClick="Command1_Click">
    Login</mobile:Command>
</mobile:Form>

<script runat="server">
  private void Command1_Click(object sender, System.EventArgs e)
  {
    if (FormsAuthentication.Authenticate(txtUserName.Text,txtPWD.Text))
    {
      FormsAuthentication.RedirectFromLoginPage(txtUserName.Text,false);
    }
    else
    {
      Label1.Text = "Please check your Username and Password.";
    }
  }
</script>
```

2. Save the file as `Login.aspx` in a virtual directory configured as a web application.

3. Create a new file and enter the following code, before saving it as `Menu.aspx` in the same directory as the first. This page is optional, and is included just to show you that even a page with no explicit authentication code is still protected:

```
<%@ Page Inherits="System.Web.UI.MobileControls.MobilePage" Language="C#"%>
<%@Register TagPrefix="mobile" Namespace="System.Web.UI.MobileControls"
Assembly="System.Web.Mobile" %>

<mobile:Form id="Form1" runat="server">
  <mobile:Link id="Link1" runat="server"
    NavigateURL="SecretPage.aspx"
    SoftkeyLabel="GO!">
    Go to the Secret Page!
    </mobile:Link>
</mobile:Form>
```

4. Create another new file in your text editor, enter the following code and save it in the same directory as the other two as `SecretPage.aspx`:

```
<%@ Page Inherits="System.Web.UI.MobileControls.MobilePage" Language="C#"%>
<%@Register TagPrefix="mobile" Namespace="System.Web.UI.MobileControls"
Assembly="System.Web.Mobile" %>

<mobile:Form id="Form1" runat="server">
  <mobile:Label id="Label1" runat="server">
  </mobile:Label>
</mobile:Form>

<script runat="server">
  private void Page_Load(object sender, System.EventArgs e)
  {
    if (User.Identity.IsAuthenticated)
    {
      Label1.Text = "Hello " + User.Identity.Name +
            " you made it to the special Secret Page using the " +
            User.Identity.AuthenticationType + " authentication type";
    }
  }
</script>
```

5. And finally we create/amend our `web.config` file, saving it in the same directory as the others:

```
<?xml version="1.0" encoding="utf-8" ?>
<configuration>
  <system.web>
    <compilation defaultLanguage="c#" debug="true" />
    <authentication mode="Forms">
      <forms name="WroxFormsTest" path="/" loginUrl="Login.aspx">
        <credentials passwordFormat="Clear">
          <user name="wrox" password="pass" />
        </credentials>
      </forms>
    </authentication>
    <authorization>
      <allow users="MAtt" />
      <deny users="?" />
    </authorization>
  </system.web>
</configuration>
```

6. It doesn't matter which of the three ASPX files you try and access, you'll be sent straight to the login page, just the same:

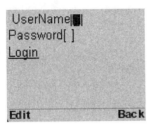

7. The next few screenshots show the remaining steps in the process of providing login credentials, and then being allowed access (we'll leave it to you to discover what happens if you don't get them right):

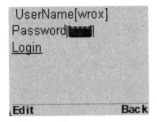

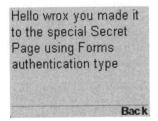

How It Works

This code for this example is very similar to that in the previous example, but with one major difference. Namely, in this example we have to write the user login code ourselves – it is not handled automatically like it was previously. The good news is it takess only a small amount of code to a call to a method on the intrinsic FormsAuthentication object. We did this in the Login.aspx page, as follows:

```
FormsAuthentication.Authenticate(txtUserName.Text,txtPWD.Text))
```

Here, the Authenticate method compares the submitted username and password against the configuration of user entries in the web.config file.

If the user passes the authentication process they will need to be sent to the page that was originally requested. The way we handled this was using the RedirectFromLoginPage method of the FormsAuthentication object. The first argument in this method is the username, the second is a Boolean that indicates whether to write a cookie so the state of being 'logged in' persists across browser sessions. We've indicated this to be false, so users will have to login each time they request the page:

```
FormsAuthentication.RedirectFromLoginPage(txtUserName.Text, false);
```

The URL that the user is redirected to is based on the **ReturnUrl** variable in the query string. This variable simply contains the URL of the page we requested before we were redirected to the login page. Ours looks something like this:

http://localhost/Login.aspx?**ReturnUrl**=http%3a%2f%2flocalhost%2fWroxFormsAuthentication%2fSecretPage.aspx

Of course, if we fail authentication because we mis-spelt our username or password we get a message saying so:

```
else
{
    Label1.Text = "Please check your Username and Password.";
}
```

Once we reach SecretPage.aspx we are again greeted by a customized welcome message. The code we've used here (residing in the Page_Load method) is exactly the same as the code we used to do this in the Windows authentication example.

```
private void Page_Load(object sender, System.EventArgs e)
{
    if (User.Identity.IsAuthenticated){
        Label1.Text = "Hello " + User.Identity.Name +
                " you made it to the special Secret Page using the " +
                User.Identity.AuthenticationType + " authentication type";
    }
}
```

The big difference between Forms authentication and Windows authentication lies in the information provided in the web.config file. We'll look at this now:

First we set the authentication mode to Forms:

```
<authentication mode="Forms">
```

Then, within the <authentication> elements we find (unique to Forms authentication) the <forms> element set. Here we set the name of the authentication cookie, the cookies path, and the URL of the login page (which unauthenticated users are redirected to):

```
<forms name="WroxFormsTest" path="/" loginUrl="Login.aspx">
```

Then, within the <forms> elements we find the <credentials> element set. In here we configured the user access list, which in our example consisted of only one <user> element, though if you want more, you could just add more <user> elements:

```
<credentials passwordFormat="Clear">
  <user name="wrox" password="pass" />
</credentials>
```

> *If seeing the password in plain view makes you nervous or is not secure enough you can change the passwordFormat to MD5 or SHA1. This will tell ASP.NET to expect to find the user's password encrypted by a specific algorithm, the key to decrypt it with can either be a default value derived from the computer or a value set in the decryptionkey attribute in the <forms> set. These both offer much better security by using an encryption algorithm to handle the password. There are currently no tools to create a hashed password for insertion into the web.config file but there is a handy method in the FormsAuthentication class itself that is called HashPasswordForStoringInConfigFile. Give this method a password and the format to return it in, and it will return the result as a string which you can then insert into your web.config file.*

Finally we have the now familiar <authorization> tag set that we set user permissions in. We set this one to <allow> wrox and <deny> all anonymous users:

```
<authorization>
  <allow users="MAtt" />
  <deny users="?" />
</authorization>
```

Passport

Passport is a subscription based user profile service that allows the centralization of user authentication. Passport enables a user to float between protected resources across multiple domains without having to login multiple times. Unfortunately, at this time, Passport only supports HTML devices, so it would not be appropriate for Mobile Web Form application development. The passport homepage is at www.passport.com, where you will be able to find the latest information.

Further Reading

We have now implemented mobile versions of some of the basic security functionality that ASP.NET provides but have nowhere near scratched the surface of what it means to truly secure an application. I have already encouraged you to take a deeper look at what the .NET Framework provides for security. But, it does not stop there though, there are still other steps that can be taken, such as SSL and digital certificates, to further protect your environment. Securing an application extends out as far as the physical security of the hardware it runs on and everything in between. Developing, deploying, and maintaining a secure application can only be done with cooperation between the developers, the network administrators, and security-aware employers.

There is no 'best' authentication solution; it is a matter which is subjective to the environment that the application lives in. Always be sure to look at the big picture of where you application lives and what it does. Take this into consideration when deciding what type of security solution is appropriate.

Session State

We saw in the last section how to maintain the users' authenticated state throughout their session, now we will look at how .NET helps maintain the users **ViewState** as well. It is through this mechanism that we are able avoid the manual 'pack your bags' type of session state management that was prevalent with traditional ASP (do any of you remember passing hidden variables everywhere your user went?)

We define ViewState as an accumulation of the property values of a control throughout its lifetime. These name/value pairs are then stored in an instance of the `StateBag` class. ViewState is enabled for a page by default.

ViewState In Mobile Pages

The Microsoft Mobile Internet Toolkit has most of the functionality of the extensive state management system that ASP.NET provides. We will be looking at a small part of it: **ViewState management**. By now you have no doubt already seen this in action when working with Mobile controls, because the state management functionality is switched on by default. For example, if we created a Mobile Web Form with a `TextBox` on it; populated this `TextBox` with a value, and then hit *Enter*, when the page refreshed, the value would still be in the box.

Here's why: Hitting *Enter* caused the page to automatically submit to the server, when this happened the value in the TextBox was stored in the user's session on the server as part of their ViewState. In ordinary Web Form pages the state is written out to the client as hidden variables and cookies, but due to current bandwidth and software limitations on mobile clients it is not – instead an identifier is attached to the query string for retrieval of the stored session state.

When rendering things such as static content you may want to turn `ViewState` off to conserve resources. In order to explicitly enable or disable view state for a page you can set the **EnableViewState** property to `true` or `false`, respectively, in the `@Page` directive for the page. If you need more granular control you can set the `EnableViewState` property at the control level as well, as follows:

```
<%@ Page EnableViewState = "false" …
```

ViewState Session History

During the course of a user's interaction with your application the Back button may be hit a few times. This could cause the view the client has and the one on the server to get out of sync. To prevent this from happening, mobile Web Forms maintain a history of the ViewState information in the user's session. There is a small identifier that is sent to the client to keep track of where in the history the user currently is. The size of this history is configurable in the web.config file by setting the sessionStateHistorySize attribute in the <mobileControls> element like this:

```
<configuration>
    <system.web>
        <mobileControls sessionStateHistorySize="12" />
    </system.web>
</configuration>
```

The higher the number, the more pages are stored on in the browser, so be aware of this and consider your target clients so as to not bog down the client browser with more than it can handle. The default value is 6.

Cookieless Sessions

As we know, there are some limitations with WAP gateways and some client devices regarding cookies. In order for session state management to work we must configure the application to use **cookieless** session state in the web.config file. The tag that this is configured in is <sessionState>. You have four options for the mode attribute; to cover each one in depth is beyond the scope of this book, but none of these fall prey to the limitations of client browsers or WAP gateways:

❑ InProc – this is the default for ASP.NET. Session state is stored in-process with the application

❑ Off – session state is disabled

❑ SQLServer – the mechanism is using an out-of-process SQL Server to store session state

❑ StateServer – session state is being store on an out-of-process NT server. (This is used for storing session state on web forms)

Other Considerations

There are a few other points to be raised about ViewState when working with mobile Web Forms. They are:

❑ Because View State is saved in a session, it is possible for it to expire if the page is not posted back to the server before the expiration time limit is up.

❑ As well as the state of the controls on the mobile Web Form, there is more data about the state of the application that needs to be stored. This includes information such as which form is active, and pagination information. This is called **Private ViewState**.

❏ You cannot use member or static variables to store state between trips to the server. The former loses its value on every trip (because the page is destroyed every time) and the latter is accessible across requests from many clients, and has an unpredictable lifetime.

Summary

In this chapter we looked at some of the ways that we can secure mobile Web Form applications by using what we have already learned from our past experience with ASP.NET Web Forms. We also talked about how mobile Web Forms can maintain their session state in a very similar way to ordinary Web Forms. We are now aware of some of the changes in mindset that are necessary when applying our knowledge of Web Form security and session state to mobile Web Forms.

In varying degrees of detail, we looked at:

❏ A brief review of .NET/ASP.NET security

❏ Windows authentication

❏ Forms authentication

❏ Passport

❏ Session State

❏ View State

❏ ViewState Session History

❏ Cookieless sessions

In the next chapter we will look at the functionality provided by the Microsoft Mobile Internet Toolkit for caching.

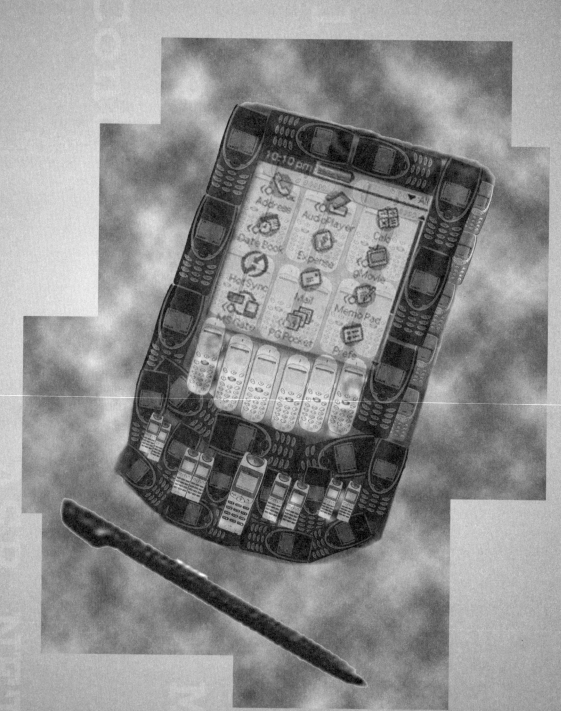

Introducing Visual Studio .NET

This chapter provides a gentle introduction to Visual Studio .NET. We'll spend some time discussing how to navigate through some of the more important menus and provide a general sense of how to work with the tool. This will prepare us for the next chapter, which focuses on how to use Visual Studio .NET to create ASP.NET mobile applications.

Throughout this book, we've been working with ASP.NET mobile applications using a standard text editor. To its credit, it has helped us to adequately complete our programming tasks. However, we have had to know which HTML tags, attributes, and code to use. Even those of us who feel comfortable with ASP.NET code have our moments when trying to remember syntax. Fortunately, Microsoft has given us a tool with which to create programs in a more intuitive, graphical, way. Enter Visual Studio .NET!

No doubt you've heard about Visual Studio .NET. Microsoft's latest Integrated Development Environment (IDE) for creating applications is causing quite a stir. Why? Visual Studio .NET is truly integrated now, allowing developers to build various types of Web-based and Windows-based applications in one place. It also provides a more graphical development interface and a rich set of tools and wizards, promising to make building applications a more productive process.

Another key selling point is Visual Studio .NET's ability to be integrated with any language supported by the .NET Framework. At this time, the following compilers can be included with the initial installation: Visual Basic .NET, C# (C Sharp), C++ .NET, and JScript .NET.

In this chapter, we'll cover the following topics:

- ❏ Installation
- ❏ The Start Page
- ❏ Creating a Web-based project
- ❏ Creating a Windows-based project
- ❏ Testing and debugging
- ❏ Advanced Topics

> The examples we present in this chapter, and the next, assume that you have access to Visual Studio .NET Professional Edition.

Installation

To begin, the installation disc should be inserted. Simply double-click on the Setup icon which is found in the root directory on the disc. The next screen asks the user to accept the licensing agreement. Following that, there is the option within the Setup program to select which of the three default languages to install: Visual Basic. NET, C++. NET and C#. There are additional items to select as well. Unless the machine has limited space, the user should simply select Install Now!.

> Please ensure you have the .NET Runtime Framework on your machine prior to installing Visual Studio .NET. Also verify that Internet Information Services and FrontPage Extensions are configured and functioning properly.

Once the installation has been successfully completed, a screen appears that indicates that the setup has no errors. To run Visual Studio .NET, go to Start | Programs and choose Microsoft Visual Studio .NET 7.0 from the folder of the same name.

Start Page

After Visual Studio .NET is launched, the following screen appears:

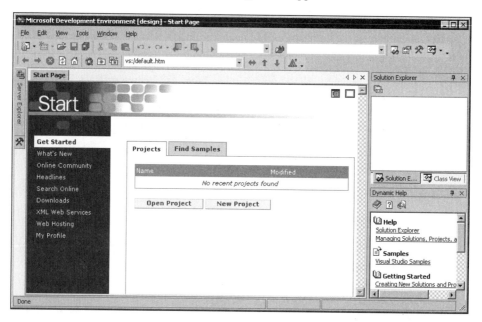

This Start Page allows users to customize the look-and-feel of Visual Studio .NET based on how they plan to use it. It also provides a link to general information about the .NET Framework.

Please note that this link may not be available in the final release.

As we can see, there are a number of options available. Let's take a look at each of these in turn:

> To view the latest information about Visual Studio .NET and download software from Microsoft, make sure that you have an established connection to the Internet. This provides the user with the most current information located directly on Microsoft's web site.

Getting Started

Within the Get Started tab on the Start Page, we have the ability to create a new project, or open an existing one:

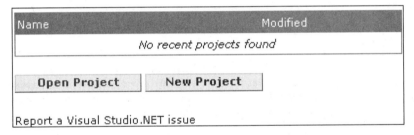

As we begin to create projects, past project names will appear as hyperlinks where No recent projects found is currently shown.

What's New

This option shows any recent changes or additions to Visual Studio .NET and other .NET products. Below is just a portion of the hyperlinks available:

What's New
What's New in Visual Studio.NET
What's New in Visual Studio Tools
What's New in Visual Basic
What's New in Visual C++
What's New in Visual C#
Locating Readme Files

Online Community

A predefined list containing web sites and newsgroups pertinent to .NET is shown. These links can be clicked to visit the appropriate area of the Microsoft web site for research and discussion forums.

Headlines

This section provides current events and information about Microsoft products. All of this information is gathered from the Microsoft site:

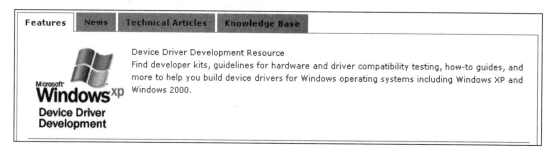

Search Online

The search feature allows us to look for items in the Microsoft Software Development Library (MSDN). This library provides developers with a resource for software downloads, samples, assistance and a discussion amongst other developers. For those that have the MSDN knowledge base installed on a local machine, this link provides the most up-to-date information:

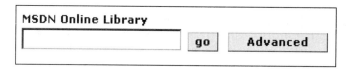

With an Internet connection established, click on **Advanced** to view the actual MSDN search screen on the Internet. If you have questions about Visual Studio .NET, this is a great support tool:

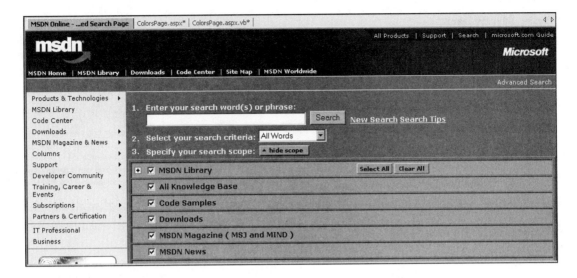

Downloads

This option provides us with a fairly comprehensive listing of .NET software and utilities available for download, as well as examples for, and documentation about, Visual Studio .NET:

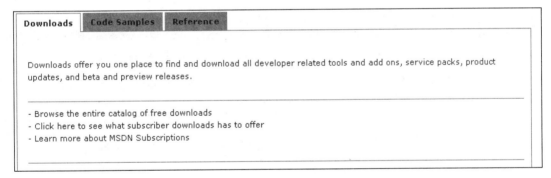

Simply click on any of the links shown and follow the instructions.

Web Hosting

Microsoft takes the opportunity to publicize its cooperatives with various providers, who will allow you to take advantage of their .NET-related services:

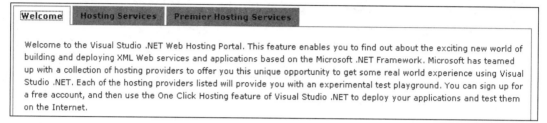

My Profile

Visual Studio .NET allows users to customize their own settings to facilitate the most productive use of the environment, viewing only those help topics we wish to see and having the IDE laid out in a comfortable way for each developer. This permits developers to tailor the environment to the types of projects and languages they work with most:

Now that we've had a quick overview, let's spend some time setting up our Visual Studio .NET configuration:

Try It Out – Customizing Your Visual Studio .NET Environment

1. Complete the installation of Visual Studio .NET Professional Edition.

2. Click on My Profile in the left-side column once the Visual Studio .NET Start Page appears:

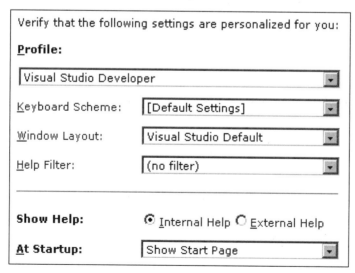

3. For the Profile setting, select Visual Studio Developer.

4. For the Keyboard Scheme, leave this as [Default Settings].

5. For the Window Layout, leave this as Visual Studio Default.

6. For the Help Filter, leave this as (no filter).

7. Set Show Help as Internal Help.

8. Select Show Start Page for the At Startup option.

How It Works

Right away, Visual Studio .NET gives us the ability to wade through the mass of functionality that Microsoft has provided so that we can use only what we need. We'll take a look at each of the options provided on the My Profile page:

The Profile setting allows us to indicate what application look-and-feel we'd like to use. We selected Visual Studio Developer for this setting. As soon as we chose this option, you should notice that Visual Studio .NET automatically set the screen layout (for example, expanded the Toolbox, displayed the Solution Explorer window, Dynamic Help, and so on):

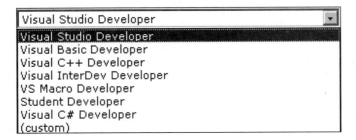

Don't worry, we're not permanently committed to this setting after we've chosen it. We have the option of going back and changing it at any time.

Next, with the Keyboard Scheme setting, we can take advantage of keyboard layouts that previous versions of Visual Studio already use, and that we may already be familiar with:

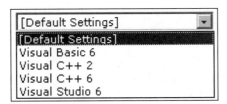

The Default Settings option was automatically set when we selected Visual Studio Developer as our default profile.

Using the Window Layout preference, we can control the initial setting for our window display inside of Visual Studio .NET (such as the Form Designer, Solution Explorer, and Properties windows):

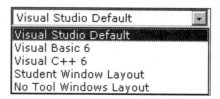

We'll leave this as the Visual Studio Default.

Even the Help Content can be customized, using the Help Filter:

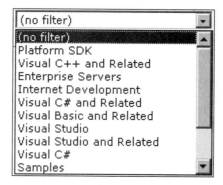

By filtering our help information, this reduces the amount of overhead needed by Visual Studio .NET to dynamically respond with help as we work in the environment. We've selected (no filter) for easy access to all help topics.

Note, that unfortunately we are not able to select multiple items from this list.

We also have the ability to retrieve help information from a local source as part of the .NET installation (Internal Help) or a different source (External Help) such as CD. We specified Internal Help so that we could avoid always needing the Visual Studio .NET installation CD for accessing help items. (Here, we're assuming that the help files were installed during setup):

Finally, we have a setting that allows us to specify the action that occurs when Visual Studio .NET is first launched:

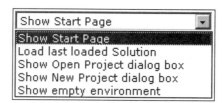

We selected Show Start Page. Again, you may change these preferences at any time.

Now we have the environment set the way we wish. The next step is actually to use Visual Studio .NET to create the type of application we want, using the language we want. The following section explains how.

Creating a Project

To start a new project, File | New | Project is selected from the Menu Bar at the top of the screen. (If the Start Page appears, you may also click on the New Project button, under Get Started):

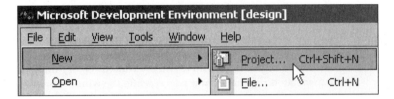

The following screen will appear which permits the developer to choose from various **project templates**. As we can see below, on the left, there are a number of different languages available:

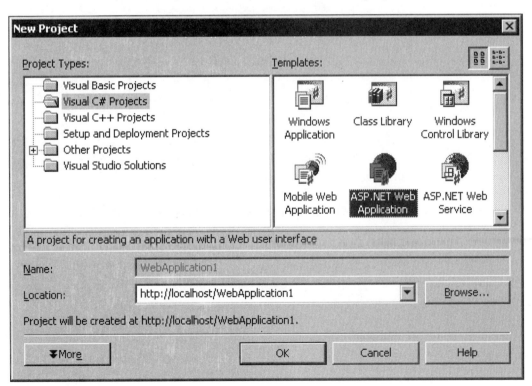

The primary language for the project is selected by clicking on one of the folders in the **Project Types** pane. We then click on one of the icons in the right-hand pane, which are specific kinds of project we can build in each language. Finally, the name and the location for the project are entered.

To create an ASP.NET web application using C#, the **ASP.NET Web Application** icon is chosen from the **Templates** pane. Next, the application name is entered in the **Name** field, and the virtual directory where our application will reside is entered in the **Location** field as shown below:

Ensure that the location and project name combination does not currently exist.

Once **OK** is pressed, an associated physical directory, and a virtual directory under the web root will be created, together with the associated references and pages, while the window below is displayed:

Once the project is established, the Visual Studio .NET application screen appears containing menus and other items needed to create a web application:

Your environment may appear differently depending on your configuration.

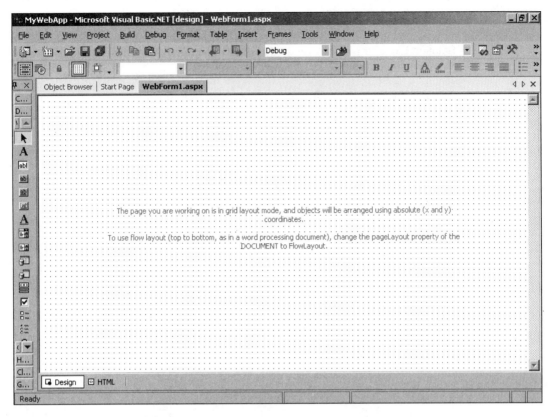

This may seem a bit daunting, but don't be concerned. We'll introduce each of the major items within the environment, in turn. For those who have used any of the applications in the Visual Studio 6 suite, the general screen layout should be familiar. While we won't discuss every window and function within Visual Studio .NET, we will familiarize you enough so that you feel comfortable working with it.

In our next example, we'll create a simple Web-based application to show you how easy it can be:

Try It Out – Form Colors Web Application

The Form Colors web application is comprised primarily of a simple form containing ASP.NET server-side controls and some C# code in the background. The form will have a dropdown list which contains names of colors, a button to execute the logic to determine which color was selected, and a label which will hold the message indicating which color was chosen by the user:

1. Launch Visual Studio .NET.

2. Select File | New | Project.

3. Select Visual C# Projects as the Project Type and ASP.NET Web Application as the Template.

4. Enter FormColors in the Name field and http://localhost as the Location. Click OK.

5. If the Solution Explorer is not currently displayed, select View | Solution Explorer from the main menu (or press *Ctrl-Alt-L*).

6. In the Solution Explorer, right-click on the filename WebForm1.aspx, and select Rename. Change the name to ColorsPage.aspx.

7. If the Toolbox does not appear, select View | Toolbox to display controls available for a Web Form (or press *Ctrl-Alt-X*):

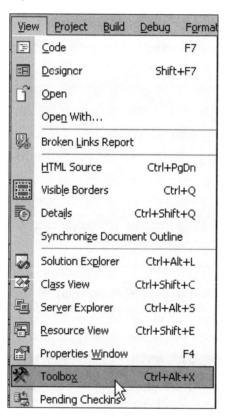

8. Using your mouse pointer, drag the DropDownList control from the Toolbox onto the Designer as shown below:

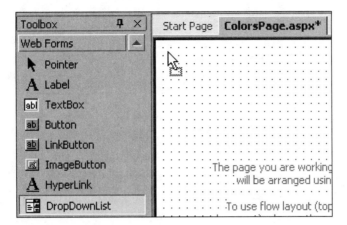

9. Drag a Button control onto the grid, just below the DropDownList control (see next screenshot).

10. Drag a Label control onto the grid, below the Button control (seen next screenshot).

11. Right-click on the DropDownList in the Designer, and select Properties:

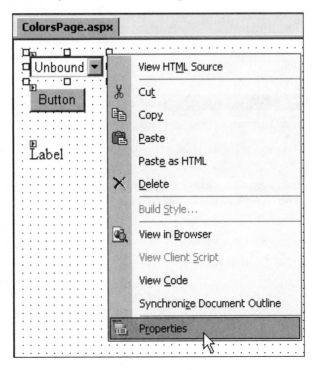

When the Properties window appears, scroll to (ID) at the bottom of the list in the Misc section. Change the (ID) to ddlColorChoices:

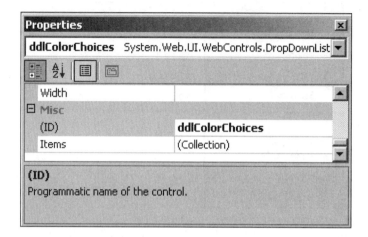

12. Click on the Items property to highlight it. Then click on the ellipsis (...) button next to Items as shown below:

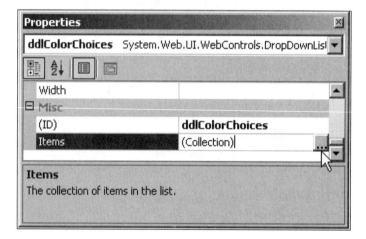

13. Once the ListItem Collection Editor appears, press the Add button to insert items into the dropdown list:

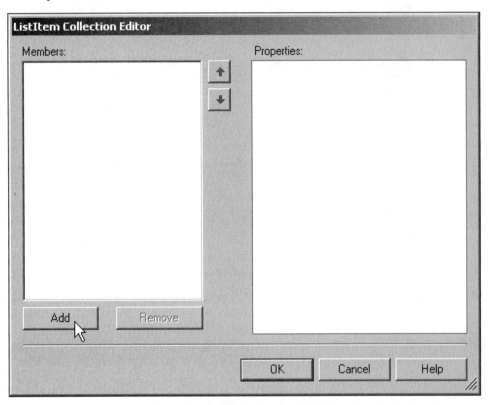

14. Add an item with a Text property of Red by clicking in the field next to Text. Click in the field next to Value and Red will automatically populate it. Then Press OK:

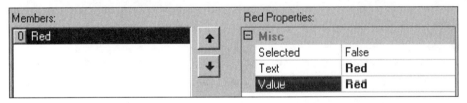

Repeat this process for the following items so that there are three items in all. Once the Text value is entered, the Value field will automatically populate with that same value:

❑ Text property of **Yellow**

❑ Text property of **Blue**

15. Click OK to save these properties of the drop-down list box.

16. Right-click on the Button control and select Properties in the Designer. Change the (ID) property to btnChangeColor, and the Text property to Change Color:

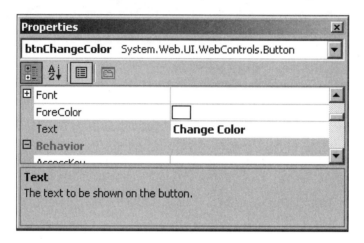

17. Right-click on the Label control and select Properties. Change the (ID) to lblColorResult and remove the label's text.

18. Press the HTML button at the bottom of the Designer window to display the following HTML automatically generated by Visual Studio .NET based on our display in the Designer:

```
<%@ Page language="c#" Codebehind="ColorsPage.aspx.cs" AutoEventWireup="false"
Inherits="FormColors.WebForm1" %>
<!DOCTYPE HTML PUBLIC "-//W3C//DTD HTML 4.0 Transitional//EN" >
<HTML>
  <HEAD>
    <meta name="vs_showGrid" content="False">
    <meta name="GENERATOR" Content="Microsoft Visual Studio 7.0">
    <meta name="CODE_LANGUAGE" Content="C#">
    <meta name="vs_defaultClientScript" content="JavaScript
            (ECMAScript)">
    <meta name="vs_targetSchema"
            content="http://schemas.microsoft.com/intellisense/ie5">
  </HEAD>
  <body MS_POSITIONING="GridLayout">
    <form id="Form1" method="post" runat="server">
      <asp:DropDownList id="ddlColorChoices" style="Z-INDEX:
                101; LEFT: 16px; POSITION: absolute; TOP: 16px"
                runat="server">
```

```
            <asp:ListItem Value="Red">Red</asp:ListItem>
            <asp:ListItem Value="Yellow">Yellow</asp:ListItem>
            <asp:ListItem Value="Blue">Blue</asp:ListItem>
        </asp:DropDownList>
        <asp:Button id="btnChangeColor" style="Z-INDEX: 102; LEFT:
                    16px; POSITION: absolute; TOP: 48px" runat="server"
                    Text="Change Color"></asp:Button>
        <asp:Label id="lblColorResult" style="Z-INDEX: 103; LEFT:
                    16px; POSITION: absolute; TOP: 104px"
                    runat="server"></asp:Label>
    </form>
  </body>
</HTML>
```

19. Double-click on the **Change Color** button:

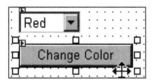

The following code will appear:

```
using System;
using System.Collections;
using System.ComponentModel;
using System.Data;
using System.Drawing;
using System.Web;
using System.Web.SessionState;
using System.Web.UI;
using System.Web.UI.WebControls;
using System.Web.UI.HtmlControls;

namespace FormColors
{
  /// <summary>
  /// Summary description for WebForm1.
  /// </summary>
  public class WebForm1 : System.Web.UI.Page
  {
    protected System.Web.UI.WebControls.DropDownList
      ddlColorChoices;
    protected System.Web.UI.WebControls.Label lblColorResult;
    protected System.Web.UI.WebControls.Button btnChangeColor;

    public WebForm1()
    {
      Page.Init += new System.EventHandler(Page_Init);
    }
```

```
      private void Page_Init(object sender, EventArgs e)
      {
        //
        // CODEGEN: This call is required by the ASP.NET Web Form Designer.
        //
        InitializeComponent();
      }


      #region Web Form Designer generated code
      /// <summary>
      /// Required method for Designer support - do not modify
      /// the contents of this method with the code editor.
      /// </summary>
      private void InitializeComponent()
      {
          this.btnChangeColor.Click += new
System.EventHandler(this.btnChangeColor_Click);
          this.Load += new System.EventHandler(this.Page_Load);

      }
      #endregion

      private void Page_Load(object sender, EventArgs e)
      {
        //Put user code to initialize the page here
      }

      private void btnChangeColor_Click(object sender, EventArgs e)
      {

      }

    }
}
```

Note that the code within the region *section will be hidden until it is expanded by pressing the +
to the left of the section.*

20. Type the following code inside of the Page_Load subroutine structure automatically created
by Visual Studio:

```
      private void Page_Load(object sender, EventArgs e)
      {
        //Put user code to initialize the page here
        lblColorResult.Text = "Current selection: " +
                                    ddlColorChoices.SelectedItem.Value;
      }
```

21. Add this code inside of the `btnChangeColor_Click` subroutine structure automatically created by Visual Studio:

```
private void btnChangeColor_Click(object sender, EventArgs e)
{
   lblColorResult.Text = "Current selection: " +
          ddlColorChoices.SelectedItem.Value;
}
```

22. Change the `private` declaration to `public`, and Press **Save**:

```
public void btnChangeColor_Click(object sender, EventArgs e)
```

23. Right-click on **ColorsPage.aspx** in the **Solution Explorer** and select **Build and Browse** (or simply press *F5*):

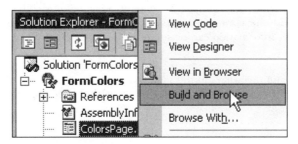

24. The following screen will appear. To test your code, select **Blue** from the dropdown list and press **Change Color**. The result will be displayed just below the button:

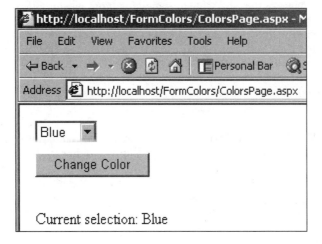

How It Works

Visual Studio .NET makes creating a web application very easy. Creating a new project, using File I New I Project, is very similar to creating items in other Microsoft Windows-based tools.

First, we selected C# Projects as our Project Type. As other language compilers are installed within the .NET Framework, the appropriate Project Type folders will appear on the left-hand side of the New/Open Projects dialog. As we can see within the Templates pane, each of the icons displays according to which language is used. For instance, if we had chosen a Visual Basic ASP.NET Web Application project, the following icon would have been displayed in the project type:

Next, we had to assign a name to the project. By default, Visual Studio .NET creates a folder beneath the web root-directory with the same name as the project we create here. The project is also connected to http://localhost so your information can be served.

> For this example, and the others in this chapter, we've assumed that
> C:\inetpub\wwwroot is the web root-directory with the virtual root,
> http://localhost.

All of the files associated with this project appeared automatically in the Solution Explorer. We'll talk about how Visual Studio .NET automatically creates these files a little later in the chapter.

Once we changed the name of the ASPX file to something more meaningful, we began adding controls from the Toolbox to the form. We then changed the name of DropDownList1 to ddlColorChoices, right-clicked on the control and selected Properties to display the ListItem Collection Editor. Instead of having to enter the HTML for the <asp:DropDownList> control using individual <asp:ListItem> controls, we added items to the dropdown list using this simple wizard.

We changed the control's name because DropDownList1 doesn't give us much indication of its purpose. ddlColorChoices is more meaningful.

Next, we took a quick look at the HTML that Visual Studio .NET automatically generates. To view this, we clicked on the HTML button shown beneath the Designer window to display the sourcecode.

As we remember, the first line, known as the **Page directive**, is necessary for any ASP.NET web page. The Codebehind attribute in the Page directive is important. Visual Studio .NET uses this technique to separate out presentation code from business logic, making for much cleaner and more easily maintainable code:

```
<%@ Page language="c#" Codebehind=" ColorsPage.aspx.cs " AutoEventWireup="false"
Inherits="FormColors.WebForm1" %>
<!DOCTYPE HTML PUBLIC "-//W3C//DTD HTML 4.0 Transitional//EN" >
```

In this case, the code-behind file is called `ColorsPage.aspx.cs`. We will look at the code that it contains shortly.

> **We discuss the Code-behind concept in more depth in the next chapter.**

The next things to notice in our ASPX page the `<meta>` tags. These are automatically generated by Visual Studio .NET with certain default settings (for example, Javascript as the default client script language). Also, we can see that the `<body>` tag has an attribute called `MS_POSITIONING`. We have one option for this attribute: GridLayout. The GridLayout value allows elements to be dragged across the Design view surface. If the `MS_POSITIONING` attribute is omitted then it assumes FlowLayout behavior. With FlowLayout, web browsers arrange elements in the order that they occur on the page, from top to bottom, rather than being positioned aesthetically by the designer.

```
<HTML>
  <HEAD>
    <meta name="vs_showGrid" content="False">
    <meta name="GENERATOR" Content="Microsoft Visual Studio 7.0">
    <meta name="CODE_LANGUAGE" Content="C#">
    <meta name="vs_defaultClientScript" content="JavaScript
            (ECMAScript)">
    <meta name="vs_targetSchema"
            content="http://schemas.microsoft.com/intellisense/ie5">
  </HEAD>
  <body MS_POSITIONING="GridLayout">
```

Finally, we have the ASP.NET server-side controls that comprise the page. Nothing new here, except it is interesting to see how Visual Studio .NET keeps the position of the controls we placed on the form by using a `style` attribute:

```
<form id="Form1" method="post" runat="server">
  <asp:DropDownList id="ddlColorChoices" style="Z-INDEX:
              101; LEFT: 16px; POSITION: absolute; TOP: 16px"
              runat="server">
    <asp:ListItem Value="Red">Red</asp:ListItem>
    <asp:ListItem Value="Yellow">Yellow</asp:ListItem>
    <asp:ListItem Value="Blue">Blue</asp:ListItem>
  </asp:DropDownList>
  <asp:Button id="btnChangeColor" style="Z-INDEX: 102; LEFT:
              16px; POSITION: absolute; TOP: 48px" runat="server"
              Text="Change Color"></asp:Button>
  <asp:Label id="lblColorResult" style="Z-INDEX: 103; LEFT:
              16px; POSITION: absolute; TOP: 104px"
              runat="server"></asp:Label>
  </form>
  </body>
</HTML>
```

> **For additional information on ASP.NET server-side controls, and more, please refer to *Beginning ASP.NET Using C#* from Wrox Press (ISBN 1-861006-15-2). Alternatively, see *Professional ASP.NET*, also by Wrox Press (ISBN 1-861004-88-5).**

We added code to the button, btnChangeColor, in the form by double-clicking on the button control in the **Designer**. We were taken to the code-behind file (ColorsPage.aspx.cs) for the entire page, where we simply made our changes within the subroutine structure, btnChangeColor_Click. We also made a change to the Page_Load event, while we were there:

We'll look at code-behind in more detail in the next chapter. Essentially, it is a way of moving code that would normally reside within <script> tags on the .aspx file to a separate file, making it easier to separate presentation and layout from the code.

```csharp
using System;
using System.Collections;
using System.ComponentModel;
using System.Data;
using System.Drawing;
using System.Web;
using System.Web.SessionState;
using System.Web.UI;
using System.Web.UI.WebControls;
using System.Web.UI.HtmlControls;

namespace FormColors
{
  /// <summary>
  /// Summary description for WebForm1.
  /// </summary>
  public class WebForm1 : System.Web.UI.Page
  {
    protected System.Web.UI.WebControls.DropDownList
      ddlColorChoices;
    protected System.Web.UI.WebControls.Label lblColorResult;
    protected System.Web.UI.WebControls.Button btnChangeColor;

    public WebForm1()
    {
      Page.Init += new System.EventHandler(Page_Init);
    }

    private void Page_Init(object sender, EventArgs e)
    {
      //
      // CODEGEN: This call is required by the ASP.NET Web Form Designer.
      //
      InitializeComponent();
    }
```

```
#region Web Form Designer generated code
/// <summary>
/// Required method for Designer support - do not modify
/// the contents of this method with the code editor.
/// </summary>
private void InitializeComponent()
{
   this.btnChangeColor.Click += new
                      System.EventHandler(this.btnChangeColor_Click);
   this.Load += new System.EventHandler(this.Page_Load);

}
#endregion

private void Page_Load(object sender, EventArgs e)
{
   //Put user code to initialize the page here
   lblColorResult.Text = "Current selection: " +
                  ddlColorChoices.SelectedItem.Value;
}

public void btnChangeColor_Click(object sender, EventArgs e)
{
   lblColorResult.Text = "Current selection: " +
                  ddlColorChoices.SelectedItem.Value;
}

   }
}
```

One thing to note is the #region segment, which is code that is automatically generated by Visual Studio .NET. The #region directive lets you specify a block of code that you can expand or collapse when using the outlining feature of the **Visual Studio Code Editor**. #region statements support block semantics (such as #If...#End If), meaning that the start and end must be in the same code block. In addition, when we dragged and dropped the button control from the **Toolbox** to the form, the Private Sub btnChangeColor_Click subroutine was automatically created. This code only contained the subroutine framework for executing code when the form was loaded. To make this routine visible to other segments of the code, we changed its declaration from private to public.

Finally, we used Visual Studio .NET to test our code. Our browser setting was Microsoft Internet Explorer (the default). When we selected **Browse and Build**, the sourcecode was compiled and the result was displayed in a new browser window:

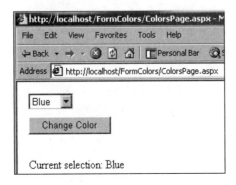

Since we've now had some exposure to the general Visual Studio .NET environment, let's take a closer look at some of its primary windows. The first one we'll discuss is the Designer.

The Designer Window

When an application with a front-end is created, this area is used to layout the interface screen. Unlike a text editor, we can speed up development by being able to see what the screen looks like as we work. While this is very much like the Visual Basic 6 environment, we don't need experience with Visual Basic to use the Designer.

Each project template causes a specific Designer to appear when the project is opened. For a Web Application, the Web Form Designer appears. A Windows Application displays the Page Designer. While a Web Service only displays a message where the Designer area (which cannot be modified) would be located because it has no front-end interface:

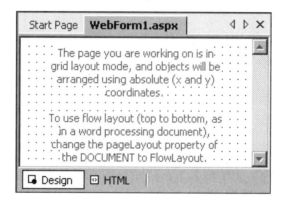

As we can see, the Designer window has a grid of dots (the default Designer area is much bigger but we've reduced it to fit on the screen). We begin the development process by dragging and dropping controls onto the form and inserting code behind them as needed.

The tabs above the Designer allow us to move quickly and easily through the various files that our project might comprise:

The buttons below the Designer allow us to toggle between the Designer view and the HTML view for the page:

As we use the Designer to make a form, Visual Studio .NET automatically generates the source HTML. In addition, it automatically handles control instance names of objects entered directly into the code. Those of you that are more comfortable working with HTML may bypass the Designer completely and enter code to build the front end (in exactly the same manner as with a text editor).

Now we've seen the window provided to allow us to layout controls on our form, let's move on to look at the window that provides us with access to those controls:

The Toolbox Window

The Toolbox is separated into different categories, each pertaining to a specific function. Clicking on each category reveals each one's appropriate controls. The tab categories will also vary depending on the project template used. For instance, with our web application, we have the following controls:

We employ the Toolbox by using our mouse pointer to drag-and-drop items onto the Designer. The above graphic shows only a sample of the controls available. We also have the ability to add controls.

The Solution Explorer Window

The Solution Explorer contains all of the files necessary for a project. For a web application, these files include the actual web pages with code-behind files containing the sourcecode, referenced modules, global.asax and web.config files, and default styles.css style sheet, among others. This window can be viewed by selecting it from the View option on the menu bar or by pressing *Ctrl-Alt-L*.

When we create a new project, on the right-hand side of the screen we see the Solution Explorer that contains the following entries:

We won't delve into each of these files too deeply, since some have been covered in previous chapters or are not within the scope of this discussion. However, we will show the references that Visual Studio. NET includes within an ASP.NET Web Application. When we create mobile applications in the next chapter, we'll see that there will be unique references:

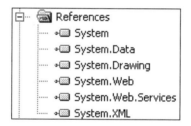

You may recognize the names of some of these items from earlier chapters. These modules have to be referenced when creating an ASP.NET web page. When we used a standard text editor, we had to remember to include these in our sourcecode. Fortunately, Visual Studio .NET automatically handles this for us.

The other item of interest in the list is ColorsPage.aspx. As we see, this was automatically created by Visual Studio .NET. Again, if we had chosen a different project template, the default name of the page would differ. (We can change its name by right-clicking on it in the **Solution Explorer** and selecting **Rename**.)

The Properties Window

Now we'll see how we can change the characteristics of the various controls in the Designer:

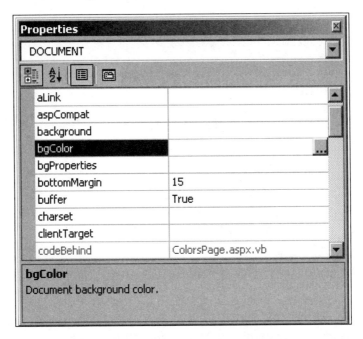

The Properties window allows us to view and modify appearances and behaviors for a selected object. In this window, property names can be sorted and sections collapsed as needed. Each control possesses properties specific to its type. For instance, we can use Properties to add items to a dropdown list; however, adding list items isn't available for a label since this control doesn't use items.

As we make changes to the control within the Properties window, the code is changed to reflect them. This makes our development much more straightforward by having all properties visible (since we don't have to remember each control's properties).

The Dynamic Help Window

The **Dynamic Help** feature in Visual Studio .NET provides developers with a great facility to see context-sensitive help:

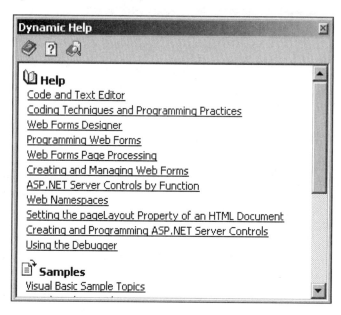

This is a definite improvement over the previous version of Visual Studio, which required users to search through all of the help links and samples included with the entire suite.

Based on settings in the **Start Page**, a user can establish what help information is initially available. Then, as actions are performed within the environment (entering code, clicking menu options, and so on), the **Dynamic Help** window makes the appropriate information available. However, keep in mind that there is a performance penalty attached to having this feature available, since Visual Studio .NET must constantly monitor the user to be able to respond accordingly.

To turn this feature off, select Tools | Options, and then from the Environment folder, select Dynamic Help. The following dialog will appear:

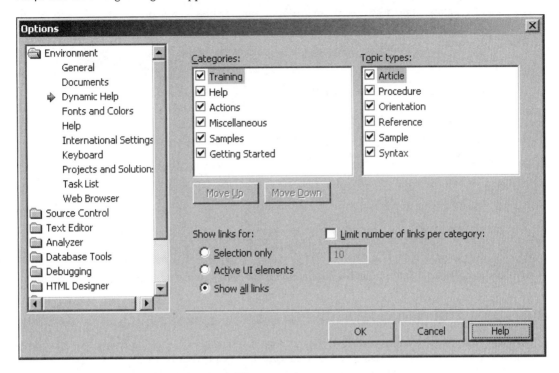

Deselect all of the categories, then press OK to save these settings.

Testing A Project

Visual Studio .NET provides some good features to assist in the testing of our projects. Many of these will be familiar to users of previous versions of Visual Studio.

The Output Window

The Output Window allows us to see the status of our application as we compile its sourcecode. The information provided in this window indicates whether or not the build was successful:

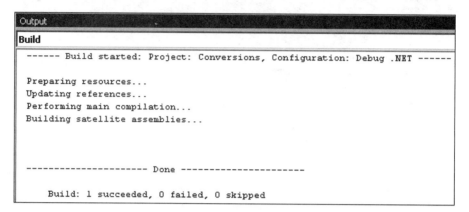

The Output Window also shows whether or not the list of modules was successfully loaded into the debugger at runtime. If this window is not open you can find it at View | Other Windows | Output.

The Task List Window

The Task List is a great way to handle debugging when entering or compiling sourcecode. To view the Output Window, select View | Other Windows | Task List or press *Ctrl-Alt-O*.

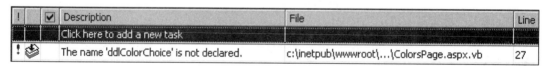

Here's an example of when the Task List may be useful. Suppose we have made reference to a control that does not exist in our code. In this case, the "s" was omitted from ddlColorChoices. The Task List points out this error, indicating the file name and the line number causing the problem. If we double-click on the error in the list, we will be taken directly to that segment of code. As our errors are corrected and the code recompiled, the items will be removed from the Task List.

In addition, user-defined comments can be displayed in the Task List as well using the TODO command in our sourcecode, as shown below:

```
'TODO: This comment will be displayed in the Task List
```

This function will appear as a line item in the Task List, enabling us to follow the program flow.

We may also add our own identifiers and even set their priorities. This can be done by selecting Tools | Options | Environment | Task List.

The Debugging Window

The debugging capabilities in Visual Studio .NET are quite similar to those in previous versions of Visual Studio. The ability to set breakpoints, step into code, and view the call stack, is all available. You can get to this information by selecting Debug from the menu bar. Within this menu the Start button (shown below) allows us to compile our sourcecode with, or without, debugging:

If you wish to stop the program at a particular line in your logic, you can simply click to the left of that line to display a breakpoint (denoted by a red dot). Your program will stop executing at this point:

Please note that a breakpoint cannot be set on a line that does not execute.

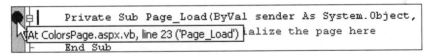

Once we reach this line, and our program stops, we can press the Step Into key (*F11* in our Visual Studio .NET profile) to move to the next line. We can continue stepping through like this until our program ends. The *F5* key can also be pressed to continue running until either the next breakpoint is reached or the application has finished.

Now that we've seen how to create applications, and test them, as well as some of the useful features provided with Visual Studio .NET, we'll build a small Windows application using C#:

Try It Out – Word Search Windows Application Using C#

The Word Search Application will allow a user to enter a keyword, press a button, and have it search the content of a text box to find that string. Once it's found, the string will appear in a larger font and underlined:

1. Outside of Visual Studio .NET create the following directory: `C:\WordSearch`.

2. Within the `C:\WordSearch` directory, create a text file called `WordSearchContent.txt` containing the following text (or similar):

The Lord is my Shepherd; I shall not want. He maketh me to lie down in green pastures; he leadeth me beside the still waters.

3. Launch Visual Studio .NET.

4. Create a C# Windows Application. Enter `WordSearch` as the **Name** of the project and `C:\WordSearch` as the **Location**.

5. View the **Solution Explorer**. After it appears, right-click on `Form1.cs` and select **Rename**. When the cursor appears, rename this file to `WordSearch.cs`.

6. In the **Designer**, right-click on `Form1` and choose **Properties**. Change the **Name** to `frmSearch`. Change the **Text** property to `Word Search`.

7. Drag the following items from the **Toolbox** onto `frmSearch`:

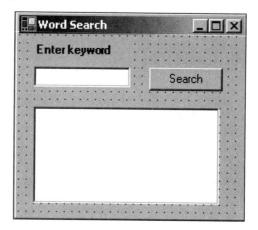

Label: Right-click on it and select **Properties**. Change the Name to lblCaption. Change the Text to **Enter keyword**. Make the font bold by selecting the Font property and choosing Bold.

Textbox: Right-click on it and select **Properties**. Change the Name to txtKeyword. Delete the value for Text.

Button: Right-click on it and select **Properties**. Change the Name to btnSearch. Change the Text to Search.

RichTextBox: Right-click on it and select **Properties**. Change the Name to rtbContents. Delete the value for Text.

8. Double-click on btnSearch to display the code-behind the form.

9. Add the following statement at the top of the code, below using System;:

```
using System.IO;
```

10. Within the Main routine, change Form1 to frmSearch:

```
static void Main()
{
    Application.Run(new frmSearch());
}
```

11. In the WordSearch.cs file, add the following code to the Load event:

```
private void frmSearch_Load(object sender, System.EventArgs e)
{
    FileStream fs = new FileStream("c:/WordSearch/ WordSearchContent.txt",
                                    FileMode.Open, FileAccess.Read);
    StreamReader r = new StreamReader(fs);
    r.BaseStream.Seek(0, SeekOrigin.Begin);
    while (r.Peek() > -1)
    {
        rtbContents.Text = rtbContents.Text.Trim().ToString() + " " +
            r.ReadLine().Trim().ToString();
    }
    r.Close();
}
```

12. Then add the following code in the btnSearch_Click structure created by Visual Studio:

```
private void btnSearch_Click(object sender, System.EventArgs e)
{
    rtbContents.Find(txtKeyword.Text, 0, RichTextBoxFinds.MatchCase);
    rtbContents.SelectionFont = new Font("Courier", 12, FontStyle.Underline);
}
```

13. Click on View Designer in the Solution Explorer:

14. Right-click on `frmSearch` and choose Properties. Click on the Events button:

15. Set the Load property value to `frmSearch_Load`:

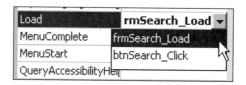

16. Click on View Code in the Solution Explorer:

17. Set a breakpoint on the following line:

```
136        private void btnSearch_Click(object sender, System.EventArgs e)
137        {
138            rtbContents.Find(txtKeyword.Text, 0, RichTextBoxFinds.MatchCase);
139            rtbContents.SelectionFont = new Font("Courier", 12, FontStyle.Underline);
140        }
```

18. Now press the Start button at the top of the screen.

19. Once the WordSearch application begins, enter the word "want" in the textbox:

20. Press Search.

21. When the breakpoint in the code is reached, press *F11* to continue to the next statement:

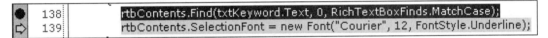

```
138    rtbContents.Find(txtKeyword.Text, 0, RichTextBoxFinds.MatchCase);
139    rtbContents.SelectionFont = new Font("Courier", 12, FontStyle.Underline);
```

22. Press *F5* to continue execution, and the form will display the following result:

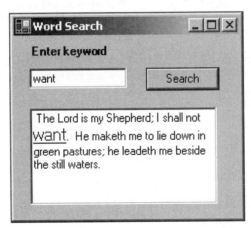

How It Works

As adept as it is in developing web applications, Visual Studio .NET does equally well with Windows programs.

We began by selecting File | New | Project. Then we entered the name WordSearch as the application name with a physical location of c:\WindowsApp, as shown below:

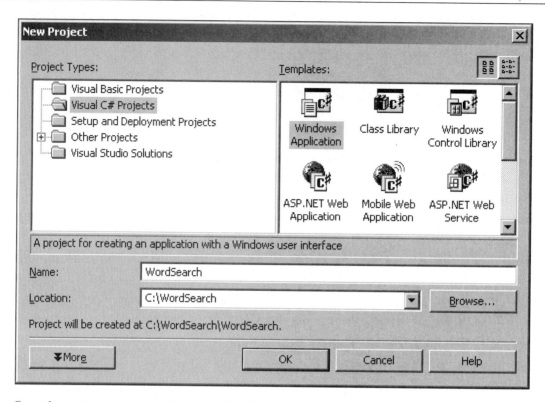

Once the main screen appeared, we used the **Toolbox** to drag and drop controls onto the **Designer** area. Just as with a web application, we were able to set properties for the controls and insert new code into the existing code automatically generated by Visual Studio .NET.

When we clicked on **View Code** in the **Solution Explorer**, we could see this generated code. The code in the `frmSearch_Load` routine is automatically run when the form is first loaded. We entered additional lines to read a text file and loaded its contents into a `RichTextBox`. The code uses the `FileStream` object, which allows us to open and read the file, `WordSearchContent.txt`, which contains our sample text:

```
private void frmSearch_Load(object sender, System.EventArgs e)
{
  FileStream fs = new
      FileStream("c:/WordSearch/WordSearch/WordSearchContent.txt", _
      FileMode.Open, FileAccess.Read);
  StreamReader r = new StreamReader(fs);
  r.BaseStream.Seek(0, SeekOrigin.Begin);
  while (r.Peek() > -1)
  {
    rtbContents.Text=rtbContents.Text.Trim().ToString() + " " +
    r.ReadLine().Trim().ToString();
  }
  r.Close();
}
```

Next, this C# routine opens the file in read-only mode and instantiates a `StreamReader`:

```
FileStream fs = new FileStream("c:/WordSearch/WordSearch/WordSearchContent.txt ",
                               FileMode.Open, FileAccess.Read);
StreamReader r = new StreamReader(fs);
```

Next, it positions the read at the first line:

```
r.BaseStream.Seek(0, SeekOrigin.Begin);
```

Then it reads the file line by line and finally closes the `StreamReader`. As the file is read, the routine puts the data into the `Text` property of the `rtbContents RichTextBox` as a string value:

```
while (r.Peek() > -1)
{
   rtbContents.Text=rtbContents.Text.Trim().ToString() + " " + _
                              r.ReadLine().Trim().ToString();
}
r.Close();
```

The second routine, `btnSearch_Click`, performs a search on the text in `rtbContents` when the `btnSearch` button is pressed.

The first line in the routine uses the keyword we entered in the textbox as a parameter. It indicates that we start before the first character (0) and specifies that any matches should match the case of the keyword. The second line indicates what to do with the text if we find it. In this example, we change the matching text to have the font face `Courier`, the font size `12` and underline the text so that it stands out:

```
private void btnSearch_Click(object sender, System.EventArgs e)
{
   rtbContents.Find(txtKeyword.Text, 0, RichTextBoxFinds.MatchCase);
   rtbContents.SelectionFont = new Font("Courier", 12, FontStyle.Underline);
}
```

In this example, we also took the opportunity to use the debugging functionality. We began setting a breakpoint at:

```
rtbContents.Find(txtKeyword.Text, 0, RichTextBoxFinds.MatchCase);
```

When we ran the application, the code stopped at the point we set and allowed us to step through it line by line from then on. Also the **Autos** window appeared, which displayed all of the properties available within the scope of the execution. We stepped to the next line by pressing the *F11* key.

When we looked in the Autos window, we saw that the Text property for txtKeyword contained the value of "want":

Autos		
Name	Value	Type
⊞ rtbContents	{System.Windows.Forms.RichTextBox}	System.Windows.Forms.RichTextBox
⊞ rtbContents.Selectic	{System.Drawing.Font}	System.Drawing.Font
⊞ this	{WordSearch.WordSearch}	WordSearch.WordSearch
⊞ txtKeyword	{System.Windows.Forms.TextBox}	System.Windows.Forms.TextBox
txtKeyword.Text	"want"	string

We then had the ability to change this value for testing purposes. For instance, if we had had code that trapped particular types of inputs, we could have clicked inside of the Value cell for txtKeyword.Text and changed it to meet the trapping condition.

Advanced Topics

Visual Studio .NET provides several more advanced features which we'll discuss briefly. We'll see that these are extremely useful in building our applications.

> **If you require more information about Visual Studio .NET, please see *Professional Windows Forms* by Wrox Press, ISBN 1-861005-44-7 .**

The Server Explorer

The Server Explorer is a new feature available with this version of Visual Studio. Its window can be found beneath the View option on the main menu. With this option, users have the ability to work with server components on the network without having to leave the boundaries of the application:

For instance, developers consistently work with databases. Visual Studio .NET is "component-aware", which means it looks for these connections on startup, and we have the database's structures (table, views, and so on) available to use in our code. We can drag-and-drop them on our forms and bind them to controls. There's no need to worry about creating code for database connections and transactions. This is handled automatically.

The Object Browser

The Object Browser is an extremely useful tool, especially when researching the properties and methods of .NET modules and components. This too can be found beneath the View option on the main menu:

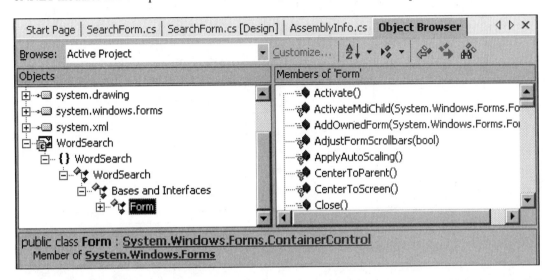

It allows us to see the available properties of a form. As we may be working with some types of control for the first time, the Object Browser allows us to click on an item and see all of its members. These can be sorted or searched for the property we need in our application.

Setting Options In Visual Studio .NET

Visual Studio .NET also gives the ability to set additional options, such as the font faces, sizes, and colors for the code editor, the way the Debugging tools behave, and how source control is handled, to name but a few. Explaining all of the options available would require a separate chapter alone:

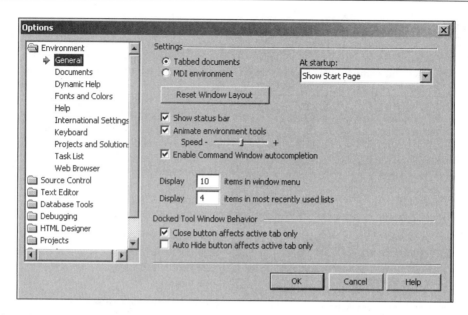

We'll quickly show you how to set two helpful options within the Visual Studio .NET environment:

Try It Out – Setting Visual Studio .NET Options

With this exercise, we'll initiate the setting to display line numbers in our code and cause the Designer to default to the HTML view upon start up:

1. Launch Visual Studio .NET

2. Select Tools | Options from the menu bar

3. In the left pane, select Text Editor

4. Select All Languages

5. In the Display frame, click the checkbox next to Line numbers

6. Select HTML Designer from the menu bar

7. From General, in the Start Web Form pages panel, select the radio button next to HTML View, and press OK

8. Create a new web application project in C#

9. Select the View Code button from the Solution Explorer

How It Works

We have several options available for customization. This can make the development experience in Visual Studio .NET much more enjoyable by providing you with a few extra conveniences.

By selecting **Text Editor** from the folders list, we have the ability to choose settings for all of the languages in Visual Studio .NET, as well as for each language. Now, each time we launch Visual Studio .NET, these settings are saved so that we can have the environment behave as we wish, without having to change them each time:

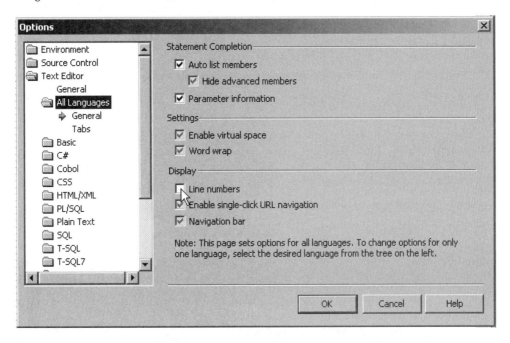

As we've chosen the **Line Numbers** option from the **Display** frame (shown above), we will be able to see the corresponding lines number for the code when we select **View Code** in our examples. This provides us with an easy way to reference code as we work with our application:

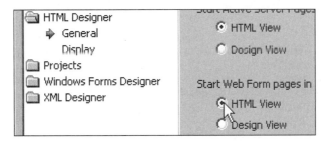

Finally, because we set the **Start Web Form** page option to HTML, we saw that the HTML view appeared first instead of the **Designer**. Again, for those who would rather work with the HTML to create a form, this is a good feature as we avoid having to click on the HTML button each time we create or open a project.

Summary

In this chapter we've seen how powerful Visual Studio .NET is in creating Web and Windows applications. It becomes our one-stop shop for building the kinds of applications we need using the languages we prefer. Features such as the Designer, debugging, sourcecode management and dynamic help allow us to be more productive. Visual Studio .NET gets the novice programmer up and running quickly with ASP.NET development and allows the expert to be more productive as less emphasis is placed on creating the presentation and more is placed on the actual logic.

In the next chapter we will continue our Visual Studio .NET theme, as we look at how it can be used to create ASP.NET Mobile Applications.

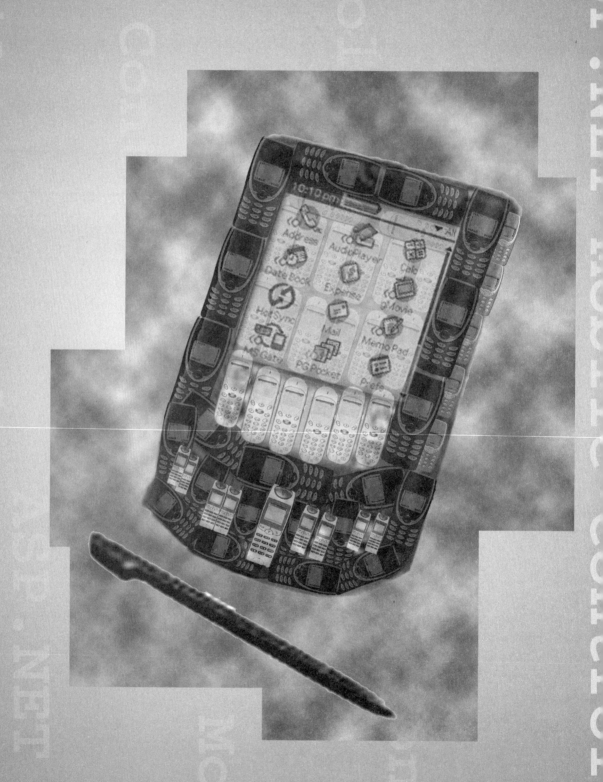

Using Visual Studio .NET For Mobile Applications

Visual Studio .NET was gently introduced to us in Chapter 17. We saw how front-end development, using its drag-and-drop environment allows us to rapidly produce Web and Windows-based applications. We were exposed to creating an individual user's profile to make his/her development experience more productive and enjoyable. We also learned how tools, such as the Designer, dynamic help, and formatting capabilities, make Visual Studio .NET a great alternative to the standard text editor.

In this chapter, we'll discover just how easy it is to build ASP.NET mobile applications using Visual Studio .NET. We'll go through the process of creating a project, setting properties for mobile controls, writing code behind the controls, and finally testing, all within the Visual Studio .NET environment. Along the way, we'll delve into the techniques Visual Studio .NET uses to structure code and the specific items that are available within the Mobile Controls Toolbox.

Let's take a look at how we can use VS .NET within the context of creating ASP.NET mobile applications.

Introduction

Throughout this book, we've seen that developing mobile applications using Notepad is possible and works quite well in tandem with the Mobile Internet Toolkit. However, entering line upon line of display code can be cumbersome, not to mention difficult for keeping track of the syntax for tags and their attributes. Testing a mobile application can be an adventure all of its own.

Fortunately, Visual Studio .NET is a friendly IDE (Integrated Development Environment) where we can construct mobile web applications in a much more graphical and controlled way. The Mobile Internet Toolkit, which we've worked with in the previous chapters, is tightly integrated with Visual Studio .NET with support for creating .NET mobile applications.

When we launch Visual Studio .NET (assuming it's already installed), we see the Microsoft Mobile Explorer Content Toolkit icon at the bottom of the splash graphic.

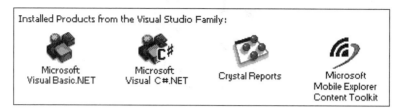

Within Visual Studio .NET, we create a mobile application by selecting File | New | Project, as shown below.

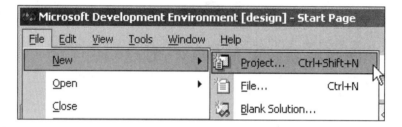

As we've seen in the previous chapter, the following screen appears from which we can choose from among various project templates.

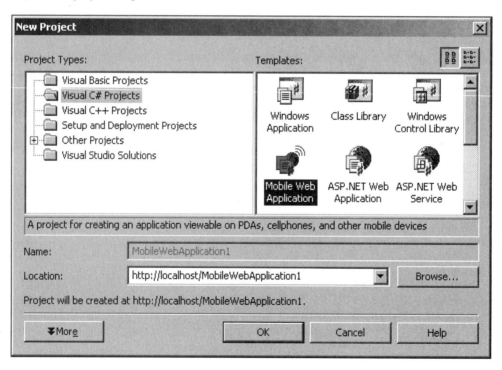

For our purposes, we will select the Mobile Web Application template within the C# Projects folder. In the **Name** field, we replace `MobileWebApplication1` with the name of our project.

Note the Location in the drop-down list. The line below displays the virtual path including the folder where the application will reside.

To show how easy it is to create an ASP.NET mobile application, let's try this example:

Try It Out – Your First ASP.NET Mobile Application Using Visual Studio .NET

1. Launch Visual Studio .NET, and then within the C# Projects folder, create a Mobile Web Application. Give your project the name, `MyMobileApp`, and press OK. Once `MobileWebForm1.aspx` appears, you will see `Form1`.

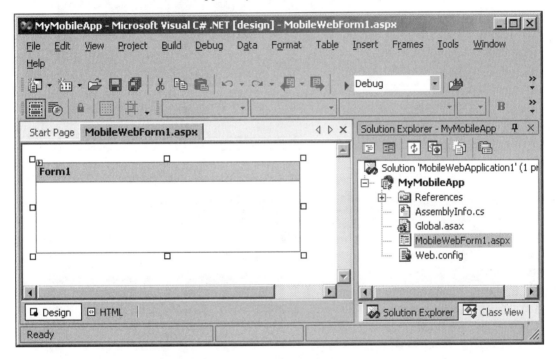

2. Right-click on `MobileWebForm1.aspx`, and select `Delete`, then press *Ctrl-Shift-A* to create a new item. We then select the Mobile Web Form template with the name, `ConversionsForm.aspx`.

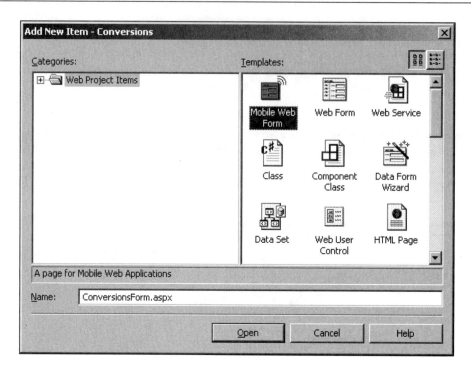

3. Next, we go to View | Toolbox (or press *Ctrl-Alt-X*). The Mobile Controls **toolbox** will appear.

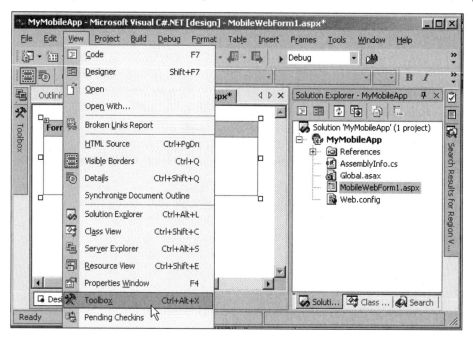

4. Right-click on `Form1`, and Select **Properties**.

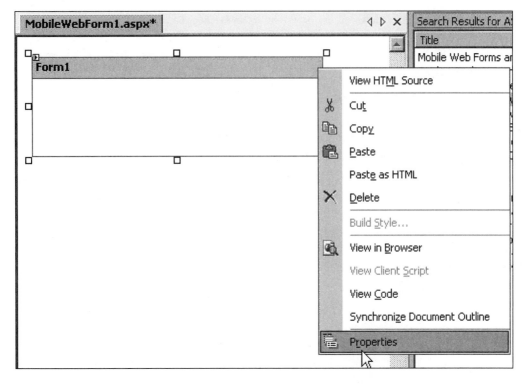

5. In the **Properties** pane, change the `ID` property to `frmMain`.

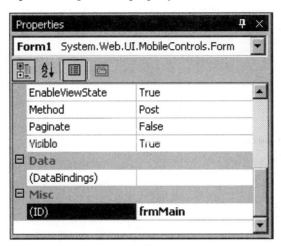

6. Drag a Label mobile control from the Toolbox to frmMain.

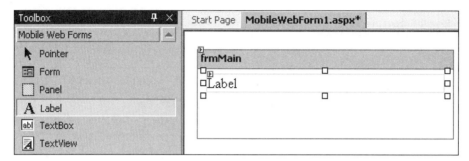

7. Right-click on the Label in frmMain. Select Properties. In the Properties pane, change the ID property to lblCaption. Change the Text property to read "Press button to go to next form". Drag a Command button from the Toolbox to frmMain, just below the Label.

8. Right-click on the command button in frmMain. Select Properties. In the Properties pane, change the ID property to btnGo. Change the Text property to Go. Drag a new form from the Toolbox, just below frmMain.

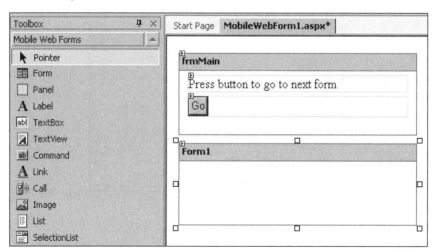

9. Right-click on `Form1`. Select `Properties`. In the **Properties** pane, change the (`ID`) property to `frmTwo`. Drag a label from the **Toolbox** and place it on `frmTwo`.

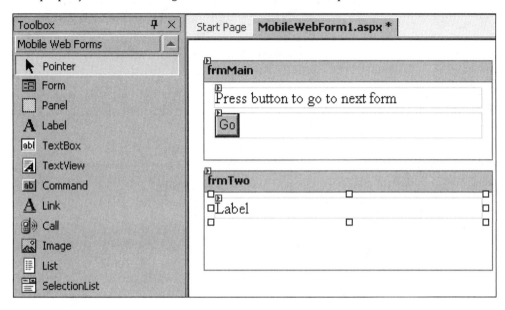

10. Change the label's `ID` to `lblCaptionTwo` and its `Text` property to "This is the second form". At the bottom of the Mobile Designer, select the **HTML** button to view the code for this page.

```
<%@ Page language="c#" Codebehind="MobileWebForm1.aspx.cs"
Inherits="MyMobileApp.MobileWebForm1" AutoEventWireup="false" %>
<%@ Register TagPrefix="mobile" Namespace="System.Web.UI.MobileControls"
Assembly="System.Web.Mobile" %>
<meta content="Microsoft Visual Studio 7.0" name="GENERATOR">
<meta content="C#" name="CODE_LANGUAGE">
<meta content="Mobile Web Page" name="vs_targetSchema">
<body xmlns:mobile="Mobile Web Form Controls">
    <mobile:Form id="frmMain" runat="server">
        <mobile:Label id="lblCaption" runat="server">Press button to go to next
form</mobile:Label>
        <mobile:Command id="btnGo" runat="server">Go</mobile:Command>
    </mobile:Form>
    <mobile:Form id="frmTwo" runat="server">
        <mobile:Label id="lblCaptionTwo" runat="server">This is the second
form</mobile:Label>
    </mobile:Form>
</body>
```

11. Click on the View Designer button in the Solution Explorer.

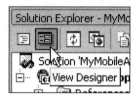

12. Double-click on the Command button, Go, on frmMain. The following code will appear.

```csharp
using System;
using System.Collections;
using System.ComponentModel;
using System.Data;
using System.Drawing;
using System.Web;
using System.Web.Mobile;
using System.Web.SessionState;
using System.Web.UI;
using System.Web.UI.MobileControls;
using System.Web.UI.WebControls;
using System.Web.UI.HtmlControls;

namespace MyMobileApp
{
    /// <summary>
    /// Summary description for MyMobileApp.
    /// </summary>
    public class MobileWebForm1 : System.Web.UI.MobileControls.MobilePage
    {
        protected System.Web.UI.MobileControls.Form frmMain;
        protected System.Web.UI.MobileControls.Label lblCaption;
        protected System.Web.UI.MobileControls.Command btnGo;
        protected System.Web.UI.MobileControls.Form frmTwo;
        protected System.Web.UI.MobileControls.Label lblCaptionTwo;

        public MobileWebForm1()
        {
            Page.Init += new System.EventHandler(Page_Init);
        }

        private void Page_Load(object sender, System.EventArgs e)
        {
            // Put user code to initialize the page here
        }
        private void Page_Init(object sender, EventArgs e)
        {
            //
            // CODEGEN: This call is required by the ASP.NET Windows Form
                                                        Designer.
            //
            InitializeComponent();
        }
```

```
        #region Web Form Designer generated code
        /// <summary>
        /// Required method for Designer support - do not modify
        /// the contents of this method with the code editor.
        /// </summary>
        private void InitializeComponent()
        {
            this.btnGo.Click += new System.EventHandler(this.btnGo_Click);
            this.Load += new System.EventHandler(this.Page_Load);

        }
        #endregion

        private void btnGo_Click(object sender, System.EventArgs e)
        {

        }
    }
}
```

13. Change the `private` declaration for btnGo_Click to `public`, and enter this line of code within the `Private Sub btnGo_Click` subroutine framework:

```
this.ActiveForm = frmTwo;
```

14. Then, we press the Run button at the top of the screen.

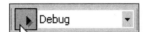

A new instance of Microsoft Internet Explorer will appear.

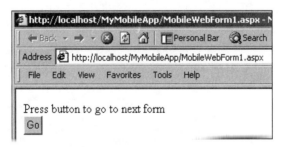

15. Finally, press Go to view the second form:

How It Works

By dragging and dropping mobile controls from the Toolbox onto the Mobile Designer with a little C# code behind the command button, we created a functioning (albeit not very powerful) ASP.NET mobile application using Visual Studio .NET. We didn't have to enter a single line of HTML!

As we saw in Chapter 17, the initial dialog appears allowing us to create a specific type of project using C#. We pressed OK, and a message appears indicating that a connection was being made. While this was occurring, a folder was created in the associated physical directory. For example, if you use c:\inetpub\wwwroot as your default web directory on your local machine, the new application folder will be c:\inetpub\wwwroot\MyMobileApp.

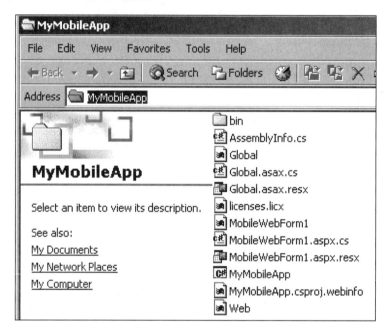

Once the connection is complete, the Visual Studio .NET environment appears. We saw this layout in Chapter 17.

However, if we examine the References folder, we note a subtle difference from examples we've already seen. When the folder is expanded, we see namespaces that are available within our mobile project.

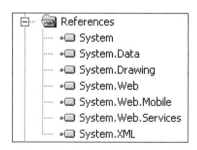

Notice the namespace System.Web.Mobile, which enables us to import classes from its namespace and instantiate objects using code. Whether Visual Studio adds a reference or we do it manually (refer to the 'Reference' folder in solution explorer), it copies the imported namespaces to the current assembly. However, to use the classes contained in the imported namespace(s), we must indicate our intention to the compiler, by inserting the using statement in our current namespace.

We've also learned that we have the ability in ASP.NET to have multiple mobile forms within one ASPX page. This reduces the number of pages on the physical site, which improves performance during runtime.

In this exercise, we have two mobile forms on the Designer grid, frmMain and frmTwo. We dragged one label and one command button onto frmMain. A second label was placed on frmTwo. When the mobile form design was complete, we simply added the ActiveForm statement behind btnGo. This allowed us to make frmTwo active when we pressed the command button, btnGo.

In previous chapters, we had to enter a lot of code by hand. Fortunately, Visual Studio shields us from handling some of this tedium. As we used the Designer, the HTML for the forms was built dynamically. We viewed it after we clicked on the HTML button in the Designer.

```
<%@ Page language="c#" Codebehind="MobileWebForm1.aspx.cs"
Inherits="MyMobileApp.MobileWebForm1" AutoEventWireup="false" %>
<%@ Register TagPrefix="mobile" Namespace="System.Web.UI.MobileControls"
Assembly="System.Web.Mobile" %>
<meta content="Microsoft Visual Studio 7.0" name="GENERATOR">
<meta content="C#" name="CODE_LANGUAGE">
<meta content="Mobile Web Page" name="vs_targetSchema">
<body xmlns:mobile="Mobile Web Form Controls">
    <mobile:Form id="frmMain" runat="server">
        <mobile:Label id="lblCaption" runat="server">Press button to go to next
form</mobile:Label>
        <mobile:Command id="btnGo" runat="server">Go</mobile:Command>
    </mobile:Form>
    <mobile:Form id="frmTwo" runat="server">
        <mobile:Label id="lblCaptionTwo" runat="server">This is the second
form</mobile:Label>
    </mobile:Form>
</body>
```

Let's take a look at the top two lines, since they have some attributes we may not have seen to this point.

```
<%@ Page language="c#" Codebehind="MobileWebForm1.aspx.cs"
Inherits="MyMobileApp.MobileWebForm1" AutoEventWireup="false" %>
```

The Page compiler directive indicates that this is an ASP.NET page (as opposed to a control, a Web Service, etc.). We can see that, since we created this mobile application as a C# project, the Language attribute specifies that any script associated with this page will be written in C#.

The AutoEventWireup attribute is set to False by default. The Web Form designer wires up the event handlers for the page events explicitly. The Web Forms designer adds the following code for the Page_Load event handler into the InitializeComponent function of the Web Forms code-behind file.

377

```
// C#
private void InitializeComponent()
{
  this.Load += new System.EventHandler(this.Page_Load);
}
```

Visual Studio .NET uses a default event handler name to assist the developer in understanding what is going on during the explicit wire-up of object events to event handlers. This method can be coded to include any valid method name.

The next attribute, `Codebehind`, specifies the assembly that contains the logic for our page. We'll spend some time with this particular item in the next section. The final attribute, `Inherits`, indicates the class upon which this page is based.

```
<%@ Register TagPrefix="mobile" Namespace="System.Web.UI.MobileControls"
Assembly="System.Web.Mobile" %>
```

As we've learned, the `Register` directive associates aliases with namespaces and class names for concise notation for use with custom server controls. In our case, the prefix `mobile` allows us to point directly to those mobile controls available within the assembly.

There are also <meta> tags that are automatically generated, indicating the environment this page was created in, the language used, and the type of page.

Also hidden behind this page is the actual logic. We saw it briefly when we switched to the code view after double-clicking on the Go button. As you remember, we can also see this code by clicking on the View Code button in the Solution Explorer.

In this code, we have several namespaces included at the top:

```
using System;
using System.Collections;
using System.ComponentModel;
using System.Data;
using System.Drawing;
using System.Web;
using System.Web.Mobile;
using System.Web.SessionState;
using System.Web.UI;
using System.Web.UI.MobileControls;
using System.Web.UI.WebControls;
using System.Web.UI.HtmlControls;
```

We also have the class name, `MobileWebForm1`, which matches the name of the mobile web page.

```
public class MobileWebForm1 : System.Web.UI.MobileControls.MobilePage
```

Within this class, we inherit the ability to use mobile controls with a mobile page as well as have access to the behaviors of the mobile page itself. This is a compiled class that will reside in the \bin directory within our application directory. When it is executed, the ASPX page will look for the code specified in the Codebehind attribute in the Page processing directive. Also, by including the line above, our page now has access to functionality and display properties for a web page containing mobile controls.

Next, each of the controls on the mobile forms (as well as the forms themselves) are declared.

```
Protected WithEvents frmMain As System.Web.UI.MobileControls.Form
Protected WithEvents lblCaption As System.Web.UI.MobileControls.Label
Protected WithEvents btnGo As System.Web.UI.MobileControls.Command
Protected WithEvents lblCaptionTwo As System.Web.UI.MobileControls.Label
Protected WithEvents frmTwo As System.Web.UI.MobileControls.Form
```

The code below is automatically created by Visual Studio.

```
#region Web Form Designer generated code
/// <summary>
/// Required method for Designer support - do not modify
/// the contents of this method with the code editor.
/// </summary>
private void InitializeComponent()
{
    this.btnGo.Click += new System.EventHandler(this.btnGo_Click);
    this.Load += new System.EventHandler(this.Page_Load);

}
#endregion
```

If there are behaviors that should occur when this page is called, code will be inserted into the InitializeComponent() subroutine.

The initial structures for the two methods below is also created:

```
private void Page_Load(object sender, System.EventArgs e)
{
    // Put user code to initialize the page here
}

public void btnGo_Click(object sender, System.EventArgs e)
{

}
```

The last step was to add the line:

```
this.ActiveForm = frmTwo;
```

Fortunately, Visual Studio handles a lot of the code creation without our intervention!

Since we've gotten a look at how to create a simple mobile application using Visual Studio .NET, we can now talk about each of the areas within Visual Studio that are specific to mobile development. Let's begin discussing how to design a mobile application.

Designing A Mobile Application

As with the other Designers within Visual Studio .NET, the Mobile Designer allows us to see graphical representations of screens as we create them. This tool keeps us from entering code, browsing to the page, examining the output, making revisions, re-examining the output, and on and on. The goal is to increase our productivity and reduce our errors.

As we look at the Mobile Designer, the name of the file appears in a tab just above the design field.

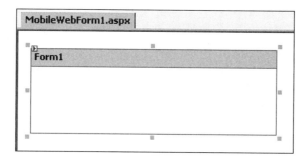

When a mobile application is created, the default name for the page is `MobileWebForm1.aspx`. This file should be renamed to something more indicative of our application. We can do this by right-clicking on the name of the file in the Solution Explorer.

Note that, within the Mobile Designer, we have a mobile form called `Form1`, which always appears when a mobile project is created. `Form1` is currently the selected object (since there are no other items in the Mobile Designer's field). If the Properties pane is not visible, press **F4**. When we look at the Properties pane (below the Solution Explorer), information appears for `Form1`.

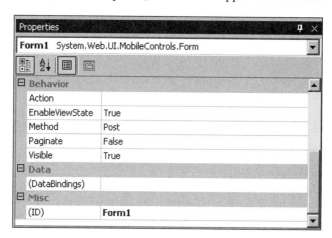

In Chapter 17, we used the Toolbox to display and specifically make use of the mobile controls available to us (View | Toolbox or *Ctrl-Alt-X*). The mobile controls shown in the Toolbox were introduced in previous chapters. As we use them, keep in mind that these controls will be rendered based on the particular mobile device. For instance, the Nokia 6210 mobile phone will display a selection list containing two elements as two radio button options.

With Notepad, we entered HTML within our ASPX file and hoped that we made no syntax mistakes. With Visual Studio .NET, it is extremely easy to design mobile applications. Simply drag and drop items from the Mobile Controls Toolbox, and the base code is automatically generated.

Now that the mobile form has been created, how do we get it to behave as we wish. In the next section, we'll discuss how to include custom logic.

Adding Logic

We've seen how a mobile application is designed; the Visual Studio .NET environment makes this quite simple. Next, we can begin adding logic in the ASPX.CS file created by Visual Studio. We click on the tab displaying the ASPX.CS file just above the Mobile Designer if it's shown. Otherwise, the View Code button can be clicked in the Solution Explorer when the ASPX is open to view the code or when the page is double-clicked in Design mode.

As we enter code, we have features available such as Intellisense, Auto Complete, and automatic formatting to assist us with creating error-reduced code. As the developer types, Intellisense displays properties, methods, and events available for an object. Since we are learning about controls, this comes in handy. Autocomplete allows us to enter the first few unique letters of a property, method or event, and VS .NET will complete the word for us. The automatic formatting structures our code for easy viewing. These are 'carry-overs' from the previous version of Visual Studio.

> **Visual Studio .NET conveniently color codes keywords and automatically indents nested statements based on language for easy reading. We also have the ability to collapse sections of code.**

The logic can be entered within this file, making reference as needed to mobile controls on the form.

One thing to note is that, when discussing how Visual Studio structures code, we must address a concept called **Code behind**. We'll cover this below.

Code-behind

When we worked with Notepad, we entered the code for mobile controls directly within the ASPX. This required us to create <SCRIPT> blocks that would appear at the top or bottom of the ASP.NET page.

Visual Studio .NET by default handles our script using the concept of a code-behind file. Code-behind is a construct that allows us to separate our programming logic from our display code. This is definitely progress, compared with the intermingled HTML/Server-side code of classic ASP. Visual Studio .NET automatically creates two files for a mobile application, one with the ASPX extension and the other with the ASPX.CS extension (which is our code-behind file, assuming we were using C# of course!). To look at the code behind the page, we can click on the View Code icon in the Solution Explorer.

We see that creating an ASP.NET mobile application with Visual Studio. NET is fairly straightforward. Since we've just used it to create a basic application, you should now be feeling a bit more comfortable with the Visual Studio .NET environment. Now let's walk through an example with a little more complexity, explaining items pertinent to our discussion.

Try It Out – Conversions Mobile Application

This exercise will have you create a mobile application called **Conversions** (for the mathematician on the go), which will allow a user to select from among two formulae. Based on the selection, the user will be taken to the appropriate screen to convert one measurement to another.

1. Launch Visual Studio .NET, and within the C# Projects folder, create a Mobile Web Application. Name the project Conversions. (If the Solution Explorer does not appear, press Ctrl-Alt-L.)

2. Within the Solution Explorer, left-click on MobileWebForm1.aspx, and delete it.

3. Select a New Item by pressing *Ctrl-Shift-A*, then select the Mobile Web Form template with the name, ConversionsForm.aspx.

4. Right-click on ConversionsForm.aspx and select Set As Start Page.

5. Drag and drop a new form control onto the Designer from the Toolbox. In the Properties window, rename Form1 to frmMain.

6. Drag and drop a label control from the Toolbox onto frmMain. Change the label's ID to lblConversionsCaption and set the Text property to "Choose to see formula".

7. Drag and drop a selection list control from the Toolbox onto frmMain, below the label. Change the selection list's ID to slFormulas.

8. Right-click on the new selection list, slFormulas, and choose Property Builder.

9. Click on Items, then click on Create New Item. Enter "Fahrenheit to Celsius with the value of FC". Press OK.

10. Repeat this process in #9 for Pythagorean Theorem, with the value PT.

11. Drag the Command button from the Toolbox to the form as shown below. Change its ID to btnDisplay. Then we change the **Text** property to Display.

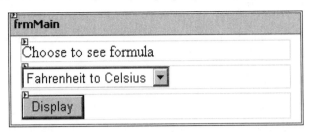

12. Drag another form from the Toolbox and drop it just below frmMain. Rename this new form from Form1 to frmFahrenheitCelsius.

13. Drag a label from the Toolbox onto frmFahrenheitCelsius. Change the label's Text property to "Convert Fahrenheit to Celsius" and the ID to lblFtoCCaption.

14. Drag a textbox from the Toolbox onto frmFahrenheitCelsius. Leave the textbox's Text property blank and set the ID to txtFahrenheitValue.

15. Drag a label from the Toolbox onto frmFahrenheitCelsius. Make the label's Text property blank and its ID to lblCelsiusValue.

16. Drag the Command button from the Toolbox to the form as shown below and rename it to btnFtoCConvert. Change the Text property to Convert.

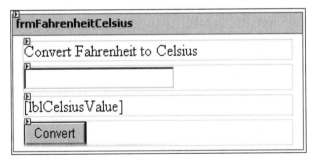

17. Drag another form from the Toolbox just below frmFahrenheitCelsius. Rename this new form from Form1 to frmPythagorean.

18. Drag a label from the Toolbox onto frmPythagorean. Change the label's **Text** property to "Enter each side to display hypotenuse" and the ID to lblPythagoreanCaption.

19. Drag another label from the Toolbox onto frmPythagorean. Change the label's **Text** property to Side A and the ID to lblSideA.

20. Drag a textbox from the Toolbox onto `frmPythagorean`. Make the textbox's **Text** property blank and the `ID` to `txtSideAValue`.

21. Drag a label from the Toolbox onto `frmPythagorean`. Change the label's **Text** property to `Side B` and the `ID` to `lblSideB`.

22. Drag a textbox from the Toolbox onto `frmPythagorean`. Make the textbox's **Text** property blank and the `ID` to `txtSideBValue`.

23. Drag a label from the Toolbox onto `frmPythagorean`. Make the label's **Text** property blank and the `ID` to `lblHypotenuse`.

24. Drag a command button from the Toolbox onto `frmPythagorean`. Change the button's **Text** property to `btnPythagoreanConvert` and the `ID` to `Convert`.

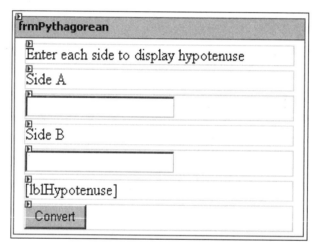

25. Double-click on the `btnDisplay` command button on `frmMain`.

26. When the code appears, enter the following in the `btnDisplay_Click` routine automatically created by Visual Studio.

```
private void btnDisplay_Click(object sender, System.EventArgs e)
{
    if (slFormulas.Selection.Value == "FC")
    {
        this.ActiveForm = this.frmFahrenheitCelsius;
    }
    else if (slFormulas.Selection.Value == "PT")
    {
        this.ActiveForm = this.frmPythagorean;
    }
}
```

Change the `private` declaration for `btnDisplay_Click` to `public`.

27. Below the `btnDisplay_Click` routine, add the following code:

```
private string ConvertFahrenheitToCelsius(double decDegreesF)
{
    double decDegreesC;
    string strMessage;
    decDegreesC = (decDegreesF - 32) / 1.8;
    strMessage = decDegreesF + " degrees Fahrenheit = " +
                       decDegreesC.ToString() + " degrees Celsius";
    return strMessage;
}

public void ReturnCelsiusConversion(object sender, System.EventArgs e)
{
    this.lblCelsiusValue.Text =
      ConvertFahrenheitToCelsius(double.Parse(txtFahrenheitValue.Text));
}

private string CalculateHypotenuse(int intSideA, int intSideB)
{
    double intHypotenuse;
    string strMessage;
    intHypotenuse = Math.Sqrt(Math.Pow(intSideA,2) +
                                     Math.Pow(intSideB,2));
    strMessage = "A right triangle with Side A of length " +
        intSideA.ToString() + " and Side B of length " +
        intSideB.ToString() + " has a hypotenuse of " + intHypotenuse;
    return strMessage;
}

public void ReturnHypotenuseCalculation(object sender, EventArgs e)
{
    lblHypotenuse.Text =
            CalculateHypotenuse(int.Parse(this.txtSideAValue.Text),
                            int.Parse(this.txtSideBValue.Text));
}
```

28. Click on the View Designer button in the Solution Explorer, then click on the HTML button to view the code for the controls. Then, within the `btnFtoCConvert` item, enter the following attribute:

```
OnClick="ReturnCelsiusConversion"
```

The resulting line is shown below:

```
<mobile:Command id="btnFtoCConvert" runat="server"
OnClick="ReturnCelsiusConversion">Convert</mobile:Command>
```

29. Within the `btnPythagoreanConvert` item, enter the following attribute:

```
OnClick="ReturnHypotenuseCalculation"
```

The resulting line is shown below:

```
<mobile:Command id=" " runat="server"
OnClick="ReturnHypotenuseCalculation">Convert</mobile:Command>
```

How It Works

Once we created a new Mobile Application project using C#, we deleted and renamed the application `ConversionsForm.aspx`. There are problems with renaming the form within the existing page, since Visual Studio .NET does not automatically make appropriate form name changes in the Codebehind file. Thus, it is much cleaner to simply delete the initial mobile web page and add a new one.

We then viewed the Properties window by pressing **F4**, and clicked within the cell to the right of (ID). When the cursor appeared, we entered its new name: **frmMain**. As we could see, the name of the form changed in the Mobile Designer as well. Once these changes have been made, we're ready to begin adding mobile controls to our form.

When we selected View | Toolbox to display the mobile controls available to us, we saw the various intrinsic controls available for mobile applications.

There is a significant list of mobile controls shown (we've seen most of these before in previous chapters).

To begin, we dragged a label from the Toolbox onto `frmMain`. Within our Properties pane, we changed the label's ID to lblConversionsCaption and set the Text property to Choose to see formula: (as shown below):

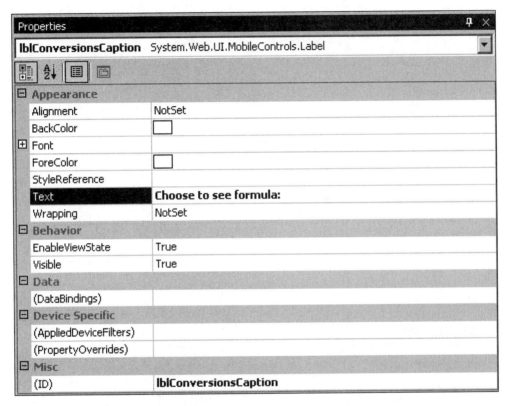

Then we dragged and dropped a selection list control from the Toolbox onto the mobile form, below the label we just added. We went to the Properties pane, scrolled down, and changed the ID to slFormulas.

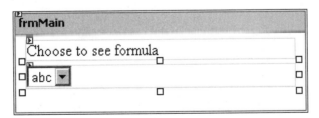

To add items to a selection list in Notepad, we entered our HTML with `<mobile:SelectionList>` tags and its associated `<Item>` tags. However, using Visual Studio .NET, we have the ability to add items to the list using the Property Builder. To do this, we right-clicked on the new selection list and chose Property Builder.

The wizard appeared with this default view.

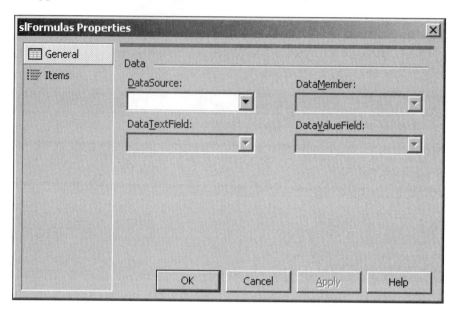

We have the ability to bind this mobile selection list to a data member from a data source or simply skip this step to manually add static elements to the list. We chose the latter option to keep our example somewhat simple.

We then added individual items to our selection list by clicking on Items.

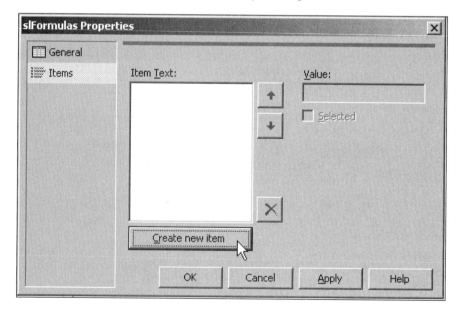

With the Property Builder, we have the ability to add or delete list elements, as well as move them in sequence.

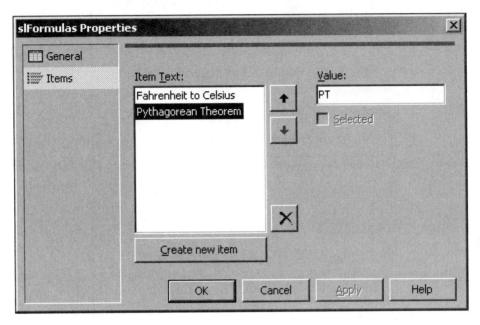

Finally, we pressed OK to finish adding items to slFormulas.

The last item we added to this mobile form is a command button. When the user presses this button, it fires off an event that takes the user to the appropriate conversion form. There, they can enter input values and receive a converted value.

To do this, we dragged the Command button from the Toolbox to the form and renamed its Text property to Display and ID to btnDisplay. We then had three mobile controls placed on the form.

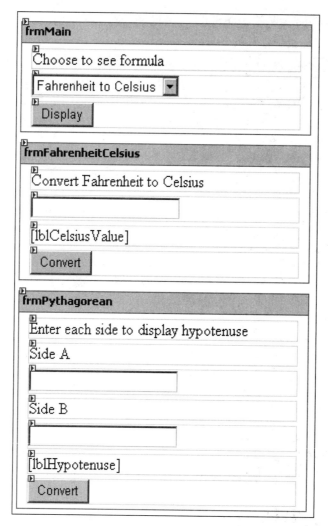

Visual Studio .NET made designing our mobile forms a cinch!

Prior to this chapter, we've been working with Notepad to create our applications. Having dealt first-hand with the code, you may be wondering what the HTML looks like for this page. With Visual Studio .NET, we can see the code simply by clicking on the HTML button below the Mobile Designer:

The Code Editor displays the following:

```
<%@ Page language="c#" Codebehind="ConversionsForm.aspx.cs"
Inherits="Conversions.ConversionsForm" AutoEventWireup="false"%>
<%@ Register TagPrefix="mobile" Namespace="System.Web.UI.MobileControls"
Assembly="System.Web.Mobile" %>
<%@ Page language="c#" Codebehind="ConversionsForm.aspx.cs"
Inherits="Conversions.ConversionsForm" AutoEventWireup="false"%>
<meta name="GENERATOR" content="Microsoft Visual Studio 7.0">
<meta name="CODE_LANGUAGE" content="C#">
<meta name="vs_targetSchema" content="Mobile Web Page">
<body xmlns:mobile="Mobile Web Form Controls">
    <mobile:Form id="frmMain" runat="server">
            <mobile:Label id="lblConversionsCaption" runat="server">Choose to see
                                                    formula</mobile:Label>
        <mobile:SelectionList id="slFormulas" runat="server">
            <Item Value="FC" Text="Fahrenheit to Celsius"></Item>
            <Item Value="PT" Text="Pythagorean Theorem"></Item>
        </mobile:SelectionList>
                        <mobile:Command id="btnDisplay" OnClick="btnDisplay_Click"
                                    runat="server">Display</mobile:Command>
    </mobile:Form>
    <mobile:Form id="frmFahrenheitCelsius" runat="server">
            <mobile:Label id="lblFtoCCaption" runat="server">Convert Fahrenheit to
                                                    Celsius</mobile:Label>
        <mobile:TextBox id="txtFahrenheitValue" runat="server"></mobile:TextBox>
        <mobile:Label id="lblCelsiusValue" runat="server"></mobile:Label>
            <mobile:Command id="btnFtoCConvert" onclick="ReturnCelsiusConversion"
                                    runat="server">Convert</mobile:Command>
    </mobile:Form>
    <mobile:Form id="frmPythagorean" runat="server">
            <mobile:Label id="lblPythagoreanCaption" runat="server">Enter each side to
                                            display hypotenuse </mobile:Label>
        <mobile:Label id="lblSideA" runat="server">Side A</mobile:Label>
        <mobile:TextBox id="txtSideAValue" runat="server"></mobile:TextBox>
        <mobile:Label id="lblSideB" runat="server">Side B</mobile:Label>
        <mobile:TextBox id="txtSideBValue" runat="server"></mobile:TextBox>
        <mobile:Label id="lblHypotenuse" runat="server"></mobile:Label>
                                <mobile:Command id="btnPythagoreanConvert"
    onclick="ReturnHypotenuseCalculation" runat="server">Convert</mobile:Command>
    </mobile:Form>
</body>
```

Visual Studio .NET created the majority of the HTML for us!

To see the complete code for this application, we click on the **View Code** button in the Solution Explorer:

The following C# code appears:

```csharp
using System;
using System.Collections;
using System.ComponentModel;
using System.Data;
using System.Drawing;
using System.Web;
using System.Web.Mobile;
using System.Web.SessionState;
using System.Web.UI;
using System.Web.UI.MobileControls;
using System.Web.UI.WebControls;
using System.Web.UI.HtmlControls;

namespace Conversions
{
    /// <summary>
    /// Summary description for Conversions.
    /// </summary>
    public class ConversionsForm : System.Web.UI.MobileControls.MobilePage
    {
        protected System.Web.UI.MobileControls.Label lblConversionsCaption;
        protected System.Web.UI.MobileControls.Form frmPythagorean;
        protected System.Web.UI.MobileControls.Label lblPythagoreanCaption;
        protected System.Web.UI.MobileControls.Label lblSideA;
        protected System.Web.UI.MobileControls.TextBox txtSideAValue;
        protected System.Web.UI.MobileControls.Label lblSideB;
        protected System.Web.UI.MobileControls.TextBox txtSideBValue;
        protected System.Web.UI.MobileControls.Label lblHypotenuse;
        protected System.Web.UI.MobileControls.Command btnPythagoreanConvert;
        protected System.Web.UI.MobileControls.SelectionList slFormulas;
        protected System.Web.UI.MobileControls.Form frmFahrenheitCelsius;
        protected System.Web.UI.MobileControls.Label lblFtoCCaption;
        protected System.Web.UI.MobileControls.TextBox txtFahrenheitValue;
        protected System.Web.UI.MobileControls.Label lblCelsiusValue;
        protected System.Web.UI.MobileControls.Command btnFtoCConvert;
        protected System.Web.UI.MobileControls.Command btnDisplay;
        protected System.Web.UI.MobileControls.Form frmMain;
```

```
    public ConversionsForm()
    {
        Page.Init += new System.EventHandler(Page_Init);
    }

    private void Page_Load(object sender, System.EventArgs e)
    {
        // Put user code to initialize the page here
    }

    private void Page_Init(object sender, EventArgs e)
    {
        //
        // CODEGEN: This call is required by the ASP.NET Windows Form Designer.
        //
        InitializeComponent();
    }

    #region Web Form Designer generated code
    /// <summary>
    /// Required method for Designer support - do not modify
    /// the contents of this method with the code editor.
    /// </summary>
    private void InitializeComponent()
    {
        this.Load += new System.EventHandler(this.Page_Load);

    }
    #endregion

    }
}
```

Now that we've seen the skeletal code for this form, let's continue on with developing our example. To complete our application, we must add the three additional mobile forms to our web page, one for each of the formula choices in our drop-down list on the frmMain mobile form.

When the user initially browses to our site, she/he will encounter the mobile form on their device. They select from the drop-down list and press **Display**. In order to handle this event, we must include some code.

By clicking on the **HTML** button in the **Designer**, we inserted the onclick attribute for the btnDisplay mobile command button, which fires off a subroutine called btnDisplay_Click.

```
<mobile:Command id="btnDisplay" onclick="btnDisplay_Click"
runat="server">Display</mobile:Command>
```

When we select the formula and press the **Display** button on frmMain, we go to the ConversionsForm.aspx.cs assembly based on the Codebehind attribute (in our previous HTML listing) and perform some action. The action in this case is to make one of our three "sub-forms" the active form on the device.

393

```
public void btnDisplay_Click(object sender, System.EventArgs e)
{
    if (slFormulas.Selection.Value == "FC")
    {
        this.ActiveForm = this.frmFahrenheitCelsius;
    }
    else if (slFormulas.Selection.Value == "PT")
    {
        this.ActiveForm = this.frmPythagorean;
    }
}
```

When the mobile application is run, what happens when the user selects the Fahrenheit to Celsius formula?

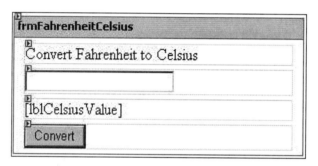

This screen will appear and await the user's entry of a number in degrees Fahrenheit.
The user will input it and press the Convert button. The result will appear in the lblCelsiusValue
mobile:Label control. We must create logic that will handle this operation.

The conversion formula for Fahrenheit to Celsius is: $C = (F - 32) / 1.8$

Let's insert this logic just below the btnDisplay_OnClick routine in
ConversionsForm.aspx.cs;

```
private string ConvertFahrenheitToCelsius(double decDegreesF)
{
    double decDegreesC;
    string strMessage;
    decDegreesC = (decDegreesF - 32) / 1.8;
                        strMessage = decDegreesF + " degrees Fahrenheit = " +
                                decDegreesC.ToString() + " degrees Celsius";
    return strMessage;
}

public void ReturnCelsiusConversion(object sender, System.EventArgs e)
{
                                            this.lblCelsiusValue.Text =
            ConvertFahrenheitToCelsius(double.Parse(txtFahrenheitValue.Text));
}
```

We've just created two methods (so we could re-use the conversion calculation if need be). One performs the conversion calculation (`ConvertFahrenheitToCelsius`) and the other (`ReturnCelsiusConversion`) places the result as Text into the `lblCelsiusValue` mobile control.

The next form is `frmPythagorean`, where users can calculate the hypotenuse for a right triangle.

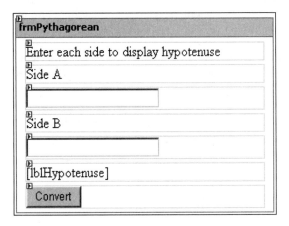

The formula for determining the hypotenuse is: $C = (A^2 + B^2)^{1/2}$ (where A is one side of the triangle, B is another side of the triangle).

Once the values for each side are entered, we press the Convert button, and the result will appear in the `lblHypotenuse mobile:Label` control.

The logic to handle this operation appears below:

```
private string CalculateHypotenuse(int intSideA, int intSideB)
{
    double intHypotenuse;
    string strMessage;
    intHypotenuse = Math.Sqrt(Math.Pow(intSideA,2) + Math.Pow(intSideB,2));
        strMessage = "A right-angled triangle with Side A of length " +
    intSideA.ToString() + " and Side B of length " + intSideB.ToString()
                        + " has a hypotenuse of " + intHypotenuse;
    return strMessage;
}

public void ReturnHypotenuseCalculation(object sender, System.EventArgs e)
{
    lblHypotenuse.Text =
CalculateHypotenuse(int.Parse(this.txtSideAValue.Text),
int.Parse(this.txtSideBValue.Text));

}
```

Great! We've used Visual Studio .NET to create the design for each mobile form and then used the Code-behind technique automatically employed by Visual Studio to control the application's behavior. So now that we've created a mobile application, how do we know it works? Let's take a look at how to test it using Visual Studio .NET.

Testing A Mobile Application

Once we have created our mobile application, we have some great ways in Visual Studio .NET to test it. There are a variety,browsers available within the Visual Studio as well as additional emulators available from vendor sites. Since the code in the ASPX is rendered differently to accommodate different mobile devices, it's always important to check a thorough representation before making the application available to the public.

To launch a browser/emulator, we'll go to the Solution Explorer and right click on `MobileWebForm1.aspx`. The following menu will appear. Choose **Browse With...** to see a list of currently available emulators.

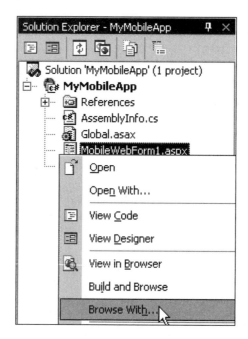

The following screen will appear with a list of browser choices (based on those that are installed on the machine):

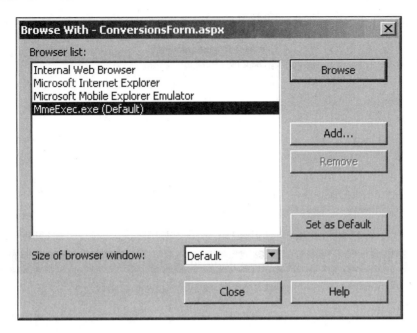

In our case, there is a list of four browsers shown above (your configuration may provide a different list). The final item appears with the name MmeExec.exe, which is the Microsoft Mobile Explorer (MME)

We have the ability to add and remove browsers and emulators to this list as we wish. Currently, the MME is set as our default browser within VS.NET. Let's leave the settings as is and close this window.

In the Solution Explorer, we can right-click on MobileWebForm1.aspx, and select **Build and Browser** to launch MME with the initial form, frmMain.

Since **Go** is highlighted, we must simply press the **OK** softkey to fire the btnGo_Click subroutine in the MyMobileApp.aspx.cs file.

The second form will appear in the display window:

This is the second form

⇄ Complete

Testing a mobile application is quite simple. Let's try it out with the Conversions application.

Try It Out – Testing The Conversions Application

1. Launch Visual Studio and open the Conversions mobile project.

2. In the Solution Explorer, right-click on `ConversionsForm.aspx`. Select **Browse with**....

3. Click on **Set as Default** for `cdk_mbr_vs`.

4. Press **Close**.

5. In the Solution Explorer, right-click on `ConversionsForm.aspx`. Select **Build and Browse**.

6. When the MME appears with the `Fahrenheit to Celsius` option active, press **OK**.

7. On the `Fahrenheit to Celsius` form, use your mouse pointer to click on textbox. Enter `98.6`. Press **OK**.

8. When the MME appears, press the down arrow key to highlight **Convert**. Press **OK**.

How It Works

The MME gives us a realistic feel for how our application will appear and behave. We began this exercise by selecting it as our emulator. Once this was chosen, we selected the Browse and Build option.

With no breakpoints set, as the application is building, we'll see the following in the Output Pane. This provides us with information on the status of the build, whether successful or failed.

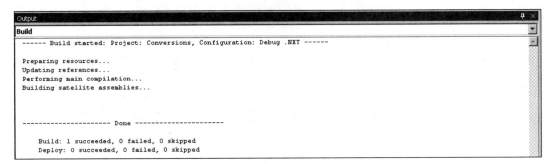

Once this is successfully built, the MME appears with the initial form, frmMain.

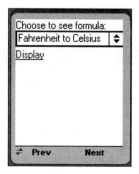

You can see how the rendering within the MME differs from our design using the Mobile Designer in VS. NET. The .NET Framework is intelligent enough to adapt the page display based on a supported device.

The <mobile:SelectionList> is rendered as a one-line scrolling list. Notice the **Prev** and **Next** buttons at the bottom of the screen. These will allow users to scroll through the formula list to select the one they want. Also, see that the **Display** button is shown as a hyperlink. Once the formula is chosen, we can press the down arrow button in the MME to place the focus on the **Display** link. Finally, the left button (softkey) will appear with a caption of **OK**.

Press that button to go to the frmFahrenheitCelsius mobile form (shown below).

The Fahrenheit to Celsius Conversion form displays the heading at the top. The <mobile:TextBox> appears as a field with an enter arrow. To input a value in this field, we must use the mouse pointer to click on the box in the MME. A script dialog box appears with a place to enter the value.

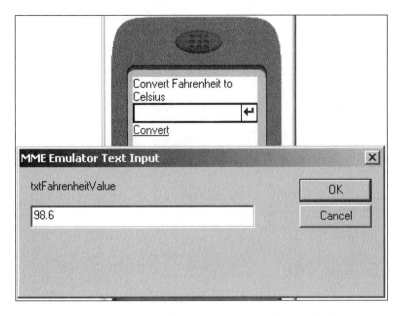

To verify that our logic works correctly, we'll enter the average human body temperature in Fahrenheit (98.6) since we know that it is equivalent to 37 degrees Celsius. Then, we press the OK button.

Now we press the down arrow button. Once the Convert link is highlighted, we'll press the OK softkey.

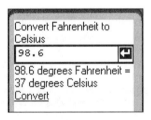

We can see that the conversion formula works as we expect. Let's go back to `frmMain` (the Main Menu). We can repeat the same steps for the Pythagorean Theorem. We'll enter Side A with a value of 3 and Side B with a value of 4.

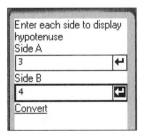

401

Once both values are entered, we press the down arrow button to highlight **Convert** and press **OK**. The following result will then appear in the MME.

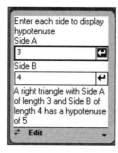

The Pythagorean formula appears to be coded correctly.

Now that we've verified that our mobile application behaves as expected, we can see how it displays using Microsoft Internet Explorer.

We can press the Stop button to return to Design Mode.

Next, go to the Solution Explorer and right-click on ConversionsForm.aspx to display the menu again. Select **Browse with...**, then select **Microsoft Internet Explorer** as the browser type. Once this has been done, right-click on ConversionsForm.aspx again, and choose **Build and Browse**.

A new window should appear like the one shown below.

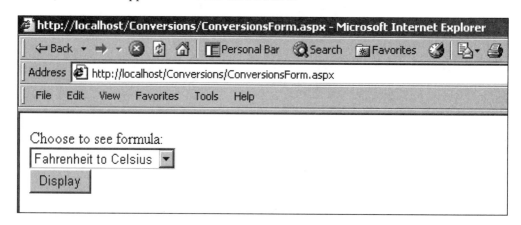

This browser renders the output differently from the MME. The `<mobile:SelectionList>` is shown as a drop-down list box. The Display button appears as an actual button, as opposed to the link we saw in the previous example.

Assume that we'll go to the Fahrenheit to Celsius form, we'll simply press Display with the current formula selected. The next form will appear in its place with a label, textbox, another label (for the result), and a Convert button.

Again, we enter 98.6 in the text field and press the Convert button.

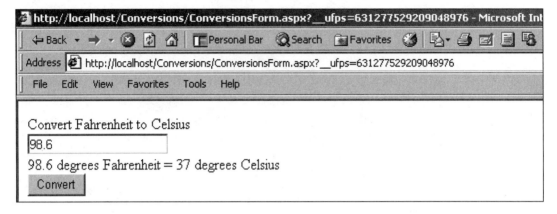

Similar to the MME example, the conversion message is returned and displayed as before, just above the button.

Summary

Visual Studio .NET makes quick work of ASP.NET mobile application development. We've looked at how Visual Studio .NET encourages through its use of wizards and drag-and-drop functionality offering two major advantages:

❑ It brings the non-developer closer to creating his/her own applications

❑ It fosters a separation of code and content so that graphics specialists can work with greater autonomy while developers can focus much more on creating logic.

As long as the mobile development team at Microsoft continues to continually support current mobile devices, Visual Studio .NET has the potential to be a powerful tool for efficiently creating .NET mobile applications for some time to come.

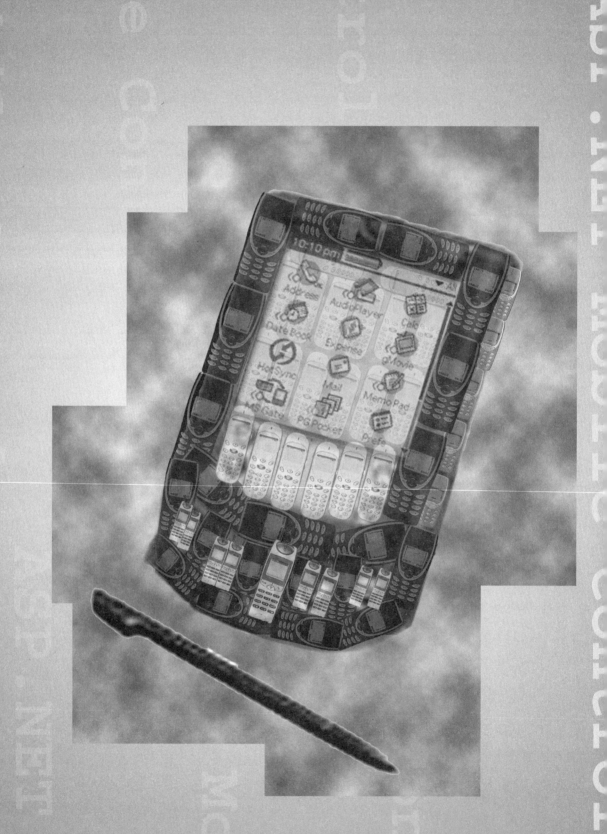

Maître D' Mobile Application

Throughout this book, we've been looking at simple examples of how to develop ASP.NET Mobile Control-based applications. We have created them using both Notepad and the Mobile Designer in Visual Studio .NET. We've also had introductions to ADO.NET and Web Services in preparation for this Case Study. In this chapter, the use of ASP.NET mobile controls is integrated with an XML web service to manipulate data in a Microsoft Access database. This collective application, called 'Maître d', will be used by consumers to make reservations and place carryout orders from a restaurant.

Overview of the Application

The Maître d' application provides a restaurant with functionality for making reservations, pre-ordering food and placing carryout orders. Its purpose is to streamline the common commercial bottleneck of restaurant administration, and allow the company to move employees away from answering telephone calls, and into more productive areas.

> As with all the other chapters of this book the files for this application are available to download from **www.wrox.com**. Full installation and setup instructions are also included in the download.

Maître D'

The application will showcase how to build a commercial-quality mobile application using ASP.NET in C#. The functionality has been scaled down so that we may focus on specific areas of interest for mobile development, without becoming distracted by too much application-level information.

Target Audience

Our enterprising restaurateur has had enough of missed sales. His heralded restaurant is known for its elegant dinner combinations. Busy families have passed by his establishment, tempted by its ambience and the smell of its food. However, they saw the long lines that haunted the entryway and decided to dine at a place with faster service. Potential customers also learned that the restaurant is often short-staffed during peak hours and that there could be a lengthy wait between the time it took to be seated and the time it took the waiter/waitress to take the order.

Since the restaurant is located in a thriving technological metropolis, the owner has done his research and found that many of his potential customers routinely use mobile devices in their daily lives.

Gathering Requirements

The owner has relayed that he wants a mobile application to showcase his complete array of services. The .NET Framework, with its rendering capabilities for multiple mobile devices, looks to be the best bet for providing the functionality he needs on varied client browsers. His customers are time-aware, so he wants speed to be the top priority without a lot of glitz. He also needs a cost-sensitive solution and doesn't want to spend a great deal of capital on software. In his words: "Something simple...something effective".

Architecture

The application that we have devised to suit the owner's requirements is comprised of three principal sections:

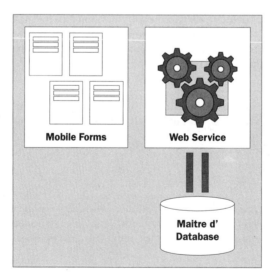

❑ A **web page** containing all of the mobile forms displayed on the user's client devices

❑ A **Web Service** containing WebMethods to retrieve and store database information

❑ A **Microsoft Access database** housing the data used by the application.

We'll take a look at each of the application's components.

Maître D' Database

Since this application will contain a small volume of data (and for the purposes of this case study), we'll use a Microsoft Access 2000 database to store our customer information as well as any data needed to complete the orders.

Below is the entity-relationship diagram for this database schema:

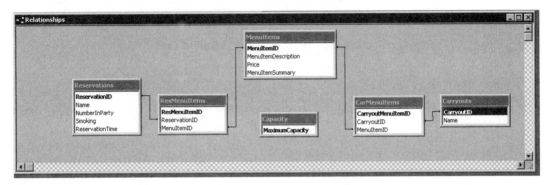

The following database tables are used within the Maître d' application:

The Reservations Table

The Reservations table contains information about each individual who has made a reservation:

Column Name	Type	Length	Description
ReservationID (primary key)	Autonumber	Long Integer	A unique key for the reservation
Name	Text	100	The unique name associated with a reservation
NumberInParty	Number	Long Integer	The number of people in the party
Smoking	Yes/No	--	Indicates whether you prefer smoking or non-smoking seating
ReservationTime	Date/Time	--	The time when the party is to arrive

The ResMenuItems Table

The ResMenuItems table contains a combination of ReservationID and MenuItemID (from the Reservations table) for each reservation made. This scheme is used since multiple menu items may be ordered for each reservation:

Column Name	Type	Length	Description
ResMenuItemID (primary key)	Autonumber	Long Integer	A unique key for the reservation/menu item combination
ReservationID	Number	Long Integer	A key used to identify a particular reservation
MenuItemID	Number	Long Integer	A key used to identify a particular menu item

The Carryouts Table

The Carryouts table contains information about each individual that has placed a carryout order:

Column Name	Type	Length	Description
CarryoutID (primary key)	Autonumber	Long Integer	A unique key for the carryout order
Name	Text	100	The unique name associated with a carryout order

The CarMenuItems Table

CarMenuItems contains a combination of CarryoutID and MenuItemID for carryout orders:

Column Name	Type	Length	Description
CarMenuItemID (primary key)	Autonumber	Long Integer	A unique key for the carryout order/menu item combination
CarryoutID	Number	Long Integer	A key used to identify a particular carryout order
MenuItemID	Number	Long Integer	A key used to identify a particular menu item

The MenuItems Table

The MenuItems table contains information about each menu item made available by the restaurant:

Column Name	Type	Length	Description
MenuItemID (primary key)	Autonumber	Long Integer	A unique key for the menu item
MenuItemDescription	Text	150	The name of each dinner combination
Price	Currency	--	The price of each dinner combination
MenuItemSummary	Text	200	A description of all sides available with the dinner entrée.

This database structure contains all the application's information about its customers, their orders, and the menus. A Web Service is used to manipulate the database, and we will be looking at this in the next section:

The Maitre D' Web Service

Following the philosophy of an *n*-tier architecture, our business and data retrieval logic is isolated from our application's display code. To handle this, a Web Service was created containing functions needed to populate our Mobile Forms and handle database manipulation. Its individual WebMethods perform specific tasks, which occur when called by the Mobile Forms' application logic within an ASP.NET web page.

MaitreDWebService.asmx

The code for the Web Service is quite extensive, and may seem a little off-putting. Don't worry, it is simply a collection of simple WebMethods, each performing a slightly different operation on the data that we're holding. We've broken the code up, and discussed each section in turn.

Since this project was created using Visual Studio .NET, the modules needed for system-related, data and Web Service object references were automatically included. However, the System.Data.OleDb module needed to be inserted manually:

```
using System;
using System.Collections;
using System.ComponentModel;
using System.Data;
using System.Data.OleDb;
using System.Diagnostics;
using System.Web;
using System.Web.Services;
```

Next, comes Visual Studio .NET's auto-generated code that sets the namespace to `maitreD`. Within it, the Web Service class name is also set and creates an instance of itself when it is first called. The `objConnection.Open()` was inserted manually into the `InitializeComponent` routine. This statement actually opens the connection to our Microsoft Access database:

```
namespace maitreD
{
  /// <summary>
  /// Summary description for Service1.
  /// </summary>
  public class maitreDWebService : System.Web.Services.WebService
  {
    public maitreDWebService()
    {
      //CODEGEN: This call is required by the ASP.NET Web Services
                    Designer
      InitializeComponent();
    }

    #region Component Designer generated code
    /// <summary>
    /// Required method for Designer support - do not modify
    /// the contents of this method with the code editor.
    /// </summary>
    public void InitializeComponent()
    {
      objConnection.Open();
    }
    #endregion
```

Now comes the main logic section of the Web Service, beginning with the code used by `objConnection.Open()` to instantiate a connection object to the database. We're using a DSN-less connection with the Microsoft Jet database engine that gives us the ability to interact with the Access database. Also, the ADO.NET connection object, `OleDbConnection`, is instantiated for use by subsequent database commands:

You'll need to change the `Source` element to where your database is situated.

```
OleDbConnection objConnection = new
OleDbConnection("Provider=Microsoft.Jet.OLEDB.4.0; Data
Source='c:\\inetpub\\wwwroot\\maitreD\\maitreD.mdb'; User ID=admin;
Password=;");
```

The next segment of code is the first `WebMethod` in the Web Service. It is named `GetMenuItems`, and selects all values from the **MenuItems** table using the ADO.NET `OleDbDataAdapter` command. The resulting data is stored in a dataset called `MenuItems` and returned to the calling program. In this case, the data will be returned to the mobile forms page for display purposes:

```
[WebMethod]
public DataSet GetMenuItems()
{
  OleDbDataAdapter objCommand = new OleDbDataAdapter("select * from
               MenuItems order by MenuItemID ", objConnection);
  DataSet dsMenuItems = new DataSet();
  objCommand.Fill(dsMenuItems, "MenuItems");
  return dsMenuItems;
}
```

The next `WebMethod` is used to find the total number of people who have a reservation for a particular time (which is stored in the **Reservations** table). This is compared with the predefined seating capacity for the restaurant. When this capacity is exceeded, no more reservations can be taken for that time. It accepts the date and time for a particular reservation, as well as the capacity for the restaurant:

```
[WebMethod]
public string CheckExistingResTime(DateTime dtTime, int intCapacity)
{
  DataSet dsReservation = new DataSet();
  OleDbDataAdapter objCommand = new OleDbDataAdapter
    ("SELECT Sum(NumberInParty) As ReservationCount from Reservations
               WHERE ReservationTime = #" + dtTime + "# GROUP BY
                                ReservationTime ",objConnection);
  objCommand.Fill(dsReservation, "Reservations");
  DataView dvResCount = new
               DataView(dsReservation.Tables["Reservations"]);
  if (dsReservation.Tables["Reservations"].Rows.Count > 0)
  {
    if ((int)dvResCount[0].Row[0] < intCapacity)
    {
      return "Capacity exceeded";
    }
    else
    {
      return "OK";
    }
  }
  else
  {
    return "Failed";
  }
}
```

With the `GetExistingReservation` routine, two operations are performed. Since the **ReservationID** is the unique key, the name is used to retrieve this value from **Reservations** table. The **ReservationID** is then used against the **ResMenuItems** table to retrieve each of the items ordered. The reservation information for the customer is then returned in the form of a dataset:

```
public DataSet GetExistingReservation(string strName)
{
  DataSet dsReservation = new DataSet();
  DataSet dsReservationDetails = new DataSet();
  OleDbDataAdapter objCommand = new OleDbDataAdapter("SELECT
    ReservationID FROM Reservations WHERE Name = '" + strName +
                                       "'", objConnection);
  objCommand.Fill(dsReservation, "Reservations");
  if (dsReservation.Tables[0].Rows.Count > 0)
  {
    DataView dvReservation = new
                       DataView(dsReservation.Tables["Reservations"]);
    OleDbDataAdapter objJoinCommand = new OleDbDataAdapter("SELECT
      RES.Name, RES.NumberInParty, RES.Smoking, RES.ReservationTime,
      count(MI.MenuItemDescription) as ItemQty, MI.MenuItemDescription,
      MI.Price, sum(MI.Price) as TotalPrice from MenuItems MI,
      ResMenuItems RMI, Reservations RES where RES.ReservationID =
      RMI.ReservationID AND RMI.MenuItemID = MI.MenuItemID AND
      RES.ReservationID = " + dvReservation[0].Row[0] + " GROUP BY
      MI.MenuItemDescription, MI.Price, RES.Name, RES.NumberInParty,
      RES.Smoking, RES.ReservationTime order by MI.MenuItemDescription
      asc ", objConnection);
    objJoinCommand.Fill(dsReservationDetails, "ReservationDetails");
    return dsReservationDetails;
  }
  else
  {
    return null;
  }
}
```

Similarly, the following WebMethod is used to retrieve data about a carryout order for a customer:

```
// Returns a dataset containing information for an active carryout order
[WebMethod]
public DataSet GetExistingCarryout(string strName)
{
  DataSet dsCarryout = new DataSet();
  DataSet dsCarryoutDetails = new DataSet();
  OleDbDataAdapter objDataAdapter = new OleDbDataAdapter("SELECT
          CarryoutID FROM Carryouts WHERE Name = '" + strName + "'",
                                       objConnection);
  objDataAdapter.Fill(dsCarryout, "Carryout");
  if (dsCarryout.Tables[0].Rows.Count > 0)
  {
    DataView dvCarryout = new DataView(dsCarryout.Tables["Carryout"]);
    OleDbDataAdapter objJoinCommand = new OleDbDataAdapter("SELECT
        CAR.Name, count(MI.MenuItemDescription) as ItemQty,
        MI.MenuItemDescription, MI.Price, sum(MI.Price) as TotalPrice,
        MI.MenuItemSummary from MenuItems MI, CarMenuItems CMI,
        Carryouts CAR WHERE CAR.CarryoutID = CMI.CarryoutID AND
        CMI.MenuItemID = MI.MenuItemID AND CAR.CarryoutID = " +
```

```
                    dvCarryout[0].Row[0] + " group by MI.MenuItemDescription,
                    MI.Price, MI.MenuItemSummary, CAR.Name ORDER BY
                    MI.MenuItemDescription asc", objConnection);
                objJoinCommand.Fill(dsCarryoutDetails, "CarryoutDetails");
                return dsCarryoutDetails;
            }
            else
            {
                return null;
            }
        }
```

To create a record containing general information about a new reservation (not each of the menu items at this point), the `AddNewReservation` WebMethod is available. It accepts the name, the number in the party, the smoking preference, and the reservation time as input parameters. A check is initially performed to see if a reservation currently exists under that name. If a record does not exist, the routine inserts the new reservation into the **Reservations** table. A string is returned indicating whether the transaction failed or was successful:

```
    // Creates a new reservation
    [WebMethod]
    public string AddNewReservation(string strName, int intNumberInParty,
                bool bSmoking, System.DateTime dtTime)
    {
        DataSet dsReservation = new DataSet();
        OleDbDataAdapter objDataAdapter = new OleDbDataAdapter("select
                    ReservationID from Reservations where Name = '" +
                                        strName + "'", objConnection);
        objDataAdapter.Fill(dsReservation, "Reservations");
        OleDbCommand objCommand = new OleDbCommand("Insert Into
                Reservations (Name, NumberInParty, Smoking, ReservationTime)
                    values ('" + strName + "'," + intNumberInParty + "," +
                            bSmoking + ",#" + dtTime + "#)", objConnection);
        if (dsReservation.Tables[0].Rows.Count <= 0)
        {
            objCommand.ExecuteNonQuery();
            return "OK";
        }
        else
        {
            return "Failed";
        }
    }
```

The following code is used to create the basic information for a carryout order. This routine returns OK if the insertion is successful and Failed if it doesn't work:

```
// Creates a new carryout order
[WebMethod]
public string AddNewCarryout(string strName)
{
  DataSet dsCarryout = new DataSet();
  OleDbDataAdapter objDataAdapter = new OleDbDataAdapter("select
                CarryoutID from Carryouts where Name = '" + strName +
                                    "'", objConnection);
  objDataAdapter.Fill(dsCarryout, "Customer");
  if (dsCarryout.Tables[0].Rows.Count == 0)
  {
    OleDbCommand objCommand = new OleDbCommand("Insert Into
                Carryouts (Name) values ('" + strName + "')",
                objConnection);
    objCommand.ExecuteNonQuery();
    return "OK";
  }
  else
  {
    return "Failed";
  }
}
```

To delete a reservation from the database, the following WebMethod is used. It accepts the customer's name as an input parameter. It first retrieves the associated ReservationID from the Reservations table based on the customer's name, and then deletes the record for that key. Finally, it removes all corresponding records from the ResMenuItems and returns a string indicating the success or failure:

```
// Deletes a reservation from the database
[WebMethod]
public string DeleteReservation(string strName)
{
  DataSet dsReservation = new DataSet();
  OleDbDataAdapter objDataAdapter = new OleDbDataAdapter("SELECT
      ReservationID FROM Reservations WHERE Name = '" + strName +
                                    "'",objConnection);
  objDataAdapter.Fill(dsReservation, "Reservation");
  DataView dvReservation = new
                DataView(dsReservation.Tables["Reservation"]);
  OleDbCommand objCommand = new OleDbCommand(
            "Delete from Reservations where ReservationID = " +
                    dvReservation[0].Row[0], objConnection);
  if (dsReservation.Tables[0].Rows.Count > 0)
  {
    objCommand.ExecuteNonQuery();
    OleDbCommand objJoinCommand = new OleDbCommand(
            "Delete from ResMenuItems where ReservationID = " +
                    dvReservation[0], objConnection);
```

```
          objJoinCommand.ExecuteNonQuery();
          objJoinCommand = null;
          return "OK";
      }
      else
      {
          return "Failed";
      }
  }
```

The next WebMethod handles deletions for carryout orders within the **Carryouts** and **CarMenuItems** tables:

```
// Deletes a carryout order from the database
[WebMethod]
public string DeleteCarryout(string strName)
{
    DataSet dsCarryout = new DataSet();
    OleDbDataAdapter objDataAdapter = new OleDbDataAdapter("SELECT
                CarryoutID FROM Carryouts WHERE Name = '" + strName +
                                              "'", objConnection);
    objDataAdapter.Fill(dsCarryout, "Carryout");
    DataView dvCarryout = new DataView(dsCarryout.Tables["Carryout"]);
    OleDbCommand objJoinCommand = new OleDbCommand("DELETE FROM
                                  CarMenuItems where CarryoutID = " +
                                  dvCarryout[0].Row[0], objConnection);
    if (dsCarryout.Tables[0].Rows.Count > 0)
    {
        OleDbCommand objCommand = new OleDbCommand("DELETE FROM Carryouts
            WHERE CarryoutID = " + dvCarryout[0].Row[0], objConnection);
        objCommand.ExecuteNonQuery();
        objJoinCommand.ExecuteNonQuery();
        return "OK";
    }
    else
    {
        return "Failed";
    }
}
```

To add items to a reservation, the following WebMethod is available. It accepts the customer's name and **MenuItemID** as input parameters. It checks the **Reservations** table to see if the reservation currently exists. If so, it associates the **MenuItemID** with the **ReservationID** and inserts the record into the **ResMenuItems** table:

```
// Adds individual menu items to a reservation
    [WebMethod]
    public string AddMenuItemToReservation(string strName, int MenuItemID)
    {
        DataSet dsReservation = new DataSet();
        OleDbDataAdapter objDataAdapter = new OleDbDataAdapter("SELECT
                    ReservationID FROM Reservations WHERE Name = '" +
```

```
                                    strName + "'", objConnection);
     objDataAdapter.Fill(dsReservation, "Reservations");
     DataView dvReservation = new
                     DataView(dsReservation.Tables["Reservations"]);
     if (dsReservation.Tables[0].Rows.Count > 0)
     {
       OleDbCommand objCommand = new OleDbCommand("Insert Into
                     ResMenuItems (ReservationID, MenuItemID)
                     values (" + dvReservation[0].Row[0] + "," +
                     MenuItemID + ")", objConnection);
       objCommand.ExecuteNonQuery();
       return "OK";
     }
     else
     {
       return "Failed";
     }
   }
```

Finally, to add items to a carryout order, we can use the following WebMethod:

```
   // Adds individual menu items to a carryout order
   [WebMethod]
   public string AddMenuItemToCarryout(string strName, int MenuItemID)
   {
     DataSet dsCarryout = new DataSet();
     OleDbDataAdapter objDataAdapter = new OleDbDataAdapter("SELECT
                 CarryoutID from Carryouts where Name = '" + strName +
                 "'", objConnection);
     objDataAdapter.Fill(dsCarryout, "Carryout");
     DataView dvCarryout = new
                 DataView(dsCarryout.Tables["Carryout"]);
     if (dsCarryout.Tables[0].Rows.Count > 0)
     {
       OleDbCommand objCommand = new OleDbCommand("Insert Into
                 CarMenuItems (CarryoutID, MenuItemID) values (" +
                 dvCarryout[0].Row[0] + "," + MenuItemID + ")",
                 objConnection);
       objCommand.ExecuteNonQuery();
       return "OK";
     }
     else
     {
       return "Failed";
     }
   }
```

Testing

Before we go any further into our application, we'll pause and test that the WebMethods we've created are functioning properly. We can do this using its automatically created Web Service Description Page, which lists all the available WebMethods of a Web Service, and allows you to view their WSDL and invoke them with test data.

Navigate your browser to the directory where your `MaitrDWebService.asmx` file resides, and you should see the following:

As an example, let's take a look at the `GetAllItems` WebMethod. When you scroll down, and click its hyperlink, you will be presented with a screen like this:

Since the WebMethod has no input parameters, only an Invoke button appears. Once it is pressed, the WebMethod performs the act of retrieving all of the records from the MenuItems database table. The screen below shows the results, in XML format, which our code can use for display purposes:

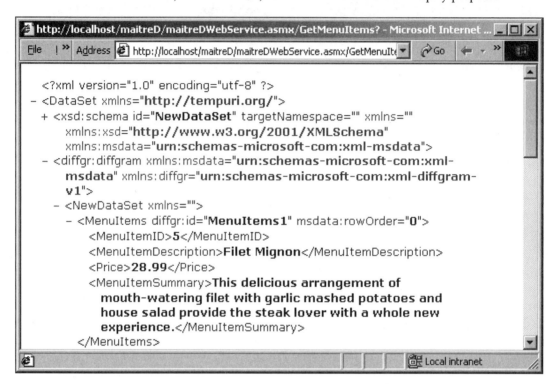

We can see that the XML data, shown above, contains tags that correspond to the names of the database fields in the MenuItems table. We can see that this table has been populated with three of the combination dinners available at the restaurant. For instance, the Roast Beef dinner has a summary describing what is available with the meal and a price for the complete combination, as well as its unique key (MenuItemID).

Before we go on to discuss the presentation logic, we're going to pause for a moment, and look at what the end result looks like when viewed with the Microsoft Mobile Explorer 3.0 (which has enough functionality to provide a good user experience). Then, once we've seen what it looks like, we'll be in a better position to explain how it works.

The User Interface

Let's take a stroll through the Web Forms that make up the front-end of our application. There are four main things that you can do with our application, and we'll look at each in turn:

Making A Reservation

Here's the sequence of screens that show how a reservation is made:

Once **Make Reservation** and **Go!** are selected, the next screen displays fields to enter the name, the number in the party, the time and the smoking preference for the reservation. The down arrow is used to go to each field so it can be populated. Then, we select **Go!** to view the mobile form for pre-ordering dinner combinations.

The next screen allows the user to select from the available dinners and the quantity for each. The item is selected from the list and the value is entered (for instance, **Chicken Cordon Bleu** with a quantity of 1). Once these are populated, the down arrow key is pressed to highlight **Add To Order**, followed by the **OK** button. Confirmation appears on the screen. Adding items to the reservation can be repeated as needed (since there may not be a one-to-one relationship between each member of the party and a dinner). If no more are desired, the **Home** link can be highlighted and **OK** pressed to go to the main menu.

Placing A Carryout Order

To create a carryout order, the **Place Carryout Order** option should be selected from the main menu:

Once **Go!** is selected, the next screen displays a panel to enter the name for the carryout order. As with a reservation, select **Go!** to view the mobile form for pre-ordering dinner combinations. The item is selected from the list and the value is entered (in this case, **Grilled Swordfish** with a quantity of 2). The down arrow key is then pressed to highlight **Add To Order** and the **OK** button is pressed. Confirmation appears on the screen and allows the user to enter additional items. If no more are desired, the **Home** link is highlighted and **OK** pressed to go to the main menu.

Seeing An Existing Order

Once a reservation or carryout order has been created, the See Existing Order option can be selected:

Select Go! to see the next screen containing a link to view the complete order. Once the carryout order name appears with the link, we can highlight the associate item as shown above. The next screen appears with the quantity ordered and the price.

View Menu

Finally, we can see what menu items are available from the restaurant by selecting View Menu from the main menu:

Click on Go! to see a list of all of the items. As the down arrow is pressed, we can highlight each of them. Press OK to view a summary of the items included in the dinner combination with its price.

Now that we've seen what the end-result should look like, we can go back and view the sourcecode with a better grasp of what is going on.

The Display Logic – MaitreDMobileForm.aspx

The first section of the code is automatically generated by Visual Studio .NET. As you can see from the `Page` directive, we are employing a code-behind technique to separate out display logic from our application logic:

```
<%@ Register TagPrefix="mobile" Namespace="System.Web.UI.MobileControls"
Assembly="System.Web.Mobile" %>
<%@ Page language="C#" Codebehind="maitreDMobileForm.aspx.cs"
Inherits="maitreD.maitreDMobileForm" AutoEventWireup="false" debug="true"%>
<meta content="Microsoft Visual Studio 7.0" name="GENERATOR">
<meta content="C#" name="CODE_LANGUAGE">
<meta content="Mobile Web Page" name="vs_targetSchema">
<body xmlns:mobile="Mobile Web Form Controls">
```

As we can see, the "Main Menu" form makes use of some basic mobile controls:

A `<mobile:Image>` command is use to display the Maitre d' logo (or alternate text), a `<mobile:SelectionList>` contains the option choices available to the user, and a `<mobile:Command>` button returns their input:

```
<mobile:form id="frmMain" runat="server">
  <mobile:Image id="imgLogo" runat="server" AlternateText="maitre d'"
          ImageURL="file:///C:\Inetpub\wwwroot\maitreD\maitreD.wbmp"
                              Alignment="Center"></mobile:Image>
  <mobile:Label id="lblmaitreD" runat="server" text="maitreD">
    How may I help you?</mobile:Label>
  <mobile:SelectionList id="dllOrderType" runat="server">
    <item Text="Make Reservation" Value="R" />
    <item Text="Place Carryout Order" Value="C" />
    <item Text="See Existing Order" Value="O" />
    <item Text="View Menu" Value="M" />
  </mobile:SelectionList>
  <mobile:Command id="cmdGoToForm" onclick="GoToForm_OnClick"
                          runat="server" text="Go!"></mobile:Command>
</mobile:form>
```

The "New Reservation" form contains the following code. There are mobile controls for capturing the information needed to create a new record. The user can either enter the information and press Go! to add menu items, or press the Home link to return to the main menu:

```
<mobile:form id="frmReservation" runat="server">
  <mobile:Label id="lblReservationName" runat="server"
                                      text="Please enter your name:">
  </mobile:Label>
  <mobile:TextBox id="txtReservationName" runat="server"></mobile:TextBox>
  <mobile:Label id="lblNumberInParty" runat="server" text="No. in Party:">
  </mobile:Label>
  <mobile:TextBox id="txtNumberInParty" runat="server"></mobile:TextBox>
  <mobile:Label id="lblReservationTime" runat="server" text="Time:">
  </mobile:Label>
  <mobile:SelectionList id="slReservationTime" runat="server">
```

```
                <item Text="12:00pm" Value="12:00" />
                <item Text="1:00pm" Value="13:00" />
                <item Text="2:00pm" Value="14:00" />
                <item Text="3:00pm" Value="15:00" />
                <item Text="4:00pm" Value="16:00" />
                <item Text="5:00pm" Value="17:00" />
                <item Text="6:00pm" Value="18:00" />
                <item Text="7:00pm" Value="19:00" />
                <item Text="8:00pm" Value="20:00" />
                <item Text="9:00pm" Value="21:00" />
                <item Text="10:00pm" Value="22:00" />
                <item Text="11:00pm" Value="23:00" />
        </mobile:SelectionList>
        <mobile:SelectionList id="ddlSmoking" runat="server">
            <item Text="Smoking" Value="true" />
            <item Text="Non-Smoking" Value="false" />
        </mobile:SelectionList>
        <mobile:Label id="lblReservationMessage" runat="server"></mobile:Label>
        <mobile:Command id="cmdReservationItem"
            onclick="NewReservationItem_OnClick" runat="server" text="Go!">
        </mobile:Command>
        <mobile:Command id="cmdBackReservation"
            onclick="ReturnTofrmMain_OnClick" runat="server" text="Home">
        </mobile:Command>
    </mobile:form>
```

The "New Carryout Order" form is much simpler, only capturing the name, and providing a Go! button to move on to the form for pre-ordering items.

```
    <mobile:form id="frmCarryout" runat="server">
      <mobile:Label id="lblCarryoutName" runat="server"
                        text="Please enter your name:"></mobile:Label>
      <mobile:TextBox id="txtCarryoutName" runat="server"></mobile:TextBox>
      <mobile:Label id="lblCarryoutMessage" runat="server"></mobile:Label>
      <mobile:Command id="cmdCarryoutItem" onclick="NewCarryoutItem_OnClick"
                        runat="server" text="Go!"></mobile:Command>
      <mobile:Command id="cmdBackCarryout" onclick="ReturnTofrmMain_OnClick"
                        runat="server" Text="Home"></mobile:Command>
    </mobile:form>
```

The "Menu Item" screen provides a list of all available dinner combinations.

To do this the <mobile:ObjectList> control is populated with data from the MenuItems database table. We'll see in the next section (Application Logic) how this happens. Also note that the LabelField attribute provides the list with a header.

The MenuItemID, MenuItemDescription, MenuItemSummary, and Price for each item are contained in the returned dataset. Within the <mobile:ObjectList> control, the Field attribute allows us to specify which fields will appear in the list. User-friendly titles are specified to be displayed in the list with the Title attribute. The table fieldname is then bound to the Field item with the DataField attribute. The Visible attribute determines whether each field will be displayed (the DataFormatString is {0:C}, which is the format for currency).

```
<mobile:form id="frmMenu" runat="server">
  <mobile:Label id="lblMenuMessage" runat="server"></mobile:Label>
  <mobile:ObjectList id="olMenuItems" runat="server"
                  AutoGenerateFields="false" LabelField="fMenuItem">
    <Field Title="Menu Items" DataField="MenuItemDescription"
                               Name="fMenuItem" Visible="false" />
    <Field DataField="MenuItemSummary" Name="fDescription"
                                                Visible="true" />
    <Field Title="Price" DataField="Price" Name="fPrice" Visible="true"
                               DataFormatString="{0:C}" />
  </mobile:ObjectList>
  <mobile:Command id="cmdBackMenuItems" onclick="ReturnTofrmMain_OnClick"
                  runat="server" Text="Home"></mobile:Command>
</mobile:form>
```

When **See Existing Order** on the main menu is selected, the code for the name entry will be rendered on the device. The name and the type of order are specified to springboard to the order display using basic Mobile Controls. Since the reservation information differs from the carryout information, we will use two separate detail forms:

```
<mobile:form id="frmOrder" runat="server">
  <mobile:Label id="lblOrderTitle1" runat="server" text="Name:"
                           >Please enter your name:</mobile:Label>
  <mobile:TextBox id="txtOrderName" runat="server"></mobile:TextBox>
  <mobile:SelectionList id="slCurrentOrderType" runat="server">
    <item Text="Reservation" Value="R" />
    <item Text="Carryout Order" Value="C" />
  </mobile:SelectionList>
  <mobile:Command id="cmdDisplayOrder" onclick="cmdDisplayOrder_Click"
                           runat="server" Text="Go!"></mobile:Command>
  <mobile:Command id="cmdBackOrder" onclick="ReturnTofrmMain_OnClick"
                           runat="server" Text="Home"></mobile:Command>
</mobile:form>
```

The first is the "Existing Reservation Detail" form. Here we have a `<mobile:ObjectList>` control. Unlike the "Menu Items" list, this one is populated with data from a join between the **ResMenuItems** and the **Reservations** database tables. There are specific fields for the time, the number in the party, the quantity, the menu item description, price, and the total price for each associated menu item. This form also provides the user with the ability to delete his or her reservation from the database. That sounds quite complicated, but if you look at the code, you'll see it is really very simple·

```
<mobile:form id="frmExistingReservationDetail" runat="server">
  <mobile:Label id="lblReservationDetailMessage"
                                    runat="server"></mobile:Label>
  <mobile:ObjectList id="olExistingReservation" runat="server"
                     AutoGenerateFields="False" Alignment="Left"
                  TableFields="frMenuItem;frItemQty;frTotalPrice">
    <Field Title="Name" DataField="Name" Name="frName" Visible="false" />
    <Field Title="Reservation Time" DataField="ReservationTime"
                        Name="frReservationTime" Visible="true" />
```

```
              <Field Title="No. in Party" DataField="NumberInParty"
                              Name="frNumberInParty" Visible="true" />
              <Field Title="Smoking" DataField="Smoking" Name="frSmoking"
                                                    Visible="true" />
              <Field Title="Quantity Ordered" DataField="ItemQty" Name="frItemQty"
                                                    Visible="true" />
              <Field Title="Menu Item" DataField="MenuItemDescription"
                                    Name="frMenuItem" Visible="true" />
              <Field Title="Price" DataField="Price" Name="frPrice" Visible="true"
                                      DataFormatString="{0:C} ea" />
              <Field Title="Total" DataField="TotalPrice" Name="frTotalPrice"
                              Visible="false" DataFormatString="{0:C}" />
        </mobile:ObjectList>
        <mobile:Command id="cmdDeleteReservation"
                    onclick="DeleteReservation_OnClick" runat="server"
                                Text="Delete"></mobile:Command>
    <mobile:Command id="cmdBackResDetail" onclick="ReturnTofrmMain_OnClick"
                        runat="server" Text="Home"></mobile:Command>
    </mobile:form>
```

The code below renders a corresponding detail screen for use with Carry Out orders. It is populated with data from a join between the **CarMenuItems** and the **Carryouts** database tables. There are specific fields for the quantity, the menu item description, price, and the total price for each associated menu item. Once again, this form also provides the ability to delete the order:

```
    <mobile:form id="frmExistingCarryoutDetail" runat="server">
      <mobile:Label id="lblCarryoutDetailMessage"
                                    runat="server"></mobile:Label>
      <mobile:ObjectList id="olExistingCarryout" runat="server"
                        AutoGenerateFields="False" Alignment="Left"
                    TableFields="fcMenuItem;fcItemQty;fcTotalPrice">
        <Field Title="Name" DataField="Name" Name="fcName" Visible="false" />
        <Field Title="Quantity Ordered" DataField="ItemQty" Name="fcItemQty"
                                                    Visible="true" />
        <Field Title="Menu Item" DataField="MenuItemDescription"
                                    Name="fcMenuItem" Visible="true" />
        <Field Title="Price" DataField="Price" Name="fcPrice" Visible="true"
                                      DataFormatString="{0:C}ea" />
        <Field Title="Total" DataField="TotalPrice" Name="fcTotalPrice"
                              Visible="false" DataFormatString="{0:C}" />
      </mobile:ObjectList>
      <mobile:Command id="cmdDeleteCarryout"
                                    runat="server">Delete</mobile:Command>
      <mobile:Command id="cmdBackCmdDetail" onclick="ReturnTofrmMain_OnClick"
                        runat="server" Text="Home"></mobile:Command>
    </mobile:form>
```

Finally, our last form is the one allowing customers to "Add Menu Items" to their order. This form is able to add items to both reservation orders and carryout orders since the function is identical. The `<mobile:SelectionList>` list pulls information from the **MenuItems** table, and a `<mobile:Textbox>` is there to enter the number of each item. Press **Add To Order** to associate these with the order, which is determined by the value in the `onclick` event. As each is added, a message appears confirming it. Once complete, the **Home** link takes the user back to the main menu:

```
<mobile:form id="frmSelectionMenu" runat="server">
  <mobile:Label id="lblSelectionMenuItems" runat="server"></mobile:Label>
  <mobile:SelectionList id="slMenuItemsToSelect"
                              runat="server"></mobile:SelectionList>
  <mobile:Label id="Label1" runat="server">Qty</mobile:Label>
  <mobile:TextBox id="txtItemQty" runat="server" Font-Size="Small"
                      MaxLength="2" Numeric="True"></mobile:TextBox>
  <mobile:Label id="lblSelectionMenuMessage"
                                runat="server"></mobile:Label>
  <mobile:Command id="cmdAddToOrder" onclick="AddToOrder_OnClick"
                      runat="server">Add To Order</mobile:Command>
  <mobile:Command id="cmdBackSelectionMenu"
                  onclick="ReturnTofrmMain_OnClick" runat="server"
                                Text="Home"></mobile:Command>
</mobile:form>
```

Now that we have the display format for the mobile forms, we must have a way to control their behavior. The next section addresses how this occurs.

Application Logic – MaitreDMobileForm.aspx.cs

For Maitre d' to perform the way we expect, we must have underlying code to support user events. In our application this is stored in a code-behind file, called maitreDMobileForm.aspx.cs. We will discuss its functionality here:

At the beginning of the code, we have all of the modules needed to use short-cut references within our mobile forms. In the interest of space, all but two of the control declarations have been cut out, as they lend no value to this explanation. You can, of course, view them in full in the code download from www.wrox.com.

```
namespace maitreD
{
  public class maitreDMobileForm : System.Web.UI.MobileControls.MobilePage
  {
    protected System.Web.UI.MobileControls.TextBox txtName;
    ...
    protected System.Web.UI.MobileControls.SelectionList slOrderType;

    public maitreDMobileForm()
    {
      Page.Init += new System.EventHandler(Page_Init);
    }

    public void Page_Load(object sender, System.EventArgs e)
    {
      olMenuItems.DataSource = maitreDFunctions.GetMenuItems();
      olMenuItems.DataBind();
      lblSelectionMenuMessage.Text = "No items selected";
    }
```

```
private void Page_Init(object sender, EventArgs e)
{
  InitializeComponent();
}

#region Web Form Designer generated code
/// <summary>
/// Required method for Designer support - do not modify
/// the contents of this method with the code editor.
/// </summary>
private void InitializeComponent()
{
  this.Load += new System.EventHandler(this.Page_Load);
}
#endregion
```

In addition to these, Visual Studio .NET has created declarations for all of the mobile controls used within the mobile forms, as well as the forms themselves. The constructor routine creates an instance of the page when it is initially called. Note that the following lines have been inserted into the Page_Load routine. This code loads the <mobile:ObjectList> on the "Menu Item Display" form and sets the initial message in the "Menu Selection" form.

```
olMenuItems.DataSource = maitreDFunctions.GetMenuItems();
olMenuItems.DataBind();
lblSelectionMenuMessage.Text = "No items selected";
```

The next line creates an instance of the maitreDWebService, which allows all of the mobile forms to have access to its WebMethods. This is followed by a counter declaration:

```
maitreDWebService maitreDFunctions = new maitreDWebService();
int i;
```

The GoToForm_OnClick routine is executed after the desired action is selected and the Go! button pressed. This routine will take the user to the form so they can begin creating a new reservation or a carryout order. It checks the value selected in the actions list on the main menu. Based on that choice, the user is taken to one of four possible forms: the New Reservation general information entry screen, the New Carryout screen, the Existing Order display screen, and the Menu Items display screen. If the latter is chosen, the WebService method, GetMenuItems, is called and retrieves and loads all of the menu items from the database into the object list.

```
public void GoToForm_OnClick(object sender, System.EventArgs e)
{
  if (slOrderType.Selection.Value == "C")
  {
    ActiveForm = frmCarryout;
  }
  if (slOrderType.Selection.Value == "R")
  {
```

```
        ActiveForm = frmReservation;
    }
    if (slOrderType.Selection.Value == "O")
    {
        ActiveForm = frmOrder;
    }
    if (slOrderType.Selection.Value == "M")
    {
        olMenuItems.DataSource = maitreDFunctions.GetMenuItems();
        olMenuItems.DataBind();
        ActiveForm = frmMenu;
    }
}
```

The following code shows the routines for creating new reservations and carryout orders. Let's take a look at how we create a new carryout order:

```
public void NewCarryoutItem_OnClick(object sender, System.EventArgs e)
{
    DataSet dsExistingCarryout =
            maitreDFunctions.GetExistingCarryout(txtCarryoutName.Text);
    if (dsExistingCarryout == null)
    {
        string strStatus =
                maitreDFunctions.AddNewCarryout(txtCarryoutName.Text);
        lblSelectionMenuItems.Text = "Select items for " +
                txtCarryoutName.Text + " carryout order";
        slMenuItemsToSelect.DataSource =
                maitreDFunctions.GetMenuItems();
        slMenuItemsToSelect.DataValueField = "MenuItemID";
        slMenuItemsToSelect.DataTextField = "MenuItemDescription";
        slMenuItemsToSelect.DataBind();
        lblSelectionMenuMessage.Text = "No items selected";
        ActiveForm = frmSelectionMenu;
    }
    else
    {
        lblCarryoutMessage.Text = "Carryout order under " +
            txtCarryoutName.Text + " already exists. Please re-enter.";
    }
}
```

The first thing that occurs is that a dataset is created from the results of a call made to the GetExistingCarryout WebMethod in the maitreDWebService. Following this, it checks to see if the dataset is null which, if it is, means that no current carryout order has been placed under that name. This logic keeps the user from attempting to save a carryout order under a duplicate name. If the order is new, it saves the name in the **Carryouts** database table.

We then pre-populate the menu item selection list, specifying that the **MenuItemID** will serve as the value attribute and the **MenuItemDescription** as the text value for the initial message. Finally, we are taken to the next screen. If a carryout order already exists, then a message is displaying indicating this.

Next comes similar code for creating a new Reservation, however, it differs from the carryout order creation by requiring additional items: number in the party, the smoking preference, and the reservation time, that are needed to book seats.

```
public void NewReservationItem_OnClick(object sender,
                                       System.EventArgs e)
{
    DataSet dsExistingReservation =
                maitreDFunctions.GetExistingReservation
                (txtReservationName.Text);
    if (dsExistingReservation == null)
    {
        string strStatus = maitreDFunctions.AddNewReservation
                    (txtReservationName.Text,
                     int.Parse(txtNumberInParty.Text),
                     bool.Parse(ddlSmoking.Selection.Value),
                     DateTime.Parse(txtReservationTime.Text));
        slMenuItemsToSelect.DataSource =
                    maitreDFunctions.GetMenuItems();
        slMenuItemsToSelect.DataValueField = "MenuItemID";
        slMenuItemsToSelect.DataTextField = "MenuItemDescription";
        slMenuItemsToSelect.DataBind();
        lblSelectionMenuMessage.Text = "No items selected";
        ActiveForm = frmSelectionMenu;
        lblSelectionMenuItems.Text = "Select items for " +
                    txtReservationName.Text + " reservation";
    }
    else
    {
        lblReservationMessage.Text = "Reservation under " +
            txtReservationName.Text + " already exists. Please re-enter.";
    }
}
```

The next two routines are very small, and simply serve to take users to the Order and Main Menu screens, respectively, when the Home button is pressed:

```
public void ReturnTofrmOrder_OnClick(object sender, System.EventArgs e)
{
    ActiveForm = frmOrder;
}

public void ReturnTofrmMain_OnClick(object sender, System.EventArgs e)
{
    ActiveForm = frmMain;
}
```

Next comes the cmdDisplayOrder_Click routine. This is activated when the user wants to view the Order Detail screen. Once the Go! button is pressed, a check is made to see if the order is a reservation, or a carryout:

```
public void cmdDisplayOrder_Click(object sender, System.EventArgs e)
    {
        if (slCurrentOrderType.Selection.Value == "R")
        {
            if (maitreDFunctions.GetExistingReservation
                        (txtReservationName.Text) != null)
            {
                lblReservationDetailMessage.Text = "Reservation for "
                                    + txtOrderName.Text;
            }
```

Following this is code to load the object list containing the data resulting from a call to the `GetExistingReservation.` WebMethod:

```
            olExistingReservation.DataSource=
                    maitreDFunctions.GetExistingReservation(txtOrderName.Text);
            olExistingReservation.DataBind();
            ActiveForm = frmExistingReservationDetail;
        }
```

Very similar code exists for retrieving information about Carry Out orders as well.

```
        else if (slCurrentOrderType.Selection.Value == "C")
        {
            if (maitreDFunctions.GetExistingCarryout
                        (txtCarryoutName.Text) != null)
            {
                lblCarryoutDetailMessage.Text = "Carryout Order for "
                                    + txtOrderName.Text;
            }
            olExistingCarryout.DataSource=maitreDFunctions.GetExistingCarryout
                                            (txtOrderName.Text);
            olExistingCarryout.DataBind();
            ActiveForm = frmExistingCarryoutDetail;
        }
    }
```

This next routine checks to see if a carryout name exists. If so (by checking the value of `txtCarryoutName.Text`), we can acquire the item quantity that the user entered and use a for loop to add each selected menu items to the associated Carryout Order ID:

```
public void AddToOrder_Click(object sender, System.EventArgs e)
    {
        if (txtCarryoutName.Text != "")
        {
            int intItemQty = int.Parse(txtItemQty.Text);
            for(1;i<intItemQty;i++)
            {
```

```
      string strStatus =
          maitreDFunctions.AddMenuItemToCarryout(txtCarryoutName.Text,
                    int.Parse(slMenuItemsToSelect.Selection.Value));
      if (strStatus == "OK")
      {
        lblSelectionMenuMessage.Text = "Item added: " +
                                    slMenuItemsToSelect.Selection.Value;
      }
      else
      {
        lblSelectionMenuMessage.Text = "Item not saved";
      }
    }
  }
}
```

For a reservation, the code below takes care of similar actions:

```
      else if (txtReservationName.Text !="")
      {
        //ActiveForm = frmAddToResult;
        int intItemQty = int.Parse(txtItemQty.Text);
        for(1;i<intItemQty;i++)
        {
          string strStatus =
                          maitreDFunctions.AddMenuItemToReservation
                          (txtReservationName.Text,int.Parse
                          (slMenuItemsToSelect.Selection.Value));
          if (strStatus == "OK")
          {
            lblSelectionMenuMessage.Text = "Item added: " +
                                    slMenuItemsToSelect.Selection.Value;
          }
          else
          {
            lblSelectionMenuMessage.Text = "Item not saved";
          }
        }
      }
    }
```

Finally, we have the last two routines, which permit users to delete their existing reservation or carryout order. Each calls its corresponding WebMethods within the Web Service to delete the reservation and any associated menu items already chosen with their order. Once this is complete, the user is returned to the Main Menu.

```
      public void DeleteReservation_OnClick(object sender,
                                            System.EventArgs e)
      {
        string strStatus =
                  maitreDFunctions.DeleteReservation(txtOrderName.Text);
        ActiveForm = frmMain;
      }
```

Once again, we have a similar routine for handling carry out orders:

```
public void DeleteCarryout_OnClick(object sender, System.EventArgs e)
{
  string strStatus =
                maitreDFunctions.DeleteCarryout(txtOrderName.Text);
  ActiveForm = frmMain;
}
```

Summary

In this Case Study, we've seen how the ASP.NET Mobile Controls we've been discussing throughout the book can be used in conjunction with other project types to create a viable commercial solution on the .NET Framework.

Hopefully it will serve to show that developing a mobile application requires us to alter our mindset from creating a few functionality-rich web pages to creating many more mobile web forms, with a minimal amount of terse information on each. If this different method of thinking about the way you present information to your users is followed, it also, hopefully, shows that Mobile Controls have a great potential to influence the way people deal with information, and the environments within which it can be accessed and employed.

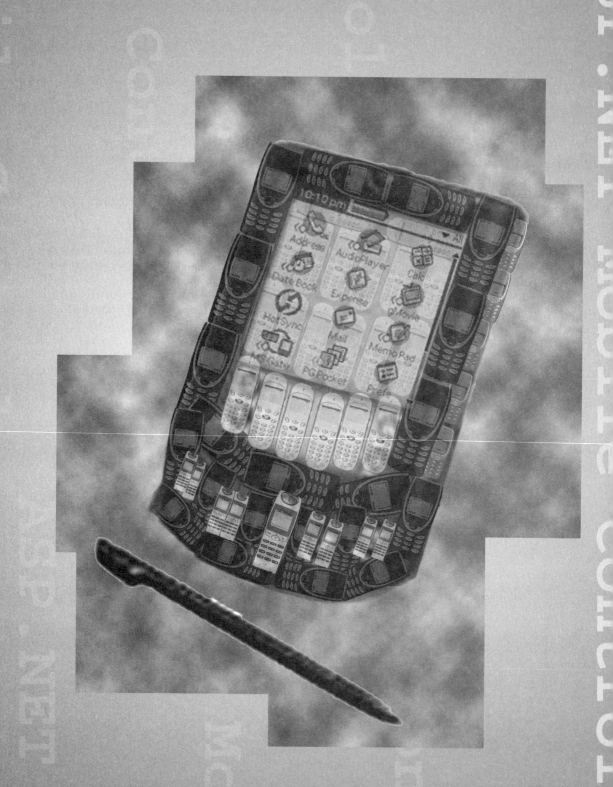

Configuring Environment Variables

If you have had trouble getting command line compilation to work, then the chances are that you may need to manually configure your environment variables on your system to point to the correct path to your .NET installation. This will act like a shortcut to the compiler files (csc.exe for the C# compiler, and vb.exe for the VB .NET compiler). After you've created these shortcuts, your system will be able to locate csc.exe whenever you type csc, for example.

Let's have a go at getting our environment variables set up.

Try It Out – Configuring your Environment Variables

Before you can compile any .NET components, you need to configure your system to locate some files. These files are vbc.exe, and the System.dll files that are required by the compiler. This is a one-off process, and needs to be done before you attempt to compile any assemblies. There's no harm done if you forget to do this, but these examples will not work correctly without going through this process.

1. Right-click on the My Computer icon on the desktop, and select Properties. In the dialog that appears, select the Advanced tab from the top, then click on the Environment Variables button. A new dialog will appear:

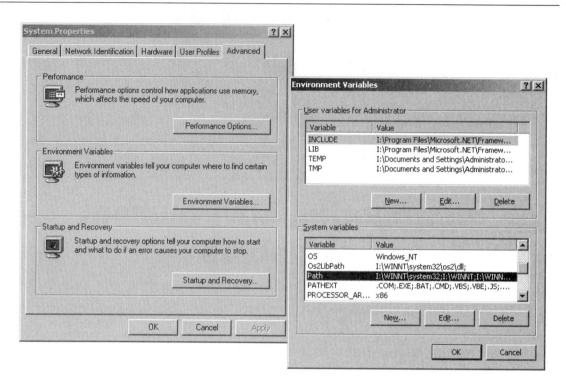

2. You need to highlight the Path statement in the bottom window of the Environment Variables dialog, and then click on the Edit button. Your path may look something like this:

```
%SystemRoot%\system32;%SystemRoot%;%SystemRoot%\System32\Wbem
```

You need to add to this the following text:

```
;%SystemRoot%\Microsoft.NET\Framework\v1.0.3328
```

So that the path now reads:

```
%SystemRoot%\system32;%SystemRoot%;%SystemRoot%\System32\Wbem;%SystemRoot%\Microso
ft.NET\Framework\v1.0.3328
```

> You'll need to substitute the number at the end of the path to correspond to the build
> number of the .NET Framework running on your system (the release candidate of
> .NET is 3328, but the final released product number will be a different number – this
> chapter was written based on release candidate of the .NET Framework).

Once you've done this, close the three windows in turn by clicking on their respective OK buttons. You will now be able to use command-line compilers without a problem.

How it works

This command should tell the computer exactly where to look when you compile your applications using the vbc.exe file, or any of the other compilers for other languages. Once this has been done, you shouldn't have to do this again. By entering this information, our operating system will know where to look if we simply type vbc to compile a file.

```
;%SystemRoot%\Microsoft.NET\Framework\v1.0.3328
```

The first part of the additional information we entered is the semi-colon, which simply indicates that there is another item to be stored in the path declaration of the environment variables. The %SystemRoot% declaration is a short-hand notation that corresponds to the location of the WinNT directory on your hard drive. If your copy of windows is installed on your C drive, this will be C:\WinNT. The remainder of the path is simply the path to the location of your .NET system files

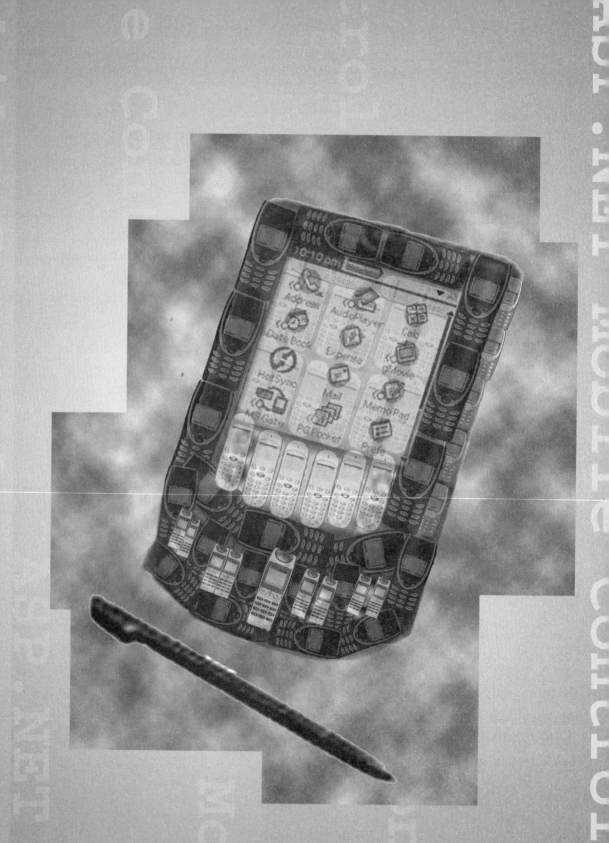

Index

A Guide to the Index

The index is arranged hierarchically, in alphabetical order, with symbols preceding the letter A. Most second-level entries and many third-level entries also occur as first-level entries. This is to ensure that users will find the information they require however they choose to search for it.

X

p2p.wrox.com
The programmer's resource centre

A unique free service from Wrox Press
With the aim of helping programmers to help each other

Wrox Press aims to provide timely and practical information to today's programmer. P2P is a list server offering a host of targeted mailing lists where you can share knowledge with four fellow programmers and find solutions to your problems. Whatever the level of your programming knowledge, and whatever technology you use P2P can provide you with the information you need.

ASP Support for beginners and professionals, including a resource page with hundreds of links, and a popular ASP.NET mailing list.

DATABASES For database programmers, offering support on SQL Server, mySQL, and Oracle.

MOBILE Software development for the mobile market is growing rapidly. We provide lists for the several current standards, including WAP, Windows CE, and Symbian.

JAVA A complete set of Java lists, covering beginners, professionals, and server-side programmers (including JSP, servlets and EJBs)

.NET Microsoft's new OS platform, covering topics such as ASP.NET, C#, and general .NET discussion.

VISUAL BASIC Covers all aspects of VB programming, from programming Office macros to creating components for the .NET platform.

WEB DESIGN As web page requirements become more complex, programmer's are taking a more important role in creating web sites. For these programmers, we offer lists covering technologies such as Flash, Coldfusion, and JavaScript.

XML Covering all aspects of XML, including XSLT and schemas.

OPEN SOURCE Many Open Source topics covered including PHP, Apache, Perl, Linux, Python and more.

FOREIGN LANGUAGE Several lists dedicated to Spanish and German speaking programmers, categories include. NET, Java, XML, PHP and XML

How to subscribe
Simply visit the P2P site, at http://p2p.wrox.com/

Programmer to Programmer™

Wrox writes books for you. Any suggestions, or ideas about how you want information given in your ideal book will be studied by our team.
Your comments are always valued at Wrox.

Free phone in USA 800-USE-WROX
Fax (312) 893 8001

UK Tel.: (0121) 687 4100   Fax: (0121) 687 4101

ASP.NET Mobile Controls – Registration Card

Name _____

Address _____

_____

_____

City _____ State/Region_____

Country _____ Postcode/Zip_____

E-Mail _____

Occupation _____

How did you hear about this book?

❏ Book review (name) _____

❏ Advertisement (name) _____

❏ Recommendation _____

❏ Catalog _____

❏ Other _____

Where did you buy this book?

❏ Bookstore (name) _____ City_____

❏ Computer store (name) _____

❏ Mail order_____

❏ Other _____

What influenced you in the purchase of this book?

❏ Cover Design ❏ Contents ❏ Other (please specify):

_____

How did you rate the overall content of this book?

❏ Excellent ❏ Good ❏ Average ❏ Poor

What did you find most useful about this book? _____

_____

What did you find least useful about this book? _____

_____

Please add any additional comments. _____

_____

What other subjects will you buy a computer book on soon?

_____

What is the best computer book you have used this year?

_____

Note: This information will only be used to keep you updated about new Wrox Press titles and will not be used for any other purpose or passed to any other third party.

wrox

Programmer to Programmer™

Note: If you post the bounce back card below in the UK, please send it to:

Wrox Press Limited, Arden House, 1102 Warwick Road,
Acocks Green, Birmingham B27 6HB. UK.

Computer Book Publishers